Poetry as Re-Reading

AGM STUDIES

AVANT-GARDE & MODERNISM

Poetry as Re-Reading

American Avant-Garde

Poetry and the Poetics

of Counter-Method

M I N G - Q I A N M A

Northwestern

University Press

Evanston

Illinois

Northwestern University Press
www.nupress.northwestern.edu

Printed in the United States of America

10 9 8 7 6 5 4 3 2 1

Library of Congress Cataloging-in-Publication Data

Ma, Ming-Qian.
   Poetry as re-reading : American avant-garde poetry and the
poetics of counter-method / Ming-Qian Ma.
      p. cm. — (Avant-garde and modernism studies)
   Revised version of the author's thesis—Stanford University.
   Includes bibliographical references and index.
   ISBN-13: 978-0-8101-2483-7 (cloth : alk. paper)
   ISBN-10: 0-8101-2483-1 (cloth : alk. paper)
   ISBN-13: 978-0-8101-2485-1 (pbk. : alk. paper)
   ISBN-10: 0-8101-2485-8 (pbk. : alk. paper)
   1. American poetry—20th century—History and criticism.
2. Postmodernism (Literature)—United States.   I. Title.
II. Series.
PS323.5M225 2008
811.509113—dc22

                                        2008000308

♾ The paper used in this publication meets the minimum
requirements of the American National Standard for Information
Sciences—Permanence of Paper for Printed Library Materials,
ANSI Z39.48-1992.

For my parents, Ke-Qin Ma and Yun-Xian Wang

Contents

Acknowledgments

Grown out of my dissertation, this book owes its existence to the members of my dissertation committee at Stanford University. I wish to express my gratitude to Marjorie Perloff for her scholarly insight and rigorous criticism, to Albert Gelpi for his sympathetic challenge and incisive commentary, and to Robert Harrison for his philosophical inquiry and constructive feedback.

I am also grateful to my colleagues at the State University of New York at Buffalo. In particular, I wish to thank Mark Shechner for his administrative support as the Interim Chair, Joseph Conte for his professional wisdom, Stacy Hubbard for her generous mentorship, and Neil Schmitz for his unfailing confidence. The publication of this book has also received important assistance provided by the Julian Park Fund, the College of Arts and Sciences, SUNY-Buffalo.

The writing of this book has benefited from support from many scholars through publications, conferences, written exchanges, and conversations, for which I wish to thank, among others, Charles Altieri, Gerald Bruns, Michael Davison, Rachel Blau Duplessis, Stephen Fredman, Alan Golding, Robert von Hallberg, Burton Hatlen, Lynn Keller, Peter Quartermain, Mark Scroggins, and Susan Vanderborg.

I am indebted, in a way beyond words, to Joseph Perloff, whose unconditional support, unreserved confidence, and continuous encouragement have been instrumental in every stage of writing this book.

The anonymous readers' reports have provided invaluable criticisms for the improvement of the book. Donna Shear, Henry Carrigan Jr., Anne Gendler, and Mairead Case at Northwestern University Press have been most understanding, patient, supportive, and helpful throughout the publication process.

Special thanks to Geoffrey Hlibchuk for his unreserved dedication, trustworthiness, mature professionalism, editorial rigor, and computer expertise, which have given the book its current form; and to James Maynard for his impeccable ethics, thoughtful management, and the responsible approach with which he has handled all other details imperative in making this publication a success.

Some of the chapters herein have appeared previously under the same titles in journals and anthologies, and they have all been revised to various degrees and updated in areas pertinent to the overarching thesis of the book. For permission to include here revised versions of the essays originally published by them, acknowledgment is made to the following journals and university presses:

Chapter One, "A 'No Man's Land': Postmodern Citationality in Zukofsky's 'Poem beginning "The,"'" in *Upper Limit Music: The Writing of Louis Zukofsky*, ed. Mark Scroggins (Tuscaloosa: University of Alabama Press, 1997), 129–53.

Chapter Two, "A 'Seeing' Through Refraction: The Rear-View Mirror Image in George Oppen's *Collected Poems*," in *Sagetrieb* 10, nos. 1–2 (Spring and Fall 1991): 83-97.

Chapter Three, "Be Aware of 'the Medusa's Glance': The Objectivist Lens and Carl Rakosi's Poetics of Strabismal Seeing," in *The Objectivist Nexus: Essays in Cultural Poetics*, ed. Rachel Blau DuPlessis and Peter Quartermain (Tuscaloosa: University of Alabama Press, 1999), 56–83.

Chapter Five, "Articulating the Inarticulate: Singularities and the Counter-Method in Susan Howe," in *Contemporary Literature* 36, no. 3 (Fall 1995): 466–89. Copyright 1995 by the Board of Regents of the University of Wisconsin System.

Chapter Six, "Reflection upon *My* [Unreflected] *Life*: M. Merleau-Ponty and Lyn Hejinian's Poetics of 'Genetic Phenomenology'," in *Analecta Husserliana: The Yearbook of Phenomenological Research* 69 (2000): 17–37. Reprinted with kind permission of Springer Science and Business Media.

Chapter Seven, "'Nonsense Bargains': Inversely Proportional Writing and the Poetics of 'Expenditure without Reserve' in Bruce Andrews's Work," in *Textual Practice* 18, no. 2 (2004): 297–316. http://www.informaworld.com.

The author wishes to thank Bruce Andrews, Charles Bernstein, Lyn Hejinian, Susan Howe, and Steve McCaffery for kind permission to quote from their work. Additionally, grateful acknowledgment is made to the following copyright holders for permission to reprint material published or owned by them:

Stanford Gann Jr. Permission to quote from "Patriarchal Poetry" granted by the Estate of Gertrude Stein through its Literary Executor, Mr. Stanford Gann Jr., of Levin and Gann, P.A.

Green Integer Books. Excerpts from Lyn Hejinian's *My Life*, copyright © 1980, 1987 by Lyn Hejinian, and *Writing Is an Aid to Memory*,

Poetry as Re-Reading

All method is a fiction.

 —Stéphane Mallarmé, *Mimique*

It is not the victory of science that distinguishes our nineteenth century, but the victory of scientific method over science. . . . The most valuable insights are arrived at last; but the most valuable insights are *methods*.

 —Friedrich Nietzsche, *The Will to Power*

What we observe is not nature in itself but nature exposed to our method of questioning.

 —Werner Heisenberg, *Physics and Philosophy*

It is necessary, *at a certain moment,* to turn against Method, or at least to regard it without any founding privilege, as one of the voices of plurality: as a *view,* in short, a spectacle, mounted within the text.

 —Roland Barthes, *The Rustle of Language*

Introduction. "The Medium Is the 'Method'": Toward a Postmodern Poetics of Counter-Method

From Modernism to Postmodernism: The Polemic of Method

In *Five Faces of Modernity,* Matei Calinescu's theorizing of the modern-postmodern divide raises an issue rarely engaged, except tangentially perhaps, in the critical discourse on postmodernism.[1] Implicitly underlying his view is the issue of method as mediator: its centrality in the modernist ethos, and its subsequent critique in postmodernist aesthetics. The point of departure of his contention is contextualized in the philosophy of science, which has, since the turn of the last century, undertaken a self-reflexive rethinking that begins to reckon with and acknowledge the historical contingency of its own paradigms.[2] "The more comprehensive presentations of the issues of postmodernism," Calinescu observes from the outset, "sometimes include references to epistemological problems and concepts" which, as he quickly specifies, result from the "important changes that have occurred in the ways science views itself and the legitimacy of its procedures of inference."[3] Due to what Ilya Prigogine and Isabelle Stengers refer to, in *Order Out of Chaos,* as "man's new dialogue with nature,"[4] new concepts or worldviews, such as chaos theory, the scientific field theory, quantum physics, Werner Heisenberg's uncertainty principle, and Kurt Gödel's incompleteness theorem, have emerged, causing what is now commonly referred to as an epistemological crisis by calling into question the Cartesian methodology as the very foundation of positivist and empiricist thinking.[5] As the birthmark of postmodernism, radical changes as such in scientific paradigms, asserts Calinescu, "cannot be without analogies" in philosophy and the arts.[6]

Philosophically, Calinescu proceeds to argue, the paradigm change in science finds its corresponding manifestation in "a major shift in contemporary thought from epistemology to hermeneutics."[7] Positioning himself against the background of the epistemological crisis, he then describes the difference between epistemology and hermeneutics as grounded essentially in different methodological orientations. Whereas epistemology is characterized as deterministic and ahistorical, as "[tending] to reach beyond history: it normally takes the trans-historical implications or claims of theory seriously," hermeneutics is seen from Calinescu's standpoint as anti-universalistic, as deeply rooted in a "historical self-consciousness."[8] Such a self-acknowledged historicity or contingency presents itself fundamentally as a counter-methodical sensibility, thus approaching the world through a particular kind of procedure different from that of epistemology. To substantiate his argument, Calinescu invokes as his example the Italian philosopher Gianni Vattimo, who posits from a Heideggerian-Gadamerian position the notion of method as hegemonic and deterministic. According to Calinescu's synthesis of Vattimo, there are two different kinds of thought. On the one hand, there is the modernist "'metaphysics' or 'strong thought' (a thought that is domineering, imposing, universalistic, atemporal, aggressively self-centered, intolerant in regard to whatever appears to contradict it, etc.)"; and on the other hand, in direct opposition to this modernist "strong thought," there emerges at the end of modernism "'*il pensiero debole*' or 'weak thought,' a typically postmodern mode of reflection."[9] The difference between the methodological underpinnings of the two lies in that "the most adequate expression of weak thought," argues Calinescu, "is the 'right' hermeneutical attitude in which, as Gadamer suggests in *Truth and Method,* the interpreter practices, as it were, a methodical weakness."[10] The features of this so-called methodical weakness are then summed up as "attentiveness and compliance to the inner demands of the object of interpretation, respect for its essential fragility, willingness to listen to what it says before questioning it, and renewed efforts not to impose on it one's 'rationality' or convictions."[11]

Artistically, the paradigm shift in science, with its questioning of the legitimacy of its own procedures of inference, is mirrored in a highly self-reflexive use of what Calinescu calls postmodern devices. Taken mainly from prose fiction, such devices include, among many others, "a new existential or 'ontological' use of narrative perspectivism," "duplication and multiplication of beginnings, endings, and narrated actions," "the parodic thematization of the author" and "the reader," "the treatment on an equal footing of fact and fiction, reality and myth, truth and lying, original and imitation, as a means to emphasize un-decidability," and "self-referentiality and 'meta-fiction' as means to dramatize inescapable circularity."[12] When applied to writing, these postmodern devices are foregrounded in such a way as to highlight, beyond the modernist-formalist aesthetics best articulated in a Brechtian "alienation effect," their own nature and function as nothing but "contrivance" from which "there simply is no escape."[13] With postmodern devices thus deployed, "what is ultimately fore-grounded," Calinescu announces, "is not a convention but conventionality itself";[14] that is, not method as an instrument but the very instrumentality of method.

Calinescu's assessment of postmodernism resonates, in a measure, with N. Katherine Hayles's thesis in *The Cosmic Web: Scientific Field Models and Literary Strategies in the 20th Century* that "the breakdown of the Cartesian dichotomy" between "the *res cognitans* and the *res extensa,* the thinking mind and the physical object," has, among other issues, "methodological implications."[15] What is particularly important about Calinescu's perspective, however, is his awareness that the Cartesian dichotomy is, in essence, a methodological construct, and that its breakdown is, first and foremost, the breakdown of methodology itself. His insight, when viewed in this light, lies not so much in his understanding of these methodological implications as in his consciousness of *the implications of method.* In contrast to the popular understandings and approaches that tend to perceive the issue of method in terms of cultural symbiosis, seeing scientific models and literary strategies as methodical manifestations mutually reflexive of and comparable to one another,[16] Calinescu seems to call attention to method itself, postulating method as foundational, perceiving it as that which constitutes both the structural and the functional mechanisms of any given domain of inquiry, mechanisms that first render possible and then secure the ultimate realization of their philosophical premises. At the heart of the crisis of epistemology, it follows then, exists the crisis of method; and the movement from modernism to postmodernism, in this view, presents a change well beyond the parameters of a simple paradigm shift in method. Rather, it stages a historical-conceptual transformation from what might be described as the "fetishism" of method to the questioning and rethinking of method proper, foregrounding the issue of method so as to call into question modernist hypotheses and understandings of reality modeled on the methods of the natural sciences.

In this sense, the diverse experiments in postmodern literature in general and in American avant-garde poetry in particular, variously described as formal, stylistic, or generic, can be read as aiming not at a "methodical rhetoricity" or "methodical expressivity"—that is, an expressive capability and efficacy resulting from the method used—but at a critical inquiry into method itself. Among the questions thus raised, what, for instance, is the nature of method? What are its structural-functional components that sustain its end-oriented efficacy? Can a method, scientific, philosophical, or communal, ever be "purposeless" or "innocent"? What does it mean, culturally and sociopolitically, to use a method? Is there a methodical "outside"? In view of its universal presence and applicability, what is the most basic level of methodical performance? Further, is it viable, either in concept or in praxis, that the appropriation of an old method or the invention of a new one presents a means sufficient enough to sidestep the self-referential mechanism embedded therein? Finally, if it is imperative to negate traditional method by ways other than appropriation or invention, what is the form of this negation, and what position does this negation take vis-à-vis the method under negation?

Toward a Critical Understanding of Method

The etymology of the word *method,* as Justus Buchler points out, contains "the ancient notion of the 'way,'" in that "the Greek *methodos* suggests a way followed, the pursuit of a path" and, by extension, "a 'way' of applying."[17] Defined in the *Oxford English Dictionary* in two major categories, *method* means "I. Procedure for attaining an object" and "II. Systematic arrangement, order." The former, which covers science and art, designates "in a wider sense: A way of doing anything, esp. according to a defined and regular plan; a mode of procedure in any activity, business, etc.," whereas the latter, which deals with logic, rhetoric, and literary composition, designates "orderliness and regularity in doing anything; the habit of acting according to plan and order." The fundamental principle of any method, as the *Oxford English Dictionary's* definition makes clear, can thus be described by three adjectives: subject-oriented, premeditated, and purposive, which in turn connote the fourth one: deterministic. But a fuller understanding of method, especially its relation to the domain of truth and knowledge, did not find a better and more focused development until what David Antin calls "experimental modernism," a modernism represented historically by "the twin theorists" of Descartes and Bacon on the one hand and by Kant on the other.[18] Though arguing mainly from the perspective of art, Antin nevertheless offers a succinct yet comprehensive definition of a modernism predicated on method:

> First, I would like to suggest that Modernism is definable in terms of a single fundamental axiom: *that it is necessary to begin from a radical act of definition or redefinition of the domain of the elements and the operations of the art or of art itself.* I would like to suggest that this axiom is both necessary and sufficient to define modernism in the grand sense that goes deep into certain aspects of Romanticism—this axiom more generally to determine the domain of human knowledge, its relation to truth (the object of knowledge), the appropriate methods for discovering it, representing it and communicating it, you arrive at the modernism of Bacon and Descartes as you pass backwards through Kant.[19]

In *The Advancement of Learning,* for instance, Bacon, in his theorizing of "the true method of the sciences," idealizes method as a form of reason constitutive of not only the origin but also the delivery of knowledge, positing that "knowledge that is delivered as a thread to be spun on, ought to be delivered and intimated, if it were possible, in the same method wherein it was invented: and so is it possible of knowledge induced."[20] Bacon's notion of method, considered by Michel Serres as based upon a "command-obedience couplet"—that is, "One commands nature only by obeying it," which presents nothing but "the circle of ruse and productive hypocrisy"—is replaced in due course by that of Descartes, who assumes an offensive posture by suppressing the "Baconian obedience" and by turning method into an infinite game of strong reason, always endowed with a winning strategy.[21] More emphatically in *Rules for the Direction of the Mind,* Descartes establishes method as the founding mediator in "Rule Four," claiming that *"we need a method if we are to investigate the truth of things*" and that "it is far better never to contemplate investigating the truth about any matter than to do so without a method."[22] Identifying it with "mental intuition or deduction," he then defines method as an administrative projection and regulation, as the "reliable rules which are easy to apply, and such that if one follows them exactly, one will never take what is false to be true or fruitlessly expend one's mental efforts."[23] The nature of method as the reduction of the multiplicity to a set of universal rules from a subject's standpoint is explicated further in "Rule Five":

> *The whole method consists entirely in the ordering and arranging of the objects on which we must concentrate our mind's eye if we are to discover some truth. We shall be following this method exactly if we first reduce complicated and obscure propositions step by step to simpler ones, and then, starting with the intuition of the simplest ones of all, try to ascend through the same steps to a knowledge of all the rest.*

> This one Rule covers the most essential points in the whole of human endeavour. Anyone who sets out in quest of knowledge of things must follow this Rule as closely as he would the thread of Theseus if he were to enter the Labyrinth.[24]

But this "Labyrinth" exists only as a figure of speech, for in Descartes' scheme of things it is already mapped out. Identifying Descartes' own method "as a variant of the method of analysis which was used in Greek mathematics" in general and tracing it back to Pappus in particular, Jaakko Hintikka, in "A Discourse on Descartes's Method," pinpoints a common denominator: both share the assumption that the unknown is already known.[25] "Descartes's general methodological paradigm," he argues, is thus based on "a network of functional dependencies between the known and the unknown."[26] Geometrical in nature, this "functional dependency" is then explained by Descartes as one that is itself dependent in essence on reason:

> First, in every problem there must be something unknown; otherwise there would be no point in posing the problem. Secondly, this unknown something must be delineated some way, otherwise there would be nothing to point us to one line of investigation as opposed to any other. Thirdly, the unknown something can be delineated only by way of something else which is already known.[27]

The "functional dependency," then, foregrounds a self-serving construct of predetermined necessity, in which the "dependency" amounts to nothing but reason's self-addressed invitation to "function." In other words, the known "depends on" the unknown only insofar as it has already known the unknown. It bespeaks a conceptual a priori which determines the unknown by projecting itself onto the latter, and to which the latter testifies. Cartesian method, as Justus Buchler asserts, is therefore "prescriptive," and its rule, "designed to lead one ahead . . . both points and defines. . . . The rule is thus not merely a launching or a promising beginning; it is not merely the way but the whole way. It ensures economy."[28] Or, as Descartes himself puts it succinctly in "Rule Ten," method is the order "ingeniously read into" the matter.[29]

Descartes' method as formal logic presents a conceptual artifice akin to Kant's doctrine of transcendental method elaborated in the *Critique of Pure Reason*. In the "Preface to Second Edition," Kant states explicitly that the book is "a treatise on the method," the main purpose of which is to revolutionize the hitherto prevalent procedure in metaphysics "in accordance with the example set by the geometers and physicists."[30] The entire transcendental project, he claims, aims at "rendering a service to reason . . . [by] discovering the path upon which it can securely travel."[31] Perceived as "a part of logic, that is, inquiry,"[32] Kantian method, in this sense, is reason itself in action, always "[sheltering] an anticipated view of the sense of the being which one encounters."[33] Kant thus brings to the fore the primacy of reason in the preface:

> Reason, holding in one hand its principles, according to which alone concordant appearances can be admitted as equivalent to laws, and in the other hand the experiment which it has devised in conformity with these principles, must approach nature in order to be taught by it. It must not, however, do so in the character of a pupil who listens to everything that the teacher chooses to say, but of an appointed judge who compels the witnesses to answer questions which he has himself formulated.[34]

And with such as his major premise, Kant refines, in a sense, the Cartesian "rules" by firmly establishing their transcendental status:

> Understanding has rules which I must presuppose as being in me prior to objects being given to me, and therefore as being *a priori*. They find

expression in *a priori* concepts to which all objects of experience necessarily conform, and with which they must agree.[35]

Kant's transcendental method, furthermore, finds its expression in two different kinds of execution: the synthetic or progressive, and the analytic or regressive.[36] While the former, as Norman Kemp Smith explicates it, proceeds "from given, ordinary experience . . . to discover its conditions, and from them to prove the validity of knowledge that is *a priori*," the latter starts "from the existence of *a priori* synthetic judgments, and, assuming them as valid, would determine the conditions under which alone such validity can be possible."[37] To put it another way, the distinction between the two, according to Smith, lies in that "in the synthetic method the grounds which are employed to explain *a priori* knowledge are such as also at the same time suffice to prove its validity. In the analytic method they are grounds of explanation, but not of proof. They are themselves proved only in so far as the assumption of validity is previously granted."[38] Whichever the case, the nature of either method is specified by Kant himself as "the system of rational psychology" constructed as a complete circle and committed to idealism.[39] In this sense, Smith argues, Kant's transcendental method, "rightly understood, does not differ in essential nature from the hypothetical method of the natural sciences" precisely because "the very essence of his transcendental method consists in the establishment of *a priori* elements," and the "proof of their *a priori* validity presupposes the phenomenal character of the objects to which they apply."[40] In Kant's transcendental philosophy, the basis of his method is, in short, "the proposition 'I think,'"[41] according to which to "dis-cover" anything means, in actuality, to "re-cover" it.

It is neither the place nor the intention of this study to take up the metaphysical nuances underlying the methodical constructs in Descartes, Bacon, and Kant. Suffice it to say, in light of the discussion so far, that method, be it Cartesian, Baconian, or Kantian, presents a generative device, a self-fulfilling game of reason for recovering its predesignated prey. In *The Tain of the Mirror*, Rodolphe Gasché offers a comprehensive and lucid definition of method when he encapsulates both the concept and the function of method in the traditions of science and philosophy:

Methods are generally understood as roads (from *hodos:* "way," "road") to knowledge. In the sciences, as well as in the philosophies that scientific thinking patronizes, method is an instrument for representing a given field, and it is applied to that field from the outside. That is, it is on the side of the subject and is an external reflection of the object. It is an instrumental approach to knowledge from an entirely subjective position. . . . For genuine philosophical thought, methods are always *determined* methods, which have their source in the region to which they apply and which are dependent on the nature and the specificity of that region. For this reason the ultimate method—that is, the method that represents the philosophical itinerary to truth—must be one that describes the intrinsic and spontaneous movement of truth itself. The philosophical method, as the road toward truth in a domain that is itself determined in terms of truth, implies philosophy's self-implication, and the necessity to reflect itself into self-consciousness. Since Plato such a method has been called *dialektike,* the science of dividing (*diairesis*) and reunification (*synagoge*). Such a method is nothing other than the patient pursuit of the conceptual activity of truth as it develops its own coherence. It is thus not a formal procedure or rule separate from the content of truth. Method, then, is no longer simply the way to truth; it is truth itself. This is what Hegel means when, in the last chapter of the greater *Logic,* entitled "The Absolute Idea," he finally thematizes the concept of method: "From this course the method has emerged as the *self-knowing Notion that has itself,* as the absolute, both subjective and objective, *for its subject matter,* consequently as the pure correspondence of the Notion and its reality, as a concrete existence that is the Notion itself."[42]

Although this notion of method as the foundational mediator, centered on the proposition of "I think" and committed to a self-fulfilling prophecy, has been explicated and theorized quite extensively both in science and in philosophy, the generative mechanism of a method, or its self-referential structure, has been left largely unexamined, particularly—and rather oddly, too, given the fact that a method makes sense only in a dialogical (i.e., relational) situation, various as it may be in context and degree—in discourses on or pertinent to organizational behavior.[43] The question thus remains as to how a method ever becomes a method, or how it works.

In his study of the theories of method in Karl Popper, Imre Lakatos, and Larry Laudan, Husain Sarkar presents what could be considered as a model in this regard, and his delineation of a framework of method contributes to one's understanding of this issue by amplifying, in a way, the Cartesian,

Baconian, and Kantian concepts in terms germane to a structural, socio-logical reading of method.[44] In *A Theory of Method,* for instance, he argues from the outset that "a method has three distinct components," which he christens respectively "the *objective component,* the *normative component,* and the *illustrative component*"; but what in fact defines a method "*correctly and clearly,*" he insists, are the former two, each of which is, in turn, "ex-haustively divided into two parts."[45] Functioning essentially as the defini-tion of the "concept of a method," the objective component, according to Sarkar, consists of "the *logical part* and the *conventional part.*"[46] The logical part deals with problems such as "the old and new problems of induction, the paradox of confirmation, the issue of contra-factual conditionals, the problem of verisimilitude, and the problem of incommensurability and counter-comparison," thus containing in itself "statements that *do* have a truth-value"; whereas the conventional part tackles problems "the answers to which can be neither true nor false," in the sense that it "defines by convention its [own] key terms, such as ad hoc, corroboration, empiri-cally progressive problem-shift, and problem-solving effectiveness."[47] Also endowed with "a truth-value," the normative component is divided, in a similar fashion, into "the *acceptability* part and the *evaluative* part."[48] The acceptability part, asserts Sarkar, "lays down the conditions under which theories classified in one way or another by the method's conventional part can be accepted," thus becoming entitled to the right to "give advice" by being, rather paradoxically, "dependent on the conventional part."[49] The evaluative part, on the other hand, "defines rational action"; and "since the rationality of actions is closely connected to the acceptance or rejection of theories, it follows that an act is rational, according to a method, if, and only if, it is carried out in accordance with the injunction laid down in the acceptability part."[50] Thus outlined, the anatomy of method can be seen in the structural diagram shown in figure 1.

Furthermore, these parts of a method, as indicated in the figure, are by no means parallel sectors isolated from one another. They are, Sarkar points out further, "linked" in a specific way in that some "are parasiti-cally dependent on others."[51] Sarkar's choice of expression ("parasitically dependent on") here pinpoints the nature of method as incestuous, as a self-serving, self-sustaining, and self-promoting construct in which this parasitic dependency, also referred to earlier as the functional dependency in Descartes, is manifested in a structural circularity. There are, in this sense, two levels of self-referential mechanism embedded in Sarkar's struc-

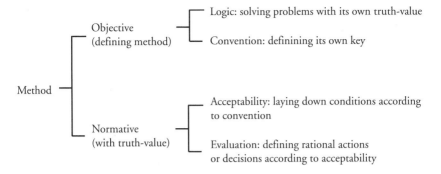

Figure 1

ture of method: the directive and the operative. The directive level, for instance, can be seen in the objective-normative axis in figure 1, where a method sanctions itself into existence by defining its own objective, the truth-value of which is established, legitimated, and realized through the normative defined by none other than the objective. The operative level is shown in the logic-convention-acceptability-evaluation axis, where the closed circle becomes blatantly self-evident. Following Sarkar's sequence of description of the links between the four parts but in a reverse order, one finds a chain of "parasitical dependency": the evaluation of any rational action, which carries out the enforcement of logic, "cannot be made independently of" the injunction laid down in "the advice-giving acceptability," which establishes the conditions of rejection or acceptance in conformity with the regulations based on agreement or custom known as convention, which defines its own key terms as a form of logic with a truth-value that can be "evaluated in its own right," which in turn is articulated through evaluation.[52] In the structure of method, what Kant refers to as the system of rational psychology constructed in a complete circle and committed to idealism can be illustrated in figure 2.

Thus formulated, Sarkar's structure of method sheds considerable light on a dimension of method that has not yet been addressed directly. Its four component parts of logic, convention, acceptability, and evaluation, while pointing to method itself as an arbitrary, closed, generative construct with a reason of its own, also define it simultaneously and explicitly as social. Method is social as it is contextual. It is a way of thinking and functioning situated at the level of society, employed by a social mentality, and justified in terms of social interests.[53] For the structure of method

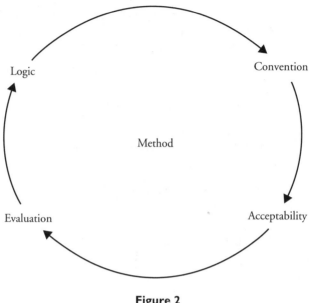

Figure 2

mirrors, to a great extent, the structure of a society, of an organized cognitive and epistemological enterprise following a regulatory procedure aiming at self-validation on the one hand and maximum efficiency on the other, with its own rationale routinized as convention, which in turn sets its own criteria of assessment and judgment. Method, in other words, is a system; it is a system of rational psychology in which the Kantian proposition of "I think" is refashioned as that of "group think," articulating, as such, communal choices and decisions grounded in a social context and based upon a collective consensus. It is a shared mind-set so formulated as to pit itself against anarchy and uncertainty, an autotelic construct in which, as Robert E. Shiller observes, "ends and means move into each other" to ensure an economy of closure, or foreclosure, to be more accurate.[54] As much as there is private use of method, there is no private method. And regardless of one's original intention or initial occasion, any private use of method is always already a social act, since to use a method is to follow a social logic, to submit to an established convention, thus subscribing to as well as enacting the cultural ideology inscribed therein. To put it differently, one tends to take method as a given precisely because method constitutes a socially determined and socially sanctioned "self-expressivity" whereby an individual finds his or her "own," "private" voice only insomuch as he or she has already joined the collective chorus. By the same token, the invention of a new method is possible if, and only if, it is carried out within the social parameters of logic, convention, acceptability, and evaluation, social parameters in which, and in which alone, a method can be conceptualized and recognized as such in the first place. To invent a new method is, in the same vein, to reassert one's social position by updating the social convention in conformity with the public consensus. As a social construct, method always "introduces fixity."[55] It does not have an "outside" in that, though it "promises production," as Don Byrd argues, "it produces only what is implicit in its rules."[56] It is, in this sense, the opposite of possibility. A socio-teleological totality, method embodies then a "continuing proliferation of conventions" that predetermines the contextual boundaries of any organized activity.[57]

Methodological Bifurcation in Modernism: Pound versus Stein

Calinescu's general thesis of the centrality of method in modernism as constitutive of a cognitive-epistemological totality and its subsequent critique in postmodernism does not stand alone, and it finds its more concrete counterpart in the criticism of poetry. In his study of modernism in American poetry, David Antin takes a similar position, arguing, rather trenchantly, for an aesthetic-methodological bifurcation that signals the distinction between the high modernists and the postmodernists. Antin's critical stance on this issue is, as Stephen Fredman points out, Gadamerian, in that he shares with the latter, among other positions, "the claim that method is not value-free but rather that the method chosen prejudices the truth one can achieve."[58] In Antin's view, the bifurcation in question is represented, on the one hand, by Ezra Pound and other high modernists, whose "interest was concentrated at the level of rhetoric," and, on the other hand, by Gertrude Stein, "the only one with an interest in language as language."[59] The fundamental issue that separates the interests in rhetoric from that in language is the received status and function of method in avant-garde experiments.

The modernist aesthetic of "making it new" is, in this sense, an aesthetic pivoting on method. As is the case with Pound's notion of the image as a "psychological ensemble," which is employed "as a rhetorical element rather than a linguistic one," Antin perceives Pound and Eliot as literary methodologists who concern themselves primarily "with presentational and narrational strategies, the manipulation of sequences of pieces of discourse and their arrangement."[60] These presentational and narrational strategies, as Sarkar has contended, "are nothing but the normative components of a method the scientists espouse."[61] They are the normalizing measures for evaluation and acceptability, the purpose of which is, in Buchler's words, to "manipulate complexes characteristically within a perspectival order."[62] As such, the entire Poundian project, Antin goes on to claim, presents an attempt to "construct a literary methodology, a 'language' that Americans could use out of a nearly random array of foreign excellences";[63] or, for that matter, a literary methodology anyone could use.

Antin's observation proves to be a suggestive index to Pound's art, the poetics of which—be it imagist, ideogramic, or vorticist—is indeed a poetics of what Geoffrey Grigson calls "Methodism,"[64] modeled in principle after those of the sciences.[65] It is a well-known fact that Pound himself is markedly vocal, often in a manifesto fashion, about the founding status of method in the great works of art and more specifically in his own aesthetics, about what Buchler calls the "methodic process as an influence," that is, as "manipulative possibilities" to be "realized in a specific form of (methodic) activity."[66] "The ideogramic method," for instance, "consists of presenting one facet and then another," Pound thus defines it, "until at some point one gets off the dead and desensitized surface of the reader's mind, onto a part that will register."[67] Theoretically for Pound, method presents then a twofold objective: epistemological and communicative. Epistemologically, its Cartesian purchase becomes unmistakably manifest through the analogy Pound draws repeatedly between poetry and science, and through his no less repeated emphasis on having recourse to scientific methods as the sure-footed way to establishing his perspectival order in literature. In *ABC of Reading,* which is in essence a book of methodology or pedagogy, Pound begins the first chapter with the statement that "the proper METHOD for studying poetry and good letters is the method of contemporary biologists," which is promptly illustrated by "the anecdote of Agassiz and the fish."[68] He then ends this chapter with a section titled "The Ideogrammic Method or the Method of Science," with the conjunction "or" denoting an equivalent or substitutive relation between the two kinds of methods in that both facilitate, in an explicit Cartesian sense, "the efficiency of verbal manifestation" and "the transmittibility of a conviction."[69] Moreover, he avowedly espouses Fenollosa's privilege of "the method of science, 'which is the method of poetry' ";[70] and the ideogramic method, which is always "based on something everyone KNOWS"[71] and "can give a man an orderly arrangement of his perception," functioning in this way "as an implement for acquisition and transmission of knowledge."[72]

"The arts, literature, poesy, are a science," Pound declares emphatically, "just as chemistry is a science."[73] To the extent that poetic method is, for Pound, identical with the scientific method, Pound's equation of art with science is perhaps most literally and most academically articulated in his theory on vorticism, which he tries to formulate in *Gaudier-Brzeska: A Memoir*. "I can explain my meaning best by mathematics," he writes, in his effort to clarify what he means by vorticism as an "intensive art."[74] "There are four different intensities of mathematical expression known to the ordinarily intelligent undergraduate," Pound continues, "namely: the arithmetical, the algebraic, the geometrical, and that of analytical geometry."[75] Applicable to his concept of vorticism therein is the fourth form of intensity: analytical geometry, which, like art, offers "a new way of dealing with form," a new way, that is, of handling life.[76] To show Pound's position accurately, the following passage on analytical geometry in relation to artistic creation is worthy of being quoted in full:

> *Fourthly,* we come to Descartian or "analytical geometry." Space is conceived as separated by two or by three axes (depending on whether one is treating form in one or more planes). One refers points to these axes by a series of co-ordinates. Given the idiom, one is able *actually to create.*
>
> Thus, we learn that the equation $(x - a)^2 + (y - b)^2 = r^2$ governs the circle. It is the circle. It is not a particular circle, it is any circle and all circles. It is nothing that is not a circle. It is the circle free of space and time limits. It is the universal, existing in perfection, in freedom from space and time. Mathematics is dull ditchwater until one reaches analytics. But in analytics we come upon a new way of dealing with form. It is in this way that art handles life. The difference between art and analytical geometry is the difference of subject-matter only. Art is more interesting in proportion as life and the human consciousness are more complex and more interesting than forms and numbers.
>
> This statement does not interfere in the least with "spontaneity" and "intuition," or with their function in art. I passed my last *exam.* in mathematics on sheer intuition. I saw where the line *had* to go, as clearly as I ever saw an image, or felt *caelestem intus vigorem.*
>
> The statements of "analytics" are "lords" over fact. They are the thrones and dominations that rule over form and recurrence. And in

like manner are great works of art lords over fact, over race-long recurrent moods, and over to-morrow.

Great works of art contain this fourth sort of equation. They cause form to come into being.[77]

In other words, great works of art are those that transcend the fluxes of the contingents onto the level of perfection and universality once the creative intuition forms a methodological alliance with science; once, that is, spontaneity recognizes its own methodical mirror image in analytics.

The same holds true for communication, which is, as Pound has argued consistently, most effective with a certain methodical grounding. "The attraction of method," in this respect, "is that it creates a context for writer and reader to stand in the place of commonality," as Don Byrd thus clarifies, albeit in a different context; "It establishes a synthetic intimacy by legislating the rules of a language which can bear a complex poetry."[78] "Language is a means of communication,"[79] Pound thus defines it, and "great literature is simply language charged with meaning to the utmost possible degree."[80] It follows, then, that the function of literature is to communicate clearly and effectively. "It has to do with the clarity and vigour of 'any and every' thought and opinion," Pound specifies further. "It has to do with maintaining the very cleanliness of the tool, the health of the very matter of thought itself," a thought whose purpose is, in turn, to "keep language efficient as it is in surgery to keep tetanus bacilli out of one's bandages."[81] The model is, in this respect, mathematics. "Poetry," Pound writes in *The Spirit of Romance,* "is a sort of inspired mathematics";[82] and if "bad art is inaccurate art," good art is then "the art that is most precise," he continues to argue, a precision characterized by a "maximum efficiency of expression," a "complete clarity and simplicity" achievable only by way of a perfect control.[83] That being said, Pound wastes no time offering methods of such perfect control, both general and concrete. To write at all, for instance, there are "the three chief means" of "phanopoeia, melopoeia, logopoeia."[84] "All writing is built up of these three elements," Pound explains, "plus 'architectonics' or 'the form of the whole.'"[85] Should one wish to write poetry in "a new fashion"—that is, poetry of the imagist persuasion—there are, then, "three principles" to follow:

1. Direct treatment of the "thing" whether subjective or objective.
2. To use absolutely no word that does not contribute to the presentation.

3. As regarding rhythm: to compose in the sequence of the musical phrase, not in sequence of a metronome.[86]

"The serious artist is scientific," Pound reiterates;[87] and his critical writings abound with mandates, manifestos, instructions, and advice on diverse categories of methods, either stated in general or explicated in detail. For purposes both epistemological and communicative, Pound's poetics of method, which foregrounds "the thinking word-arranging, clarifying faculty," can thus be epitomized in his own motto: "Consider the way of the scientists rather than the way of an advertising agent for a new soap."[88]

In overt contrast to Pound, who is preoccupied with a rhetoricity or expressivity contingent strictly upon a rhetorical-methodical efficacy of presentation, Gertrude Stein seems to have concentrated on experimenting with and searching for an experiential expression freed from language as a method of interlocking constraints. This exploratory valence in Stein is predicated, as its precondition, upon a critical one that takes language itself to be none other than the medium of method "in and through" which, as Jayne Walker puts it, experience is reductively processed.[89] "The essence of grammar," Stein writes in *How to Write,* "is that it is freed of following."[90] Hence a double valence of critical investigation and exploratory search; and hence a paradox with regard to Stein's avant-garde position: a new way of writing freed from any methodical restrictions of language ("freed of following") is possible when, and only when, the nature and function of language as method ("The essence of grammar") is thoroughly and critically scrutinized and understood.[91] Stein "was the writer in English with the deepest interest in language," as Antin asserts emphatically, the only writer, of all high modernists, who "had a philosophical commitment to the problematic double system of language—the self ordering system and the pointing system," and who demonstrates, in *The Making of Americans* in particular, a "refined grasp of the language as medium—and of language as medium."[92] Although Antin does not explain in detail therein all the "problematicalness" that Stein is committed to investigate,[93] his professed distinction between Pound and Stein, as evidenced in a distinction between rhetoric and language, between effectiveness of expression and the medium of expression, between presentational-narrational strategies and grammar, makes a tacit statement concerning the issue of method in Stein's work.

Insofar as Stein's attitude toward the nature and function of method is concerned generally, the only piece of writing in which her stance could be discerned in a recognizable form is "Patriarchal Poetry," where there is one long sentence in which the word *method* is foregrounded:

> Patriarchal Poetry to be filled to be filled to be filled to be filled to method method who hears method method who hears who hears who hears method method method who hears who hears who hears and method and method and method and who hears and who who hears and method method is delightful and who and who who hears method is method is method is delightful is who hears is delightful who hears method is who hears method is method is method is delightful is delightful who hears who hears of of delightful who hears of method of delightful who of whom of whom of of who hears of method method is delightful.[94]

"This sentence is remarkable, among other things," observes Peter Quartermain, "for its method."[95] It is a method whereby "method," as a conceptual, structural, and functional mechanism constitutive of "the authoritarian power of conventional, Anglo-centric, and male literary values," is chanted, as if sacrilegiously, to the point of absurdity where it itself is teased out, satirized out of its routinized transparency into visibility.[96] As such, "method," as is also the case with the term "Patriarchal Poetry," "virtually loses all meaning" in the poem, having been dethroned from its position of the authority of administrative hierarchy and sent into exile as a quotidian, paratactical element.[97] Thus composed, "the whole poem" in general, and this sentence in particular, becomes "a form of deconstruction," as Quartermain rightly argues, "in which the discourse demolishes the term—and the authority and stability of the cipher—embedded within it and shaping it, acting out as it does *non*patriarchal modes of writing."[98] Considered as "a referential work,"[99] "Patriarchal Poetry" presents, however, only a rare case of a Steinian "clarity."

Of all Stein's work, that which comes closest to a theory of method is arguably the essay titled "Composition as Explanation." Recalling her own writing experience, Stein mentions therein three "things" which bring her "to composition," and which she has "naturally done."[100] "Continuous present is one thing," she writes, "and beginning again and again is another thing. These are both things. And then there is using everything."[101] Stein's wording in this statement, insofar as it is purportedly a statement on her method of writing, is indeed suggestive. First, she never refers to "continuous present," "beginning again and again," and "using everything" as "methods" or "principles," as Pound would have; rather, they are, and Stein is quite emphatic about this point, "things." Second, the chief attribute of these "things," or the reason they are called "things," is that they are natural, in the sense that "a natural composition" is a composition "in the world," where "things [are] naturally simply different."[102] Composing is, from this perspective, "doing natural phenomena."[103] Stein brings this point to the fore when she thus summarizes:

> The composition is the thing seen by every one living in the living they are doing, they are the composing of the composition that at the time they are living is the composition of the time in which they are living. It is that that makes living a thing they are doing. Nothing else is different, of that almost any one can be certain. The time when and the time of and the time in that composition is the natural phenomena of that composition and of that perhaps every one can be certain.[104]

Following and enacting the moment-to-moment changing fluxes of time and of situated perceptions in the life world,[105] Stein's way of composition can be understood, in this sense, as what Jayne Walker calls "the epistemological model of present-tense vision" without the Cartesian circle;[106] it is a phenomenological approach that dispenses with the phenomenological methods of reduction. Differently put, Stein's is, to borrow a phrase from Barrett Watten's *Total Syntax,* "the method that is no method"—that is, a method devoid of its "dialectical frame" and, consequently, emptied of its "predicative potential."[107]

At work in Stein's writing is what might be referred to as a poetics of counter-method, one that resists any methodical directives in writing on the one hand and any methodical reappropriations in reading on the other. So "anomalous" is such a "position among the various modern schools," observes F. W. Dupee, that "a knowledge of Joyce's and Eliot's methods"—and of Pound's methods for that matter—would only prove to be "wrong" if or when applied to reading Stein.[108] This problem is compounded further by the fact that Stein consistently refused to theorize her own method regardless of an occasionally tantalizing gesture. It is a general consensus that, though written in the imperative mood and in declarative sentences, Stein's *How to Write,* for instance, is "misleadingly labeled,"[109] argues Kostelanetz, because, as Patricia Meyerowitz has made clear, "it certainly does not tell you how to write."[110] Such "elusiveness" on the part of Stein is by no means whimsical, however;[111] rather, it articulates a postmodern perspective. "If the artist *knows exactly what he is going to do*," Meyerowitz thus comments on Stein's lack of a methodological anchoring, "*and more importantly how it will be done and what it will become then there really is no use in doing it since there will be nothing new in it.*"[112] Viewed in this light, the modernist motto of "making it new" can be seen as taking on a genuinely radical spin in the hands of Stein who, contra Pound, conducts the avant-garde experiments in a manner yet inaccessible to existing methodologies, identifying the site of "making it new" in a realm beyond the methodically known and knowable.

Both critical and exploratory, or critical as exploratory, Stein's position on the issue of method is, as such, exemplarily postmodern, and its characteristic features herald a poetics of counter-method soon to be recognized as one of the most important precursory modes of innovative praxes in the twentieth century, a poetics whose method-resistance invokes Jean-François Lyotard's theorizing of the postmodern artists in relation to their modalities of composition:

> A postmodern artist or writer is in the position of a philosopher: the text he writes, the work he produces are not in principle governed by pre-established rules, and they cannot be judged according to a determining judgment, by applying familiar categories to the text or to the work. These rules or categories are what the work of art itself is looking for. The artist and the writer, then, are working without rules in order to formulate the rules of what *will have been done.* Hence the fact that work and text have the characters of an *event;* hence also, they always come too late for their author, or, what amounts to the same thing, their being put into work, their realization (*mise en oeuvre*) always begins too soon.[113]

Toward a Philosophy of Counter-Method

Stein's poetics of counter-method, so understood in light of Lyotard's concept of the postmodern, thus presents an aesthetic-methodological significance that transcends the parameters of the literary. It can be read as articulating a critical rethinking symbiotic with the epochal ethos of radical inquiry. Among other issues, it resonates, in particular, with a philosophical critique of method and methodology in terms of instrumental reasoning in the sciences, a critique that has, from diverse perspectives and with various degrees of iconoclasm, taken the center stage in the intellectual arena since the turn of the last century.

Having credited Friedrich Nietzsche with being "the first to recognize" and to "[gain] this insight into the relation of method to science,"[114] Martin Heidegger, for instance, continues the criticism of method in *On the Way to Language.* He again calls into question the nature and function of method at work in science, epitomizing method as having metamorphosed into a power at once deterministic and constitutive:

The sciences know the way to knowledge by the term "method." Method, especially in today's modern scientific thought, is not a mere instrument serving the sciences; rather, it has pressed the sciences into its own service. . . . In the sciences, not only is the theme drafted, called up by the method, it is also set up within the method and remains within the framework of the method, subordinated to it. . . . Method holds all the coercive power of knowledge. The theme is a part of the method. . . . The object of knowledge is part of the method.[115]

More importantly, he identifies—and this is, both in theory and in practice, particularly pertinent to the understanding not only of the difficulty of Stein's work but also of the objectives of formal experiments in American avant-garde poetry later, experiments that are often articulated, understood, and executed precisely in those terms—the working mechanisms of method in four reciprocally interlaced aspects of research, procedure, investigation, and experiment. In an essay titled "The Age of the World View," Heidegger begins his analysis with a question: "The essence of what we call science is research. What is the essence of research?"[116] To this question, the answer is "procedure," which he thus explains:

It is the fact that knowledge establishes itself as a procedure in a realm of the existent, of nature or of history. Procedure means here not only method, a way of proceeding—for every procedure needs a sphere in which it can move—but, more precisely, the opening of such a sphere; this is the basic procedure of research. It is accomplished through the projection of a definite ground plan of natural processes in a sphere of the existent, for example, in nature. The projection indicates the way in which the cognitive procedure must adhere to the sphere it has opened up for itself. This adherence is the discipline of research.

Through the projection of the ground plan and the condition of exactitude the method secures for itself its proper area within the sphere of being.[117]

As method at its most ambitious and most deterministic, procedure, Heidegger argues, constitutes the essence of research by legitimating itself as the ultimate point of reference from which, and from which alone, to prescribe a rule-guided investigation which consists, structurally, functionally, as well as teleologically, of an automatic verification of its projected objectives and a guaranteed clarification of its predetermined findings. Hence a self-referential circle:

> Science becomes research through the projection and through the verification of the projection in the discipline of the procedure. But projection and discipline develop into what they are only in the procedure. . . . Only within the boundaries of rule and law are facts revealed as the facts they are. The investigation of facts in the sphere of nature is in itself the establishment and preservation of rule and law. The procedure through which an object area is apprehended has the character of clarification. It always remains twofold. It founds an unknown by means of a known, and at the same time preserves this known through that unknown. Clarification is carried out in investigation.[118]

In this context, experiment is anything but capricious, for "natural science does not become research through experiment," Heidegger continues; "on the contrary, experiment becomes possible where, and only where, natural knowledge has already been transformed into research."[119] He then explains, in more concrete terms, the nature and function of experiment in research procedure, outlining the methical and methodological structure that sustains a representational foreclosure:

> To set up an experiment means to assume a situation where it becomes possible to trace a definite nexus of motions in the necessity of its course, that is, to control its calculation in advance. But the determination of the law occurs with a view to the ground plan of the object area. The latter gives the measure and fixes in advance the representation of the situation. Such representation, in which and with which the experiment starts, is no capricious imagining. That is why Newton said: *hypotheses non fingo,* the bases are not arbitrarily invented. They

are developed out of the ground plan of nature and are written into it. The experiment is that procedure which in its arrangement and execution is borne and guided by the law basic to it, in order to produce the facts which confirm the law or deny confirmation. The more exactly the ground plan of nature has been projected, the more exact will be the possibility of the experiment.[120]

Such being the case, Heidegger's critical insight that "the real system of sciences rests on the consistency of its methods,"[121] his critique of methodology as instrumental reasoning, his philosophical alternative in terms of thinking, and his postulate of counter-method that "in thinking there is neither method nor theme, but rather the region, so called because it gives its realm and free reign to what thinking is given to think,"[122] lead to a rather mythopoetic speculation on the meaning of the Tao or "way" in "Laotse's poetic thinking."[123] Imagining what is left unsaid in the word "way," he envisions, then, a different method: it is a method whose power originates from that of the world rather than from being imposed onto the world. "Perhaps the enigmatic power of today's reign of method also, and indeed preeminently, stems from the fact that the methods, notwithstanding their efficiency, are after all merely the runoff of a great hidden stream which moves all things along and makes way for everything," he thus speculates, rather poetically, "All is way."[124]

Heidegger's critique of scientific methods as such and his search for alternatives find a corresponding expression in Hans-Georg Gadamer and his theory of hermeneutics. "The logical self-reflection which accompanied the development of human sciences in the nineteenth century," Gadamer states from the outset in *Truth and Method,* "is wholly dominated by the model of the natural sciences."[125] Central to this model, he specifies further, is "Descartes' idea of method," one that represents "the fundamental presupposition of the enlightenment, according to which a methodologically disciplined use of reason can safeguard us from all error."[126] For Gadamer, it is this privilege of the founding status of methodology, which is none other than the privilege of "the pure transcendental subjectivity of the ego" as an omniscient methodologist,[127] which must be called into question. "In modern science this metaphysical idea of the way in which the knowing subject is adequate to the object of knowledge is without justification," Gadamer thus contends, for "its methodological ideal ensures for every one of its stages a return to the elements from which its knowledge is built up."[128]

To such a Cartesian methodology, Bacon's "methodological sugges-tions,"[129] Gadamer observes, have failed to present themselves as adequate options. They turn out to be "too vague and general and have produced little, especially when applied to the study of nature."[130] Predicated upon Bacon's "goal of conquering nature through obedience, the new attitude of attacking and forcing nature's secrets from it, which makes him the predecessor of modern science," Bacon's method is, its "obedience" and "new attitude" notwithstanding, equally and no less characteristically "programmatic."[131] Positioning himself against "the theory of induction on the basis of the enumeratio simplex" and of the "anticipatio" general-ization, Bacon, Gadamer points out, differs from other philosophers of "modern scientific theory and logic" in that he opts for "what he calls in-terpretatio naturae," which means "the expert explication of the true being of nature."[132] However phrased, Bacon's "expert explication" is "expert" precisely because it itself remains a methical operation, a procedure followed through "by means of methodically conducted experiments," and executed "step by step."[133] In addition, the chief purpose of these methodically conducted experiments, which are purported to discipline the mind by "carrying out a methodical self-purification of the mind," is rather modest, as it aims at eschewing no more than just "overhasty generalization":

> The required method Bacon himself describes as experimental. But it must be remembered that by "experiment" Bacon does not always just mean the scientist's technical procedure of artificially induced pro-cesses in isolating conditions and making them capable of being mea-sured. An experiment is also, and primarily, the careful directing of our mind, preventing it from indulging in overhasty generalizations, and consciously confronting it with the most remote and apparently most diverse instances, so that it may learn, in a gradual and continuous way, to work, via the process of exclusion, toward the axioms.[134]

Following his methodology of conquer-through-obedience, Bacon thus maps out a methodical procedure refashioned as new, and his experi-ments take the form of his own "method of induction," which, as is the case with all methods, "seeks to rise above the unruly and accidental way in which daily experience takes place."[135] In this sense, Bacon remains "profoundly involved in the metaphysical tradition and in the dialectical forms of argument that he attacked,"[136] Gadamer observes; and consequently, his revisionist approach to "the pure use of our reason, proceeding according to methodological principles," proves to be inadequate and "disappointing."[137]

In contrast to modern science and its foregrounding of method and methodology, as evidenced in the works of Descartes and Bacon, "a philosophical theory of hermeneutics," Gadamer makes it emphatically clear, "is not a methodology."[138] Insisting on the fundamental distinctions between natural sciences and human sciences, between ratified knowledge and practical knowledge, he argues that "from its historical origin, the problem of hermeneutics goes beyond the limits that the concept of method sets to modern science," and that "the experience of the sociohistorical world cannot be raised to a science by the inductive procedure of the natural sciences."[139] That being said, Gadamer then finds his alternative of counter-method in "the humanistic tradition" in general and in the art of rhetoric in particular, with both represented by Vico and his idea of "sensus communis."[140]

For Gadamer, the predilection for counter-method in Vico's humanistic tradition is conditioned by and manifested in two aspects of life experience. Hermeneutically, on the one hand, it is shown not only in its embrace of "the positive ambiguity of the rhetorical ideal," but also in its returning to and reappropriation of one "element from the classical tradition."[141] Aristotelian in nature, this one element central in Vico's thinking is the emphasis on "the practical ideal of phronesis" over "the theoretical ideal of sophia"—that is, the privilege of the "knowledge of the concrete" over the "knowledge from general principles":[142]

> The old Aristotelian distinction between practical and theoretical knowledge is operative here—a distinction which cannot be reduced to that between the true and the probable. Practical knowledge, phronesis, is another kind of knowledge. Primarily, it means that it is directed towards the concrete situation. Thus it must grasp the "circumstances" in their infinite variety. This is what Vico expressly emphasizes about it. It is true that his main concern is to show that this kind of knowledge is outside the rational concept of knowledge, but this is not in fact mere resignation.[143]

In this sense, Gadamer asserts, practical knowledge, or *phronesis,* is method-resistant because it consists entirely of pragmatic variables; and concrete knowledge is beyond the rational administration of methodology because it is situation-specific and circumstances-dependent, both being, moreover, infinite in varieties.

Ethically, on the other hand, *phronesis* defies methodological principles in that it is locally and communally constituted, and in that its status as practical knowledge is contingent upon *sensus communis,* which is itself always concretely situated and historically contextualized in a given segment of the spatiotemporal continuum. Inasmuch as it is part and parcel of the life experience in a sociohistorical world, Gadamer points out, this *sensus communis* should be properly understood as also constitutive of the ethics of life:

> Sensus communis here obviously does not mean only that general faculty in all men, but the sense that founds community. According to Vico, what gives the human will its direction is not the abstract generality of reason, but the concrete generality that represents the community of a group, a people, a nation, or the whole human race. Hence the development of this sense of the community is of primary importance for living.[144]

Viewed from this perspective, "an argument based on universals, a reasoned proof, is not sufficient," Gadamer adds, "because what is important is the circumstances."[145]

In the critique of scientific method and methodology, one of the most forthright and most powerful voices is, without any doubt, that of Paul Feyerabend. With his position already announced frontally in the title of his book *Against Method,* Feyerabend, himself a philosopher of science, begins and ends his study by emphatically reiterating his argument that *"all methodologies, even the most obvious ones, have their limits."*[146] These methodological limits are immanent and inevitable, he points out, due to the nature of what is called knowledge. Be it scientific or humanistic, knowledge is neither a conceptual package nor an empirical data set, neatly wrapped, cleanly completed, and ready for pickup at a place designated and pointed to by a given road sign of method, he argues; on the contrary, it itself is an ongoing dynamics of diverse human experiences grasped only momentarily and relationally in an equally ongoing complexity of understanding ceaselessly shaping, de-shaping, and reshaping itself:

> Knowledge . . . is not a series of self-consistent theories that converges towards an ideal view; it is not a gradual approach to the truth. It is

rather an ever increasing *ocean of mutually incompatible alternatives,* each single theory, each fairy-tale, each myth that is part of the collection forcing the others into greater articulation and all of them contributing, via this process of competition, to the development of our consciousness.[147]

As such, knowledge "defies analysis on the basis of rules which have been set up in advance and without regard to the ever-changing conditions of history," Feyerabend continues; it is, by nature, beyond "the naïve and simple-minded rules which methodologists take as their guide," and by which facts "enter our knowledge [as] already viewed in a certain way and [as], therefore, essentially ideational."[148] Insofar as any new discoveries or new findings are concerned, "such as the invention of atomism in antiquity, the Copernican Revolution, the rise of modern atomism (kinetic theory; dispersion theory; stereochemistry; quantum theory), the graduate emergence of the wave theory of light," they are not the results of faithful adherence to and rigorous implementation of methods and methodologies, he contends; rather, they "occurred only because some thinkers either *decided* not to be bound by certain 'obvious' methodological rules, or because they *unwittingly broke* them."[149]

But what is most important in Feyerabend's thinking in *Against Method*—and this is also most pertinent to the thesis of this study—is his critical insight with regard to the practicality of his own position specified by the preposition "against," and the feasibility of any methodical and methodological alternatives. In other words, he raises the vexed issue of "how" in terms of a critical counter-strategy vis-à-vis method per se, method, that is, which has itself become the constitution of humanity. Feyerabend puts forth this insight in the form of a question, one indicative of the seemingly insuperable difficulty:

Now—how can we possibly examine something we are using all the time? How can we analyze the terms in which we habitually express our most simple and straightforward observations, and reveal their presuppositions? How can we discover the kind of world we presuppose when proceeding as we do?[150]

To this question "the answer is clear," he nevertheless responds unequivocally: "We cannot discover it from the *inside,*" from, that is, within the "circle" of any type of methodical foreclosure.[151]

That being granted, Feyerabend's alternative from the outside finds its form in a radically critical and intensely self-reflexive reappropriation of none other than the scientific method as such. "The problems of scientific rationality," he insists, "are not solved by a change of standards but by taking a different view of standards altogether"[152]—that is, by rethinking method as a form of instrumental reasoning, and by looking into method itself, into its conceptual predispositions and concomitant structural blueprints, as constitutive of scientific rationality. To do so, Feyerabend then terms his own approaches respectively as "anarchistic methodology" and *"pluralistic methodology"*; and the only principle that characterizes these methodologies alike is summed up as *"anything goes."*[153] In addition, they are further defined specifically by the prefix "counter-," as in "counter-rules" and "counterinduction," among others.[154] Functioning, in one sense, as the second-order observations, these counter-methods are deployed so as to bring into visibility what has hitherto remained methodically and habitually invisible, and they accomplish this task by de-ontologizing methods under scrutiny through their own explicitly denatured identities as methods, with their "counter-" operations functioning as mirror images implicating both. Or, as Feyerabend himself puts it, counter-methods are used to "expose familiar rules of the scientific enterprise" by "tracing the consequences of 'counterrules'" or counter-methods.[155] Anarchistic, pluralistic, and counter-, Feyerabend's methodology thus resorts to a transdisciplinary use of "historical examples," of "a multiplicity of theories, metaphysical views, fairy-tales."[156] It is a use intended not to "replace one set of general rules by another such set," Feyerabend again makes clear, but to "demonstrate the limits and even the irrationality of some rules"[157] by having each set of rules "serving as [others'] 'bad conscience.'"[158] In this sense, a counter-methodologist "is like an undercover agent," he summarizes by way of an analogy, "who plays the game of Reason in order to undercut the authority of Reason (Truth, Honesty, Justice, and so on)."[159]

Feyerabend's methodology, so conceived of as counter-, anarchistic, and pluralistic, seems to have found its working model in the philosophy of Michel Serres, whose "anti-method" is personified in Hermes, the mythological figure reappropriated as its operative metaphor.[160]

A contemporary philosopher of the history of science, who is also referred to, very interestingly indeed, as "a poet-philosopher of science," Michel Serres is well known for his rather unconventional engagement in a trans-disciplinary study of science, philosophy, and literature, an approach that "runs counter to the prevalent" disciplinary thinking, be it scientific, philosophic, or humanistic.[161] More specifically, his work is based on "abandoning the methods of traditional philosophy," as Maria L. Assad observes, so much so that, in principle, it "cannot be explained and analyzed, it can only be implied."[162] Famous for its storytelling, mythological episodes, game plays, and poetic renditions of scientific phenomena, it defies any methodological mapping, making it nearly impossible to locate any passages of metalanguage quotable as his theoretical statements. Such a formal and textual formation is not whimsical, however. It is predicated, in fact, upon Serres's belief that "order is not the law of things but their exception," upon his understanding of an epistemology best described as "pluralistic" or "encyclopedic," and upon a different concept of knowledge thinkable "not in terms of its laws and its regularities, but in terms of perturbations and turbulences," "not in terms of order and mastery but in terms of chance and invention."[163] As such, epistemology, from Serres's standpoint, thus provides "access not only to a field of knowledge but," and more importantly in a Steinian sense, "to the world as well."[164] Epistemology is, in other words, doing natural phenomena.[165]

It follows then that Serres's "method of thinking," more accurately defined as "anti-method," is "fundamentally antithetical" to existing scientific and philosophical methods and methodologies.[166] For example, in contrast to the conventional method of the "stance," which foregrounds "the singular position taken, the unifying locus attained, in short, rational unity," Serres's method is, as Assad argues, that of "the circum-stances."[167] In other words, it is a method that "leads to, and is the chaotic encounter with, the multiple."[168] Also referred to as the "Ulyssean method," this method of circumstances, according to Serres's own explanation in *Les cinq sens,* presents a "route that is oblique, tortuous and complicated"; it dramatizes, therefore, not a reduction or a predication of the world but a faithful articulation of it: "Circumstances express a multiplicity that is irreducible to unity."[169]

Serres's anti-method receives perhaps the most concrete description from Bruno Latour who, in an obvious effort to understand it, puzzles over Serres's novel orientation by contrasting it with the standard moves of conventional methodology. In an essay titled, rather tellingly, "The Enlightenment Without the Critique: A Word on Michel Serres' Philosophy," Latour, as if soliloquizing in a tone not without a tinge of frustration and impatience, characterizes Serres's overall position of anti-method as "so totally un-French, that is to say, un-German, in his philosophical tradition".[170]

Instead of believing in divides, divisions, and classifications, Serres studies how *any* divide is drawn, including the one between past and present, between culture and science, between concepts and data, between subject and object, between religion and science, between order and disorder and also of course, divides and partitions between scholarly disciplines. Instead of choosing camps and reinforcing one side of the divide, of the crisis, of the critique—all these words are one and the same—Serres sits on the fence. Instead of dealing with a set, he always takes as the only object worth the effort the extraction of the set *from its complement.* If Serres were choosing the inside of the set, he would be a rationalist; were it to take the side of the complement, he would be called an irrationalist. How would you call someone who chooses the extraction of the set from its complement? Hyper- or infra-rationalist?[171]

His frustration and impatience aside, the difficulty Latour faces in trying to classify Serres in the established taxonomy of methodology makes an illuminative statement. More important, then, is his observation of Serres's fence-sitting position, from where to focus on "how *any* divide is drawn" and on "the extraction of the set from its complement." Though unwittingly, perhaps, Latour's own phrasal choice of "how" and "extraction from" proves to be abundantly indicative, shedding light on an investigative objective at work in what seems to be an unnameable approach. Central to Serres's "anti-method" is, as Latour has thus implicitly suggested, the critical awareness of the constitutive status of method. "The medium is the 'method,'" as Harari and Bell have also brought it to focus; and its nature and function as organized, disciplinary, and administrative violence have been manifested, since the classical age, in diverse aspects of the human construction of reality such as, among others, legitimating knowledge, forming power relations, and establishing ideological dominations.[172] The analogy Serres himself draws to characterize method as such is one of a military operation. Alluding pointedly to Descartes' theory on method, he defines method as a military science: "The most general knowledge that can be formed, the most exact, the most faithful, and the most effective, can be deciphered by a military model. The discourse on method is a science of war."[173] With much less figurative and rhetorical flare, Harari and Bell, in their effort to explain Serres's "anti-method," offer a simpler and yet more straightforward description of how method works and what its concomitant problems are in both concept and practice:

> In Serres's work, method is found in the construction of models and in their applications and variations according to mathematical operations. Method is the illustration of a given type of knowledge through the set of results that the method can produce. But the term method itself is problematic because it suggests the notion of repetition and predictability—a method that anyone can apply. Method implies also mastery and closure, both of which are detrimental to invention. On the contrary, Serres's method invents: it is thus an *anti-method*.[174]

Sketched in this description is an implied mandate concerning what Serres's anti-method would entail. First, anti-method takes its point of departure by calling into question method itself as a constitutive agency. In order to engage anti-method at all as a form of critical-exploratory inquiry, Harari and Bell seem to assert, one has to be, first and foremost, method-savvy, sensitive to its omnipresence, knowledgeable of its forms of manifestation, wary of its efficacy, and critical of its results. In other words, not only does one have to possess the knowledge of the nature, function, and working mechanisms of method, but one also has to acquire the critical ability to discern the workings of method in different fields by reconstructing their operative models out of invisibility. Second, anti-method, by virtue of its prefix *anti-*, does not have any illusionary purchase whatsoever on the notion that "method invents," which is, after all, Cartesian; and invention, viewed from this perspective, should at this point be properly understood as counter-invention—that is, as a self-reflexively inventive ingenuity that inquires into method itself as the hitherto traditional form of human invention. Third, when implementing this anti-method with its double valence of reconstruction and/as deconstruction, one locates one's entry point in the form or the structure of the target object. In his own practice, what Serres looks for specifically, for instance, is "a formal set of operations of interference, transformation, and passage," an "identical structure," or "formal equivalences—isomorphisms," which establish "convergences and alliances" across disciplines; and what is "in question" for Serres in this critical-exploratory maneuver is "precisely the structure of the text itself."[175]

As is indicated by the title of his book *Hermes: Literature, Science, Philosophy,* Serres's metaphor for his anti-method is Hermes. A versatile figure, Hermes presents for Serres not a system but a motion or a movement, one that traverses the boundaries of disciplinary methods and methodologies. Moreover, Hermes' movement is not a direct, planned itinerary to truth but a *randonnée,* which connotes etymologically the notion of impetuosity, chance, and randomness.[176] It is therefore not a "systematic and genetic exposition" of the world,[177] the presence of which would then be conjured up a priori by a coherent thought-structure exterior to the world; rather, it is construed as a journey, a voyage, an excursion, an expedition in the world, "the outcome of which," as is also the case with Serres's own writing, "cannot be predicted."[178] "Filled with random discoveries," this Hermesian voyage proceeds by unfolding "*the sum of all displacements,*"[179] displacements that enact and intensify a ceaseless reorientation followed by an immediate de-orientation, a continuous positioning, repositioning, and de-positioning that resist any methodization. First recognizing and then traversing the established methodical boundaries, Hermes thus finds its multiple, changing identity in a re-connector/de-connector, in "the weaver . . . at the crossroads," and in the "exchanger,"[180] always insinuating satirically its own possibility, or promise, of becoming a method. As a metaphor for Serres's anti-method tailored to his advocate for a pluralistic or encyclopedic epistemology based on "a quantitative model," Hermes presents "a philosophy of transport over one of fixity in order to counter the dogmatism of unified and systematic knowledge."[181]

The Poetics of Counter-Method:
The Case of Postmodern American Poetry

Following Antin's postulate of an aesthetic-methodological bifurcation that separates Pound from Stein, and distinguishes modernism from postmodernism, one finds that Stein's poetics of counter-method, with Hermes as its metaphor embarking on a critical-exploratory voyage, presents a model most enthusiastically received and most favorably invoked in diverse innovative experiments in the postmodern American poetry scene.

More specifically, at the level of practice, the compositional foregrounding of method as the medium in avant-garde writing can be argued as having manifested itself in yet another bifurcation. There is, on the one hand, what might be called a use/production-oriented approach bent on generating surprises of unforeseen results. Curiosity driven, it is an approach in which method takes on the role of play, whereby its "determined" character is perceived as having been dismissed, and its "predicative potential" is assumed as having given way to propositionless possibilities accessible via compositional games. In his introduction to *Postmodern American Poetry: A Norton Anthology*, Paul Hoover, for one, identifies such a deployment of "method" as one of the defining features of postmodern poetry, a feature contributory to "a constructionist rather than an expressionist theory of composition" by replacing "intention."[182] This approach, be it called productive or constructionist or generative, is predicated upon a dual premise. Philosophically, it follows the Gadamerian principle that advocates, as Stephen Fredman has pointed out, "the elevation of play to a philosophically meaningful description of art and science."[183] In other words, having been brought back from the kingdom of metaphysics to the playground of the quotidian,[184] method, in its artistic or playful use, is allowed once again "to dominate with relativistic flash and brilliance."[185] It is then offered a seat in the pantheon of hermeneutics, endowed once more with a generative power construed as philosophical in essence.[186] Aesthetically, it adopts the Oulipian theory of what Raymond Queneau calls *littérature potentielle;*[187] it is a literature whose potentiality results from the deliberate and strict imposition of various methods and arbitrary constraints. By "erecting the aesthetic of formal constraint, then," so explains Warren Motte, "the Oulipo simultaneously devalues inspiration,"[188] which in turn allows constraints to function, as Joseph Conte argues, "as a generative, or exploratory, device."[189] Hence the "seeming paradox" in Oulipian aesthetics, and hence the appropriated tenet for practice in American avant-garde poetry, which is put in a nutshell by Motte: "Systems of formal constraint—far from restricting a writer—actually afford a field of creative liberty."[190]

On the other hand, there is a critique/exploration-oriented approach to method. Resonating with the philosophical preoccupations of the entire historical epoch "since Nietzsche," it is an approach that has, by Don Byrd's account, perceived the function of method and methodology as being "reactive, theorizing and narrativizing its moment of crisis."[191] And this particular manifestation of the poetics of counter-method in postmodern American poetry is the critical focus of this study.

Since the first generation of postmodernists, the self-reflexive character typical of the intellectual ambience of the period finds its expression, among others, in an intensified skepticism of, if not an overt obsession with, the issue of method. This critical sensitivity to method, which is articulated in the pages of both poetry and poetics in a manner more Derridean than Bloomian, more analytical than psychological, indicates unmistakably that certain poets, alongside of those pursuing the use/production-oriented approach, do view method suspiciously,[192] calling into question, from different perspectives, the "dialectical frame" as well as the "predicative potential" of method. Thus, this critique/exploration-oriented approach is the one in which method, with its philosophical, epistemological, and sociopolitical implications fully recognized and acknowledged, is dissected so as to probe into its structural and functional mechanisms that are constitutive of any hierarchal totality. In this sense, the "exploration" component of this approach is understood as committed to a double mission. First, exploration joins the critique as the initial, preparatory stage of the latter in that it investigates, studies, and analyzes the actual makeup of method's dialectical frame as well as its predicative structure, providing its findings for critique. Second, it presents itself as a Hermesian voyage, venturing into the unknown and gesturing toward potential discoveries, all in its very own act of investigation and critique; and the more radical and more thorough its investigation and critique, the closer and more approximate it is to a negatively dialectical new, to an a-predicative potential, to a threshold onto a methodical exteriority.

Pursuing this critique/exploration-oriented approach of counter-method, the selected poets included in this book can be seen as sharing, both in principle and in practice, the following critical dispositions. For one thing, they problematize two types of methods in their works. Inextricably intertwined with one another, these methods are writing's methods and "language's methods."[193] For another, resorting to Serres's model, they identify both types of methods and their working mechanisms in the structures of conventional texts of various kinds, and they convert their own texts into the conceptual-structural sites where the problems of method in terms of writing and language are investigated and theorized. For yet another, as a corollary of the aforementioned two dispositions, these poets regard poetry, or the writing of poetry, as an active, counter-methodical performance defined by Bruce Andrews as "rereading"; more concretely put, for these poets, poetry, to the extent that it is a critical-analytical reengagement with method as a problem, is the *"rereading* [of] the reading that a social status quo puts us through."[194]

This book, with its title taken from Andrews's critical-poetical formulation, is an attempt, in a limited fashion, to map the diverse perspectives from which the issue of method is addressed or re-read. The eight essays included here fall roughly into two categories. The first four essays bring to the fore one feature of the poetics of counter-method, one that is predicated in principle upon a theorem formulated by Louis Zukofsky. One of the first-generation postmodernists, Zukofsky states, resonating with Stein's notion of writing as doing natural phenomena: "Writing occurs which is the detail, not mirage, of seeing, of thinking *with* the things as they exist."[195] This postmodernist, appositional poetics of "with," rather than the modernist, hierarchal poetics of "of" or "about," is then examined respectively in Zukofsky's rethinking of the method of citation, in George Oppen's questioning of the objectivists' own method of seeing, in Carl Rakosi's critique of language as the method of epistemology, and in John Cage's parodic appropriation of chance operation and the mesostic method. The second set of four essays concentrate on a similar or related aspect of the poetics of counter-method, one that is articulated by a theorem put forward by Charles Bernstein. A later-generation postmodernist, Bernstein posits that "all writing is a demonstration of method," which is boiled down inevitably to concrete "language practice,"[196] sociopolitically mediated and ideologically routinized. This postmodern sensitivity to the tripartite formation of "writing practice-method practice-language practice" is then analyzed in terms of Susan Howe's questioning of the method of grammar and historiography, of Lyn Hejinian's inquiry into the method of memory and time, of Bruce Andrews's insight into the method of contextual redundancy as constitutive of conventional writing and communication, and of Charles Bernstein's investigation of the method of meaning production by way of a general economy of idling language.

That being said, this book is not a comprehensive, historical survey of postmodern American poetry. Nor is it a diachronic study of the opus of some poets from artistic inception to aesthetic maturity. Rather, it focuses on some selected poets whose writings in poetry and poetics present, at certain moments in the trajectory of their creative and critical valences, a most articulate and most intense sensitivity toward the polemics of method. Due to its positioning best described as radical, such sensitivity may or may not continue in the works of these poets, and more often than not, the latter is the case. But that is exactly the point: precisely because this postmodern moment of critical intensity is only transient, its insight is genuinely avant-garde. These essays here are but a modest attempt to capture and grasp this avant-garde moment in postmodern American poetry.

The "present" essay is but a tissue of quotations.

—Editor's note from *Critique* (1969) for the first version of Jacques

Derrida's text, reproduced in *Dissemination*

The text is a tissue of quotations drawn from the innumerable centres of culture.

—Roland Barthes, *Image, Music, Text*

I. A "No Man's Land": Postmodern Citationality in Zukofsky's "Poem beginning 'The'"

In his essay titled "American Poetry, 1920–1930," which addresses the issue of the imagistic diction employed by his modernist precursors Pound, Eliot, William Carlos Williams, Marianne Moore, and H.D., Louis Zukofsky makes the following observation: "Whatever one's preferences, the diction of these poets remains their fully varied material"; and he quickly adds, "which includes quotations from sources apparently useful in preserving poetry wherever it is found."[1] Zukofsky's description of modernist poetics as, among other features, a poetics of quotation, teleologically selective and artistically mimetic, points toward his own rethinking of modernist praxis. As Rainer Nägele proclaims, "Radical thought emerges from the deepest immersion into tradition. It is never a creation *ex nihilo,* but the effect of translation and interpretation."[2] If this is true, then Zukofsky, himself a "brilliant disciple" of the Pound tradition,[3] is also, and to no lesser degree than Pound or his contemporaries, an ambitious innovator. With his own poetics "rooted in Pound's 'Grand Collage,'"[4] Zukofsky's critical insight into the modernist tradition—a tradition that Michael André Bernstein describes as "carrying" a "load of embedded quotations," the interaction of which "constitutes a central thematic concern and narrative convention"[5]—foregrounds a concomitant inquiry beyond the parameters of modernism. More specifically, it is an inquiry that explicitly anticipates a postmodern perspective, one articulated in his poetry

39

through an exploration of what Hugh Kenner describes as the "strange possibility" that "whatever is sayable has already somewhere been said."[6] "Poem beginning 'The,'" in this sense, marks Zukofsky's departure from the modernist poetics of citation oriented toward "a conceptual reorganization and a new linguistic encoding of the real world" to a postmodernist poetics of intertextuality,[7] of a "generalized citationality" featuring,[8] in the poet's own words, "chorál out / of random input," which is "made / with an assemblage of naught."[9]

In his *ABC of Reading*, Pound begins the section titled "Exhibits" with a statement that might be read as an encapsulated and yet systematic theorizing or rationalizing of the modernist use of quotations. He writes:

> The ideal way to present the next section of this booklet would be to give the quotations WITHOUT any comment whatever. I am afraid that would be too revolutionary. By long and wearing experience I have learned that in the present imperfect state of the world, one MUST tell the reader. I made a very bad mistake in my INSTIGATIONS, the book had a plan, I thought the reader would see it.[10]

The issue at stake here is not *what* but *how* to quote. It is, in other words, an issue of methodology. Designed primarily to educate, to enlighten, to communicate, Pound's poetics, however he may describe or define it, is intended in light of this passage to be the poetics of "exhibits." In the Poundian project of "Make it new," in which the antecedent for "it" points, as Leonard Diepeveen observes, to "the past poetic/political tradition,"[11] to exhibit is to quote, in that quotation is, ideally for the poet, the most eloquent and most effective form of articulation bodying forth a built-in "plan." Semantically self-evident and communicatively self-sufficient, quotations constitute, in the Poundian scheme of things, the methodological underpinning of the imagist aesthetic. Not only do quotations, for instance, provide the most viable (i.e., the most direct) routes to Pound's "direct treatment of the 'thing' whether subjective or objective," but they also satisfy the need "to use absolutely no word that does not contribute to the presentation."[12] For economically, quotations, due to their concreteness and precision, help to achieve what Pound calls the "maximum efficiency of expression" by saving the modernists from the burden and embarrassment of "saying the same thing with less skill and less conviction";[13] rhetorically, they establish for the poet "a strategic position" in a given context, functioning as "luminous details";[14] and ideologically, quotations "bear true witness" to cultural and historical manifestations,[15] thus presenting what Diepeveen describes as "a formalist, a-temporal version of originality."[16] Such a description seems even more apt in light of Pound's conception of the nature of poetry. For one thing, "logopoeia," asserts Pound, "does not translate, though the attitude of mind it expresses may pass through a paraphrase."[17] For another, poetry, as "the most concentrated form of verbal expression,"[18] will not allow the verbiage of paraphrase. Commenting on "how complete is Mr. Eliot's depiction of our contemporary condition" in *Prufrock and Other Observations,* for instance, Pound emphatically draws one's attention to Eliot's "method of conveying a whole situation and half a character by three words of a quoted phrase."[19] "Great poets," Marianne Moore recalls Pound saying, "seldom make bricks without straw. They pick up all the excellences they can beg, borrow, or steal from their predecessors and contemporaries and then set their own inimitable light atop the mountain."[20]

Somewhat similar is Eliot's theorizing of the modernist use of quotations, whose aesthetic premises consist of two principles: a "historical sense [as] a perception, not only of the past-ness of the past, but of its presence," as he writes in "Tradition and the Individual Talent," and a "conception of poetry as a living whole of all the poetry that has ever been written."[21] Such a diachronic trajectory opens, by its all-embracing "oneness," a synchronic field in which a new synthesis takes place.[22] "When a poet's mind is perfectly equipped for its work," remarks Eliot in "The Metaphysical Poets," "it is constantly amalgamating disparate experience. . . . In the mind of the poet these experiences are always forming new wholes."[23] Equally amalgamated into new constellations are quotations, and how this is done, according to Eliot in "Philip Massinger," suggests a poet's quality. He writes:

> One of the surest of tests is the way in which a poet borrows; immature poets imitate, mature poets steal; bad poets deface what they take, and good poets make it into something better, or at least something different. The good poet welds his theft into a whole of feeling which is unique, utterly different from that from which it was torn; the bad poet throws it into something which has no cohesion.[24]

Much, however, of what Pound has originally envisioned as the poetics of exhibits remains, to a great extent, only ideal or "too revolutionary."

When applied "in the present imperfect state of the world," such "directness of presentation" has to be compromised,[25] made less direct with modifications; that is, the poetics of exhibits, of showing, of presentation, must be supplemented by and, in turn, subordinated to, a poetics of commentary, of telling, of representation.[26] Pervaded by what Michele J. Leggott calls "the spirit of breezy opinionation,"[27] the modernist use of quotations in Pound and Eliot thus follows, by necessity, a method, which is a quadruple formula characterized by the "coincidence" of what Meir Sternberg labels as the four "universals" defining the working mechanisms of quotations: "representational bound, structural framing, communicative subordination, and perspectival montage or ambiguity."[28]

To quote is, first and foremost, to serve the purpose of representation. The referential function of the quoted material is appropriated in a given context in order to illustrate, to prove, to argue, to annotate, or to exemplify a particular point highlighted in an overall scheme of representation. And whichever the specific case might be, "the evocation of the past always occurs in such a way as to illuminate the present," as Herbert Grabes points out; "The situation presented in the poem forms the common meeting-point for all the levels and phases of reality evoked by quotations."[29] As a means of achieving Pound's "triumph of total meaning over detail," or as a way to establish his "new synthesis,"[30] a quotation thus circumscribes a representational bound at two mutually reciprocal levels: local/microcosmic and universal/macrocosmic. While functioning as what Jennifer Clarvoe calls a "local, small scale introduction to the dynamics of the poem as a whole,"[31] a quotation also asserts, by the same token, that "the particular and local bears universal significance without forfeiting its concreteness."[32] A case in point is Pound's use of quotations from Confucius. At the center—whether thematic or structural—of "Canto XIII," for instance, is posited the Confucian ethics of order, an idea that represents or, according to Albert Gelpi, "speaks for the side of Pound which is conservative, traditional, sexist, mandarin, rationalist," and an idea that Pound, expediently enough, has summarized and appropriated from *The Great Digest* in order to articulate his own sociopolitical concerns:[33]

> If a man have not order within him
> He can not spread order about him;
> And if a man have not order within him
> His family will not act with due order;

And if the prince have not order within him
He can not put order in his dominions.[34]

With the Confucian ethics of order thus centrally established, all the quotations in the poem are then deployed, both strategically and rhetorically, to pertain to this Confucian social philosophy, each favoring "order" from a different angle, and each articulating a strong, individual sense of initiative and moral responsibility, regardless of one's sphere of application or social position.[35] Tseu-lou's personal view of "I would put the defences in order" is juxtaposed with Khieu's royal standpoint: "If I were lord of a province / I would put it in better order than this is"; and Tchi's emphasis on humbleness—"I would prefer a small mountain temple, / With order in the observances, / with a suitable performance of the ritual"[36]—is endorsed by Kung himself, who then further specifies it in terms of moderation: "Anyone can run to excesses, / It is easy to shoot past the mark, / It is hard to stand firm in the middle." Whichever way one may pursue, to restore and maintain order, one must, as Kung's reprimand of Yuan Jang states perspicuously, "get up and do something useful."[37] Dominating Pound's own thinking, such a Confucian position on order and action has become, as Gelpi observes, "an early formulation of Pound's maxim of translating 'ideas into action.'"[38] In this sense, Lawrence Rainey is right when he claims that in *The Cantos* "the new culture is presented as a ritual recovery of quotations. New culture and new poem are consecrated in a ceremony that ratifies and is ratified by quotations, as if citation were the discursive counterpart to the theme of human and cultural regeneration."[39]

The modernist preoccupation with quotations as representational bound entails, in turn, a structural patterning, an organizational interaction between two kinds of texts that have been named respectively "host" and "found" or "frame" and "inset."[40] Though they are presented as integral parts of the host texts, quotations as found texts or insets nonetheless demand that they maintain their own status, and that they must be identified and acknowledged in one way or another in the host text or its overall frame. In other words, "their boundaries—their beginnings and ends—must be clear."[41] Consider the following excerpt from "Canto VI":

What you have done, Odysseus,
        We know what you have done . . .

And that Guillaume sold out his ground rents
(Seventh of Poitiers, Ninth of Aquitain).
"Tant las fotei com auzirets
"Cen e quatre vingt et veit vetz . . ."[42]

The image for quotations as found texts thus employed in the modernist praxis becomes, rather fittingly, that of a legal immigrant: a permanent resident in a host country with an alien registration number, documented either semiotically, or photographically, or discursively, as the case might be, by way of quotation marks, italics, foreign words, or various forms of notes and indexes. For the modernists, to maintain such a distinction or boundary is a psychological imperative, in that their intention in the use of quotations is not simply to "draw upon a canonic tradition," as Michael André Bernstein contends, so much as to "seek to establish one,"[43] one that is based on what Pound believes to be "a return to origins . . . a return to nature and reason."[44] This return, however urgent and powerful in its ambition, finds itself in need of a sign of confirmation. Manifestos and programs aside, it needs, in other words, a visual or formal facade to buttress, by showcasing, its own sense of unquestionable and undeniable literalness or actuality authorized as well as authenticated by history and tradition. If, as Diepeveen argues, "for most quoting poets the quotation is a fact, not a symbol,"[45] modernist poetry, by its grand "synthesis of heterogeneous 'origins,'"[46] presents such a fact, demonstrating that it not only makes history anew but also, and more importantly, makes history.

Yet for the modernist message to be communicated, quotations have to forfeit their independence in use in order to facilitate the construction of a textual hierarchy. In this respect, the modernist use of quotations takes on an explicitly Emersonian overtone.[47] "Whatever the formal autonomy conferred by [the frame]," argues Sternberg in the same vein, "the inset is communicatively subordinated to the frame."[48] Hence the paradox: the inset's textual territory is acknowledged in the frame only to be invaded, its sovereignty is recognized only to be violated, and its original context is accepted only to be recontextualized. "The supreme control lies with the frame," with its specific "norms and premises," writes Sternberg, for "to quote is to mediate, to mediate is to frame, to frame is to interfere and exploit."[49] Successful communication in modernist poetry results, then, from the successful colonization of the found texts by the host texts.

Out of this communicative subordination emerges the perspectival montage or ambiguity. The modernist montage, however, is hardly an entirely random mosaic; and in Pound's work the selection and the arrangement of quotations, never arbitrary to begin with, constitute in fact what Andrew Kappel describes as the poet's "vast programmatic shuffling and sifting of world literature into a usable selective order."[50] Nor is the ambiguity completely opaque; for a quotation, once colonized, "[exhibits] an intrinsic integrity in a new context provided by Pound's poem," and its original context, now having been exploited, helps the quotation "[make] its point as it stands" by offering "the missing links that make the [host text] intelligible."[51] Take Pound's portrait of Henry James in "Canto VII":

> And the great domed head, *con gli occhi onesti e tardi*
> Moves before me, phantom with weighted motion,
> *Grave incessu,* drinking the tone of things,
> And the old voice lifts itself
>   weaving an endless sentence.[52]

This excerpt corresponds almost word for word to Pound's personal memories of the novelist related in his essay "Henry James,"[53] and later in the essay Pound exalts James as a literary figure of global significance:

> As Armageddon has only too clearly shown, national qualities are the great gods of the present and Henry James spent himself from the beginning in an analysis of these potent chemicals; trying to determine from the given microscopic slide the nature of the Frenchness, Englishness, Germanness, Americanness. . . . We may rest our claim for his greatness in the magnitude of his protagonists, in the magnitude of the forces he analyzed and portrayed.[54]

The image Pound paints here of James is, "only too clearly shown" indeed, that of a classical literatus dealing with his subjects from a transnational or transcontinental perspective, an image whose magnitude finds its articulation in the canto not only in James's stylistic grandeur ("drinking the tone of things, / And the old voice lifts itself / weaving an endless sentence") but also in his physical massiveness ("And the great domed head . . . / Moves before me, phantom with weighted motion"). A context as such then naturalizes, so to speak, the two quotations from Dante and Virgil. Originally referring to Sordello, for instance, *"con gli occhi onesti e tardi"* ("with eyes honest and slow")[55] adds to and completes, in physical as well as moral terms, James's otherwise faceless image, and "*Grave incessu*" ("solemn movement"), which describes "Homer, Horace, and Ovid, three of the four great shades of antiquity approaching Dante and Virgil (Virgil himself being the fourth),"[56] identifies James as one of them, accepting and inducting him into a historical-literary summit. With their original contexts providing matching personal attributes (physical, moral, artistic) and an allegorical gathering of literary giants (Homer, Horace, Ovid, Virgil, Dante), both quotations contribute, in a way, to Pound's view that recognizes and recontextualizes James as part of that grand tradition.[57] In what Sternberg terms "transpacity," then, "mimetic and perspectival interference go together,"[58] which in turn renders quotations "specific" or even "self-explanatory."[59] Such is the case with "Canto VII." In this version of modernist poetics, quotations thus employed, as Clarvoe notes, "anchor the poem to implied confirmation."[60]

In contrast to modernist poems, in which quotations are used instrumentally as stage lighting for "the dance of intellect among words,"[61] Zukofsky's "Poem beginning 'The'" presents itself as an exemplar of postmodernist citationality whereby quotations themselves constitute the dance, occupying the center stage of the poem. This dance of quotations among themselves is realized as the result of a radical break from the four universals defining the modernist conception and method of quotations, and it visualizes, through this dance, a dazzling move from the representational bound to a presentational freedom, from the structural framing to a structural opening, from the communicative subordination to an a-communicative equality, and from the perspectival montage or ambiguity to an all-perspectival panorama and clarity. That being the case, Zukofsky's ontological treatment of quotations begins, in one sense, with the poet's theorizing of poetry itself. Poetry, he thus redefines it, "is precise information on existence out of which it grows, and information of its own existence, that is, the movement (and tone) of words."[62] Zukofsky's departure from modernism is suggested in this statement by a fundamental shift of the hitherto conceptual-philosophical groundings: epistemologically, from a position external to the world to a position internal to it, from message or meaning to information, from history or tradition to existence; aesthetic-methodologically, from poetry as a referential entity always in closure to poetry as a physical movement forever in progress; and, most germane to the topic under discussion here, from precision in terms of a teleologically controlled selection of quotations to precision in terms of synchronously aggregated occurrences of citationality.

To equate poetry with information is to return poetry to the general flux of existence, and to situate one's perspective from within that flux. For the term *information,* following Norbert Wiener's definition, "is a name for the content of what is exchanged with the outer world as we adjust to it, and make our adjustment felt upon it. The process of receiving and of using information is the process of our adjusting to the contingencies of the outer environment, and of our living effectively within that environment."[63] It is, as N. Katherine Hayles puts it in her discussion of Claude E. Shannon's work, "a statistical measure of uncertainty,"[64] or, in William Paulson's words, "a measure of a quantity of possibilities."[65] Information as such does not constitute meaning; rather, it concerns "the formal conditions of transmitting messages and not the eventual meaning or significance of messages that might be actually sent."[66] Viewed from this perspective, poetry, for Zukofsky, does not encode existence into what Paulson describes as a "uniquely defined, in a sense expected . . . specific message of given quantity";[67] instead, it presents itself as an adjustment to, and, at the same time, as part and parcel of, the dynamics that is existence, with all its uncertainties and possibilities.

In this sense, Zukofsky's definition of poetry presupposes a particular kind of temporal relationship between writing and its material. If, on the one hand, poetry grows out of information on existence, the poem's material exists prior to the poem's own coming into being and, consequently, takes on the status of found object when used in the poem. In other words, poetry is itself nothing but found material. If, on the other hand, poetry is information of its own existence, then its form and content—that is, "the movement (and tone) of words"—become synchronous, thus defying any attempt at finding an inherent, logical, hierarchal arrangement of details. In other words, poetry ("Poem") occurs when writing synchronizes both the "present continuousness" ("beginning") of its action and the "prior-ness" ("The") of its found material. Hence "Poem beginning 'The'": a poem whose own existence lies in its continuous beginning with the already existing material. A poem as such then demands a structure or an objectification "committed," as Charles Altieri argues, "to composition rather than interpretation."[68] "Good poetry," in this view, "does not argue its attitudes or beliefs," contends Zukofsky; "It exists independently of the reader's preferences for one kind of 'subject' or another."[69]

"Poem beginning 'The'" can be seen, then, as unfolding a world in which the poet "lives with the things as they exist," to put it in Zukofsky's own words, "thinking with the things as they exist."[70] The three-word title of the poem, for instance, recapitulates Zukofsky's objectivist rendering of poetry or information as found texts. Featured prominently in the title is, of course, the word "The," the definite article whose semantics and function are, in general, "controlled by the basic notion [of] 'a previously recognized, noticed, or encountered'" person, object, and so forth.[71] To illustrate further its denotative "previous-ness," the definite article is itself put in quotation marks, the awkward redundancy of which suggests, as Robert Duncan notes, "a kind of self-consciousness in which not the poet but the act of writing was this 'self.'"[72] Differently put, the act of writing, in its continuous beginning, is keenly aware of its own "with-ness," which is simultaneously a sort of belatedness, in relation to its material. Since poetry is the "precise information on existence out of which it grows," and since it always begins, as a result, with what has already begun, it establishes its own identity as quintessentially intertextual, as a continuously growing composite of found texts.

Zukofsky further emphasizes, with an exaggerated satirical overtone, his conception of the poem as an aggregate of found texts by prefacing the poem with an elaborate dedication, one that appears to be as much an acknowledgment of its indebtedness as it is an index to the sources of the poem. In either case, however, this dedication is intended not so much to highlight a controlled, purposeful selection of source materials pertinent to a certain message conveyed in the poem as to confess, apologetically indeed, its own lack of comprehensiveness vis-à-vis the quantity of precise information on existence out of which the poem has grown. So incomprehensive, in fact, is this poem of found texts that the dedication has to be made not to what the poet remembers therein but to what he does not. "Because I have had occasion to remember, quote, paraphrase," Zukofsky writes, "I dedicate this poem to Anyone and Anything I have unjustifiably forgotten."[73] So much so that, in order to compensate for the poem's indebtedness to preexisting information, the poet feels obliged even to resort to a "default" approach, announcing that whatever is not named should be otherwise "Obvious—Where the Reference Is Obvious."[74] Coupled with this lack of comprehensiveness, there is yet another kind of lack, with a similar magnitude: a pervasive lack of specificity insofar as an index is concerned. In contrast to Pound's and Eliot's concrete, explicit indexes and notes oriented to "use-context,"[75] this lack of specificity in Zukofsky's index can be read as making a rather specific statement. The index's vagueness ("*The Bible*—1–3, 9, 313, 314"), pointlessness ("The French Language—31, 33, 51, 292"), and all-inclusiveness ("Power of the Past, Present, and Future—Where the reference is to the word Sun") seem to insist that this index, contra that of Pound and Eliot, seeks to attain neither the roots nor the routes of the poem's references;[76] rather, they unveil, paradoxically, a "rested totality," a "complete appreciation. . . . The apprehension satisfied completely as to the appearance of the art form as an object."[77] Whether a "travesty"[78] or a "parody"[79] of the Poundian tradition, the poet's dedication as index thus presents a direct reversal of modernist textual practice. In beginning the poem with an all-encompassing dedication-index, Zukofsky destabilizes his own text by calling into question its host status and, in so doing, privileges a postmodernist poetry that is a found text, an ontological entity, a quantitative measure on existence, over a modernist poetry that is a message, a teleological construct, a "qualitative intuition"[80] of existence.

But poetry is also a quantitative measure of its own existence, synchronous with its "movement (and tone) of words." To the extent that poetry is considered in terms of a "measure" at all, its "care for the detail" then demands, at each passing moment, a "structure," as Zukofsky makes clear.[81] More specifically, it is a structure that is not, to use Altieri's words, a "controlling imposition"; rather, it is "a mode of attention."[82] As such, sincerity and objectification merge into a single act of writing which is "the detail, not mirage, of seeing, of thinking with the things as they exist,"[83] and which, treating cultural artifacts as phenomenal movements rather than conceptual stases, creates an open field of undifferentiated multiples. Altieri brings this point into focus when he thus summarizes it:

> Sincerity is usually not self-expression. Rather it involves insistence on the surface of the poem as concerned primarily with direct acts of naming as signs of the poet's immediate engagement in the areas of experience made present by conceiving the act of writing as a mode of attention. Sincerity involves refusing the temptations of closure— both closure as fixed form and closure as writing in the service of idea, doctrine, or abstract aesthetic ideal.[84]

In this sense, "Poem beginning 'The'" indeed resists closure, either thematic or structural, by its insistence on its own surface, a surface that unfolds a horizontal geography of quotations without a vertical geology of interpretative depth armed with the four universals.[85] It is a surface on which the objectivist sincerity as attention to details is focused, as Michele Leggott puts it, though in a slightly different context, on "the unearthing of contingencies, those places where one voice had been, or seemed to have been, listening to another."[86]

Rather emphatic of the postmodern notion of intertextuality, the poem begins with the following lines, headed by the definite article "The":

1   The
2   Voice of Jesus I. Rush singing
3   in the wilderness
4   A boy's best friend is his mother,
5   It's your mother all the time.
6   Residue of Oedipus-faced wrecks
7   Creating out of the dead,—
8   From the candle flames of the souls of dead mothers
9   Vide the legend of thin Christ sending her
                out of the temple,—
10   Books from the stony heart, flames rapping
                the stone,
11   Residue of self-exiled men
12   By the Tyrrhenian.[87]

Quoted respectively from "*The Bible*—1–3, 9," "Popular Non-Sacred Song—4, 5," "Sophocles—6," "D. H. Lawrence—8," and from other purportedly "Obvious" sources (7, 10, 11, 12),[88] the twelve entries herein present what the poet calls, in a letter to Pound, "a matter of sequential statement."[89] However, as Zukofsky's punning on the word "matter" seems amply to suggest, it is a sequence of "facts as order" rather than ordered facts.[90] Although the word "mother," for instance, which stands for the "Symbol of Our Relatively Most Permanent Self, Origin and Destiny,"[91] either appears or is implicated in most of the quoted lines, it nevertheless does not create or represent a thematic bound with a concomitant structural framing. The movement from line 1 to line 12 shows instead a physical lineup of cultural artifacts in which "mother" happens to be figured, but the lineup itself delineates neither a logical progression nor a communicative subordination of the details in a way that contributes to a theme on "mother." The same holds true for Zukofsky's numbering of these quoted lines. While seemingly guiding the poem forward in an ordered, linear progression, these numbers demonstrate a remarkable disrespect for their currently designated positions in the sequence by allowing themselves to be rearranged, thus turning the poem from a sequential ordering to a spatial configuration. With a pace of their own, they "enumerate themselves, write themselves, read themselves. By themselves,"[92] totally indifferent to each line's—or each quotation's—yearning for a logical as well as a contextual relocation. As a result, these numbers dramatize "neither tradition nor past," as Robert Duncan observes, "but immediate presentation."[93] Indeed, Zukofsky's use of numbers as such could be described as staging what Marjorie Perloff calls a "number anomaly," also evidenced in "the often illogical numbering" of propositions in Wittgenstein's *Tractatus;* such a number anomaly functions as "a kind of clinamen," she explains, "a bent or swerve where logic gives way to mystery."[94] It is a mystery of existence, that is, out of which "Poem beginning 'The'" is being emerging as its precise information, with an all-perspectival, panoramic clarity.

Central to the four universals that define the modernist conception and textual method of quotations is the idea and function of context, and Pound's acknowledgment that he is unable to use quotations without any commentary indicates his understanding of context as imperative for effective communication. His extensive, repeated exposition of this subject throughout his critical writings further suggests, rather unequivocally, that modernist poetry, given its level of difficulty, is fundamentally context-dependent or context-sensitive.[95] This is because, for Pound, any serious work of art is one that embodies a "total perception of relations,"[96] which functions, he insists, as "a sort of energy, something more or less like electricity or radioactivity, a force transfusing, welding, and unifying."[97] In poetry, which is "the more highly energized" form of verbal expression,[98] this total perception of relations is established and specified by what Grabes calls "a controlling perspective,"[99] one that determines not only its own contextual circumference but that of its material, including quotations. In order that poetry "bears true witness" and is "most precise,"[100] the poet, accordingly, must choose "words for their 'meaning,'" meaning that is not simply "a set, cut-off thing" but "comes with roots, with associations, with how and where the word is familiarly used, or where it has been used brilliantly or memorably."[101] The meaning of a word is, to put it differently, its contextual meaning. For a poet engaged in "the dance of the intellect among words," this emphasis on context appears even more crucial, in that logopoeia, Pound argues, "employs words not only for their direct meaning, but it takes count in a special way of habits of usage, of the context we *expect* to find with the word, its usage concomitants, of its known acceptances, and of ironical play. It holds the aesthetic content which is peculiarly the domain of verbal manifestation, and cannot possibly be contained in plastic or in music."[102] The same holds true for choosing quotations, the efficacy of which lies not in quotations per se but in their attached contexts, in their contextual implications as well as ramifications. So central a position, in fact, does context occupy in the modernist textual praxis that "if there is anything about justice," Pound announces with regard to the use of quotations in a specific reading of Seneca, "it must be in the context, not in the two lines quoted."[103] Hence a tripartite equation: a total perception of relations = a controlling perspective = an overarching context.

Pound's theorizing of the context, as is reflected in the above equation, can be boiled down to a methodical formula undergirding the modernist use of quotations: the text-context dichotomy. Directed by a controlling perspective, to quote is to form a total perception of relations by contextualizing the quoted texts into a new synthesis so as to initiate a communicative context, a context that is, as Alan Durant describes, "translated, up-dated, for a new historical moment."[104] The establishment of a critical resonance across time and space then requires that both the context of the host text and the original context of the found text be impregnated with a certain conceptual overlap, a sort of "echo chamber," as it were, in which the untranslatability of logopoeia in each text becomes eventually translatable in a shared context, which functions to "converge and interact through quotations."[105] In other words, between these two kinds of contexts, there must be "a simultaneously commemorative and projective bound."[106] As such, the subordination of the found text to the host text in modernist poetry turns out to be a theatrical gesture, for the former's willingness to give up its autonomy and the latter's capability to appropriate it results from the fact that they share a stable, identical, and universal context. Viewed from this perspective, the relationship between the frame and the inset becomes, to be more accurate, "a ruse, a *mise-en-scène* by which the belated writer establishes the worth of his discourse," as Claudette Sartiliot puts it, "a form of complicity,"[107] whose pragmatic function, armed with a Platonic intention, is to massively reduce the modernist "field of equivocality."[108]

In addition, for the effective transmission and communication of a contextual meaning or knowledge, quotations have to be used economically. Their deployment in the text, that is, has to take into consideration not only their quality but also, and perhaps more importantly, their quantity. The presence of a certain number of found texts proportional to the contextual scope of the host text contributes to the latter qualitatively as an organizing, hierarchical system, and any fluctuation of the number of quotations above or below the gauge of appropriateness would destroy the host text quantitatively by overwhelming it or isolating it. Properly maintained and manipulated, the ratio between these two texts helps to sustain, instrumentally, a textual as well as conceptual space where the two different kinds of contexts are able to engage in a communicative conspiracy, generating as a result what Paulson calls "a contextual redundancy," which "implies a certain degree of expectability or predictability built into its structure."[109] This contextual redundancy then provides the host text with a "capacity for self-correction" and a "margin of intelligibility."[110] Failure to achieve and maintain such a ratio leads to confusion and ambiguity, resulting in "entropy of message."[111]

Although it is generally considered as more fragmented and more ambiguous than other cantos, "Canto LXXIV" exemplifies Pound's creation of a textual mosaic with a contextual rendezvous point whereby, as Diepeveen observes, "control occurs only through a seeming lack of control."[112] The overall context of the poem, given the autobiographical backdrop of the Pisan detention camp in which Pound was imprisoned temporarily at the end of World War II, is the poet's own psychological complexity, a complexity articulated through a sharp juxtaposition of a mind still intensely engaged in a political debate and a consciousness ruthlessly bombarded by the sense of its own futility and irrelevancy. The tension between his impulse to continue his argument and his forced resignation to reality is such that the poet has to resort to a textual strategy as a self-defense mechanism whereby to rescue himself from either situation before he is hurt. The result throughout the poem is a constant thought ruptured by inserted alien materials, by interruptions of quotations, the contextual meanings of which work therapeutically for the poet's state of mind in turmoil.

Several pages into the canto, for instance, there are the following lines:

Les Albigeois, a problem of history,
and the fleet at Salamis made with money lent by the state to the
shipwrights

> Tempus tacendi, tempus loquendi.
> Never inside the country to raise the standard of living
> but always abroad to increase the profits of usurers,
> dixit Lenin,
> and gun sales lead to gun sales
> they do not clutter the market for gunnery
> there is no saturation[113]

The entire excerpt here, except for the quotation in the middle ("Tempus tacendi, tempus loquendi"), is the continuation of the poet's passionate exposition of the issue of money in relation to the state, which can be traced back to cantos XLII, XLIII, and XLV. While Pound, in the section preceding the quotation, uses "the fleet at Salamis made with money lent by the state to the shipwrights" as an example to "illustrate a major thesis of Social Credit, that the extension of credit should be the prerogative not of private banks but of the state, which should benefit from the interest,"[114] in the part following the quotation he condemns current corruptions through the mouth of Lenin. The quotation intrudes halfway through the poet's otherwise consistent argumentative trajectory.

Translated as "A time to be silent, a time to speak," "Tempus tacendi, tempus loquendi" is "the personal motto of Sigismundo Malatesta,"[115] whom Pound admires for his achievements and identifies as "a constructive and self-constructive force," and who therefore is, as Gelpi argues, a persona "for Pound's questing ego."[116] The motto's context takes shape in Malatesta's love for Isotta degli Atti, which "discloses his highest and noblest self,"[117] and becomes crystallized when he inscribed the motto on her tomb in Rimini.[118] Equipped with this context, "Tempus tacendi, tempus loquendi" thus expresses eloquently yet laconically a sense of nobility transcending the mundane, of a fated tragedy beyond language and understanding, in the face of the irretrievable loss of one's love.

Pound's use of the quotation of Malatesta's personal motto here forms a contextual correspondence with his own text. Methodically, such a use of quotations presents a variation of what Hugh Kenner identifies in *The Pound Era* as the poet's "heuristic device" in the form of the "subject-rhyme"—that is, to elucidate one thing by comparing it with another.[119] Vis-à-vis Pound's passionate pursuit of a political issue, his loss of any prospect of putting it to use, and his painful resignation to silence, there is Malatesta's noble love for Isotta degli Atti, his loss of her through death, and his stoic handling of a forced silence. As they thus contextually in-form each other, Pound's canto is able to elevate therapeutically a down-trodden soul onto a level of moral and historical significance by transplanting into its own structure Malatesta's motto, which in turn bespeaks economically the poet's state of mind in quiet desperation, struggling to remind itself that "beauty is difficult."[120] "Good writing," Pound remarks, "is perfect control."[121] It is a control rendered possible, as is evidenced in Pound's own practice, by "detailed specifications of context and circulation,"[122] by the "precise sense," whether of words or of quotations, "as understood at that particular epoch that one would like to have set before one."[123]

To the modernist "leitmotif" of quotations and context, "Poem beginning 'The'" presents itself, announces the poet, as "a direct reply."[124] If the modernist qualitative intuition of existence is always dependent on context, and if, as Alison Rieke asserts, "poems are, by definition, specific kinds of contexts,"[125] Zukofsky's poem is one in which the established text-context dichotomy collapses and the conventional function of context is subverted. The compositional strategy the poet resorts to as an alternative thus reflects a postmodernist conception and understanding of intertextuality, and its dance of quotations pushes the modernist dance of intellect among words to the edge of the stage of representation, to its ultimate limits, exposing, by default, its working mechanisms as predicated upon the logic of self-referentiality.

The form of Zukofsky's poem, for instance, can be seen as dramatizing a Baudrillardian critique of modernist binary thinking in that the aggregate of found texts, which constitute the entire poem, challenges, rather overtly, the text-context distinction as a structuralist formula based on Saussure's theory of the sign. By an "artificial separation" of a text and a context, the poem seems to argue, at least by analogy, that the modernists are able to posit, in Baudrillard's terminology, "an equivalence" between "the signifier as form" and "the signified and the referent, which are registered together as content—the one of thought, the other of reality (or rather, of perception)—under the aegis of the signifier."[126] With this separation, they succeed in putting together a system of signification in which "its second term [context as signified and referent] acts as the satellite and alibi for the first [text]"[127] and becomes, in due course, the operational prerequisite for modernist poetic license. "This discretion," Baudrillard recapitulates, "is thus the very principle of the sign's rationality," whereby what begins as "a fiction," then, "leads to a science fiction,"[128] turning into cause what is in actuality the effect.[129] For "the 'context' of any given text," as Branham and Pearce argue, is nothing but "the perception of it."[130] To put it in Baudrillard's words again, a context is that which is "carved out and projected as [the text's] function," "reflection," "effect," "shadow," "its 'pantographic' extension."[131] More specifically put, the context of any given quotation "is never replaced or subsumed but only imaged" by the host text, as Sternberg points out similarly, "where the image takes the form of an inset version."[132]

In a highly self-reflexive fashion, Zukofsky's critique of the context as the perception and projection of the text leads to his radical formal innovation in his use of quotations, a practice that Pound had conceived of earlier (for an entirely different purpose, of course) but perceived (therefore) as "too revolutionary."[133] Zukofsky's counter-method could be described as "crowding-out." By a coup d'état of excessive found texts, "Poem beginning 'The'" enacts a self-effacement, allowing the quotations to succeed in a complete takeover and, in so doing, erasing its own textual identity. With the physical disappearance of the text as the projective agency, the poem deactivates the otherwise concomitant context, which is none other than the controlling perspective that "pretends or is presumed to be exterior and external," and refuses to "reach outside of the boundaries of the writing which constitutes" itself.[134] What is left of the poem now is, literally, the half-dozen movements (and tones) of words, which form, as Hayles phrases it, a "context of no context,"[135] or in Derrida's words, a context "without any center of absolute anchoring."[136]

The absence of a text as a contextual projection frees the quotations from the four bondages of servitude of representational bound, structural framing, communicative subordination, and perspectival montage. In "Poem beginning 'The,'" quotations find themselves instead participating in a festival orgy of texture, of clusters of words devoid of any qualitative intuition.[137] Consider, for instance, the following lines of the poem:

45 For it's the hoo-doos, the somethin' voo-doos
46 And not Kings onelie, but the wisest men
47 Graue Socrates, what says Marlowe?
48 For it was myself seemed held
49 Beating—beating—
50 Body trembling as over an hors d'oeuvres—
51

52   And the dream ending—Dalloway! Dalloway—
53   The blind portals opening, and I awoke![138]

Zukofsky's dedication as index makes the reference of each line clear: "College Cheer—45," "Christopher Marlowe's *Edward II*—46, 47," "The French Language—51," and "Virginia Woolf's *Mrs. Dalloway*—52"; as for lines 48, 49, 50, and 53, they must be "Obvious—Where the Reference is Obvious."[139]

With an index as such, Zukofsky's approach to the above-quoted lines is to reduce to the absolute minimum each quotation's generality. Understood as the degree as well as the range of applicability, this generality of quotations in modernist practice is measured and adjusted by a controlling perspective in relation to other quotations' "different kinds and degrees of generality" so that a given quotation is capable of relating to others;[140] a generality, in other words, that is not only extensive or broad enough to allow a quotation to become, as Michel Serres puts it, "independent of its empirical realizations,"[141] but also strict or narrow enough for it to retain, as Diepeveen observes, its own "metaphorlike" quality and function.[142] Once reduced to its absolute minimum, however, the generality of each quotation in "Poem beginning 'The'" takes an extremely radical turn: it essentializes, rather than popularizes, the quotation, insisting on its own idiosyncrasy, its own empirical denotations, its own textual as well as contextual narcissism, which favors isolation over relation. As a result, these quotations, each in its own way, hearken back to contexts too exclusive to be shared, and point to spheres of application too restricted to allow trespassing.

All the index can offer for line 45, for instance, is a college setting. Although the colloquial expression and its singsong tone suggest a certain juvenile mischievousness, nothing else is specified. Questions such as "Cheer for what?" or "What do the 'voo-doos' refer to?" or "What is this 'somethin'?" remain unanswered. Having failed to indicate what can be expected, the radically reduced generality of this quotation then forces one's attention back to its source as the sole point of reference: the college setting. In addition, this textual-contextual self-love or self-sealing embodied by line 45 cuts any conceptual tie with lines 46 and 47, which are from Marlowe's *Edward II*. Even if one identifies these two lines as offering a glimpse of a court episode in which King Edward II's relationship with his minion Gaueston is viewed philosophically by Mortimer Senior from a historical perspective,[143] and even if one might argue that such a relationship is a kind of "voo-doo," which could relate to the "voo-doos" back in line 45, the incomparability between line 45 and lines 46–47 in terms of setting (college vs. court), magnitude of the issue (students' pranks vs. national interests), and attitude toward that issue (cheer vs. serious analysis) refuses any negotiations between the two quotations. Similarly, lines 48–50, purportedly "Obvious" in their references, are in fact far from that. Beginning with an adverbial clause of reason ("For it was myself seemed held"), these lines immediately throw one in medias res, confronting one with an overwhelming sense of emotional self-indulgence and psychological self-involvement ("Beating—beating—/ Body trembling as over an hors d'oeuvres—"), which in turn circumscribes a world too private and too personal to be anyone else's business.

Each anchoring itself firmly and hermetically in its own world, these quotations become, as Scharfstein argues, "utterly unique, which is to say, absolutely incomparable."[144] As their "referential context shrinks" to subzero, "their sphere of application grows ambiguous" proportionally.[145] Mutually isolated and unrecognizably fragmented, quotations in "Poem beginning 'The'" are busily engaged in a civil war, each claiming simultaneously its own textual-contextual boundaries only to be further "dismembered, reduced to decontextualized formulas," as Zacchi contends, making themselves unable "to testify to the identification/identity principle of the cultural system."[146] At the same time, each quotation's relentless insistence on its own context in isolation becomes as much self-serving as self-defeating, disqualifying as a result the quotation as a statement and reducing it further to a mere group of words. What the poem becomes, then, is a writing that "does not comment," as Zukofsky writes in *A Test of Poetry*, a composition that "does not linger to embroider words around a subject."[147] As such, quotations in "Poem beginning 'The'" cease to assert themselves as texts with contextual messages; instead, they offer themselves in a dance, with its own texture of movement and sounds of words.

Zukofsky's critique of the modernist method of quotations grounded in a text-context dichotomy creates, in "Poem beginning 'The,'" a textless text, a "no man's land,"[148] and his radical employment of quotations finds its most eloquent, if unwitting, explicator in Derrida. Since the "tree" onto which these found texts are supposed to be grafted "is ultimately rootless," writes Derrida, quotations as scions in such a text as "Poem beginning 'The'" "eventually [come] to be grafted onto [themselves]."[149]

But "at the same time," Derrida continues, "everything is a root, too, since the grafted shoots themselves compose the whole of the body proper, of the tree that is called present."[150] Considered from this perspective, quotations do not imply stasis or origin; they suggest, to use Derrida's words again, "both 'setting in motion'" and "solicitation, that is, the shakeup of a whole."[151] "Poem beginning 'The'" constitutes, in this sense, a radical shake-up of the whole modernist tradition's poetics of quotation. While presenting itself as a "no man's land," independent of "whatever political or religious persuasions [lie] outside the poem,"[152] the poem nevertheless finds in itself "the promise of 'shall be.'"[153] For Zukofsky's quotations do not represent, as John Taggart notes, "a group of discrete texts which will read the rewoven text for us."[154] Rather, they suggest a reconstructive potential in the poem as texture, out of which one composes one's own songs, gesturing, perhaps, toward what Edward Schelb calls "a new ordering of sensibility outside of the circumference of Modernism,"[155] toward what Zukofsky himself describes in "A"–12 as a "pinprick of contents, but an assemblage / of all possible positions."[156]

A powerful manifesto for a new poetry, Zukofsky's "Poem beginning 'The'" is more than just "an exemplar . . . for writing yet to come in 1937."[157] In a broader sense, it embodies in embryo a postmodernist poetics which will not only "bear fruit of another generation," as Zukofsky himself foresees perceptively,[158] but also herald a radical rethinking of poetry yet to come and bear fruit in the entire century.

Everyone charges what he sees with *affectivity;* no one sees things as they are, but as his desires and his state of soul let him see.

—Luis Buñuel (quoted in J. H. Matthews, *Surrealism and American Feature Films*)

To construct is the essence of vision. Dispense with construction and you dispense with vision. Everything you experience by sight is your construction. This is . . . more than a brute fact; it is a dictate of logic.

—Donald Hoffman, *Visual Intelligence: How We Create What We See*

In order to see certain things, what should we believe about them?

—T. J. Clark, *Image of the People: Gustave Courbet and the 1848 Revolution*

2. A "Seeing" Through Refraction: The Rear-View Mirror Image in George Oppen's *Collected Poems*

"The eye *sees!*" writes George Oppen in his *Collected Poems.*[1] Characteristic of the poet's signature style of minimalist brevity, this claim is nevertheless burdened, as it were, by two oddities. Thematically, on the one hand, it is overtly redundant, stating nothing short of the obvious. Stylistically, on the other hand, it is cast in an exaggerated triple emphasis, a sort of rhetorical overkill manifested in the verb "*sees*" italicized and in the sentence ended with an exclamation mark that is also italicized. Such, perhaps for Oppen, is what it takes to call attention to the polemics of vision that, since the inception of the imagist scheme of things, has been granted and elevated to the status of an aesthetic given. In light of such a blatant redundancy and an overt triple emphasis, Oppen's statement can be read as articulating what Edward Hirsch calls "the visual imperative" in Oppen's work.[2] Central to the poet's objectivist poetics of vision is a visual imperative whereby the poet is self-reflexively engaged in an intense rethinking of the act of seeing itself, of its "own limitations" and "provisional" character.[3] Viewed from this perspective, "The eye *sees!*" issues, precisely through its self-conscious rendering of the obvious, a cautionary warning against not so much what the eye sees as how the eye sees, hence bringing to the fore an underlying wariness of and an inquiry into both the nature and the method of seeing endorsed by the imagist tradition.

That being said, what, then, is Oppen's own objectivist modality of vision? If, as Kevin Power has pointed out, Oppen's poems reveal the poet's "reading of the world from a position of accepted isolation" as the result of his objectivist position,[4] how is that isolation visually constructed? And what, finally, is its significance?

When responding to an interviewer's question on the meaning of the term *objectivist* and his reference to Williams's view of the poem as an object, George Oppen offers the following summary statement of his initial understanding of the objectivist aesthetics and methodology, which are inherited directly from the imagist tradition:

> The . . . point for me . . . was the attempt to construct meaning, to construct a method of thought from the imagist technique of poetry— from the imagist intensity of vision. If no one were going to challenge me, I would say, "a test of truth." If I had to back it up I'd say anyway, "a test of sincerity"—that there is a moment, an actual time, when you believe something to be true, and you construct a meaning from those moments of conviction.[5]

Thus explained, Oppen's position as quoted above can indeed be read, especially in light of its rhetoric, as stating a "Cartesian avowal,"[6] in that the imagist intensity of vision is one and the same as a method of thought constitutive of a belief system. It delineates an epistemological mapping of the world that is none other than the subject's visual projection of it. Armed with these "methodological assumptions,"[7] Oppen, who is always "metaphysically inclined," is seen at first sight as carrying out "in effect a Cartesian investigation by imagistic rather than rationalistic means," as L. S. Dembo has argued, which is evidenced further in Oppen's own definition of the title of his book *Discrete Series*.[8] The Cartesian purchase in Oppen's poetics seems to become more perspicuously manifest when he describes the working of vision, or the act of seeing, as emotionally motivated and epistemologically channeled from an entirely subjective position. "The mind is capable not only of thinking but has an emotional root that forces it to look, to think, to see," Oppen explains to his interviewer, referring to such intellectual and emotional capabilities as the "virtue of the mind." "The most tremendous and compelling emotion we possess," he continues, "is the one that forces us to look, to know, if we can, to see."[9] Hence a linear, logical-emotional projection from the subject to the world, a projection fused with a predicative impulse whereby to look, or to see, is to know; or, what amounts to saying the same thing: a circular, causal imposition onto the world from and by a subject, whose emotional intensity finds its exclusive expression in its own irresistible desire to know, which in turn is dialectically satisfied instantly by its own act of seeing as the means of direct knowing.

It is here, however, on the imagist paradigm of vision, that Oppen parts with his precursors. His skepticism begins with his own belief system represented by the notion of the "virtue of the mind" and its relation to seeing. In a poem titled "Guest Room," for instance, he ponders on his own position, questioning the very meaning of "virtue" as the ethical grounding of seeing: "The virtue of the mind / Is that emotion / Which causes / To see. Virtue . . . / Virtue . . . ?"[10] This skepticism is then followed by "the task of rigorous thought," a task that one "must manage," as Oppen has insisted, when facing any "system of opinions and attitudes,"[11] systems such as the imagist method of thought from the intensity of vision, and his own emotion-driven necessity to see resulting from the virtue of the mind. Oppen's task of rigorously thinking this issue becomes intensified when his initial understanding of the function of vision is questioned, rethought, and explored from a different perspective. To the interviewer's question "But in a sense it's this very sensitivity that isolates the poet or makes him a lonely man, isn't it?" for instance, Oppen responds:

Yes, I quoted from a letter I received from a very young student at Columbia, Rachel Blau, "whether as the intensity of seeing increases, one's distance from them, the people, does not also increase." It was a profound and painful question that I had asked myself in her words. And that's what you are asking me again, for all that I've written a whole poem to establish, if I could, the concept of humanity, a concept without which we can't live. And yet I don't know that poetry is not actually destructive for people, because what you are applying is true. It does lead to the growing isolation of the poet; there is no question in my mind about it.[12]

Two fundamental issues emerge and beg closer scrutiny in the above exchange between the interviewer, the letter correspondent, and the poet, issues that suggest a rupture in, rather than a continuation of, Oppen's artistic affinity with the imagist tradition. First, it is crucial to point out that while "this very sensitivity" or "the intensity of seeing" in question may sound as if it still refers to the imagist vision, the effect of "isolation" or "distancing" is nevertheless not identified directly and explicitly as its visual efficacy. In fact, such effect is never theorized as part of the property of the imagist perception.[13] Viewed in this light, the use of the phrase "this very sensitivity" or "the intensity of seeing" indicates, with reasonable certainty, a switch to a different and larger context, in which each phrase refers to the act of seeing in general rather than that of the imagists in particular. It follows, then, that the effect of "isolation" or "distancing" can be construed accordingly as a conceptual insight resulting from a critical, speculative rethinking of the ramifications of the act of seeing from an aesthetic-philosophical perspective entirely different from that of the imagists. Second, the question proves to be both "profound and painful" for no other reason than the very fact that this objectivist reconceptualization of vision in terms of "isolation" or "distancing" forces Oppen into a historical position charged with an ethical obligation, a position from which to rewrite ("to establish") none other than the prevailing "concept of humanity"—hence it is "profound"—which requires a brutal, inhuman kind of honesty and sincerity with which to denounce some of the received attributes of being human—hence it is "painful."[14]

From this perspective, Oppen's departure from the imagist paradigm of perception begins, methodologically, with his rejection of the nature and function of the eye as meaning-constitutive and, philosophically, with his abandonment of the "concept of humanity" that has traditionally defined the eye as life-giving. Central to Oppen's critical concern here is, therefore, the fundamental validity of the eye as epistemological, as the sole source of knowledge, which has been conceptualized in terms of humanity and in the name of humanity. In highlighting the problem as such, no portraiture of the eye is more apt and revealing, perhaps, than its metaphorization by Claude Gandelman. "The eye is a tactile creature, an agent of human contact," he writes, in his study of visual arts from antiquity to the present. "By virtue of its mere touch, the eye gives life."[15] In other words, grounded in what Oppen has recognized as an "ego system,"[16] the life-giving power of the imagist I-eye configuration finds its perennial source in its desire to anthropomorphize, a desire that is identified by the objectivist poetics of apposition as harboring a "predatory intent."[17] Further, the way the eye touches the object, or its method of life giving, is manifested in a gaze whose visual projectile over space and time onto the object is linear, direct, and transitive. As a forward trajectory seeing implies, in this sense, a self-fulfilling prophecy in that its visual-temporal projection onto the object is itself the projection of intention disguised as expectation or anticipation, which is simultaneously fulfilled or satisfied by an answer that is itself the visual-spatial reaching to the object.

More specifically, Oppen's critique of the imagist intensity of vision as the method of thought locates its entry point, among other issues, on its predatory-anthropomorphic touch. It calls into question, in other words, the nature and the function of the touch in terms of predication, of the predicative potential, intrinsic to the act of seeing. In his study of Oppen's treatment of images vis-à-vis that of Pound, Piotr Parlej, for one, has brought this topic to the fore. As "the central issue" of the imagist methodology, he argues, predication is "understood primarily and chiefly in the philosophical, logical sense of connecting the subject with the predicate, the idea with the thing, the general with the particular, the singular with the plural."[18] The imagist tenet of "'direct treatment of the thing,'" in this sense, necessarily "describes a relationship between subjectivity and an object that carries within itself unavoidable philosophical subtexts and consequences."[19] The same holds true for the imagist intensity of seeing. Being a method of thought, the imagist eye, by virtue of its direct and transitive locking onto the object, carries out the operation of predication, simultaneously performing the precise role of the "connective" between the eye and the object, a connective whose nature is more concretely defined as "(the *synthesis*)."[20] To see, then, is to connect, which is none other than to synthesize. In this sense, one of the philosophical subtexts and the consequences carried within the imagist poetics is, both syntactically and visually, "what Kant calls synthetic judgments *a priori*,"[21] which is then further strengthened and necessitated dialectically by the imagist method itself. For, to the extent that an imagist poem, "in highlighting the question of connection," "invites the reader to interrogate" this "synthetic judgment *a priori*," as Parlej has pointed out, it itself "does not aspire to answer the question concerning the connective (the *synthesis*),"[22] thus leaving it as a tantalizing bait, so to speak; hence a paradox, a powerfully methodological effect in the form of an entrapment, in that an imagist poem, by simultaneously highlighting and evading the issue of the connective, "inspires our curiosity and stimulates us to embark on a search for one."[23] With a deft refashioning of its dialectical frame, the imagist method of thought from the intensity of vision thus perpetuates the concept of humanity favoring the logic of direct and transitive seeing as life-giving in its synthetic mapping, privileging linear visual engagement as predicative in its epistemological campaign. It is on this optics of predication that Oppen, as Parlej rightly observes in a different but related context, "disagrees with" the imagists.[24]

Predication-resistant, Oppen's objectivist poetics of vision is characterized, first and foremost, by a removal from the I-eye configuration of the component of the subject as the predator of predication, purging vision of its underlying ego-system. In Oppen's work, seeing is thus "anti-Cartesian," as Jeremy Hooker contends, in that "it denies the primacy of the self as a knowing subject, and replaces it among the things of the world."[25] Parlej makes a similar point in his reading of Oppen's poem "Psalm," and he identifies the poet's "epistemology (his 'gaze')" as "incognito."[26] Focusing on the last stanza of the poem: "The small nouns / Crying faith / In this in which the wild deer / Startle, and stare out,"[27] he presents an anti-inferential reading of "the wild deer." Contra the habitual, anthropomorphic imposition of vision whereby "the deer are said to participate in the same mechanism of perception which we, humans, enjoy," Parlej argues, Oppen deploys vision therein in such a way that it "announces the effacement of the ego, or what Chilton called Oppen's 'incognito': the gaze is permanently fixed on the outside; as the full being of the deer is affirmed, the perceiving subject, the poet's traditionally strong, vatic presence, vanishes."[28] With the absence of a predatory intent, the eye then assumes a different character. If, as Eric Mottram observes, "the life of the mind for Oppen is seeing—the articulated vision—things and facts,"[29] this seeing, as the life of the mind, is perceived as "intuitive" and not "analytical."[30] It sees objectively, in other words, in the specific sense that seeing is impersonal, or more accurately put, im-personal, which in turn allows the mind to be unfilled.[31] Anti-Cartesian or incognito or im-personal, Oppen's seeing is unpredicative and intransitive; hence the effect of distancing. It is, therefore, ethical of a different order, as it sincerely raises "the question," with regard to the physical world, "whether meaning necessarily flows from the objects of sight," and honestly acknowledges the fact, with regard to the human world, that "there are events, marvels, accidents that do not have the simple moral meaning we once ascribed to them."[32]

In this sense, Oppen's objectivist poetics of vision presents itself as fundamentally phenomenological. "I do believe that consciousness exists," Oppen makes clear, "and that it is consciousness of something."[33] More significantly, however, his consciousness of something is also accompanied by a consciousness of the impenetrability and the inexplicability of that something, and by a willing and ready acceptance of it.[34] For Oppen, phenomenology is, as such, "the philosophy of the astonished" and,[35] not surprisingly, it is characteristically anti-Husserlian in that its predication-resistance is articulated through its rejection of the phenomenological method of reduction. The task of an objectivist poet is, artistically, to "write one's perceptions," Oppen states emphatically, "not argue one's beliefs."[36] It is, ethically, to "replace by the data of experience . . . a dreary waste of lies."[37] As a result, Oppen's intensity of vision takes on concomitantly distinctive features. It is, as Dembo describes, "momentary" and "not . . . communicating" in its action and,[38] as DuPlessis observes, "disjunctive, perspectivist" in its view of the world.[39] In either case, it brings with it, if perceived from an anthropomorphic standpoint, a "sometimes chill atmosphere" as well as the effect of isolation.[40] Demethodized into a lens of "reportage," Oppen's objectivist-phenomenological act of seeing is unimposing and unpredatory, surveying the world in a fashion that "[keeps] it from being confused with Husserlian projects."[41]

Edward Hirsch, in his comparative study of "the visual imperative" and "the visual ethic" in Oppen and Tomlinson,[42] makes the following concluding observation:

> Both Oppen and Tomlinson write an austere phenomenological poetry not so much of things as of the process of the mind encountering those things. . . . Both poets continually affirm the *presence* of external reality, yet remain committed to surveying the difficult relationship between that reality and the singular perceiving self. . . . Both . . . have written a poetry of visual imperatives that simultaneously enacts and meditates on its own procedures.[43]

That being said, one question yet remains with regard to Oppen's objectivist poetics of vision. Differently put, what is the visual process, formally speaking, of the mind-eye encountering the objects? Or, how is the relationship between the singular perceiving self and the external reality visually constructed? Or, what exactly is the form of the visual procedure that is simultaneously enacted and meditated on? Finally, what amounts to asking the same question: what is the structure of Oppen's predication-resistant modality of vision?

In Oppen's poems, the ethos of the objectivist vision is articulated, to begin with, in the form of a contradiction. On the one hand, for instance, the direct, transitive thrust of the visual projectile as predication is expressed in a cluster of kinetic images of the various means of navigation or transportation, both on land and at sea: roads, cars, seas, sails, ships, and so forth. On the other hand, these images of forward movement never seem to have indicated anything other than their inability to ever reach anywhere. For the engine of the means of navigation and transportation is depicted, as in the poem "Image of the Engine," as malfunctioning if not dying:

> Likely as not a ruined head gasket
> Spitting at every power stroke, if not a crank shaft
> Bearing knocking at the roots of the thing like a pile-driver:
> . . . .
> . . . . When the thing stops,
> Is stopped, with the last slow cough[44]

Or else it is depicted as unoperational: "Endlessly, endlessly, / The definition of mortality / The image of the engine / That stops";[45] or as completely dead, resulting in a permanent stopping: "As tho all travels / Ended untold, all embarkations / Foundered."[46] What is more, the eye watching itself in a terminal paralysis is eerily portrayed in section 4 of the poem through the eyes of a bird witnessing a ship sinking:

> On that water
> Grey with morning
> The gull will fold its wings
> And sit. And with its two eyes
> There as much as anything
> Can watch a ship and all its hallways
> And all companions sink.[47]

Hence the image of the eye as a stranded vessel, without the ability to reach to the intended destination or to connect with the object; and Oppen identifies himself with this image explicitly when he writes in the poem "Confession": "I am an old ship / and leaky."[48]

As suggested by the use of images above, Oppen's objectivist vision is one whose optical trajectory does not reach the object, not, that is, directly or transitively. In stark contrast to the direct or transitive seeing that connects and synthesizes, Oppen's does not engage the seen. Conditioned visually as such, the poet then finds himself in an awkward position of isolation and distancing: he is simultaneously inside and outside the world, close to but remote from daily events, present at and absent from the human scene. Between him and the world there exists, so to speak, a glass wall that permits him to witness the latter but prevents him from any personal involvement in it. The poet functions, as a result, merely as an observer, a spectator, but not as an interlocutor, a participant. "Myself is always present," as the poet describes it himself, not without a tinge of wry humor, "and therefore invisible."[49]

Oppen's intransitive seeing of the world from this accepted position of isolation and distancing finds its expression in what might be called the rear-view mirror image, which presents the modality of an indirect seeing in the following sense: in viewing the world, the poet's optical trajectory is not projected forward to lock onto the object directly; instead, it reaches the object by being projected backward through the refraction of a rear-view mirror, which is suggested by the poet's repeated references to "glass," "water," "window," and so forth. When looking into the rear-view mirror, the poet's eye does not engage any impending or forthcoming events, or encounter any objects head-on. Much to the contrary, it sees either an incident already happened and passed, or an object still accelerating in its retreat from the eye, or itself staring back vacantly (see figure 3).

Moreover, this optical configuration has as its consequence a concomitant structure of consciousness. Since such a refracted or indirect seeing does not promise any anticipated or expected involvement in the world, the physical intensity of seeing as connecting with an Other gives way to a mental intensity which, retrospective in nature, is presented in the form of "consciousness of consciousness."[50] In other words, the physical eye is, with its failure to predicate, replaced by the mind's eye. The subsequent awareness on the part of the poet of his withdrawal from the world manifests itself in his keen attentiveness to his own state of mind rather than to the presence or the absence of an Other, in his undivided concentration on seeing itself as an act of chosen detachment rather than on the seen objects, and in his viewing things or events as already past, over, and long gone rather than impending. Seemingly narcissistic, this turn to con-

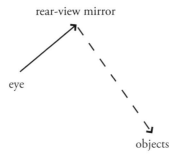

rear-view mirror

eye

objects

Figure 3

sciousness, by consciousness, and for consciousness is intended to mitigate the pain of refusing to connect and, as Hirsch has suggested earlier, to meditate on the visual procedure of the intransitive seeing, and on the new relationship between the perceiving subject and the perceived world. As the replacement of the activity of the eye in a refracted seeing, this "activity of consciousness itself" runs a parallel course that is poignantly recapitulated by Oppen when he writes,[51] with that unique objectivist clarity, about an object of the past:

The great stone
Above the river
In the pylon of the bridge

'1875'

Frozen in the moonlight
In the frozen air over the footpath, *consciousness*

Which has nothing to gain, which awaits nothing,
Which loves itself[52]

Not only do the three attributive clauses here trace the orbit of the refracted seeing through the rear-view mirror, but they also announce its unavoidable effect or outcome. For the mind's eye, when following the physical eye into the rear-view mirror, sees and realizes that there will be no communicative response ("Which has nothing to gain"), that it is itself entirely unrelating and irrelevant in the world ("which awaits nothing"),

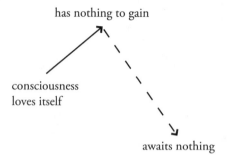

Figure 4

and that the only thing staring back with any sense of pathos is itself ("Which loves itself"). This is diagrammed in figure 4.

In this sense, both for the eye and the mind's eye, this rear-view mirror image constitutes what Charles Altieri terms "an artifact presenting the modality of things seen or felt as immediate structure of relations" between the poet and the world.[53]

In "Party on Shipboard" Oppen succeeds in portraying what he considers as "the act of the world upon the consciousness" by way of the rear-view mirror image.[54] Juxtaposing the polarities of the seeing and the seen, the poem begins with a gaze:

> Wave in the round of the port-hole
> Springs, passing,—arm waved,
> Shrieks, unbalanced by the motion——
> Like the sea incapable of contact
> Save in incidents (the sea is not
>   water)[55]

The positioning of the implied perceiving poet-subject is suggested in the first line: he stands there looking out at the sea through the porthole. But the "Wave . . . / Springs, passing" does not seem to be the only thing that catches his eye. Without turning around, he also sees (and hears), as the second and third lines show, people partying behind his back: "arm waved, / Shrieks, unbalanced by the motion." Hence a rear-view mirror in the form of the porthole, which refracts his optical trajectory to the scene behind. The objects, so arrested by the eye, are thus endowed with a flatness and a remoteness that contribute to a sense of irremediable unrelatedness: "incapable of contact" (see figure 5).

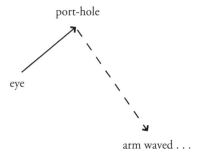

Figure 5

The same can be said about the following eight sections of the poem, which constitute an extended version of the poet's refracted seeing. Whether a glimpse of a country scene ("This land: / The hills, round under straw; / A house") or a detailed observation of a theatre setting ("Semaphoring chorus, / The width of the stage. The usher from it: / Seats' curving rows two sides by distant / phosphor"), a snapshot of motion ("Tug against the river— / Motor turning, lights / In the fast water off the bowwave: / Passes slowly") or a close-up of a still life ("Civil war photo: / Grass near the lens; / Man in the field / In silk hat. Daylight. / The cannon of that day / In our parks"), a voyeuristic recording ("She lies, hip high, / On a flat bed") or a journalistic all-embracing overview ("Bolt. . . . A ship. . . . A stone. . . . Water"),[56] all are marked with what seems to be a clinical indifference or distancing. For the perceiving poet-subject, however much he may see, never engages and synthesizes what he sees.

This optical-physical deployment, in which the sense of distancing between the eye and the objects becomes increasingly explicit and insurmountable, has its imprint upon the landscape of the mind. In its attempt to meditate on the structure of the eye-object relationship created by the refracted seeing through the rear-view mirror, consciousness asserts itself in the form of a soliloquy struggling to offer itself an explanation. Addressing itself as a "you" in a manner resembling someone talking to himself in the mirror, consciousness thus reasons:

From this distance thinking toward you,
Time is recession

Movement of no import
Not encountering you

Save the pulse cumulates a past
And your pulse separate doubly.[57]

Implicit in these three short stanzas is a structure identical to that of the rear-view mirror image, except that the spatial dimension in the latter is replaced here by a temporal one. The inability to overcome the distance between the eye and the objects ("From this distance") presents a problem to consciousness: It does not have a future in terms of an anticipated meeting with or contacting of an Other ("Movement of no import/Not encountering you"). Nor does it have a present, since the present is the actual meeting with the world and, in this sense, is the transition between a future and a past, between going to meet and having met. Nor, again, does it have a past, as the past takes its shape without its participation. For consciousness as such, time means only one thing: its own biological rhythm sounding each fleeing moment into the past ("Save the pulse cumulates a past"). Having nothing to do with what it does not have (future) on the one hand, nor with what has been completed without its involvement (past) on the other, consciousness is thus left with itself ("thinking toward you"). Such a consciousness of consciousness in turn produces a double effect in sharpening the speaker's sense of isolation ("And your pulse separate doubly"). Like its physical counterpart, the mind's eye can see only through a rear-view mirror (see figure 6).

Another case in point is the poem "Tourist Eye," in which the perceiving poet-subject again reads the world from an accepted isolation through the rear-view mirror. With the nature of the seeing already prescribed in the title of the poem, the eye sees but does not connect, witnesses but does

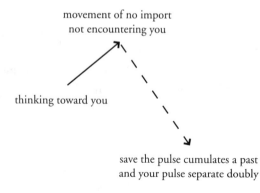

movement of no import
not encountering you

thinking toward you

save the pulse cumulates a past
and your pulse separate doubly

Figure 6

not participate. "*This activity, beginning in the midst of men . . .*"[58] ends nowhere but in the tourist's consciousness of his own status as an outsider, whose curiosity about, interest in, and concerns with the world seem only to expel him from, rather than welcome him into, a community.

A mini-series, "Tourist Eye" consists of five short, numbered, and independent poems dealing with various aspects of city life.[59] The distribution of concrete details observed in these poems seems, however, quite strangely uneven. In contrast to the physical density evidenced in poems #2 to #5, which offer images of locked doors, scarred and painted walls (#2), black windows and a child practicing piano (#3), "The red buildings of Red Hook," "the tides of Buttermilk Channel," "the Brooklyn Hardware stores" (#4), and the downtown of the oldest city (#5), poem #1 turns out to be relatively abstract. Although specific names do appear here, such as "Lever Brothers," the focus is primarily placed on "lights," "walls," and "glass."[60]

The selection of details like these in poem #1 proves to be suggestive, in that the common denominator therein seems to be the property or capacity to reflect things, especially "the lights that blaze and promise."[61] Even "the wall" is not just any ordinary one made of bricks,[62] for "this wall" in question refers to the wall of "the office / Buildings," which are made of glass, as is generally the case in modern urban architecture: "A thousand lives / Within that glass."[63] With the ability to both reflect and refract, this glass exteriority of the city not only metamorphoses from a seen object into a viewing instrument but also, logically enough, prompts the curious tourist to ask: "What is offered / In the wall and nest of lights?"[64]

In the tourist's question, the prepositional phrase "in the wall" evokes the rear-view mirror image. As it is denotatively determined, the word "in" has several meanings in this particular context. It may mean "behind or inside the wall"; it could also mean "set into the wall," in the sense that a window, for instance, might be "in the wall."[65] In either case, the emphasis falls on the object of the eye, and the wall functions as the obstacle, the overcoming of which becomes a necessity for direct seeing. But something can be "in" the wall in another sense, especially when the wall is made of glass. Just as one may say, "I saw my face in the mirror," so images reflected in the glass wall are "in the wall." The word "in" thus projects into the wall an optical, three-dimensional, perspectival interiority that is the reflection of the surrounding scene, which can in turn be seen through refraction. In this sense, the glass wall presents a rear-view mirror, in front of which stands the tourist looking into it, whose question "What is

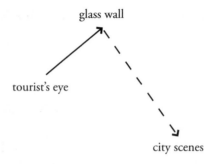

glass wall

tourist's eye

city scenes

Figure 7

offered in the wall?" can be interpreted as "What is reflected in the mirror?" or "What can I see in this rear-view mirror?" (See figure 7.)

But the tourist's question of "what is offered in the wall and nest of
lights?" has actually two parts. If "what is offered in the wall?" constructs
the image of the rear-view mirror through which the tourist's physical eye
sees the city, "What is offered in the nest of lights?" invokes a parallel image of the rear-view mirror into which the tourist's mind's eye looks and
becomes conscious of itself. "In consciousness," as Oppen himself asserts,
"objects exist in light".[66] hence light as consciousness. However, the nest
of lights, as consciousness, illuminates objects not as physical specificities
but as means by which consciousness engages itself in an unsolicited commentary or, more accurately put, a soliloquy. For the consciousness/nest of
lights, keenly aware of itself, feels the need to alleviate the intensity of its own
isolation by initiating a soliloquy. Out of this "eyeglass-wall-city scenes"
formation emerges, then, another rear-view mirror construct (see figure 8).

The result is the juxtaposition in the poem of refracted observation of
facts with soliloquized evaluative comments, as evidenced in poem #3:

Rectangular, rearing
Black windows into daylight: the sound

Of a piano in the deep bulk tying
Generations to a Sunday that holds
As the building holds, only the adamant

Nothing that the child hopes,
Laboring a tune. From any window, the day

Flawless and without exterior
Without alternative. But to the tenant

The future is all chance, all future, and the present
All inanimate, or all herself.[67]

Against the indifferent objects observed through the rear-view mirror, the
soliloquy of consciousness addressing itself sounds all the more lonely and
hollow. For the perceiving subject, seeing through refraction is understood as incurring one consequence: "The solitary are obsessed."[68]

This rear-view mirror image in "Tourist Eye" has a twin version in "Red
Hook: December."[69] The difference between these two versions lies in that
the image in the former is conceived out of semantic ambiguity, whereas
in the latter it is created out of syntactical ambiguity; both, however, are
rendered suggestive by the poet's use of the preposition "in." Thematically juxtaposing warmth ("Red Hook") with coldness ("December") in
the title, the poem begins with the speakers' lack of expectations, which
is strangely at odds with this particular time of the year, and which immediately raises a question concerning the speakers' identity in relation to
the town. Rather than having their expectations substantially but pleas-
antly altered by the extent to which the town prepares for the holiday
season ("Christmas lights," "New Year"), which would indicate a sense
of familiarity or affinity with the town, the speakers "had not expected
it."[70] Hence their status as outsiders is established in the first line of the
poem. For the word *expect* means: "1) orig. to wait, wait for; 2) to look for
as likely to occur or appear; look forward to; anticipate; 3) to look for as
due, proper, or necessary; 4) [Colloq.] to suppose; presume; guess," im-

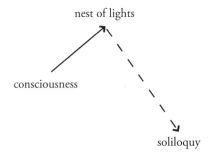

Figure 8

plying in each case "a considerable degree of confidence that a particular event will happen."[71] Failure to expect, therefore, presupposes an ignorance of a cultural poetics, of a communal environment in which the ability to expect distinguishes members of the community from outsiders. The speakers' total lack of expectations suggests, then, a kind of cultural shock they are undergoing as they enter the town, and their subsequent reading of the street scene, colored by their outsiders' perspectives, turns out to be no more than their own psychological and imaginative projection. Like the perceiving subjects in "Party on Shipboard" and "Tourist Eye," the speakers in "Red Hook: December" are, again, observers rather than participants.

As is almost always the case with Oppen, the typology of seeing is implicitly outlined at the beginning of his poems. So is it here, in the first sentence:

> We had not expected it, the whole street
> Lit with the red, blue, green
> And yellow of the Christmas lights
> In the windows shining and blinking
> Into distance down the cross streets.[72]

The syntactical ambiguity in question is caused by the prepositional phrase "In the windows," the multiple positions of which render possible two different readings and two different ocular perspectives. First, the prepositional phrase could be read as adjectival in nature, modifying "the Christmas lights" by specifying their physical location. As such, the sentence could be paraphrased as follows: "The whole street was lit with the red, blue, green, and yellow of the *Christmas lights which were in the windows,* and which were shining and blinking into distance down the cross streets." By this reading, the seeing is transitive; it synthesizes the street scene into a "whole," which is predicated upon the logic of a ritualized cultural custom, and it does so from the perspective of an insider intimately involved in the life of the town. Secondly, the prepositional phrase could be treated as adverbial in nature, functioning in this sense to modify the whole street scene by designating the place in which the entire scene is seen. That being granted, the sentence could then be paraphrased as: "*In the windows,* the whole street was lit with the red, blue, green, and yellow of the Christmas lights shining and blinking into distance down the cross streets." Positioned in this way syntactically, the prepositional phrase

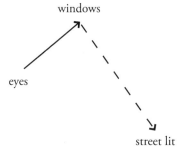

Figure 9

establishes a different visual and perspectival orientation; it dictates, in other words, a corresponding positioning of the speakers in relation to the windows, prescribing that they stand facing those windows, in which they see, through refraction, "the whole street / Lit with the red, blue, green / And yellow of the Christmas lights / . . . shining and blinking / Into distance down the cross streets." Following this reading, seeing is indirect and intransitive; it reports the street scene without predicative engagement with it, and it does so from the perspective of an outsider, or a tourist for that matter, who is only passing through. As it does in "Tourist Eye," the preposition "in" functions here not so much to point to a physical location as to transform the "windows" into a rear-view mirror (see figure 9).

Apart from establishing the rear-view mirror image, this first sentence in "Red Hook: December" also delineates, simultaneously, the life of consciousness suggested by its exclusive centering on "lights." Since the speakers have no expectations whatsoever of the town's preparation for the holiday season, which explicitly exposes them as outsiders in relation to that community, their consciousness of their own isolation intensifies. So much so that what the speakers are conscious of is not what happens in the street scene, but what occurs in their own consciousness in its very act of becoming conscious of the street scene. In other words, the details of the street scene are no more than the vocabulary of consciousness conversing with itself. One textual evidence of such consciousness of consciousness can be seen in the poet's use of affective words, words that seem to refer not so much outward to the street scene as inward to the speakers' own psyche.

In the second sentence of the poem, for instance, the speakers make an observation: "The children are almost awed in the street / Putting out the trash paper/In the winking light."[73] The key word in this sentence is "awed," which means, among other things, "a mixed feeling of reverence, fear, and wonder caused by something majestic, sublime, sacred, etc."[74] Used in the contexts of Christmas and New Year, however, the word "awed" sounds quite inappropriate, especially when applied to children young enough not to be thoroughly indoctrinated in theology but old enough to share house chores. For past experiences of the holidays, extended knowledge of the tradition, and familiarity with the conventional forms of observance would naturally and effectively abate this sensation of awe and replace it with excitement and joy. But the sense of awe never fails to secure a foothold in the hearts of those foreign to a tradition or cultural practice and, as a result, incapable of expectations of any kind. When understood contextually as such, the word "awed" seems to apply more fittingly to the speakers' own state of mind, which, struck by the spectacle, becomes conscious of its own sensation of being awed. Similar in this regard is the speakers' observation of another member of the town: "A man works/Patiently in his overcoat/With the little bulbs."[75] What seems to jar with the holiday atmosphere here is the word "patiently." Although the word means "steadily, diligently, and perseveringly," all of which appear appropriate to describe a man working in the holiday season, it also denotes "bearing or enduring pain, trouble, etc., without complaining or losing self-control" and "calmly tolerating."[76] This latter meaning, granted that it is still applicable to the man working in an overcoat, is obviously more relevant to the speakers themselves in this poem, who meanwhile are suffering "patiently" from their awareness of their own isolation that increases as their observation of the town's activities becomes more detailed. In addition, the word also means, especially in its noun form, "solitaire," "a hermit or recluse," or "card games played by one person."[77] This connotative emphasis on loneliness embedded in the word "patiently" suggests, more than anything else, the speakers' insight not into the man's mind, of which they know nothing, but into their own, which they know so painfully well. As is the case with the children, the man in the overcoat is not the object of consciousness; rather, he becomes the means whereby consciousness engages itself. Patient indeed in the true sense of the word, such consciousness of consciousness can wish for nothing for its comfort except its purportedly momentary appropriation of what belongs to the town:

And one can be at peace
In this city on a shore

For the moment now
With wealth, the shining wealth.[78]

And once again, the structure of this double consciousness is modeled after that of the rear-view mirror (see figure 10).

This mirroring process becomes, however, all the more poignant when the eye, looking into the rear-view mirror, sees nothing but itself staring back blankly. In poem #11 of "Of Being Numerous," the speaker's sense of isolation is portrayed not in his loneliness in the midst of the crowd but in his entrapment in vacant, deserted buildings: ". . . the buildings/Stand on low ground, their pediments/Just above the harbor/Absolutely im-mobile."[79] The image that emerges here is one of total emptiness or hol-lowness, which is all that the eye sees:

Hollow, available, you could enter any building,
You could look from any window
One might wave to himself
From the top of the Empire State Building—[80]

The severe sense of loneliness or isolation is treated with irony. "You could enter any building" not because of the hospitality offered by all the resi-dents there but because there is no one there: the buildings are "hollow" and, therefore, they are "available." More ironic is the statement that "one might wave to himself," out of which comes the rear-view mirror image. Similar to the act of transitive seeing, the act of waving is not only direc-tional but also target-oriented. The preposition "to," in other words, points to the object which is positioned in front of the waver, and to which the

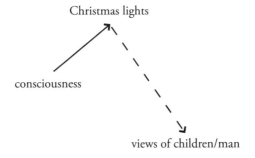

Figure 10

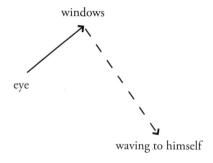

Figure 11

hand signal is intended. Since no one can be physically in two places at the same time, "One might wave to himself" in fact means, rather self-consciously, "One might wave to nobody." However, one could, perhaps, wave to himself with the help, for example, of a mirror. In this sense, the speaker's mentioning of the "window" in the previous line seems by no means casual or accidental. The fact that one can look "from" the window but see nothing "through" it may force him to look "at" the window; and this "looking at," in turn, transforms the window into a mirror, a rear-view mirror to be more exact, in which one sees himself waving to nobody but himself (see figure 11).

This escalated sense of isolation implied by "waving to nobody but himself only" is accompanied by an equally intensified consciousness, which finds its metaphor emphatically in the all-pervasive light: "It is *that* light / Seeps anywhere, a light for the times."[81] The speaker's physical entrapment in deserted buildings and his corresponding failure to contact anyone make it all the more crucial for consciousness to function beyond mere reasoning, explaining, and psychological projecting, to the point where an imaginative or inventive remedy becomes imperative. In other words, keenly aware of the tragic situation of "waving to himself," consciousness takes upon itself the responsibility of replacing that "himself" with someone else. In this light, the physical eye is immediately taken over by the mind's eye, which promptly starts a rescue game with itself. Right after the dash following "the Empire State Building," which may very well suggest the assertion of consciousness itself, there sounds a voice, imperative in tone: "Speak / If you can / Speak."[82] Upon this command, there appears, without any delay, the story of "Phyllis,"[83] a story in which the speaker is finally able not only to be told ("Her heart, she told me, sud-

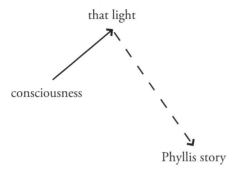

Figure 12

denly tight with happiness") but also to tell ("To talk of the house and the neighborhood and the docks"). As consciousness, he has, as it were, found someone to wave to at long last; and the working of the double consciousness is affirmed when consciousness thus reminds itself, in the last line of the poem, that all this "is not 'art.' "[84] (See figure 12.)

In Oppen's objectivist poetics of vision, the rear-view mirror image presents a modality of seeing through refraction. Intransitive or predication-resistant, disengaging or unsynthesizing, it brings with it both the affective and the pragmatic consequences of isolation and distancing. Its departure from the imagist aesthetics aside, Oppen's poetics of the rear-view mirror image, as such, asserts its significance, more importantly, beyond what has been commonly thought of as a paradigm shift in poetic thinking.

Philosophically, for one thing, it raises a methodological question with regard to systematic thinking, to any "system of opinions and attitudes,"[85] which is understood as "a rearrangement of established concepts."[86] In particular, it denatures the eye by calling attention to the act of seeing itself as an ocular system predicated upon an ego-system, and by unveiling the operation of the eye as the projection and imposition of a predatory intent in the form of logical relations.

More important is that, by de-ontologizing the eye at the level of philosophy and methodology, Oppen's objectivist poetics of vision fundamentally challenges the received concept of humanity. While the issue of "the human condition" has always occupied the center stage in Oppen's thinking,[87] his own experiences in war, politics, and exile can certainly be seen as contributory to his effort to conceptualize the alternatives. For Oppen, the question then becomes, as the poet himself implies, whether it is possible to live without sharing some of the accepted concepts and practices of humanity.[88] The answer is affirmative, painful as it is, which is evidenced in Oppen's response, when reminded of the world of isolation and distancing as the result of his seeing through refraction, "I can enter no other place."[89] In this sense, Oppen has always been writing philosophy in poetry, although he proclaims that "there wasn't any time in my life when I suddenly decided that now I'd write some philosophy."[90] More specifically, his is "the philosophy of the astonished,"[91] and the world perceived in its light is "existential,"[92] a world in which the established concepts of humanity have been found inadequate.

3. Be Aware of "the Medusa's Glance": The Objectivist Lens and Carl Rakosi's Poetics of Strabismal Seeing in "Adventures of the Head"

The objectivist movement, more than any other poetic phenomenon in the twentieth-century American poetry scene, has exhibited the true character of an avant-garde almost in the literal sense of the word.[1] If its forced and brief appearance in *Poetry* magazine in 1931, followed by *An "Objectivists" Anthology* the next year, for instance, shocked and angered the establishment with what Harriet Monroe describes as "barbed-wired entanglements,"[2] its "third or renaissance phase" after three decades of silence, as Ron Silliman points out, "restructured the entire field of American verse."[3] Probably because of its avant-garde status, the experimental nature of this radical and oppositional movement, known as the New American Poetry, has presented a territory yet to be fully explored.[4] In her theorizing of the historical position of the objectivists in the genealogy of American postmodernism, Marjorie Perloff captures a distinction crucial to one's understanding of the objectivist experiment. Responding to the question, "In what sense was the work of these poets a departure from that of the 'once revolutionary imagists,'" she argues that the objectivists represent a "larger aesthetic," one that is articulated by way of a shift "from the modernist preoccupation with *form* in the sense of imagistic or symbolist structure, dominated by a lyric 'I,' to the questioning of *representation* itself."[5] That being the case, the questioning of representation itself in objectivist poetics can be seen as having centered upon a specific focal point. What seems to have preoccupied these poets in their praxis is how to decenter the "I" as the organizing principle underpinning the scheme of mimesis. For the much-vexed complication lies in that the "I" as such also puns on the "eye," an optical agency with a corresponding linguistic structure built in.

From its inception, the objectivist consciousness is plagued by self-questioning, and its poetic emphasis on a clear, impartial, physical eye is relentlessly shadowed by a distrust of language as its reading glass. A case in point is Louis Zukofsky's "An Objective," the founding manifesto of the movement foregrounding the objectivist vision:

> *An Objective: (Optics)—The lens bringing the rays from an object to a focus. That which is aimed at. (Use extended to poetry)—Desire for what is objectively perfect, inextricably the direction of historic and contemporary particulars . . . Writing occurs which is the detail, not mirage, of seeing, of thinking with the things as they exist . . .*[6]

Two issues, more than others, take center stage in Zukofsky's "An Objective": epistemology (or the desire to know) and perception (or the use of the eye). But to a great extent, it is neither the former nor the latter alone as an isolated issue that Zukofsky is considering here. Rather, his theorizing seems to have focused on the rethinking of the nature of the relationship between the desire to know and the use of the eye, a relationship ordained by methodology, at once structured and sustained by language. Shadowing the statement, the implicit question that Zukofsky has put forth, for himself and for the objectivist experiment, is how to present "[an] object unrelated to palpable or predatory intent";[7] how, that is, to see an object in and through language when language is itself predatory, with a formal structure that materializes and objectifies what is predatorily intended. As such, Zukofsky's "An Objective," though written as a manifesto, casts a concomitant questioning look at itself as a language act capable of expressing the desire for what is objectively perfect, a look betrayed, on the one hand, by the poet's rather self-conscious phrasing and, on the other, by his much-felt need to repeat and to emphasize.

In an awkward turn of phrase, for instance, Zukofsky begins "An Objective" by reconfiguring and redefining the objectivist visual trajectory.

Rather than "the lens bringing an object to a focus," which is more acceptable in terms of usage as well as logic, he specifies the act of seeing as "the lens bringing the rays from an object to a focus." With this seemingly redundant wording, Zukofsky disarms the predatorily omniscient agency traditionally attributed to "the lens" by foregrounding the autonomous, ontological Otherness of the object. For whereas the phrase "the rays from an object" clearly asserts the separateness of and the distance between the seeing subject and the seen object, the preposition "from," in particular, further problematizes the immediacy of the object, an immediacy rendered otherwise readily available by the more "appropriate" and more "logical" preposition "of," one that denotes a projected or intended relationship from the vantage point of the predator.[8] To press his argument further, Zukofsky, as if already sensing language's predacious appetite, wastes no time reiterating the imperative of "the rays from an object." Though, for instance, "That which is aimed at" is appositional to "the rays from an object" and, therefore, dependent in grammar, it is nevertheless presented, both emphatically and suggestively, as an independent unit.

The same concern resurfaces later when Zukofsky comes to expound the objectivist theorem of sincerity, where he identifies language, seeing, and thinking as synchronous, as mutually infiltrating in a joined epistemological campaign. In accord with his emphasis on "the detail" over the "mirage," the poet, in the same vein, chooses the preposition "with" ("thinking with the things as they exist") over the predatory "of" to guide the objectivist vision. For the word "with," meaning "alongside of," "as a member of," or "in the same terms as,"[9] demystifies thinking/vision as mirage-making generalization and reduces it to a particular, to a thing or an object itself, thus establishing a parallel, coexisting, and mutually respectful relationship between the subject and the object.[10]

Such labored, self-reflexive use of language in "An Objective" seems to suggest, in this sense, an answer to the poet's question of how to see an object in and through language as a predatory mechanism. The objectivist lens, according to the Zukofskian prescription, is one that sees but does not falsify or assassinate the object.[11] It is, in other words, a two-way language lens, so structured that to see is to be seen, the one and the same movement in which the intent to prey upon the object is isolated from the mirage so that "words remain absolutely faithful to 'things' in their sensory immediacy."[12] Defined as "sincerity," this objectivist lens, with its intense "care for the detail," as Zukofsky explains in an interview,[13] resists the compulsion to absorb what it sees into a totalizing system. This particular property of the objectivist lens receives an apt description from Charles Altieri, who thus posits in "The Objectivist Tradition":

> Sincerity is usually not self-expression. Rather it involves insistence on the surface of the poem as concerned primarily with direct acts of naming as signs of the poet's immediate engagement in the areas of experience made present by conceiving the act of writing as a mode of attention. Sincerity involves refusing the temptations of closure—both closure as fixed form and closure as writing in the service of idea, doctrine, or abstract aesthetic ideal.[14]

As such, this lingual-optical configuration presents itself as an initial model of what Marjorie Perloff observes as "the questioning of representation itself." The objectivist departure from modernism, as signaled by Zukofsky's "An Objective," is marked by a radical shift from the late-imagist "act of vision" that "implicitly legitimates the existence of these things" to the objectivist act of attention that attempts to acknowledge and accept the object.[15] In this sense, the objectivist "larger aesthetic" is manifested not only in a rethinking but also in a thorough revision of a tradition far beyond the literary. It opened, to a great extent, a new area of inquiry in the early 1930s, the significance of which was to receive concentrated critical attention decades later. What Ron Silliman has designated as "objectivism's third or renaissance phase, from 1960 onward,"[16] for instance, corresponds in particular to a surge of philosophical reflection on Western culture as the culture of vision. With their emphasis on the "lens" in relation to the world, objectivist poets find themselves joined by such thinkers as Theodor Adorno, Maurice Merleau-Ponty, Martin Heidegger, Michel Foucault, Jacques Derrida, and Luce Irigaray in their critique of the construction and function of the "I/eye." In this context, there is Carl Rakosi, in whose work the objectivist lens brings into view a phenomenological landscape where the poet's "acknowledgement of the perceived arrangement of things,"[17] in Michael Heller's words, is articulated in a poetics of strabismal seeing.

"A thing can be described, but what it is can not be rendered except by variations of itself," observes Carl Rakosi in *Ex Cranium, Night;* "Man, however, is not satisfied with this. He is more obdurate than nature. Thus his own character is the mother of metaphysics and poetry,"[18] a character manifested in a craving "to find something permanent behind changing appearances, some yet unknown form of a transcendent nature," by "assigning a habitat and a character to [its] form in the mind itself."[19]

In an epigrammatic fashion, Rakosi sketches out the epistemological model underlying, since the ancient Greeks, what John Dewey describes as the "spectator theory of knowledge," one according to which to see is to know.[20] Such a convenient immediacy results from the fact that, in this "vision-generated, vision-centered interpretation of knowledge, truth, and reality,"[21] ocular vision is compromised. Particularly since Descartes, seeing becomes an auxiliary at the service of a higher entity. "The properties of the visible," as Dalia Judovitz argues, are in fact "transferred to the mental domain, whence they will illuminate metaphorically the powers of reason to attain certitude as clear and distinct ideas," thereby affirming "the arbitrary relation between the object of vision and the impression that object generates"; for what is at issue here, Judovitz continues, is "logic rather than mimesis. In other words the visible can only be addressed because its figurative character confirms to pre-given conventions."[22]

Rakosi is clearly aware of this predatory "reduction of being to being-represented."[23] "Who is like man," he writes satirically in the poem "Associations with a View from the House," "sitting in the cell / of referents, / whose eye / has never seen / a jungle, / yet looks in?"[24] His choice of verbs in his statement above from *Ex Cranium, Night,* which begins this section ("describe" vs. "render") pinpoints, for instance, the distinction between two kinds of seeing, ones that can be labeled, in Husserl's terminology, as "assertoric" and "apodeitic."[25] Referring to a "perceptual awareness of things in the ordinary sense,"[26] the assertoric constitutes a seeing *onto* the objects, thus foregrounding what Rakosi calls, citing Nicolai Akimov, "the expressiveness of *things.*"[27] By contrast, the apodeitic designates a conceptual seeing "*into* the essence of things,"[28] a seeing that performs, via desire and intention, an anthropomorphic "transmutation."[29] It is, more specifically, a transmutation "from matter to trope, into imago . . . the image of my way of knowing, of making matter conform to my mode of perception."[30]

Of these two modes of seeing, Rakosi contends further, the apodeitic, dictated by one's epistemological craving, becomes in a sense a priori, subordinating the assertoric to its own hegemony.[31] "No sooner does a person feel something," says Rakosi, "than the mind butts in: looks, describes, interprets, denatures, absorbs, controls, encapsulates. Its wit and precision make it so complacent that it assumes it has improved on the original, or at the very least, made an even exchange," thus always turning, say, "the beauty of a tree" into "the result of what is thought about it."[32] Hence an "ocular-centric paradigm,"[33] whereby the subject's access to truth and knowledge is rendered both direct and immediate by virtue of his or her visual trajectory, with desire and intention adjusting their focus on the object to extract the essence.

Rakosi's critical turn of mind here postulates a theoretical resonance with Theodor Adorno's critique of Edmund Husserl's "pure phenomenology," a phenomenology armed, nevertheless, with an "epistemological inclination to ascertain how knowledge of objecthood is in general possible and how it may be identified in the structure of consciousness."[34] In its attempt to initiate "a radically new and original beginning,"[35] a "first" seeing that purportedly presents the "object-in-itself," phenomenology, Adorno asserts, sets up its camera obscura in nowhere but the mind and resorts to epistemological methodology to secure the givenness of the world. Adorno writes:

> Since acts of thought as such may be immediate facts of consciousness just as much as impressions of sense-perception, then what for Husserl is in each case thought in acts of thought, is mediated by them, becomes for its part, immediacy. Givenness at the moment is identified in the Sixth Logical Investigation with consciousness. Hence intentionality in the pregnant sense, which Husserl gave the term, would in the end be identified with givenness. Since the mediated, what is already thought through intention, should simply be assumed, the concept of immediate givenness becomes total. Perception becomes knowledge of something, this knowledge becomes the primary, irreducible factual state of consciousness and the perceived thing world becomes, so to speak, a radical first.[36]

It is one's consciousness that determines the existence of the object, which places itself on call and will present itself instantly and automatically in its original form the moment it becomes intended. Thus the password to the "thing world," as Adorno's diction explicitly indicates, is "identity" or "recovery" granted by consciousness, and the magic verb, "become," conjures up, in Mikel Dufrenne's terms, not so much "the actual presence of the thing" as "the presence itself."[37] Phenomenology in the Husserlian scheme of things, Adorno argues, is anything but innocent, as it "falls into the fundamental position of transcendental subjectivity, or as the late Husserl called it, the ego."[38] In this sense, underlying Husserlian phenomenology one finds a different kind of optics with a corresponding methodology, one that brings the rays from the "eye/I" to a focus through a dialectical, circular movement from the ego back to the ego, bypassing, rather conveniently, the object itself. Adorno writes: "The ego constitutes things by applying categories to the sensible. . . . [What] the subject knows is true, if it corresponds with what the subject itself is constituted. The subject's knowledge of the objective leads . . . right back to the subject and is thus in a certain sense tautological."[39]

Rakosi's objectivist insight into the sense perception as always already mediated—that is, intentional in the sense that the consciousness "of" an object constitutes, in the same movement, the predatory capture of its essence—evokes Adorno's metaphor of "the Medusa's glance of a sudden 'ray of vision.'"[40] Adorno's allusion to the Medusa's eye, together with his wording of the metaphor, offers a merciless, detailed dissection of the nature of vision in the Husserlian construction of objecthood. While the word "sudden," for instance, suggests the intensity as well as the violence of such a vision that disfigures the object, the indefinite article "a" explicitly qualifies it as whimsical and arbitrary. Furthermore, the intense vision as the desire to know demands, by logic, to be objectified into method, a method as a weapon to conquer the world.

Medusa's severed head, so the mythical story goes, is used as a strategic weapon, the eyes of which turn the adversary into stone by a fixed, penetrating stare. In Husserl's "hunt for the given,"[41] this "Medusa's glance of a sudden 'ray of vision'" has a similar function: it is a deadly gaze that reduces what Adorno calls "the unformed manifold of the factical itself" to "unified conceptual structures."[42] By alluding to a visual construct from myth to illustrate the functional, administrative mechanism basic to all reduction of the "non-homonymous down to a common denominator,"[43] Adorno succeeds in showing that such a mechanism per se is fictitious.

Rakosi's poem "The Romantic Eye" presents a kind of poetic gloss of this critique of Husserl's phenomenology. Gathered in his *Collected Poems* in a section titled, rather pointedly, "Adventures of the Head," the poem is what one might call a textbook example of how the Medusa's glance works, a parody of its working mechanism:[44]

On the eight thousandth magnification
the chromosome of the Chironomus fly
stirred its microscopic nebulae into
the figure of a Greek Orthodox cross.[45]

In these four lines, the Medusa's glance assumes, in Jeffrey Peterson's words, "the 'creative' character of microscopic vision."[46] Rakosi's unhesitating switch to the scientific discourse under the heading of "Romantic" makes a statement. Not only, for instance, does he thus define the nature of science as such but he also implicates the nature of philosophy, which, as Adorno claims, "takes science as its model."[47] As an intentional and objectivating act, the creative character of the microscopic vision (science) proves, in this sense, to be identical with the no less creative character of the macroscopic vision (metaphysics). For in both, as Adorno observes, "the schema of order imposed on objects by human consciousness . . . is handled as if the need indicated in this schema were the order of the objects themselves."[48]

The four lines of the poem designate the four components constitutive of such an imposition in the form of an apodeictic seeing: the gaze ("magnification"), the object ("chromosome"), the anthropomorphic transmutation ("stirred . . . into"), and the result or creation ("a Greek Orthodox cross"). Their sequential ordering outlines the logical steps in a methodological procedure facilitating a conceptual *seeing-into,* which first projects in and then extracts from the object a preestablished, hierarchical order at the sacrifice of that object. In addition, the power of the Medusa's glance to see into things so as to "magically [transform] all becoming into being" is,[49] as the first line suggests, entirely determined and adjusted by one's desire or intention measurable in numbers, and any change in the intensity of the former or the degree of the latter will alter the end result proportionally. From this perspective, the economy of the Medusa's glance lies in a circular movement, in its intentional and judgmental capacity to establish an identity by projecting, directly and immediately, from the eye ("the eight thousandth magnification") to its creation ("the figure of a Greek Orthodox cross") across the material middle, in which the thing-object ("chromosome"), by virtue of being seen, is intimidated and subdued into servitude to the eye, becoming "the ultimate 'fulfillment' of intention," as Adorno argues, "the proof of the correctness of the judgment."[50]

In this way, through its powerful image of the Medusa's glance at work, Rakosi's "The Romantic Eye" stages, rather self-consciously, "a closed system," as the poet himself puts it in a different context, a system "not related to what is going on outside; it assumes *it* is what is going on there."[51] In such a system, assumptions take the form of methodology, whose function is, as Harari and Bell point out, none other than "the illustration of a given type of knowledge through the set of results that the method can produce."[52] Concurring with Rakosi in this regard, Adorno specifies further the anthropomorphic nature of "to see is to know" as mastery and closure:

> Thus cognition does not linger over its object for the sake of elucidating it. It does not really refer to (*meinen*) its object at all, but rather degrades it to a mere function of the schema under which it is haughtily subsumed. The more objectively cognition poses and the more purified from all delusion and supplement from the observer, the more subjective it becomes in the totality of its procedure.[53]

With "The Romantic Eye" as a reminder of the Medusa's glance at work, "Adventures of the Head," contrary to what the title seems to have suggested, assumes an ironic inversion. For the poems collected here do not indulge in portraying epic adventures in hunting for knowledge; rather, they body forth a series of meditations foregrounding Rakosi's objectivist adventures in breaking through this closed system, in resisting "the Medusa's glance of a sudden 'ray of vision.'" "We broke out of the romantic / gravitational field," Rakosi writes in "The Adventures of Varèse," "The idea / was to reach *sui generis,* / a state of random mass / above sensitivity."[54] At the point of departure of all these adventures, however, there persists this one haunting question: how to see with

the living eye?

. . . .
forever
and ever without
bias or mercy,
attrition or mystery[55]

or, to put it differently, how to realize what Rakosi himself calls, in an interview, the "fidelity to the object" through a lingual-optical construct which is itself not descriptive but prescriptive,[56] "not 'about' the world," as Burton Hatlen observes, "but constitutive of it."[57]

"I respect the external world," Rakosi states, "there is much in it that is beautiful if you look at it hard. I don't want to contaminate that; it has its own being; its own beauty and interest that should not be corrupted or distorted. But so does the poet have his own being."[58]

The ethical basis of Rakosi's objectivist approach is laid, as he has emphasized here and elsewhere, in "integrity": the integrity of the object as the seen, and of the subject as the seer.[59] But for the object to have any integrity at all, the subject must, first and foremost, assert his or her own integrity by abstaining from the apodeitic propensity, by "[fighting] against his own intellect," as Rakosi himself puts it.[60] For the integrity one accords the object originates, in actuality, only from the act of seeing that is based on respect or acknowledgment, one that resists any predatory intent. "Not to aggrandize a perception," Rakosi thus defines this ethical concept, "not to inflate the lyric impulse, that seems to go counter to one's whole romantic thrust, the thrust of poetry itself, yet that is integrity."[61] But the impulse to aggrandize a perception, Rakosi also seems to suggest, has a psychological component, which he addresses, in a way as much metaphorical as literal, through the relational condition of this integrity between a hunter and a wolf in the poem "Riddle":

> In the dead of night
> the caribou slept.
>
> The possibility of not knowing
> what you are
> had not yet been conceived.
>
> It is the original forest.
> There is peace.
>
> The wolf has eaten.
> He goes into a long howl
> to give his location.
>
> If the hunter does not find him,
> he'll live seven years.
>
> A box is a box.
> Integrity has been defined.[62]

The poem depicts a fragile, transient moment temporally balanced between two worlds: the world of objects, as represented by the caribou and the wolf, and the world of knowledge, as embodied by the hunter. What tips this balance in favor of the latter laden with potential violence, Rakosi seems to indicate here, is fear. In "The possibility of not knowing / what you are / had not yet been conceived," for instance, the construction of the verbal phrase, coupled with a tone not without a tinge of appreciation of that "not yet" moment, already foresees and anticipates a panic reaction once this possibility is conceived. While it points out, indeed, the necessary condition for the "peace" in "the original forest," it isolates, in one and the same gesture, the psychological cause of the inevitable disappearance of that condition. For the moment one conceives the possibility of not knowing what one is is also the moment that generates fear, a fear powerful enough to keep that possibility forever impossible; and with the knowing of what one is comes, as a result, the knowing of what the world is. Thus, fear, epistemology, and methodology work hand in hand, forming an intricate network of self-defense mechanisms.[63] Rakosi's implicit psychological reading in this poem finds a more explicit and pertinent articulation in Roland Barthes, who, in his chapter on "The Image" in *The Rustle of Language,* offers the following diagnosis:

> At the origin of everything, Fear. (Of what? Of blows, of humiliations?) Parody of the *Cogito* as the fictive moment when, everything having been "razed," this *tabula rasa* will be reoccupied: "I'm afraid, therefore I'm alive." An observation: According to today's *mores* (we need an ethology of intellectuals), one never speaks of fear: it is foreclosed from discourse, and even from writing (could there be a writing of fear?). Posited at the origin, it has a value as *method;* from it leads an initiatic path.[64]

And that "initiatic path" leading from fear is the one that the hunter is to travel in his pursuit of the wolf. To achieve integrity, Rakosi announces clearly at the end of the poem, one has to overcome one's fear and let the object be, be it the wolf or the box. But the hunter, Rakosi also knows very well, is always on the move, exhorted by the fear of not knowing and, concomitantly, by the desire to solve the riddle.

Viewed in this light, Rakosi's objectivist sensibility in "Adventures of the Head" centers on the tension between two kinds of desires: the *unarmed* desire for what *is* objectively perfect on the one hand, and the *armed* desire for what *should be* objectively perfect on the other.[65] Michael Heller, in his studies of Rakosi, defines the former when he writes: "In objectivist formulations, desire is unarmed and, in a sense, has no preconceived notions of the nature of the encounter; its only givens are appearances, emotions aroused, intellectual stimulations, that is, elements in the occasion."[66] It is a desire with neither the literary "overtones of strained metaphorization" nor the modernist "slight flavor of encoding and reifying reality."[67] To put it in Rakosi's own words from "Riddle," it is a desire that does not concern itself with "the possibility of not knowing." By contrast, the armed desire, as is manifested in Husserlian phenomenology, invokes its own fulfillment or satisfaction by turning the object into and then identifying it as its much-needed "evidence," evidence, as Adorno observes, "expected of the 'object'" as something given or present.[68] In other words, it is a desire to know that secures its answer through a process of *re*covery, not *dis*covery.[69] Whereas Rakosi's poems, asserts Michael Heller, "do not really attempt to capture an essence,"[70] there exist, throughout his writing, both a keen awareness of and a concomitant vigilance against "the Medusa's glance of a sudden 'ray of vision.'" As such, the encounter between the subject and the object is articulated in Rakosi's work in an "implied interrogation of the self and of any stated position or system," as Rachel Blau DuPlessis argues:[71] of the self as the epistemological hunter who knows the wolf-object by hunting it down, and of any stated position or system as ultimately the lingual-optical militarism which, as Roland Barthes asserts in terms of language's function in relation to any object, "attacks, surrounds, sizzles, hardens, and browns."[72]

Rakosi's objectivist lens, through which this "implied interrogation" is implemented, takes the form of strabismal seeing. The model of Rakosi's optics, interestingly enough, can also be traced back to the same story to which Adorno alludes; but while Adorno succeeds in revealing the predatory mechanism of the Medusa's glance, Rakosi takes a step further by pointing out that embedded in the Medusa's glance lies its own undoing. As Ovid's Perseus learns, the only means to render ineffective Medusa's fixed, one-way staring into the object is to return it a counter-look, a looking-back made possible by Perseus's bronze shield which defocuses the Medusa's glance by deflecting its deadly gaze, thus making it unable to lock onto the target directly.[73]

Rakosi finds his bronze shield in strabismal seeing, in the inability of the axes of vision to be coincidentally directed to the same object, which simultaneously forces his attention back to the act of seeing itself. As a result, this dual attention to seeing and to the act of seeing turns what was formerly a one-way vision into a two-way one: a seeing that also watches itself in action, questioning its own shaping and interpretative capacities and holding in check its own predatory intent. In other words, it is a seeing that resists the Medusa's glance as meaning, as the impulse or desire to project and to categorize. To be strabismal, then, is to break away from Medusa's one-way, self-fulfilling gaze, one in which "judging and becoming aware of a judged state-of-affairs are equivalent expressions," as Adorno puts it, "or rather the second disguises the first in metaphor"; in this sense, strabismal seeing is "becoming aware of a judged state-of-affairs" without "the immediacy of the performance of judgment."[74] This objectivist optics is mirrored, in particular, in Rakosi's use of language, which can be characterized as intransitive.

In discussing the objectivist lens in Rakosi's work, one can hardly overlook one poem that could be considered as the twin piece of "The Romantic Eye." Although included in a section titled *"Droles de* Journal" in *The Collected Poems,* a section that presents a highly parodic as well as ironic treatment of the pretentiousness and silliness of poetry in Horatian epigrams, "Objectivist Lamp" nevertheless deserves, indeed demands, one's critical attention. For one thing, in sharp contrast to the other poems' exaggerated and affected mannerism that borders upon clownery, this poem seems oddly out of place with a guarded tone and a serious subject matter. For another, while most of the poems in this section are written as monologues featuring a loud-mouthed "I" and sometimes a silent "you," as utterances of either imperatives, comments, rhetorical questions, or insults, this poem unfolds a careful observation of an object. Moreover, the title of the poem sounds too theoretically pertinent to the objectivist poetics to be simply dismissed at that. In fact, it presents a powerful redefinition of the objectivist vision by way of a critique of "The Romantic Eye" as the projector; for the word "Lamp," as the popular analogy in the romantic tradition for the perceiving mind fashioning its own experience by recovering "what it has itself partly made," alludes to M. H. Abrams's important study of romanticism and its poetics: *The Mirror and the Lamp.*[75] In this sense, "The Romantic Eye" and "Objectivist Lamp" are twin pieces in that together they form the two parts of Rakosi's objectivist demonstration: the former dissecting the romantic eye as the Medusa's glance, and the latter showing the objectivist lamp as strabismal seeing.

As is manifested in its title, "Objectivist Lamp" postulates a direct, word-for-word opposition to "The Romantic Eye." But the crucial difference that sets the tone for the objectivist poetics from the outset lies in the absence of a definite article "The," which denotes what is mentioned, designated, identified, or recognized already or previously. To expand its grammatical as well as semantic parameters slightly, "The" can also be read and employed as an adjective designating the nature or the attribute of the modified as such. "The Romantic Eye," in this sense, is the eye that always sees what it already saw; that is, it only sees what it wants to see, what it is determined to see, or what it projects to see. It follows, then, that the absence of the definite article in "Objectivist Lamp" suggests an assertoric seeing, a seeing without any preconceived notions of the nature of the encounter between the eye and the object. Instead of "[imposing] forms . . . and categories on the 'sensuous manifold'" by "throwing its beams into the external world,"[76] as the romantic mirror and lamp would do, "Objectivist Lamp" enacts a double negation of "The Romantic Eye": it sees itself, and it sees itself assertorically.

> goddess,
>   ivory carved
> Japanese
>   lady,
> hands crossed
>   over breast,
> holding
>   on her head
> electric bulbs
>   and batik
> lamp shade.[77]

Here the lamp is an object perceived but not, as Rakosi would say, aggrandized. The poem outlines a process in which language's transitive, nominating impulse is nullified at its inception, and the mirage of seeing is shattered at the moment of its suggestiveness and taken over by the detail of seeing. Rakosi's strabismal vision begins with a mythical figure, "goddess." But the apodeitic projections otherwise associated with this word are immediately called into question due to the lack of an identifiable signification caused by the letter *g* in lower case. What can be identified, then, is only the material out of which this "goddess" is made: "ivory carved." Although "goddess" is further specified by its apposition of "Japanese/lady," it is nothing more than the same physical substance that relates them, thus frustrating any attempt to see beyond the appearance. In a like manner, the ghost of a symbolic gesture suggestively promised in "hands crossed/over breast,/holding/on her head" is driven away by the rather banal "electric bulbs / and batik / lamp shade." The absence of any visionary posturing then helps to unveil a human figure as physical details carved *onto* the lamp, not as a mirage projected *into* it. With its focus on the detail of seeing, "Objectivist Lamp" sheds light exclusively on the object in its own variations, warning itself against what Michael Palmer terms "the dangers of posturing and verbal contrivance and . . . the 'larger Romantic tone of greatness.'"[78]

In "Adventures of the Head," three poems present the most appropriate testing ground for Rakosi's strabismal shield in his adventures against the Medusa's glance: "Cenozoic Time," "Man Contemplating a Rock," and "How to Be with a Rock." Rakosi's choice of a rock as the object of vision in all three poems is significant on two counts. On the one hand, it gestures, as Marjorie Perloff avers earlier, to a radical departure from the modernist poetic tradition as is evidenced, in particular, in Wallace Stevens's poem "The Rock." Grounded in the tradition of "High Romantic, Wordsworthian-Whitmanian crisis-poems," "The Rock" is not a poem about matter; rather, argues Harold Bloom, it is "Stevens's major elegy for his own poetic self."[79] The "I" in the poem, tormented by a strong desire for transcendental beyonds, is eagerly merged in a transmutational vision of either an active beholding or a passive regarding. While to behold, for Stevens, is to "[possess] the object" through a "scrutiny" so as "to drive or to set [the object] in swift motion," Bloom points out, to regard is to "watch out for something" by looking at an object "attentively or closely."[80] In either case, the result is the same as that in Rakosi's "The Romantic Eye." The rock is a "high rock" in the poem because,[81] as Stevens himself writes:

> In this plenty, the poem makes meanings of the rock,
> Of such mixed motion and such imagery
> That its barrenness becomes a thousand things
>
> And so exists no more. . . .[82]

A modernist icon, Stevens's "rock" thus bodies forth the site "where by apposition," observes Bloom, "the mind and the external realm are brought together as a dialectical alpha and omega";[83] it is that which has already been transmuted, as Rakosi has aptly epitomized earlier, "from matter to trope, into imago . . . the images as my way of knowing, of making matter conform to my mode of perception." On the other hand, it signals Rakosi's objectivist position as well as his strategy. For the "rock," while reminding one of the Medusa's glance that turns the object into stone, provides a dual perspective in each poem: that of the "rock" as an independent, ontological Otherness in its own process of becoming, and that of the "prey" as the captured, disfigured "stone" already processed into a categorized being. The juxtaposition of both perspectives, then, forces a moment of *revision*.

The poem "Cenozoic Time," it seems, carries a message almost identical to what Rakosi once warned himself: "When I sit down to write, I must not forget that one does not strike an attitude in front of a mountain."[84] Highly ironic is Rakosi's use of a geological term here. For the title of the poem refers to a time span following the Mesozoic all the way to the present, during which both the earth (rocks, mountains) and modern human culture have been in the active process of becoming, a becoming, one might hasten to add, as historic and contemporaneous particulars. Yet as a scientific term, "Cenozoic" enacts the mirage of seeing by one into the other, the Medusa's glance that freezes the becoming into being, into what the scientist-philosopher would consider as "the ultimate reality."[85] Hence "Cenozoic Time" is a title from which the rock is absent, having been subsumed under a concept. Against such a deadly gaze, the poem, both in theme and in structure, dramatizes Rakosi's strabismal seeing:

> A man looks
>   at a rock.
> The rock sits.
>   Rock and man.
> The rock is.
>   What is being?
>
> He has sensed
>   his nature,
> idea as idea
>   and trembles
> before the insoluble
>   art.[86]

The first six lines, with exactly three words in each, displays as a unit a marked terseness indicative of a conscious guard against "vision-generated, vision-centered language."[87] Rather strategically, the line break that dismembers the first sentence occurs nowhere but between "looks" and "at." For, as an intransitive verb followed by a preposition to form a transitive verbal phrase, this linguistic collocation otherwise demands, in syntax as well as in grammar, the presence of a direct object; it thus establishes and enforces a hierarchical, military control based on subjection and subordination, imposing its apodeictic gaze upon the object as its captive. Rakosi's typographical layout here serves as a counter-look, in that it obstructs the intended, straight-line *seeing-into* by demilitarizing language's mission from the transitive (look-at something) to the intransitive (look, at something).[88] "A man looks," then, suggests a man who looks in acknowledgment, who sees without magnifying the object into an immediate mirage. It signifies, in this sense, a happening as a particular, no more or less, among others; and "at a rock," read in this context, becomes an adverbial of place. Both lines claim, as such, a material moment in which intention is suspended and the detail of seeing becomes subsequently possible: "The rock sits," with the verb functioning descriptively rather than nominatively. The integrity of the rock, which is already indicated here not only by its dignified posture of sitting but also by its status as a self-sufficient syntactical unit, is highlighted further in the next line. In "Rock and man," the former is seen, by way of juxtaposition, as a particular equal to, rather than as "the sheer function of," the latter;[89] hence a *with*-relationship between the two. Indeed, that "the rock sits," by virtue of its facticity, is itself, Rakosi seems to argue, enough proof to show that "the rock is."

In contrast to the clarity of seeing as a material moment, in which the rock is witnessed in its spatiotemporality, the question in the sixth line becomes ironically as well as rhetorically self-conscious. "What is being?" does not sound here so much as a meditation attempting a "Medusian" imposition upon the rock as a self-doubt on the part of the ego reminded of its transitive seeing. For what is in fact accidental or "supervenient" is not the rock;[90] rather, it is, as the word "being" suggests, the mirage of seeing contrived ideationally to project a so-called ultimate reality.

The "inability" to see into the object and to capture its essence, as the first six lines exemplify, in turn redirects the rays of vision back to the act of seeing itself, which, already signaled by the question "What is being?" is executed in the next six lines. What occupies the subject's mind now is not how to answer the question, but rather why to ask it in the first place. And the answer the subject has found is painfully revealing. "He has sensed / his nature," which, as the apposition defines it, is none other than "idea as idea," an objectivating circle in which the predatory intent "presupposes what, by its proper *raison d'être* it should have deduced."[91] The Medusa's glance becomes, therefore, an "art" in a double sense: epistemologically, it is the "human ability to make things," "to execute a plan"; while methodologically, it is a "sly or cunning trick, wile."[92] And the source of its deadly rays lies in the intensity of one's desire and intent. It is, in other words, a self-fulfilling promise, with a guaranteed winning strategy perfected to the point of transparent immediacy. To resist the Medusa's glance as such, the subject realizes, poses a formidable task: "and trembles / before the insoluble / art."

"Man Contemplating a Rock" continues this trend of thought by bringing to the fore just how formidable or "insoluble" this "art" could be. The poem can be read, to a great extent, as a philosophical rendition of "The Romantic Eye." Whereas "The Romantic Eye" delineates, step by step, how "the immediate is also mediated" in the scientific process,[93] "Man Contemplating a Rock" makes a caricature of the philosophical process that gives birth to that ultimate form of immediacy. By doing so, it implicitly adds to the objectivist integrity that Rakosi describes when he states, "The poet is more modest than the ancient philosopher: he doesn't claim that what he has thought out is the ultimate reality":[94]

> *Incipit*
> the first
> Philosopher
> & *ad*
> *infinitum.*[95]

Here the Medusa's glance assumes the form of the transitive philosophical discourse. As the object of apodeitic seeing, the rock, though still present in the title, is literally contemplated into oblivion in the poem, the brevity of which suggests a swift movement from the deadly gaze to its prey, an immediate slaughter. The five-line verse then presents a world that begins and exists forever only in Latin, the discourse of traditional philosophy that has magically conjured up a meaning-laden universe. Lording it at the center of this universe one finds "the first / Philosopher," the origin of all origins, who authored the "*Incipit*" and authorized the "*ad / infinitum*"; hence an of-relationship between the predator and its prey. Indeed, "the relation of metaphysics to knowledge, and the relation of the latter to domination come together in the same place," as Michel Serres contends, "at the outcome provided by death."[96] And the poem, itself a demonstration of the Medusa's glance at its most predatory, encircles the burial ground of the rock.

In contrast to "Cenozoic Time" and "Man Contemplating a Rock," "How to Be with a Rock," as its title states, seems to have been written as a manual in three parts, detailing and demonstrating strabismal seeing in the form of language, a language demilitarized from saying *of* or *about* the rock to saying something *with* it. Rakosi sets up his strabismal lens in the first part:

> The explicit ends here,
> > Outer is inner.
> It is all manifest.
> > Its character is durity.
> There lies its charisma.
>
> By nature it is Pangaea.
> > It has its own face
> and its own tomb,
> > the way it stands,
> unmoved by destiny,
> > a model for the mind.
> We can only be spectators.
> > All is day within.[97]

For language to say something *with* the object is to say something *of* itself. In the first five lines, there exists a pronounced self-reflexiveness of the word cautioning itself against its own propensity to see and say more than what is there. Conditioned as such, the conceptual trajectory of the word loses its predatory momentum the moment it touches the rock and becomes defocused; it is replaced, then, by a bird's-eye view in which intention is kept at bay. "The explicit ends here," reads the first line, with "explicit" emphasizing the assertoric, not the apodeitic, nature of seeing. Further, while "here" refers to nothing but the rock in its physical entirety, "ends" means, perhaps, "completes," with both words providing what Burton Hatlen calls the "limit-point to the pretensions of the ego."[98] Furthermore, "here" designates a dimension not only horizontal but also, and more importantly, vertical: "Outer is inner," which announces the rock's material consistency and integrity that necessitate no projection or interpretation. Hence the paraphrase: the rock, in its physical entirety, speaks for itself. "It is all manifest," as Rakosi writes: the rock in its corporeality, language in its superfluity. In this sense, "The explicit ends here" suggests a language abstaining from its own Medusa's glance by acknowledging the rock's self-sufficiency, denying, as a result, any possible room for the "*Incipit*" of "the first / Philosopher."

Rakosi's strabismal lens, while bringing the rays from the rock to a focus, is turned in the next eight lines to its own consciousness, a consciousness engaged in a monologue, reminding itself of its own predatory desire. Already at work in "By nature it is Pangaea," for instance, is indeed the Medusa's glance, hypothesizing the rock into a category. But the nominating act via scientific-geological discourse is immediately negated in the following four lines. Not only does the repeated and emphatic use of the phrase "its own" ("It has its own face / and its own tomb") recognize a beginning and end independent from the "*Incipit* / . . . / & *ad* / *infinitum*" envisioned by the scientist-philosopher, but it also accepts the rock's way of existence ("the way it stands, / unmoved by destiny") as transcending the human chain of logic and laws of determinacy. The result is the awareness of a mind lacking in integrity, easily and habitually seduced by old myths or armed desires, a mind that needs, therefore, to look to the rock as its example ("a model for the mind"). Through Rakosi's strabismal lens, the traditional "ocular-centric paradigm" is thus turned upside down. "We can only be spectators," Rakosi draws the line, spectators who see without taking any part in the schemes of the Medusa's glance, and whose relation with the rock is, as such, specifically delimited by the phrase "can only." "All is day within," Rakosi thus explains his ethical decision: the rock is most articulate and expressive in its own integrity.

A husband's speech to his wife, the second part of the poem stages Rakosi's objectivist belief that "specificity pulls the most profound-looking ideas down to earth":[99]

> "Go to the village,"
>   I tell my wife,
> "and bring back a chicken,
>   an onion, a goose
> and an apple
>   and we'll lie here
> and repopulate this Siberia."[100]

Armed with irony, Rakosi's strabismal lens in the form of intransitive language works on three levels here. Discursively, the speech, voiced as an imperative ringing with a Genesis-sounding intention and purposefulness ("and repopulate this Siberia"), never receives any response. The result is a statement isolated from any mirage-generating context and, as such, reduced to a mere utterance, a vocal happening, or a physical particular. Syntactically, the excessive use of the conjunction word "and" calls into question any possible causal relation that supposedly organizes the content of the speech. Why, for instance, does the speaker demand these particular food items ("chicken," "onion," "goose," "apple")? Why "*re*populate"? And why, further, "Siberia"? Instead of setting up a tangible, logical scaffolding of some sort, "and" helps, on the contrary, to demilitarize the syntax into a series of parallel specifics, displaying, rather, the objectivist detail, not mirage, of seeing. Referentially, Rakosi's equally excessive use of the indefinite article "a/an" and his choice of the deictic "this" to designate "Siberia" create what might be called an "association-resistant" effect. Connoting "a thing not previously noted or recognized,"[101] "a/an" defamiliarizes whatever follows it by drawing attention to itself as a general, non-sequential one, as an "any one," thus making it too vague for anybody to relate. Similar in effect but reverse in function, the word "this" decontextualizes Siberia as a public domain by insinuating it into private, individual nuances inaccessible from any communal or shared perspectives. Each in its own way, both the indefinite article "a/an" and the deictic "this" foreground a life episode in concrete, seemingly arbitrary particulars that constitute what Michael Heller terms "a salient aspect of the world,"[102] not in the "profound-looking ideas" of them.

The last part of the poem articulates Rakosi's "objectivist motto" as, in Hugh Kenner's words, "No myths."[103] It is a section where Rakosi returns to myth to announce the death of myth, where, through Rakosi's strabismal lens, the mythical figures are themselves seen just as dead as unearthed human mummies, as mere inventions or imaginations parasitic on the phenomenon of death:

It is in Genesis.
A strange god,
         all torso
and without invention or audacity.

It can be accused of both plutonism
and the obvious.
        The closest human thing to it

is the novocained tooth,

                    its Medussa hair now fossilized.

It can be bequeathed to one's heirs
with the assurance that it will not depreciate
or be found irrelevant.[104]

Here, more than elsewhere, the strabismal lens proves most powerful, and the irony, most biting. It re-reads the book of myth as an excavated tomb and reexamines its content as futile preservations of highly decomposed remains. Read in the context of this section, the first line presents a succinct critical review of the epistemological tradition as the Medusian language act, mythologized as well as mythologizing. Its form as a complete sentence that ends with the loaded term "Genesis" exemplifies the apodeitic "first seeing," outlining the predatory, self-referential circle already sketched in "Man Contemplating a Rock": to write (or to use language) is to create or to invoke, and whatever is created is always born complete. With the first line setting up the thematic backdrop, the following three lines constitute a critique of the romantic eye by demythicizing a god-figure as a language construct. While the letter *g* in "god" is seen through the strabismal lens as written in lowercase, signifying the figure as, perhaps, nothing more than a historical particular, "it is in Genesis," Rakosi seems to claim, that it becomes capitalized. For "Genesis" embodies armed desires manifested in a mythmaking narrative, whose uppercase *G* invokes its own transcendent identity by projecting itself into the *G* in "God." Once demythicized, "god" turns ordinary and dead, seen as "strange," "without invention or audacity," whose headless trunk ("all torso") testifies further, by default of course, to the fact that its alleged "completeness" is no more than a language artifact.

The next five lines continue this demythicizing process in the form of an autopsy report. But it is a report that does more than just observe and record the state of the "torso": it also examines the demythicized "god" as the dead Medusa so as to reflect upon its forms of disguises and working mechanism. Rakosi's choice of words with science and myth references highlights his strabismal lens wary of a culture in which the Medusa's eye is hard to close, and of a language in which, whatever its condition, is always embedded the predatory intent. In "It can be accused of both plutonism / and the obvious," for instance, the pronoun "It" clearly points to "a strange god" in the previous sentence. This "god," as Medusa with its eyes shut, is then identified immediately as the potential or would-be defendant by the verbal phrase "can be accused of." Apart from "the obvious," the crime this "god" can be specifically charged with is "plutonism." Derived from the scientific term *plutonium* and denoting in particular the action of intense heat and radioactive destruction,[105] the word "plutonism," as its suffix dictates, also signifies a practice, a conduct, a quality, a doctrine, a belief, or an abnormal condition. It names, in other words, a logical system armed with a destructive methodology: hence science and/ as philosophy, whose intense intentions transform all becoming (life) into being (death). At the same time, science/philosophy find their roots in myth, for both "plutonism" and "plutonium" are named after the planet Pluto, which in turn receives its name from Pluto, the god ruling over the lower world. In this sense, science/philosophy are recognized further through the strabismal lens as the "gods of death," as the Medusa's glance, in whose vision an object "lives" only in its death. Not only do myth and science/philosophy share the same strategies in operation, the autopsy report reads on, but they are also reciprocal in relation. While myth provides science/philosophy with an origin, for instance, the latter offer to keep resurrecting and preserving the former as something immortal: "The closest human thing to it / is the novocained tooth." What they have failed to realize is that myth, as their epistemological cornerstone, is itself dead long since: "Its Medussa hair now fossilized."

Here Rakosi's misspelling of "Medussa" makes a thematic statement. Spelled with a double *s,* "Medussa" suggests, with each *s* referring, perhaps, to "sight" or "seeing," a split vision, a lingual-optical disfigurement of what used to be an intensely focused, deadly penetrating, apodeitic seeing. But to see all this in Medusa, Rakosi seems to indicate, the objectivist poets have to look into Medusa's eye, in which they see their own. In this sense, the double *s* also reflects the structure of Rakosi's strabismal lens, a two-way seeing that enables the poet to see Medusa's hair fossilized without being turned into a stone. It is this extra *s* in the eye, rather ironically, that makes the eye see better. This objectivist vision of strabismus is best captured in an aphorism by Adorno when he writes in *Minima Moralia:* "The splinter in your eye is the best magnifying glass."[106] For both Rakosi and Adorno, only when the apodeitic seeing *into* an object is troubled and defocused can the assertoric seeing *onto* it become possible. Indeed, if a normal eye always misses so much, an abnormal one with an additional "s/splinter" presents an alternative. Paradox thus constitutes each's position. The poem then ends with a statement of the objectivist optics. What "can be bequeathed to one's heirs / with the assurance that it will not depreciate / or be found irrelevant," Rakosi argues, is the "torso" seen in detail as a historical particular, not a "god" projected into mirage as a trans-historical abstraction.

Michael Palmer, commenting on George Oppen's objectivist position, makes the following observation: "He argues as well for a gaze turned outward, a responsibility of the self to find its realization, its form as thinking subject, in its relation to the visible and invisible things of the world. The understanding that such a realization is at best problematic is part of what informs the silences and ellipses of his lines with their particular resonance, or perhaps I mean content."[107] This objectivist understanding takes, of course, diverse forms. While it finds its expression in Oppen's emotionally charged silences and the ellipses of his lines, it assumes the form of intense meditations in Rakosi, whose poetics of strabismal seeing underscores the tension between armed and unarmed desires, between a gaze turned outward and a gaze turned inward. Indeed, in Rakosi's poems, as in Reznikoff's, "sight and directness of presentation have a priority,"[108] but it is through a relentless vigilance against Medusa's ever-greedy glance that such a priority is articulated. When asked if "there was something to the name Objectivist," Rakosi replies, "There is if you stick to the word's core, *object* . . . in this case anything and everything outside one's self . . . and to its adjective, *objective,* which has meaning along a sliding scale in proportion to how much the poet's subjective is absorbed in it or kept out . . . a useful consideration against psychological slush and sentimentality in any period and against stereotypes."[109] In this sense, an objectivist is a poet in a designated position, informed both by the necessity that "the work faces the world"[110] and by the problematic, as Barrett Watten points out in a different context, that "the mind that thinks its way into the world of things is the same mind that perceives things as having argued their way into existence. Exterior causality becomes the same as the [mind's] interior romance."[111] It is a locale of intensely self-conscious negotiations, a scale measuring and adjusting the interactions between the internal and the external, between the Medusian imposition and the strabismal countervision, between the intellectual or psychological drive toward a rational apprehension of the world on the one hand and what Oppen calls "the life of the mind" as "an awareness of the world" on the other.[112] Such, then, is the poem "The Indomitable," the title of which describes, perhaps, not only the obdurate nature of the Medusa's glance but also the very character of an objectivist against psychological slush and sentimentality:

Copulate

> < *copulare*

to join,

> to couple.

Says nothing

> of lust,

the iron master,

> sweaty,

breathless,

> fierce.[113]

With "Says nothing / of lust" as the demarcation lines sounding a warning against the Medusa's glance, the poem falls into two parts: the mirage of seeing versus the detail of seeing; or, thinking *of* an object as it *should* exist vis-à-vis thinking *with* it as it exists. It dramatizes a confrontation between the Medusa's glance and Rakosi's strabismal lens, a confrontation as a language act, in which the former's deadly gaze upon the object is defocused by the latter and the detail of seeing is restored.

The first part presents a dictionary entry on the verb *copulate*, complete with its etymology and its current usage. While the word's denotative nuances are explicitly listed ("to join, / to couple"), its meaning of uniting, linking, or connecting is nevertheless extended from mere sexual intercourse to other semantic fields by the symbol "<," meaning "derived from."[114] The word *copulare*, for instance, from which *copulate* is derived, can itself be traced to the word *copula*, which means something more than just a sexual activity. As any dictionary would show, *copula* refers, in grammar, to a form of "linking verb," like the verb "to be" or "any similar verb, as seem, appear, etc., which links a subject with a predicate complement"; in logic, it denotes the "connecting link between the subject and predicate of a proposition."[115] Whichever its semantic field, the word prioritizes the subject, and its function is to substantiate the subject by assisting it to form, to engineer, to give birth; in other words, to project elements into a construct, to configure details into a mirage. Further, the nature of this linking, whether in language, logic, or biological functioning, is defined first by the word's attached symbol "<" and then by its part of speech. The verb "to derive," which the symbol "<" stands for, has three semantic branches apart from simply "to get or receive": it means, in logic, "to get by reasoning; deduce or infer"; in genealogy or etymology, "to trace from or to a source; show the derivation of"; and in chemistry, "to obtain or produce (a compound) from another compound by replacing one element with one or more other elements."[116] Quite explicitly, both the symbol "<" and the verb "derive" as such highlight the gist of the handbook for the hunter of knowledge. Either in philosophy or in science, they thus prescribe that "to get," "to obtain," or "to produce" as a way of knowing invariably necessitates a step-by-step process, and that its operational procedure, as indicated by the preposition "by," is methodology. What is more, it is a methodology at once aggressive and predatory, for "*copulate*" is a verb, a part of speech foregrounding not only an armed desire of a certain subject by linking it into a mirage of complement or proposition, but also a single-minded drive or action toward its fulfillment. Through Rakosi's strabismal lens, Medusa's glance is revealed in this part as language, language as reasoned method and methodized reason.

The second part of this poem performs an ironic twist, in that the details listed therein contribute, rather tantalizingly, to the Medusa's glance dramatized as "*copulate*" in the first part only to tease out their own strabismal implications in keeping with the tenets of the objectivist vision. In sharp contrast to the first part, which consists of only one verb, a part that embodies Medusa's highly focused predatory intent, the second part lists a noun ("the iron master") followed by three adjectives ("sweaty," "breathless," "fierce"), thus suggesting an observation, an assertoric awareness of an object. But the three adjectives, each with its rich sensuousness, lend themselves psychologically and suggestively to the first part of the poem featuring "*copulate*," which in turn finds, rather appropriately and conveniently, all its physical, supportive manifestations in those adjectives. As such, the two parts of the poem present the Medusa's glance in action, staging a mirage of seeing in which the second part turns out to be the projection from and by the first. They portray a predatory language movement whereby there occurs a Medusian reduction of the manifold of an object to what Rakosi refers to as mere "psychological slush." Yet this Medusian imposition, Rakosi seems to argue, is rendered possible only when "the iron master" is entirely ignored or sacrificed, a step essential to all anthropomorphic transmutation of being to being-represented. For "sweaty, / breathless, / fierce" are in fact sensual details of seeing "the iron master" at work, which is itself one of the particulars constitutive of an assertoric view of a concrete work scene. In other words, the three adjectives, descriptive of an object, have nothing to do with rendering an apodeitic mirage of a sexual frenzy. "Says nothing / of lust," Rakosi announces in the middle of the poem, referring to the first part to demilitarize language as Medusa's glance bringing the rays from an "eye/I" to a focus, and pointing to the second to activate the objectivist strabismal lens bringing to a focus the rays from an object. "The Indomitable," read in this context, is indeed a poem "freed at last from psychology,"[117] not without, of course, a confrontation against the Medusa's glance.

The form of "The Indomitable," in this view, makes an important statement. It demonstrates an objectivist critique of traditional epistemology by "copulating," so to speak, two poems already discussed. Beginning, for instance, with "The Romantic Eye," the poem ends with "Objectivist Lamp," which outshines the former, releasing details from the grip of what Rakosi describes in the poem "Ground Breaking" as "the eye of abstraction."[118] For Rakosi's objectivist strabismal lens, as Michael Heller points out in his discussion of Zukofsky's use of the word *objectivist,* "is not concerned with the reified objectification of knowledge into a science . . . but with an objectification of human instance, of witnessing (active) or being witnessed."[119] However, it is by no means a given—in fact, far from it—that poems can be simply witnessing, can be "only acts upon particulars, outside of them," as Zukofsky puts it in the preface to *An "Objectivists" Anthology.*[120] For to realize the assertoric seeing, the poet has to resist his or her own impulse to render, rather than to describe, an object. And this resistance, or tension, is also articulated through objectification, which, according to Charles Altieri, "pertains to various vehicles for bringing form and resolution to the energy fields elicited in pursuit of sincerity."[121] Viewed from this perspective, Rakosi's strabismal lens, when enacted in "The Indomitable" and elsewhere, also sheds light on its own compositional strategy as a measure against the Medusa's glance. In other words, sincerity and objectification work hand in hand. For objectivist poetics "is not merely attention to objects," as Altieri recapitulates in "The Objectivist Tradition"; "it entails the construction of aesthetic objects in such a way that the conditions of desire are themselves dramatized and forced to take responsibility for their productions."[122]

Rakosi's objectivist sensibility is markedly informed by a paradox: to bring the rays from an object to a focus, one has to simultaneously defocus the authoritative rays from the "eye/I" as mediated by desire and intention. To do so, the objectivist lens has to be so constructed as to defocus the "mirage of seeing" as a way to focus on the "detail of seeing." In Rakosi's poetics, this defocusing-as-focusing figuration is cast in a mode of counter-vision best described as strabismal, a seeing that also places itself under close surveillance against its own predatory instinct. Equipped with a "bronze shield" of demilitarized language, Rakosi's poetics of strabismal seeing runs counter to a culture of vision, venturing, as a result, into a hunting ground, into a closed system, where "the Medusa's glance of a sudden 'ray of vision'" facilitates the acquisition of truth and knowledge by recovering its prey.

As such, Rakosi's objectivist poetics has ramifications far beyond the parameters of the literary. His objectivist critique of phenomenology as epistemology, in particular, finds its philosophical counterpart in Adorno's "metacritique" of Husserl. Both share the same concerns. Rakosi's belief in thinking with the things as they exist, for instance, and his sustained effort to maintain fidelity to the object by refusing to aggrandize perception, espouse, in a way, Adorno's critique of the phenomenologist as "certainly incapable of thinking objects as other than subjectively constituted."[123] Similar to Rakosi's diagnosis of the "The Romantic Eye" as circumscribing a circular movement from the ego back to the same ego, motivated by one's desire and intention, there is Adorno's conclusive statement that "phenomenology resembles a circle because it arises out of idealism and reproduces idealism at every one of its stages, as usual as a sublated moment."[124] While Rakosi considers the mirage of seeing as nothing but myth, Adorno treats the so-called first seeing as pure illusion. As much as Rakosi and Adorno see eye to eye in this regard, it is, however, their shared insight into methodology, into the essential role methodology plays in phenomenology as epistemology, that brings them together. To a great extent, Rakosi's poems such as "The Romantic Eye" and "Man Contemplating a Rock" exhibit the poet's remarkable understanding of methodology as a tautological construct, as a closed system, with preordained outcomes; and, viewed in this light, they present themselves as powerful and convincing examples or demonstrations supporting Adorno's theorem that "methodologically . . . epistemology presupposes what, by its proper *raison d'être* it should have deduced."[125] This shared realization of the "eye/I" as living, walking methodology leads, then, to shared interests as well as efforts in searching for the alternative, an alternative that describes, rather than renders, an object.

What is most revealing in Rakosi's and Adorno's choices of alternatives is the striking similarity between the two in terms of their own methodologies, methodologies that might be best specified with the prefix *counter-*.

Challenging the metaphysical foundation of a culture privileging the all-mighty "eye/I" whose "spirit [is] objectified (*versachlicht*) into method" and, concomitantly, whose "totality of consciousness, is the world,"[126] both Rakosi and Adorno find their counter-methods in optic abnormalities. Whereas Rakosi resorts to a strabismal seeing, for instance, Adorno favors the eye with a splinter in it ("The splinter in your eye is the best magnifying glass"). Against a cultural background of visionary clarity and immediacy of various kinds, this seeming absurdity of their alternatives itself makes, in fact, a powerful argument. For it is not only ironic but also paradoxical, and the aesthetic strategy underlying both methods, as the "Publisher's Note" in *Minima Moralia* makes it clear, lies in their use of "allusions [that] involve irony or inversion";[127] or rather, both. Capable of a two-way seeing that unmasks the nature of the centuries-old approach to the world through vision-generated, vision-centered interpretations of truth, knowledge, and reality, Rakosi's strabismal eye defocuses desire's deadly gaze from "Medusian" to "Medussian," turning upside down the established ocular-centric paradigm sanctioning its own mirage of seeing. Alluding to religious as well as epistemological conventions, Adorno's splintered vision not only makes a mockery of biblical morals preaching the clarity of seeing by removing the plank from one's own eyes first,[128] but also inverts Hegel's—and Husserl's, for that matter—phenomenological dictum from "the True is the whole" to "the whole is the false."[129] Each in his own way, Rakosi and Adorno deploy optic abnormality as a metaphor, as a double-edged sword: it implicates the existing sociocultural formation itself as an abnormality, as largely the result of the affection of an ideologically mediated ocular-centrism, and it points to itself, rather paradoxically, as a radical alternative. With these optic abnormalities as their counter-methods, Rakosi and Adorno attempt to break away from the Medusa's glance as closure into a world where they can be *with* the world, where they can see things as what they *are* rather than what they *should be*. In reading Rakosi and Adorno, one thus finds their counter-methods at work in a war of eye against eye: the strabismal eye or the splintered eye versus the Medusa's glance.

If the rules be well considered, we shall find them to be made only to reduce Nature into method.

—John Dryden, "Preface" to *Troilus and Cressida*

Method is the opposite of chance. It is designed to keep the domain of imagination in order, so that amidst the data it has arranged, a new discovery may be recognized.

—Justus Buchler, *The Concept of Method*

Proposing itself as a pure meta-language, [method] partakes of the vanity of all meta-language. . . . The danger of Method (of a fixation upon Method) comes from . . . a demand for responsibility: the work must increase lucidity, expose the implications of a procedure, the alibis of a language . . . here Method is inevitable, irreplaceable, not for its "results" but precisely—or on the contrary—because it realizes the highest degree of consciousness of a language, *which does not forget itself.*

—Roland Barthes, *The Rustle of Language*

4. The Politics of Critical Parody: Chance Operation and the Mesostic Method in John Cage

"All I know about method," John Cage writes in *Silence*, "is that when I am not working I sometimes think I know something, but when I am working, it is quite clear that I know nothing."[1] In his distinctively idiosyncratic vein of satire and paradox, a Swiftian-Cagean ethos yet to be fully grasped, Cage in this seemingly simple pronouncement lashes out at the Cartesian-Kantian notion of method as what Joel Weinsheimer terms "the paradigmatic expression of the condition that gave rise to epistemology."[2] Not only, for instance, is method demystified as having no intrinsic, determining value in relation to knowledge or knowledge acquisition—an awareness Cage has achieved through his own work experience ("when I am working, it is quite clear that I know nothing")—but it is also recognized as an a priori construct grounded in the proposition of "I think," a prefabricated story of what knowledge should be ("when I am not working I sometimes think I know something"). Considered by many as "an American freethinking maverick,"[3] Cage has certainly challenged, in a radical fashion, the existing sociocultural norms and conventions; but what truly distinguishes Cage as a nonconformist is his overt "iconoclasm vis-à-vis traditional methods."[4] In addition, Cage's iconoclasm, despite its manifestations in diverse fields, can be argued as resulting, more specifically, from one singular critical insight; it is an insight into the fact that "method lies deep in the roots of human affairs," as Justus Buchler contends, and that it is "a basic trait of man."[5] As such, his work foregrounds, both in concept and in praxis, a reversal of an epistemological mandate fundamental in the Cartesian-Kantian tradition, a mandate articulated most expressively, perhaps, by its neoclassical counterpart in poetry and poetics; a reversal, that is, from Pope's "Nature Methodiz'd" to Cage's "nature de-methodized."[6]

Cage's politics of demethodization, as his work demonstrates abundantly, pivots upon the position Cage takes in his relation to the world, a position indicative of a decentered subject. In his study of Cage, Daniel Herwitz sums up this position succinctly as "let it be."[7] A case in point is Cage's understanding and treatment of sound in music. "[One] may give up the desire to control sound," Cage writes, "clear his mind of music, and set about discovering means to let sounds be themselves rather than vehicles for man-made theories or expressions of human sentiments."[8] To "let it be," in this sense, is to forgo control, the "tactic faculty" which functions as the prerequisite for method.[9] For control, "common to all methods" as means to minimize risks through regulatory measures, "implies a perspective of voluntary coping, through which method confronts the indifference or recalcitrancy of existence," as Buchler has argued, thus constituting the "elemental discipline that precedes methodic consumptions."[10] In other words, to "let it be" is to let it be free from methodic impositions. For Cage, such a position is imperative in that art is, by definition, "the imitation of nature in her manner of operation" and, as such, he continues, "is an affirmation of life—not an attempt to bring order out of chaos nor to suggest improvements in creation, but simply a way of waking up to the very life we're living, which is so excellent once one gets one's mind and one's desires out of its way and lets it act of its own accord."[11]

In his study of "The Limits of Method" contended by Gadamerian hermeneutics, Weinsheimer makes a similar argument with regard to method in relation to one's perceived position in the world. In contrast to Cage's counter-method of letting it be, which is grounded in a sense of being with the world, he writes:

Method, and epistemology in general . . . is primarily a response to *Fremdheit*, the condition of being no longer at home in the world. To be at home means to belong, to live in surroundings that are familiar, self-evident, and unobtrusive; its contrary, *Fremdheit*, consists in the schism between past and present, I and others, self and the world. Method derives from this sense of living among objects to which one no longer belongs.[12]

It is this "sense of loss," he continues, "that accompanies the movement from being at home to *Fremdheit*, the movement in which one's world devolves into the materials of knowledge,"[13] or, as Samuel Taylor Coleridge puts it, "the *materials* of Method," materials meaning "the *relations of things* [that] form the prime objects" of method.[14] Citing, as his example, lines from Wordsworth's poem "The World Is Too Much with Us" ("Little we see in nature that is ours; / . . . . / For this, for every thing, we are out of tune"),[15] Weinsheimer amplifies the romantic overtone of this "no longer belongs" as the pretext for method in all domains of inquiry: "Like nature, art and history no longer belong to us, nor we to them."[16] To this crisis, he goes on to say, method rises promptly as a solution: "Method, then, aims to redeem this loss by substituting itself for the kind of understanding that is not reflective knowledge because it understands everything in advance by belonging to it, before knowing and its methodical regulation come into play."[17]

Gerald Bruns, in his comparative study of Cage, approaches this phenomenon from a similar perspective. Addressing the issue of ethics in Cage's work via a contrast between Martha Nussbaum and Stanley Cavell in terms of the former's "failure of *knowing*" vis-à-vis the latter's "forgoing or disowning knowledge," Bruns argues that Nussbaum's "sense of knowing the world intimately" results from a game of what Cage has identified as the "logical mind,"[18] a self-isolated psyche methodically romancing itself. He writes:

The pathos here is part of our Cartesian and Kantian legacy, the pathos of the disembodied, isolated subject of modernity whose knowledge of the world is purchased at the cost of its place in it. We might think of Nussbaum as one of "the last romantics," where romanticism is a general term for various experiments in re-embodying the subject, overcoming its solitude or separateness, its exile from things and from others (coping with solipsism and narcissism).[19]

This pathos, which is as much Cartesian and Kantian as it is Wordsworthian, is the founding factor of epistemology as methodology.[20] It presents a form of psychological therapy, a self-rescue "camp" for reclaiming its own "willed" loss. To overcome the subject's solitude or separation from the world, it finds its means in hunting for knowledge, the value of which, as John Dewey has argued in *The Quest for Certainty*, "depends upon the *method* by which [a cognitive conclusion] is reached, so that the perfecting of method, the perfecting of intelligence, is the thing of supreme value."[21] Emphasizing the nature of cognition as a system of method rooted in the Cartesian-Kantian legacy of the "sealed-off *ego cogito*,"[22] Bruns cites Emmanuel Levinas's definition of cognition as the "autarchy of the I" that refuses to let the world be, as the proposition of "I think" methodized into "I can":

> Cognition is the deployment of [the identity of the] same. . . . To know amounts to grasping being out of nothing, or reducing it to nothing, removing from it its alterity. . . . Cognition is "hence not a relation with the other as such but the reduction of the other to the same. Such is the definition of freedom: to maintain oneself against the other despite every relation with the other to insure the autarchy of the I. Thematization and conceptualization, which moreover are inseparable, are not peace with the other but suppression or possession of the other. For possession affirms the other, but within a negation of its independence. 'I think' comes down to 'I can'—to an appropriation of what is, to an exploration of reality. . . . Possession is preeminently the form in which the other becomes the same, by becoming mine."[23]

In this sense, Cage's aesthetics of demethodization begins with the negation of this pathos of separation as the archetype of a binary construct, as the psychological prototype of method. In order to affirm life, Cage asserts, it is imperative to de-dichotomize the world by de-psychologizing it. One should, for instance, simply let oneself be "interested in sounds just as they are, apart from psychology about them," as Cage states in his discussion of Edgard Varèse and his work, which features "an acceptance of all audible phenomena as material proper to music," thus "divorcing sounds from the burden of psychological intentions."[24] Such a de-psychologization constitutes what Cage believes to be a "psychological turning," a turning "in the direction of those [one] does not intend."[25] The form of this turn or reversal is a paradox. For while it "seems at first to be a giving up of everything that belongs to humanity"—that is, to be a violation of the epistemological-methodological conventions that have hitherto created and sustained the identity of a culture—this psychological turning in actuality "leads to the world of nature, where, gradually or suddenly, one sees that humanity and nature, not separate, are in this world together; that nothing was lost when everything was given away. In fact, everything is gained."[26] It leads to a state of *"selbstverstandlich,"* where "the things . . . are to us self-understandable, self-evident matter of course,"[27] and where method, accordingly, is never imagined. In other words, Cage's depsychologization or psychological turning enacts an erasure of the "I" as the sole reference point in which the world is perceived dualistically as the Other, and according to which nature is conceived methodologically into reflective knowledge.

To no lesser degree, Cage's politics of demethodization is also predicated upon his radical questioning of cultural norms and conventions as methods ritualized. For Cage, method presents the most fundamental form of cultural authoritarianism and conceptual gridlock. With an insight into method as constitutive of the basic trait of human disposition on the one hand and of the structural-functional fabric of a culture on the other, he identifies methodical performances right down to the level of day-to-day routines, seeing their manifestations in a panorama of phenomena ranging from behavioral patterns, such as habits, to utilitarian instincts, such as interests. So thorough, indeed, is his understanding of the nature and function of method and its deep permeation through the cultural unconscious that Cage refuses to be deluded into oversimplifying the whole issue by privileging—that is, romanticizing—certain theories of change as a handy solution at the expense of method's psycho-sociocultural specificity and complexity. For any theory of change, to the extent that it is already a form of cultural artifact, is but change methodized into a formula and rationalized into a discourse. When conversing with Joan Retallack on the topic of the "composing mind" in relation to and in terms of "a strange attractor," for instance, Cage perceives this much-idealized scientific remapping of an artistic activity as no more than a simple switch of methodical paradigms.[28] Therefore, to Retallack's proposition that "I wonder whether in its organizing of experience within certain kinds of complex aesthetic procedures, the artist is allowing the mind to behave as a strange attractor," Cage responds by reminding his interlocutor that the verb "allowing" always enacts an intentional, purpose-laden, and method-oriented proclivity incapable of a complete self-erasure.[29] Should one attempt this approach, Cage answers pointedly by way of a rhetorical question, "Well, that of course leads toward habits, doesn't it?"[30]

Cage's awareness of the "omnipresence" of method as habit-based and interest-sensitive is reflected in his concern regarding the form of his own praxis. His working method is thus oriented toward not self-expression but self-interrogation, not meaning but the methodical grounding of meaning. "Composing this way changes me," Cage has said, commenting on his method, "rather than expresses me."[31] In his experiments there persists, therefore, the relentless question as to how to break away from the gravitational pull of what is referred to in Coleridge's aesthetics as the "habit of Method" or the "methodic habit."[32] Nowhere does this issue become more imperative than in the area of improvisation, where the purported spontaneity on the spur of the moment, so realizes Cage, is but a conditioned response, always circling back to habits. When asked by Joan Retallack (JR) about his resumed interest in improvisation, Cage (JC), in a truly illuminating moment in *Musicage,* explains his decision as essentially methodical, or more accurately put, counter-methodical:

JR. You said you had never been interested in [improvisation] because you felt it returned you to habit.

JC. Well, very formerly. But lately, for a variety of reasons, I've become interested in improvisation.

JR. Why?

JC. For just that reason. I became interested because I had not been interested. And the reason I had not been interested was because one just goes back to one's habits. But how can we find ways of improvising that *release* us from our habits?[33]

The nature of Cage's methodical praxis is presented here in a nutshell. It is, as the rhetorical question makes clear, a methodical counter-move, or the stratagem of the "Trojan horse," so to speak, against the habit-forming method. Such a methodical position runs counter to an unexamined but popular assumption that Cage's work "shifts the scene of the aesthetic outside the swath of the culture's self-reflecting gaze," which grants the artist the position of a *"compleat outsider"* with a trans-cultural capability magically immune to any culture's centripetal force.[34] Much to the contrary, Cage insists that, precisely because a culture's gaze is always "self-reflecting," its narcissistic swath, be it Oriental or Occidental, does not leave an "outside" for anyone; and that, given the nature of culture as such, to resort to a different cultural mechanism constitutes not a solution but an equal entrapment—that is, a welcome reorientation, no doubt, but to yet another form of authoritarianism and gridlock alien only in its manner of operation but not in nature. The ways to release one from one's habits, argues Cage through his rhetorical question, can therefore be found only from within these habits; and to break away from any methodical gridlock, by extension, one has to deliberately mimic that method as one's point of departure. At issue, in either case, is not a simple matter of appropriation of an old form, which is sometimes naively assumed to be capable of transcending—by ignoring—its original, inherent logic of signification, since to appropriate any cultural form is to be appropriated simultaneously by that form and its concomitant implications. It is, rather, a parodic reversal of the culture's self-reflecting gaze as a form of counter-gaze conscious of itself, critically and satirically, being implicated therein.[35] The object of Cage's methodical praxis is, in short, method itself.

Cage epitomizes his counter-method laconically in the form of a paradox: "purposeful purposelessness."[36] Given the fact that method, as Buchler points out, always "rests on a purpose,"[37] the two words in Cage's aphorism can be read as forming a means-end construct aiming at self-deconstruction. Cage's methodical praxis (purposefulness), in other words, is intended to be its own critique and erasure (purposelessness). Differently put, the negation of method (purposelessness) is rendered methodically (purposefulness); hence a "methodical methodlessness." In this sense, Cage's deployment of method finds its model in Jonathan Swift, and it takes the form of satire fashioned in particular after "A Modest Proposal." Its Swiftian edge, which aims at dislodging cultural authoritarianism and logical gridlock, lies in its much-affected, mock-serious posture of authority and authenticity; and its methodical approach, which aims at shocking the cultural, habitual mind-set out of its unconscious, finds its most effective form in the strategy of extremism. "Unless we go to extremes," Cage thus professes, with regard to the condition of the mind in relation to the possibility of change, "we won't get anywhere."[38] A postmodern version of "A Modest Proposal," Cage's method, then, presents the mock-enactment of traditional methods. Both construed as the culture's self-reflecting gaze and executed as its narcissistic swath, it calls itself into question, as is the case with Swift's proposal, by drastically amplifying its own sociocultural logic and self-serving mechanism, pushing itself to the extreme where its transparent elegance turns out to be a naked absurdity recognizable by as well as shocking to even the most unthinking.

Such a Swiftian-Cagean methodical praxis exhibits some unique features, all intended to bring into visibility what has long since been taken for granted. First, it is blatantly performative and theatrical, and attempts to "re-artificialize" method out of its "naturalized" state so as to push it to the level of critical consciousness. Second, it resorts to defamiliarization as the means of self-mirroring and self-implication. By fusing the most ancient and alien (*I Ching*) with the most contemporary and familiar (computer technology), it externalizes through the former what has been hitherto internalized in the latter, thus making visible the familiar in the unfamiliar. Third, it is strictly logical and procedural, but in a way that juxtaposes, rather revealingly, both its generative capacity as objectively referential and potentially limitless and its own operational mechanism as arbitrarily self-referential and deterministically limiting. Brought into focus by this juxtaposition is, again, a paradox: the arbitrary constraint of any method constitutes the very source of its own generative power. Necessary rules and arbitrary constraints, Cage's method thus demonstrates, are in fact one and the same thing, the two sides of the same coin working hand in glove with each other. They take turns to be of service to convention, which names them either "necessary" or "arbitrary" as the occasion warrants, whatever the occasion might be. Finally, like Swift's proposal, Cage's method is both aggressively partisan and mercilessly incriminating. It imposes itself upon its readers and audience alike, forcing them either to accept and to follow its logic only to find themselves conceptually and procedurally entrapped, or to question and challenge its logic only to find themselves socially and ethically implicated. In either case, Cage's method incurs a critical awareness of its own praxis of method as Swiftian—that is, a seeming affirmation turned into a self-exposure and self-negation.

Cage's methodical praxis thus articulates, first and foremost, a critical concern with method per se at the fundamental level of cultural industries; and in Cage's compositional performance and enactment, it is therefore method itself that emerges from behind the scene onto the stage and into the spotlight, not as a king fully clothed, but as the emperor stark naked.

Chance, as any dictionary would define it, is "the happening of events without apparent cause, or the apparent absence of cause or design," "an unpredictable event or accidental happening," "a risk or gamble," an "opportunity" or "probability," and so forth. By contrast, *operation* is "the act, process or method" which functions, as its verb denotes, to "bring about a desired or appropriate effect."[39]

A signature method in Cage's work, the phrase "chance operation" presents a problem. While the postmodern ethos clearly privileges "chance," personifying it by taking "operation" as its attribute, it does so with the usual epistemological assumptions. As is dictated by the use of language therein, "chance" is acknowledged, but only in a way that it can be harnessed (operation). Hence an irony: for chance to operate at all, it has to be operated on first. In "chance operation," human intention is thus projected into a natural phenomenon that is beyond grasp, and the romantic "pathetic fallacy" takes the form of what might be called a "methodological fallacy." The phrase "chance operation" suggests, then, not an acceptance of chance but a cognition of it, a conceptualization of chance that negates its ontological independence, a retrospective methodization of what is fundamentally anti-method. In her reading of Cage's work in the context of contemporary sciences, N. Katherine Hayles, for one, raises this issue. Struck by the phrase as "passing strange" and "oxymoronic," she proceeds to offer "three interpretations of chance that present it as a concept that can be enacted through an operation."[40] In other words, chance becomes perceivable only when it is made conceivable, graspable only when it is rendered methodical. With an explicit foregrounding of method (operation) as the only means to approach chance as a concept, chance is transplanted from the realm of unpredictability into the field of disciplined knowledge, from the world of becoming into the taxonomy of being. Once framed by the epistemological assumptions of science, chance never stands a chance.

What, then, is chance? To the extent that it is that which is inaccessible to any methodical approach, chance exists only in pre-thinking. For "thinking," to paraphrase what Buchler has pointed out in his study of Coleridge, always implies method, which is "the opposite of chance."[41] It is just "another name for method" according to John Dewey, for whom "thinking," as method, is specified as "intelligence in operation."[42] If, as Buchler observes in Coleridge, a methodical process is a process in which the anticipative quality of the mind plays a steady role,[43] chance, by virtue of what it is, defies the anticipatory mind. Unpredictable, beyond expectations, and prior to awareness, it is that which disappears the moment human intelligence begins to encroach upon it. Always a surprise, it cannot be captured but only run into, assuming a certain shape only in memory, in retrospective reasoning and restructuring. To put it in Lyotard's mode of utterance, chance always comes too soon for the reasoning mind, or, what amounts to the same thing, its conceptualization or methodization always begins too late.

Cage, however, does not seem to concern himself with chance as such; in fact, he has never considered chance operation as anything other than just a method. Describing his "composing means" as always being "arranged," for instance, Cage clarifies the meaning of this phrase by specifying "the technical difference between indeterminacy and chance operation": "In the case of chance operation, one knows more or less the elements of the universe with which one is dealing, whereas in indeterminacy, I like to think . . . that I'm outside the circle of a known universe, and dealing with things that I literally don't know anything about."[44] In this sense, chance operation is by no means random. On the contrary, it is for Cage an informed operation, an operation both based on and guided by certain knowledge. In addition, it is an operation endowed with an insight into the macroscopic universe, from where to determine and shape, however arbitrarily, the microscopic world. Practical in nature, instrumental in function, and purposeful in intention, chance operation is none other than a method of epistemology, a way of knowing governed by its own logic, organized by its own procedure, operated by its own mechanism, and guaranteed of its own recoveries.

Cage identifies both the "elements of the universe" and the method of "dealing with" them in the *I Ching*, an ancient book of wisdom also titled *The Book of Changes*.[45] With the *I Ching* providing him with "just a mechanism of the chance operation,"[46] Cage's Swiftian move begins with his substituting the concept of "chance" for that of "change," a move, that is, not without a certain degree of sensationalism for a strategic purpose. Given Cage's insight into the cultural mind-set as always methodically informed, and considering his belief in going to extremes as a means to "change our present intellectual climate,"[47] chance as a form of radical unpredictability but ironically reified into an operation presents itself to Cage as a rather appropriate model of parody, the implications of which, once understood, will produce a satirical effect both shocking and, therefore, revealing. From this perspective, one finds in Cage's use of "chance" in chance operation and its enactment a rhetorical-methodical strategy similar to that of Swift's "A Modest Proposal." For one thing, in both "modest proposal" and "chance operation," the emphases are placed on the second terms: "proposal" for Swift, and "operation" for Cage. For another, the nature of the second term in either case ("proposal" or "operation") is defined by the first ("modest" or "chance"), which, adjectival in function, is used in effect to create a rhetorical double, simultaneously pointing to its opposite. Further, the purpose of this rhetorical double, by virtue of its "undercover" operation, is to incriminate and to shock the current state of mind in a rather sensational fashion. Swift's use of the word "modest," for instance, which immediately established an allied position with the then English public by offering a humble service both from the standpoint and for the benefits of the public, maximally amplifies its utter inhumanity toward the Irish in the proposed systematization of cannibalism into a national economy, thus implicating the public in its own social-political logic as the very ethical grounding of such a proposal and, consequently, shocking the public into a critical awareness of its own inhumanity. Functioning as bait, Cage's use of the word "chance" is, in a like manner, positioned from within a postmodern ethos against experimental modernism. But it chimes in with a post-Cartesian sentiment only to reveal a Cartesian ghost in its operation. In other words, chance, once employed as an operation in the name of "freeing the ego," maximally amplifies its ego-centered procedure, thus implicating the ego in its own transparent, manipulative move and, consequently, shocking it into a critical realization of its own persistent presence in/as a deeply entrenched "method-ness" even at its most liberal or utopian.

Cage's understanding of chance operation in relation to ego resonates with Justus Buchler's critique of the "wholly good method," and of the folly of divorcing method from human choices. Whatever its kind, method, as Buchler contends, is itself a form of human decision. He writes:

> In the attempt to regard a method as wholly good "in itself," the most desperate expedient is to contend that all of its practical applications, all of its technological translations, are wholly alien to its nature. But if they are really "applications," and are alien to its nature, from what other nature do they derive? And what other method makes them possible if not this one? Human decision is as much part of a methodic process as of its eventual translations. What is called the objectivity or dispassionateness of a method consists not in its exclusion of human choices, but in its patterning, regulation, or guidance of these choices, its introduction of a compulsive dimension that excludes arbitrariness. This patterning or determination sets limits and opportunities for all human decision, practical as well as theoretical, and defines the possibilities of technological no less than of intellectual choice.[48]

Buchler's argument brings to the fore the basic properties of method that are crucial to the understanding of Cage's use of chance operation. First, there is no exteriority of method, whose practical applications (coin tossing) or technological translations (computer programs), however diverse, are prescribed by none other than the nature of method. Second, the nature of any method is identical with the nature of the human ego—that is, method is itself a form of human decision and human choice. Third, human decision or choice, as method, finds its objectivity in its own logic, which constitutes a compulsive, administrative policing for the maximum power and control over the world against chance and arbitrariness. Moreover, the limits and the opportunities set by a method amount to the same thing: they are the manipulated and manipulative possibilities, both in theory and in practice, within an ego/method-determined perspectival order vis-à-vis complexities.

To a great extent, Cage's own discourse on chance operation foregrounds these basic properties of method almost verbatim. Much of what Cage has said is, in fact, intended to correct the popular misconception regarding his method. "Most people who believe I'm interested in chance don't realize that I use chance as a discipline," says Cage, not without a tinge of frustration. "They think I use it—I don't know—as a way of giving up making choices. But my choices consist in choosing what questions to ask."[49] In this statement, Cage clarifies his method from three different angles. To "use chance as a discipline," he begins by pointing out, is not to surrender to chance but to "employ [it] for or apply [it] to a given purpose," as is denoted by the verb "use."[50] Being a purpose-oriented, intention-laden action, to use anything then is to methodize an approach to it so as to achieve preestablished goals. In this sense, when using chance as a discipline, one is disciplined not by chance, for chance, by virtue of what it is, cannot be employed, much less consciously and purposefully; instead, one is disciplined by the use of chance, which is a methodical refashioning of a concept in the name of chance. Further, Cage's use of chance, as such, is of course not "a way of giving up choices"; on the contrary, it is a way of making choices. The use of chance, in other words, is itself a choice or a decision. Furthermore, Cage's "choices consist in choosing what questions to ask," and this choice of question presents, in part, what Buchler calls the compulsive dimension which, disguised as objective or dispassionate, excludes arbitrariness and sets limits.

Hence a "dialectic of question and answer," as Richard Palmer observes, who perceives it as the quintessential component of method since antiquity:

> A question, after all, posits a preliminary way of seeing; just as understanding is not placeless and empty, so questioning is not without its own horizon of expectations. . . . Analysis and methodical questioning, however, tend not to call into question their own guiding presuppositions but rather to operate within a system, so that the answer is always potentially present and expected within the system. Thus they are not so much forms of true questioning as of testing.[51]

In this sense, questions and answers are what they are only insofar as they themselves form the polar vectors of a logical system and function within that closed circle, in which it is the questions that determine the answers. For answers are nothing but questions self-constituted, self-asserted, and self-vindicated. To choose a question is, therefore, to determine a corresponding answer, and to ask a question is already to know the answer. Within this system of method, the need to choose or to ask questions at the level of an individual is demanded and satisfied at the level of the method, which is itself the human origin of all predetermined answers. The very "humanism" of method lies, then, in its ability to project itself into a sort of "objective correlative" beyond the human. Cage's statement of his use of chance thus presents no more than a latter-day version of the age-old Socratic method, whose self-referential mechanism was deciphered by Werner Heisenberg long ago when he said, "What we observe is not nature in itself but nature exposed to our method of questioning."[52]

Equally so is Cage's own praxis. As for his use of chance operation as a method of what Buchler refers to as manipulated and manipulative possibilities within the parameters of the number of sixty-four prescribed by the *I Ching*,[53] nothing is more illustrative as an example than his *Mureau*, which is composed by a "chance-determined mix" of Thoreau's "remarks in the *Journal* about sound, silence and music."[54] Worth quoting at length, the following discussion between the interviewer (I) and Cage (C) with regard to the compositional process of *Mureau* demystifies chance operation as chance by highlighting some of the fundamental properties of method evidenced therein.

c. My letters become quite interesting. Letters are either vowels or consonants. But it was the diphthong that taught me to think of letters as possibly being *in combination*. AE, for instance, is a diphthong. Therefore, *I thought if* vowels can join together to make diphthongs, *why can't* they join in larger groups and *why can't* consonants join one another? And *I decided that they would*. Then, *if* I landed, by chance, on the letter T in the word "letters," this T connected with another T. My next question would be: Do I take just the T that I landed on, or do I take the one adjacent to it also? And *if it were* B and J in the word "subject," and *if* I landed on the B, *I would accept* the J if chance said I should.

I. By what process did you land on the B?

c. Well, by counting the letters in the line, and then relating that number to the number of sixty-four and the *I Ching*, giving me the number that would give me the B.

I. *I think you've skipped a step of your process.* Let's say there are one hundred and twenty-eight letters on the line; you consult the *I Ching* and get, say, the number four. That would mean you'd use the numbers eight and nine? I'm making a very simple example—one hundred and twenty-eight letters. Let's make it really simple—sixty-four.

c. And we get the number fifty-three, *so it would be the fifty-third letter.* The letter, say, is a B and it's adjacent to a J preceded by a vowel. So we ignore the vowel, since we're dealing with consonants. . . .

I. And the word in this case is "subject."

c. And I ask whether I use just the B or the B and the J.

I. *You make it then an either/or question.*

c. *If I throw one to thirty-two, it would be the B alone, with the J being thirty-three to sixty-four.* But say there were five consonants. Here are four: N. G. C. H—the NG from the word *I Ching* and the CH from "chance." Then my question is, since I've landed on the G, do I take the N in front of it and the C and H after it? Or what do I do? *My first possibility would be* to take the G alone. *My second would be* to take the NG, because it's in the same word. *The next would be* to take NGC, and *the fourth would be* to take NGCH. *Is that right?*

I. *There are more possibilities.*

c. What are they?

I. Well, if you landed on the G, *why not* take just the G and the C that follows it?

c. *Because* the N came before and belongs in the same word. That's how I worked anyway. *I did leave out the GC; you are quite right.* Or the GH too. T took the G as being primary. . . .

I. *If* you took the G as being primary, *therefore* the G is *necessarily* connected to the N because both come from the word "*Ching*," but it is not necessarily connected to the letters of the second word.

C. *Well, you're quite right. . . . I realize I've omitted certain possibilities. I didn't mean to.* What would you do? You would have the C, the NG, the CG, the NCG, and the NGCH; *would you accept that as the limit? That's five.* Then one to twelve will be the first, thirteen to twenty-five the second, twenty-six to thirty-seven the third, and thirty-eight to fifty-one the fourth, and fifty-two to sixty-four the fifth.

I. And that's how you divide *the sixty-four options* of the *I Ching when there are five alternatives.*

C. That's how that works.[55]

It is clear that the above conversation presents a mathematical operation of permutation and combination ("in combination") within an arbitrary parameter ("the sixty-four options of the *I Ching*"), which establishes a perspectival order. Grounded in the Cartesian-Kantian ego ("I thought," "I decide") on the one hand and binary logic ("an either/or question") on the other, the entire operation consists of predetermined moves ("process"), in which each step is serialized into a fixed, causal position or relation ("because," "if I . . . it would be . . . ," "if . . . therefore . . . necessarily") and, as such, can be readily traced ("you've skipped a step of your process," "I did leave out the GC; you're quite right"). Within this methodically constructed perspectival order, possibilities become conditioned as well as conditional ("would you accept that as limit?"). They are, in other words, known possibilities ("there are more possibilities"), calculable possibilities ("that's five," "there are five alternatives"), manipulated and controlled possibilities ("I realize I've omitted certain possibilities"), and predetermined and, therefore, foreseeable or anticipated possibilities ("my first possibility would be . . . My second would be . . .").

This exchange between Cage and his interlocutor, with the former explaining and inferring his steps to the latter and the latter correcting and perfecting the procedure of the former, and with a joined effort to reach a conclusion vindicated by and satisfactory to both, sheds light on the nature and function of method in two aspects. On the one hand, "the essential function" of any methodical operation is, to put it in Buchler's words, an "assertion (saying)."[56] The self-referential trajectory of such an assertion or saying finds its working mechanism in two closed circles: first, it demands that it be "interpreted by the type of persuasion that it seeks to introduce," a persuasion which is linked to "corroboration," and which is itself that corroboration;[57] and second, Buchler continues, "It aims, moreover, to turn corroboration into an impersonal verdict imposed by the very complexes which are manipulated."[58] On the other hand, the airtight, logical procedure of Cage's method provides a powerful testimony to Hans-Georg Gadamer's insight into one particular aspect of Cartesian method. "A methodically disciplined use of reason can safeguard us from all error," observes Gadamer in *Truth and Method;* "This was Descartes' idea of method."[59] To be methodical, then, is to be error-free. Joel Weinsheimer, in his study of Gadamerian hermeneutics, elaborates Gadamer's position further when he writes:

> Method is designed rather to avoid stumbling and prevent accidents, whether serendipitous or otherwise. . . . [Whatever] has not been regularly derived or confirmed should, even if true, be held in suspicion and, for purely methodological reasons, in fact be considered erroneous. . . . Mistakes are precluded by method because the methodologically controlled mind is aware of its position at all times, knowing its origin and the rules that govern its progress; and therefore the end of method is clear and distinct, because the steps of derivation can be retraced, and rechecked at will.[60]

Or, to put it in Buchler's words again, "method is the strategic dissemination of prudence. It is not a repeatable process that seeks to arrive at the new, but a repeatable process that seeks to rectify the old. Its function is to extend the tried, to avoid lapse into the untried."[61] Of this Cartesian feature of method, nothing is more illustrative than the compositional process of *Mureau,* which is outlined by Cage and his interlocutor as a process of derivation, verification, and confirmation. Operated within the confines of the parameters of sixty-four, Cage's chance operation proves to be an operation in which chance is purposefully and accurately precluded by a methodically and mathematically controlled mind. As such, "reason and method are synonymous," as Buchler rightly states; and resultantly, "no method, if faithfully pursued, can be unsatisfactory."[62] No wonder, one realizes, Cage and his interlocutor are able to arrive at a prompt agreement on and understanding of "That's how that works," because "mathematical analysis," similar to "embroidery," observes Buchler analogically, "leaves no indeterminateness in the sequel."[63]

Cage's use of the chance operation, as evidenced in his exposition of the compositional process of *Mureau*, is based on his thorough knowledge of this "mechanism by means of which the *I Ching* works," and on his shared insight with Leibniz into the system of the "number of sixty-four, with a binary situation with all its variations in six lines."[64] Given his understanding of the conceptual-methodological sameness between Oriental philosophy and Occidental metaphysics, Cage's continuous advocation and practice of chance operation invites, or more accurately, demands and even forces a rethinking of his work beyond the surface. In fact, his straightforward and straight-faced appropriation as an alternative of an identical but more primitive method from an ancient culture can indeed be read as Swiftian; and his critical parody, which is articulated through his counter-method, foregrounds a performative poetics in which the problem of methods and methodology is staged through a Swiftian dramatization of the methodical entrapment that "goes to excess."[65] In this sense, Cage's chance operation-generated texts should be read, indeed, as a Swiftian proposal, whose structural rigidity, procedural exactitude, and semantic ambiguity are but advanced symptoms of an abnormality indicative of the logicality of method at work.

At the center of this dramatization is, of course, the image of Cage himself, carrying chance around in a briefcase, having disciplined it into computer programs and thus subjected it to the operations of rational thinking: a waking image, that is, parodying a culture in which method reigns as the supreme ruler.

To the question "Why do you write these mesostics?" Cage answers: "Questioning why we do what we do is very curious"; and when asked further "if [his] present concern with the mesostics [is] a kind of splendid isolation," Cage responds with a succinct clarification and specification: "No, it is my present concern with language. You see, language controls our thinking; and if we change our language, it is conceivable that our thinking would change."[66]

Cage's use of the mesostic method, as the artist himself stated above, is intended, first and foremost, to be a form of questioning. More specifically, it is to inquire into "why we do what we do." This concern with the logic ("why") of human activity is directed explicitly toward language, and it focuses further on the form of language and its controlling, operational mechanism. From Cage's perspective, language is perceived in this sense as a structure of forceful reasoning and violent imposition, which asserts itself through/as a methodological paradigm. The investigative critique of method embedded in Cage's formal praxis thus does not lie in his interest in the efficaciousness of language, as evidenced in its expressive capability and potential resulting from innovative manipulations of the rules of language.[67] Rather, it calls into question the enabling structure of language, that which constitutes language's expressivity in the first place. At issue, as Cage's formal praxis testifies, is not what can be generated but the generative mechanism itself, not the expressive content of a discovery but the prescriptive procedures leading to the discovery, not meaning per se but the methodical grounding of meaning.

Central to Cage's critical concern with language is the problem of syntax, whose nature is suggested by the metaphor Cage uses to characterize both its manner of operation and his own strategy of counter-method. In the preface to "Writing for the Second Time Through Finnegans Wake," Cage reveals the metaphor and its source. He writes, "Due to N. O. Brown's remark that syntax is the arrangement of the army, and Thoreau's that when he heard a sentence he heard feet marching, I became devoted to non-syntactical 'demilitarized' language."[68] Compared to an army in marching formation, the overwhelming power of syntax as the force of suppression and policing is cast here both visually and acoustically in highly imagistic terms. In addition, the metaphor of syntax as army, as the means of violence for the purpose of domination and control, is then further elaborated in a larger, theo-philosophical context by way of another metaphor. In one interview, for instance, Cage (C) answers the questions (Q) on this issue, already using military vocabulary.

Q. Do you make your experiments with non-syntactical language because you feel somehow bound by syntactical language?

C. I think we need to attack that question of syntax. My friend Norman O. Brown pointed it out to me that syntax is the arrangement of the army.

Q. Yes, that reminds me of Nietzsche's saying that our need to have grammar is proof that we cannot live without God. If you are opposed to syntax, do you think that we do not need to have God?

C. Yes, and Duchamp too, when he was asked what he thought about God, said, "Let's not talk about that. That's man's stupid idea."[69]

To use syntactical language (or grammar, for Nietzsche) is, simply put, to follow the commandments of God. Perceived in light of these metaphors, syntax, for Cage, exemplifies a comprehensive method of administration whose disciplinary power is executed by four branches of enforced control, all in one: the linguistic, the military, the religious, and the philosophical. To demilitarize syntax, in this sense, is to fundamentally break away from language as a method of indoctrination and regulation. That being granted, there is, for Cage, more than one way to demilitarize syntax, or to attack the question of syntax, as Cage himself puts it. In the foreword to his *M: Writings '67–'72*, he explains:

> Syntax, according to Norman O. Brown, is the arrangement of the army. As we move away from it, we demilitarize language. This demilitarization of language is conducted in many ways: a single language is pulverized; the boundaries between two or more languages are crossed; elements not strictly linguistic (graphic, musical) are introduced; etc. Translation becomes, if not impossible, unnecessary. Nonsense and silence are produced, familiar to lovers. We begin to actually live together, and the thought of separating doesn't enter our mind.[70]

The way Cage takes to demilitarize syntax can be described, in principle, as pulverization. His specific counter-method assumes the form of, among others, the mesostic. In his introduction to *I–VI*, Cage offers the following definition of his mesostic method:

> [A mesostic] is a string which spells a word or name, not necessarily connected with what is being written, though it may be. This vertical rule is lettristic and in my practice the letters are capitalized. Between two capitals in a perfect or 100% mesostic neither letter may appear in lower case. In an imperfect or 50% mesostic the first letter may reappear but the second is not permitted until its appearance on the second line as a capital in the string.[71]

And in Cage's own textual praxis, in addition, these capitalized letters form a vertical column down the center of each stanza.

As the term *mesostic method* indicates, Cage's demilitarization of syntax is executed at the level of method, in that syntax is more concretely understood in terms of a military configuration of "arrangement," a methodological deployment of logically and purposefully organized units. By "demilitarization" it does not mean, however, that Cage's resort to the mesostic is intended to produce, in a non-military fashion, a different set of meanings or semantic effects vis-à-vis that of syntax. Rather, the mesostic is used as a counter-method—that is, it is counter-methodically super-imposed, both literarily and metaphorically, onto the syntactical method as a way to demilitarize it or to attack it. The result is, as Buchler puts it, "exhibitive," in that the critique of syntax as a method "consists in the product"[72]—that is, what is visually presented on the page. In "Sixty-One Mesostics Re and Not Re Norman O. Brown," for instance, the first one begins and appears as follows:

there is no difference Between
        this paRking
            zOne and any other, the entire city
        is a toWaway
        zoNe.[73]

More significant in this regard is the fact that Cage chooses the mesos-tic method, and this choice itself can be seen, as is the case with his use of chance operation based on the *I Ching,* as performing the critical parody central to Cage's avant-garde work. As Joseph Conte points out in his study of Cage, the mesostic method, as "a version of the acrostic poem," is by no means a new form, and it has been familiar to writers as early as the Old Testament.[74] That being so, Cage's work presents a simultaneous engagement with two kinds of methods fundamental since the biblical beginning of the word: the mesostic as a writing method, and syntax as the language method; and Cage engages both by superimposing the for-mer onto the latter. Mimicking these two ancient methods of expression, Cage's work, as critical parody, results in a formal or methodological re-versal that is Swiftian in effect, bringing to consciousness, by exhibiting, just how syntax controls one's thought. Cage's use of mesostics, in other words, dramatizes a Swiftian modest proposal in its satirical intent, which becomes manifest with the help of a paradoxical re-reading of the received understanding of the mesostics.

When asked by John Ashbery, "What is your standard of a form being sufficiently constricting?" Harry Mathews replied: "A form that makes you write something that you wouldn't normally say, or in a way that you would never have said it. The form is so demanding that you can't get around it."[75] In principle, Cage's mesostic method, as Conte observes, "falls within this category."[76] Accepted hitherto as the standard understanding and definition of mesostics, Mathews's statement above nevertheless invites a critical scru-tiny. If, for instance, "the mesostic method does in fact constrict both what the poet says and the way it is said, simply by demanding that certain letters fall into certain places and not others,"[77] it follows, one might argue, that the mesostic functions as such when, and only when, it is realized in language as its material embodiment of expressivity, and that its identity and function are therefore intrinsically linguistic. That being the case, it follows further that the constricting property of the mesostic cannot be conceived as divorced from that of language, and that they are in fact inextricably the same. In this sense, Mathews's characterization of the mesostic as such turns out to be the characterization of none other than language itself. By virtue of its Swiftian logic, the mesostic, when superimposed onto language, forces into visibility and into one's critical consciousness language's controlling mechanism. Cage's use of the mesostic method can thus be understood as constituting a second-order observation by which to reveal the "blind spot" of language,[78] a blind spot that guarantees the successful implementation of control and regulation determining what can be said and how it is said.

In order to demilitarize syntax, Cage's counter-methodical deployment of the mesostic also foregrounds a centrifugal "image-field" against the centripetal linearization.[79] His emphatic specification of his own style of the mesostic, which capitalizes the letters stringed vertically in the middle, presents an important argument in several ways. For one thing, his graphic enhancement of the letter by capitalizing it resonates, theoretically as well as strategically, with Jacques Derrida's visual appropriation of the letter *a* in his coined word *différance*. By an exhibitive approach, or an approach of showing,[80] both men, in their philosophical rethinking, call attention to the fact that the letter "is written or read, but it is not heard."[81] In her reading of Cage's *Roaratorio*, Marjorie Perloff makes the same observation of his mesostic, which spells the name "James Joyce":

> Jilke
> begAn to
> Moult
> instEnch of
> gladSome rags
>
> poor Jink
>   fOllowing
>   roY's
>   suCh bash in patch's
>   bEyond recognition[82]

Arguing against the idea of the "imposition of hierarchy" in Cage's mesostics, Perloff then offers a Derridean reading of the above stanzas:

> [The] mesostic production of Cage's *Roaratorio* challenges precisely the Platonic doctrine that thought is prior to language and language, in its turn, prior to writing. For the name *JAMES JOYCE,* significant as it is on the page, is not *heard* at all when the poem is read aloud, and conversely the sounded *e* in "JhEm" or "hEaven" is a false externalization of the silent *e* of *JAMES.* Thus the hierarchy of thought, speech, and writing collapses. For is Cage's written text to be regarded as the secondary representation of his speaking and chanting? Or is the recital just one version of the primary written text?[83]

By ingeniously appropriating the Derridean strategy into his own modified letteristic style, Cage's use of the mesostic method suggests a model whereby the deconstructive rethinking of the sign becomes applicable at the level of syntax.

In addition, the physical placement of each graphically enhanced letter in the middle of the line-syntax presents an important counter-methodical move. For the capitalized letter, by virtue of its enlarged shape, literally cuts through the line-syntax vertically, transforming it, as a result, into a visual field. In Cage's "Composition in Retrospect," for instance, one finds the following mesostics that spell the thematic term "method":

> My
> mEmory
> of whaT
> Happened
> is nOt
> what happeneD
>
> i aM struck
> by thE
> facT
> tHat what happened
> is mOre conventional
> than what i remembereD[84]

What is counter-methodically problematized in the above stanzas is the traditional relation between attention and perception, which states that where attention is least strenuous, perception is most automatic and complete.[85] Cage's use of the mesostic method therein effectively impedes one's trained, horizontally oriented perceptual procedure by distracting it into a vertically inserted, visual-spatial expansion. Centrally positioned and visually enhanced, each letter of the word "method," for instance, forcefully demands one's heightened attention by asserting its presence frontally in the middle of each horizontal line to the extent that linear processing of semantic information is rendered so ineffective as to be nearly impossible. In this fashion, these capitalized letters, instead of contributing to the transparent procedure of perception by "disappearing" into various lexical units, disrupt, as a group, the gestalt picture with their obtrusive physicality, showcasing "method" as the foundational mediator. Moreover, each capitalized letter, functioning as the constitutive component of the word "method," determines, from its designated "methodical" positioning, the quantitative index with regard to the possible but still limited choices for the construction of its following syntactical line. Structured as such, this mesostic stanza—or any mesostic writing, for that matter—visualizes the transparent and unveils the foundational; rather than demonstrate any generative potential, it shows the methodical grounding as both the fundamental principle and the functional mechanism of any generative activity. In Cage's formal praxis, the mesostic method thus demilitarizes the otherwise invincible—because invisible—syntax as the marching army of logic by introducing the graphic.

Cage is indeed a latter-day Jonathan Swift, a cultural satirist. Among the few innovative voices of postmodernity, Cage's is heard loud and clear, announcing, through his critical parody, "But the emperor of method has no clothes on!"

Outside the central disciplines of Economy, Anthropology,
and Historiography is a gap in causal sequence. A knowledge
excluded from knowing.

> —Susan Howe, "The Difficulties Interview"

Collision or collusion with history

> —Susan Howe, "Articulation of Sound Forms in Time"

[The] double of his path, which, for him, has meaning, but when
repeated, does not.

> —Jean Baudrillard, *Please Follow Me*

5. Articulating the Inarticulate: Singularities and the Counter-Method in Susan Howe

"If Written Is Writing," the title of Lyn Hejinian's essay first published in *L=A=N=G=U=A=G=E*, bodies forth a central pronouncement of Language poetry.[1] Itself only a conditional clause, the title is, of course, incomplete both in syntax and in logic. The absence of an apodosis, while disrupting a structure as a form of reason, frees from the conventional epistemological boundaries new configurations, ones that point, as Charles Bernstein notes, to "new—in the sense of uncharted or undiscovered (unarticulated)—worlds within language."[2] Further, the resistance to syntactical/logical closure exemplified by the title can be realized only through a radical language praxis, a praxis constitutive of a shift from "written" to "writing," as is suggested in the title.

Hejinian's linguistic shift from the past participle ("written") to the present one ("writing") epitomizes the critical issue that has occupied center stage, both in theory and in practice, in Language poetry: the status of language and its concomitant implications. If conceptualized and put to use as something always already happened, completed, or established, as the definition of the past participle dictates, language, Hejinian seems to argue, is in actuality isolated from the dynamic sphere of human activity. The estrangement of language from the complexity of everyday existence, in turn, transforms it into what Michael Davidson describes as "a static

paradigm of rules and features."[3] Endowed, nonetheless, with an autonomy transcending the world, this "static paradigm" assumes an apriority
manifested in being "omniscient," the etymology of which specifies its major constituents as, rather revealingly, "ML *omniscientia, fr.* L *omni* [all] +
scientia knowledge—see more at science."[4] Formulaic in structure and
prescriptive (as descriptive) in function, language is not only "meaning-
referential," as Jerome McGann argues,[5] but also, according to Don Byrd,
"theoretical," in that it is always "biased toward the general case."[6] The
present participle, by contrast, designates language as being active, as an
ongoing process in which meaning becomes constitutive.[7] For the physicality of such language activity refuses to be selective, thus allowing for
local, contingent, or chancy occurrences, occurrences embodying "those
dimensions of the real" that are otherwise erased or glossed over.[8]

This shift from "written" to "writing" is substantiated in the essay as
a shift from what Hejinian calls, with a critical insight, "[seeking] a vocabulary for ideas" to "[seeking] ideas for vocabularies."[9] The exchange of
syntactical positions between "vocabulary" and "ideas" as the object of the
verb, together with the change of "vocabulary" from singular to plural,
bespeaks a paradigmatic turning point in language praxis that calls for a
critical reassessment of language in relation to knowledge.

In this respect, Don Byrd, in his study of postmodern poetics, presents some pertinent historical overviews. Byrd observes that deeply
rooted in the Western metaphysical tradition is "the thought of language
as an extra-ontological structure. . . . As an independent subjective structure that describes all ontological possibilities"[10]—so much so that "since
the seventeenth century, if not since the sixth century B.C.," he affirms,
"the formal structure of language has been confused with the structure
of mind and world."[11] The rapid advent and dazzling vigor of cognitive
sciences in the seventeenth century, in particular, fostered what Byrd calls
a "Cartesian position," one that "represents a change in desire, a reassessment of the relation between thought and the physical world,"[12] culminat-
ing in Descartes' statement that "there is need of a method for finding out
the truth."[13] This method, Byrd points out, is realized in a "formal system
or linguistic machine" intended and constructed to provide "a complex
descriptive model . . . substituted for nature, so *something* in the model
corresponded to *everything* in nature."[14] As such, the Cartesian method
represents a form of reason "directed toward rational control of the unruly
linguistic machine that generates its illusory worlds."[15]

In this "methodological reduction of multiplicity to universal rules," logic, the sole motor power driving the epistemological enterprise, becomes but "a collection of techniques for a theater, a representational space. It accounts adequately, therefore, for closure, for endings and deaths."[16] Epistemology, in this sense, turns into "an administrative, not a foundational, science," a policing mechanism sifting the world to construct what Byrd terms a *disciplined knowledge.*"[17] What has been consistently sifted out, or put to death, in pursuit of this "disciplined knowledge" is a "common knowledge," which Byrd defines as follows:

> The domain of the common knowledge has no preexistence. It comes into being only when contingent beings come into contingent relationship. The common knowledge leads not to certainty of mind but to confidence of action. It consists not of propositions to be communicated from A to B but of orientations in fields of meaning, measures by the scales in which humans share not a perspective or a belief but a world that opens to his or that particular vantage and practice.[18]

It is in search of this "common knowledge" that Language poetry, with its shared emphasis on but diverse forms of praxis, aims at deconstructing language as the Cartesian construct of the real. Charles Bernstein, for instance, under a Wittgensteinian premise, turns his writing into a search for new worlds within language by way of "a poetry and a poetics that do not edit out so much as edit in";[19] Ron Silliman, "recognizing [poetry] as the *philosophy of practice in language,*" writes to "search out the preconditions of a liberated language within the existing social fact";[20] and Lyn Hejinian postulates, in "The Rejection of Closure," that "a central activity of poetic language is formal," whereby, "failing in the attempt to match the world, we discover structure, distinction, the integrity and separateness of things."[21] As much similar as unique is Susan Howe's poetic praxis, a praxis committed, among other goals, to articulating the inarticulate through a counter-method of singularities.

"Poetry brings similitude and representation to configurations waiting from forever to be spoken," writes Susan Howe in her "Statement for the New Poetics Colloquium, Vancouver, 1985." "I write to break out into perfect primeval Consent. I wish I could tenderly lift from the dark side of history, voices that are anonymous, slighted—inarticulate."[22] To articulate the inarticulate, Howe's poetic praxis pivots on a lyric consciousness upon which impinges a double mission of rescuing and breaking free: rescuing

"the stutter" that Howe hears in American literature "as a sounding of uncertainty. What is silenced or not quite silenced,"[23] and breaking free from
a linguistic world in which, as Marjorie Perloff puts it in *The Dance of the
Intellect*, "the articulation of an individual language is all but prevented
by the official discourses that bombard the consciousness from all sides."[24]
Poetry as such engages its material, both in theory and in methodology,
with two major critical inquiries informing one another, namely, how to
read and how to write; that is, "How do I, choosing messages from the
code of others in order to participate in the universal theme of Language,
pull SHE from all the myriad symbols and sightings of HE," as Howe
observes in her insightful study of Emily Dickinson.[25] From this perspective, Howe's poetry can be described, to put it in Bruce Andrews's terms,
as a "*rereading* [of] the reading that a social status quo puts [her] through"
by "[rewriting] its material . . . the raw materials of a society, a collection
of practices & avowals & disavowals, governed by discourse."[26]

To articulate, in this sense, foregrounds the *re-* prefix as denotative of
"founding," "establishing," "pioneering," and "exploring." A linguistic act
of "pathfinding" regardless of an already given itinerary, "to articulate"
means, according to a standard dictionary, "to put together with joints;
to form or fit into a systematically related whole; coordinate coherently,"[27]
thus suggesting a regrounding of representation through "a recognition
that there is an other voice, an attempt to hear and speak it."[28] To articulate, then, is to assume an iconoclastic, sociolinguistic status that Howe
identifies in *Singularities* as the "Emancipator at empyrean center," "the
lean Instaurator," or "THE REVISER" wandering "on wild thought-
path" rather than the captive imprisoned in "iconic Collective . . . thought
thought out."[29]

Yet to render audible this "undervoice that was speaking from the beginning" constitutes a paradox.[30] For the inarticulate can find its forms of
articulation only within the already articulated, within, in other words,
a language which is itself a sociohistorical construct, or, as Dale Spender
puts it, a "language *trap.*"[31] "For we are language Lost / in language," Howe
aptly portrays this predatory apparatus of ultimate silencing in *The Europe
of Trusts,*[32] one that Howe subsequently describes, vis-à-vis her own writing experience, as relentlessly and incessantly lying in wait for its prey:

So I start in a place with fragments, lines and marks, stops and gaps,
and then I have more ordered sections, and then things break up again.

That's how I begin most of my books. . . . These sounds, these pieces of words come into the chaos of life, and then you try to order them and to explain something and the explanation breaks free of itself. I think a lot of my work is about breaking free. Starting free and being captured and breaking free again and being captured again.[33]

Language as a predator marks its exclusive territory by ceaselessly preying upon the consciousness of the Other. That being the case, to articulate as an iconoclastic rescue mission means, first and foremost, to escape from the linguistic roundup, to break free from grammar as "repressive mechanism," and to resist being captured and silenced by meaning as "the unconscious political element in lineal grammaticization."[34] Centering unfailingly upon issues such as these, Howe's re-reading is embodied in a rewriting that postulates an interrogation of language, of "[its] received model on its own ground."[35] "Who polices questions of grammar, parts of speech, connection, and connotation?" asks the poet in *My Emily Dickinson.* "Whose order is shut inside the structure of a sentence? What inner articulation releases the coils and complications of Saying's assertion?"[36] These questions, by interrogating the "formerly assumed and unquestioned mechanisms,"[37] force open a path through the ensnaring cobwebs of the prescriptive grammar to "an enunciative clearing," as Howe phrases it, "the poet's space. Its demand is her method."[38]

A challenge to the knowledge "always stamped PASSED BY EXAMINER,"[39] Howe's poetry of articulating the inarticulate presents itself as an index, theoretical and methodological, to Michel Serres's remarkable study of the form of knowledge acquisition in the seventeenth century. To a great extent, Howe's interests in Emily Dickinson's "process of writing" and "re-ordering of the forward process of reading,"[40] her study of "what form for the form,"[41] her reconceptualizing poetry as, in Edward Foster's words, "a different way of knowing things,"[42] and her recourse to the algebraic concept of singularity as a means to "[pull] representation from the irrational dimension love and knowledge must reach" parallel Serres's focal points in his analysis of the Cartesian construct of the real.[43] In light of this Serresian paradigm of Western epistemology as a hunt, Howe's poetry demonstrates a bent to contrive a method, or counter-method, to break free from the language trap through a "productive violence" highly informed rather than random.[44]

Titled "Knowledge in the Classical Age: La Fontaine and Descartes,"

Serres's brilliant exegesis, both structural and metaphorical, begins with the fable "The Wolf and the Lamb":

> The reason of the stronger is always the best.
> We will show this shortly.
> A Lamb quenched his thirst
> In the current of a pure stream,
> A fasting Wolf arrives, looking for adventure,
> And whom hunger draws to this place.
> "Who makes you so bold as to muddy my drink?"
> Said the animal, full of rage:
> "You will be punished for your temerity."
> "Sire," answers the Lamb, "may it please Your Majesty
> Not to become angry;
> But rather let Him consider
> That I am quenching my thirst
> In the stream,
> More than twenty steps below Him;
> And that, as a result, in no way
> Can I muddy His drink."
> "You muddy it," responded this cruel beast;
> "And I know that you slandered me last year."
> "How could I have done so, if I had not yet been born?"
> Responded the Lamb; "I am not yet weaned."
> "If it is not you, then it is your brother."
> "I do not have any." "Then it is one of your clan;
> For you hardly spare me,
> You, your shepherds, and your dogs.
> I have been told: I must avenge myself."
> Upon which, deep into the woods
> The Wolf carries him off, and then eats him,
> Without any other form of *procès*.[45]

Behind the seeming arbitrariness with which the Wolf kills the Lamb, Serres points out, there exists a logical architecture. What the fable dramatizes, to begin with, is the notion of structure. With an algebraic origin, this structure operates as an ordered structure, designating a set of elements provided with an ordering relation that is prescribed as irreflexive, antisymmetric, and transitive. When enacted in the fable, this ordered structure with an ordering relation is seen in the form of the pure stream flowing in one direction, with the Lamb positioned downstream, the absent shepherds and dogs upstream, and the Wolf in the middle. It represents, as the fable unfolds, a form of *procès*, *procès* meaning not only "process," etymologically, but also, judicially, "trial." In this sense, the form is, according to Serres, a reason, a ratio, a connection, a relation. It is a form as "a 'method' of knowledge," to put it in Don Byrd's words, the advantage of which is "precisely [its] avoidance of particular and sensuous means of expression," and in which "the Other [is] created in the image of [its] reason."[46]

This form of trial as a reason then demands, Serres proceeds to argue, that a certain possibility be established—the possibility of a party responsible for some wrongdoing or injury that a plaintiff claims to have suffered, whatever the wrongdoing or injury might be. When diagrammed onto the fable's topographical layout as a structure of causality, the responsible party, termed by Serres "the majorant," occupies the upstream position, has complete control over anyone below, and, found guilty, deserves to be punished; whereas the plaintiff, called "the minorant," occupies the downstream position, has no control over anyone above, and therefore has the right to take revenge. In other words, he who is upstream is responsible and loses. Hence the fable's strategy or the trial's law. All, from Serres's standpoint, is engendered and activated by the first word in the Wolf's first question—the "Who" in "Who makes you so bold as to muddy my drink," a use of language foregrounding not dialogue but self-interpretation, not ontology but epistemology.[47] For with "Who" as a reference to a majorant, the Wolf succeeds in positing the existence of what Serres calls the third man, that is, the shepherds and dogs in the Lamb's social group, upstream from him, which in turn enables the Wolf to change his position/status from upstream/majorant (in relation to the Lamb) to downstream/minorant (in relation to the third man). Having majorized the Lamb by identifying him with the shepherds and dogs upstream from him, the Wolf minorizes himself into a position entitled to collect, to eat the Lamb. The guaranteed winning strategy here, as executed by the Wolf, lies in the displacement of the majorant-minorant couplet within what Serres calls the "game-space," a displacement realized by reason as an absolute and constant optimization, and by following a global theorem: all the moves are maximized. The Wolf wins, to put it differently, because he plays the role of the minorant by maximizing each move in an absolute fashion—there is no place above the shepherds assisted by their dogs, and there is no place below the Lamb—whereby he freezes the game-space in a single pattern of order and hierarchy. Thus the trial is over, and the Lamb is sentenced to die.

As an animated game of strategy, with its rules and moves, this fable, Serres continues, bodies forth the hidden model of all exact knowledge, a model aimed at "discovering entire classes of phenomena that corresponded to the mathematical species of algebra."[48] Descartes, after Bacon, picked up this precept and, by rejecting the Baconian impulse to obey nature, developed it further into an agonistic relationship between humans and the exterior world, a relationship in which the weak party, with reason's verdicts, always wins, by discovering the maximum and the minimum points at the edge of the space organized by the couplet of the majorant and the minorant, and as Byrd asserts, by "putting off the proof of the premises until they can be supported by the conclusion."[49] To know nature, in this sense, becomes a deadly dangerous game. For knowledge is a hunt, as Serres's succinct conclusion reads, and to know is to put to death other forms of knowledge, that of the Lamb, for instance. These epistemologies, therefore, are not innocent: at the critical tribunal they are calling for executions. Indeed, the reason of the strongest is reason by itself. Western man is a wolf of science.

Both Howe's poetry and her criticism suggest an acute awareness of Serres's "Western man" as a Cartesian methodologist, who is in actuality "a medium—that is, language itself,"[50] with Wolfish moves which, also "drafted in . . . language,"[51] "[institute] an inherently linguistic world as [his] field of operation,"[52] resulting in the ultimate silencing of the undervoice and the killing of the knowledge of the Other.[53] Howe writes:

> Knowledge narrowly fixed knowledge
> Whose bounds in theories slay
> . . . .
> Alone in deserts of Parchment
> Theoreticians of the Modern
>
> —emending annotating inventing
> World as rigorously related System[54]

To the extent that Howe considers such "linguistic nature [as] always foreign" and herself as "a foreigner in her own language,"[55] her effort to articulate the inarticulate can be first seen in her attempt to outsmart the language trap by appropriating the Cartesian strategies, specifically, the displacement of the majorant-minorant couplet. With the word "Who" in her own interrogation "Who polices questions of grammar," for instance, she succeeds in usurping the Wolf's place along the linear trajectory of language as an ordered structure with an ordering relation, by positioning the existing sociolinguistic system, designed to render her invisible and voiceless, downstream from her, and upstream, the "third man," who prescribes rules for such a system. Concomitantly established, then, is her right to raise and pursue the issue of responsibility. For poetry, as Howe defines it, is "a search by an investigator for the point where the crime began. What is the unforgivable crime? Will I ever capture it in words?"[56] And the point her search leads to turns out to be the point where language began, where, through language, "stability and constancy of certitudes or precisions are conceived . . . as the end of a prior game."[57] "In the beginning was the Word," Howe quotes in her *Talisman* interview, "and the Word was God,"[58] thus revealing the Cartesian circle, with what Byrd calls "an idealism as the pretext for a language without etymologies or sensuous content."[59]

Such an appropriation, though successfully leading the poet-investigator to the crime scene, gets her no further. If the Wolf, by occupying the middle position, becomes entitled to assert knowledge by killing, the poet-articulator, by the same token, only finds herself entitled to be denied her own knowledge by being killed. For this appropriation constitutes nothing but the recycling of a gendered form constructed as a reason or logic, whose circularity presupposes a priori the impossibility of any countermoves. To articulate the "inarticulate true meaning/lives beyond thought/linked from beginning,"[60] then, the poet has to take another approach, one that "would mark the beginning of a new history,"[61] a history of what Howe conceives as "an actuality" rather than "some intellectual fusion or agreement,"[62] some "documents . . . written by the Masters."[63] And this new approach, as Serres suggests, is to "[attack] *the ordered structure itself*—which is the condition for the game's existence or, rather, without which the game can have neither space nor time—in order to shatter it."[64]

It is in singularity that Howe locates her point of attack on this ordered structure with its "logical determination of position,"[65] a move that reminds one of Derridean deconstruction as "operating necessarily from the inside, borrowing all the strategic and economic resources of subversion from the old structure, borrowing them structurally."[66] Talking about René Thom and his lecture at SUNY-Buffalo entitled "Singularities," Howe sketches out her understanding of the concept as follows:

> In algebra a singularity is the point where plus becomes minus. . . . The singularity (I think Thom is saying) is the point where there is a sudden change to something completely else. It's a chaotic point. It's the point chaos enters cosmos, the instant articulation. Then there is a leap into something else. Predation and capture are terms he uses constantly.[67]

Singularity, in other words, constitutes the juncture where "chaos cast cold intellect back" to show the "archaic presentiment of rupture / Voicing desire no more from here."[68] It is the site of "the struggle not to be reduced,"[69] a struggle to break free violently—as is suggested by Howe's use of words like "sudden change," "completely else," "the instant," and "a leap"—from the predation and capture of what Howe calls the "lenses and language / total systemic circular knowledge / System impossible in time."[70] In the same vein, René Thom's theorizing of catastrophe, which Howe specifically refers to in the same context, sheds further light on the poet's understanding and use of singularity.[71] To appropriate Thom's terminology, as Howe certainly does for her purpose, a singularity is a catastrophe, a sudden, violent change which, ushering "anarchy into named theory / Entangled obedience,"[72] makes itself manifest in the "morphology" or structure. Either of "conflict" or of "bifurcation," it designates "a field of local dynamics defined as the gradient of a potential," whose centrifugality outlines "a new grammar grounded in humility and hesitation," a hermaphroditic language, perhaps, for the " 'sheltered' woman. . . . [Holding] back in doubt, [having] difficulty speaking."[73]

As such, singularity becomes, as Marjorie Perloff puts it in her discussion of war in Wittgenstein, "the condition for what might best be called textual breakthrough."[74] When applied to reading and writing, it constitutes the point where linguistic fracture occurs. Howe's poems, remarks the poet herself, "fracture language, they are charged."[75] And this is done by "changing order and abolishing categories,"[76] for order and categories suggest "hierarchy" and "property."[77] To articulate the inarticulate, in this sense, is to be a "child / regical,"[78] demilitarizing language as "a martial art" by initiating singularities and incurring catastrophes at all levels.[79] In Howe's poetry, the form that singularity takes is, among others, what

DuPlessis refers to as "matted palimpsests,"[80] a writing-through which, via points of contact with and displacement of the canonized materials, "releases the coils and complications of Saying's assertion"[81] and, as a result, enables the poet to "[see] what she did not see [say] what she did not say," as is suggested by Howe's aptly entitled study "The Captivity and Restoration of Mrs. Mary Rowlandson."[82] Indeed, singularity, as an act of restoration from captivity, deconstructs so as to reconstellate:

> Deflagration of what was there to say. No message to decode or finally decide. The fascicles have a "halo of wilderness." By continually interweaving expectation and categories they checkmate inscription to become what a reader offers them.[83]

Howe's poetry, written in "matted palimpsests," embodies a three-layered linguistic deposit, or a three-dimensional language experience: (1) the source text, often excerpted or duplicated in prose and other genred language, or indicated by a footnote; (2) Howe's text as an act of writing through the source text; and (3) what this writing-through gestures toward. Resembling what Lyn Hejinian calls "field work," such a textual formation becomes "an activity."[84] The dynamics of the interweaving of all three invites or, indeed, demands a simultaneous, tripartite reading: anaphoric reading of the source text, exophoric reading of the text proper, and cataphoric reading of the inarticulate.[85] To read anaphorically is not to appeal to the source text for confirmation, but rather to "break out into [its] perfect primeval Consent."[86] The critical inquiry back into the knowledge "always stamped PASSED BY EXAMINER" thus subpoenas the source text as the established conceptual representation and investigates it as the crime scene. In this way, it reopens the case that has been long since closed by interrogating the assumptions undergirding the source text. To read exophorically, then, is to break up the logical cobwebs of captivity. With its centrifugal trajectory fracturing the linear linguistic structure, exophoric reading turns the text proper into the physical site of singularities. The sudden and violent changes in turn engender a language wilderness, where "stutter" reigns over grammar. And to read cataphorically is to reconstellate. It is, as Bernstein puts it, "to imagine new reals that have never before existed."[87] Envisioning "an open horizon,"[88] it reads the catastrophic aftermath of singularities as a potential of perceptual reknowing so as to reground representation in actuality.

The title poem of Howe's *The Nonconformist's Memorial* begins with a passage carefully footnoted as from "The Gospel According to St. John":

20.15 Jesus saith unto her, Woman,
why weepest thou? whom seekest
thou? She, supposing him to be the
gardener, saith unto him, Sir, if thou
have borne him hence, tell me where
thou has laid him, and I will take
him away.
16 Jesus saith unto her, Mary. She
turned herself, and saith unto him,
Rabboni; which is to say, Master.
17 Jesus saith unto her, Touch me
not; for I am not yet ascended to
my Father: but go to my brethren,
and say unto them, I ascend unto my
Father, and your Father; and *to* my
God, and your God.
18 Mary Magdalene came and told
the disciples that she had seen the
Lord, and *that* he has spoken these
things unto her.[89]

Otherwise taken for granted, the anaphoric reading of this passage, a reading as referring to an origin already codified, as surrendering to a discourse already authorized, as the unquestioning acceptance of a myth already objectified, is nevertheless checkmated from the outset. For this passage, identified by the footnote as a "citation," not only exemplifies this term's doctrinal use as "abbreviated / Often a shortcut / stands for Chapter,"[90] but also suggests a play on the ambiguity of its meaning as both "an official summons to appear (as before a court of law)" and "an act of quoting,"[91] a play that blends the two meanings into one. For the nonconformist whom "the Gospel did not grasp,"[92] quoting becomes, indeed, summoning: the passage, with its monologic meaning, is cited not to be followed but to face polylogic possibilities, "other similitudes / Felicities of life / . . . / dissenting storms / A variety of trials."[93]

Yet to shatter the ordered structure itself, a structure that is explicitly dictated and outlined in the cited passage, one has to strip it to its logical

In Peter she is nameless
Actual world nothing ideal

headstrong anarchy thoughts
A single thread of narrative

She was coming to anoint him
As if all history were a progress

As if all history were a progress
She was coming to anoint him

A single thread of narrative
headstrong anarchy thoughts
Actual world nothing ideal

In Peter she is nameless
The nets were not torn

The Gospel did not grasp

Figure 13

scaffold first. And the exophoric reading, in this sense, begins as an X-ray reading of the source text. Three pages into the poem, Howe then creates a textual layout stretched over two facing pages, and shown in figure 13.

What is presented here, apart from "the nets were not torn / The Gospel did not grasp," is a six-line poem repeating itself, but in such a way that the two identical parts form a perfect circle. For the repeating part, printed upside down and interlined with the repeated, begins its first line where the latter just ends and proceeds from bottom to top and from page 7 to page 6, in the current edition, thus suturing a seamless, head-to-tail-to-head, circular structure. In addition, Howe's "re-ordering of the forward process of reading," a textual move that functions sometimes by playing upon one's trained sensibility, highlights such a circular motion further by forcing one, having reached the end of the six-line poem on page 7, to turn the book upside down so as to resume "the forward process of reading" of the repeating part, thus necessitating a repagination of the former 7 as now 6, and 6 as 7. Hence the circle again.

This textual formation, then, provides a diagramming of the logical structure embedded in the cited passage. It points to the contour of such a structure as a circularity. From word to word, its self-referentiality takes the form in the Gospel of "a single thread of narrative" from Him back to Him,[94] precluding the actuality that "it is by chance that she weeps / Her weeping is not a lament / She has a voice to cry out."[95] As such, "The Narrative of Finding"[96] weaves its thread into "the nets,"[97] or what Wittgenstein calls "Newtonian mechanics" as "a net of a given form," whereby to "construct according to a single plan all the true propositions that [he needs] for the description of the world" at the expense of "*particular* point-masses."[98] As long as "the nets were not torn,"[99] she, captured and positioned accordingly in the nets, "is nameless" and is named only to signify a "Sir" or "Rabboni;[100] which is to say, Master."[101] Irreflexive, antisymmetric, and transitive, the Gospel sentence *"that* he had spoken these / things unto her" enacts an ordered structure with an ordering relation,[102] whose logic determines a priori that she cannot speak back for lack of a language of her own and, resultantly, is silenced:

> In the synoptic tradition Mary
> enters the tomb
>
> . . . .
>
> It is the Word to whom she turns
> True submission and subjection[103]

However perfectly circular, this structure, manifested in "a single thread of narrative" reiterating itself, proves to be what K. Ludwig Pfeiffer calls "fictionality (aesthetic illusion as a production of senses of the real)."[104] For just as "mathematics involves propositions that mathematical systems themselves can't prove," as Edward Foster asserts,[105] the language that materializes this circle points to itself as "the linguistic form of the fiction" and, as such, the site of singularity.[106] Not only is the circle's "singleness" already problematized by "headstrong anarchy thoughts,"[107] but its narrative progress is also impeded and disrupted within its game-space by unrelated, different uses of tense and mood, suggesting "a lack of successful *suture*":[108] the simple present ("she is nameless"), the past continuous ("She was coming"), and the subjunctive ("history were").[109] But the most devastating critique yet of the logical structure as a linguistic form of fiction, a critique that certainly incurs "the capture breaking / along the shock wave / interpreted as space-time / on a few parameters,"[110] lies in Howe's use of "as if": "As if all history were a progress / A single thread of narrative / Actual world nothing ideal / The nets were not torn." Although the "as if" construct as a form of negation appears to have been agreed upon by all, its intended conceptual representation as well as structural containment of an unreal assumption seems, in the context of these two pages, to be what Howe is driving at. In other words, Howe, with the "as if" phrase, not only repudiates history as "a progress / A single thread of narrative / Actual world nothing ideal" by appropriating the phrase's "already made and inhabited" meaning,[111] but also, and more importantly, draws one's attention to this linguistic collocation itself as a fiction-making mechanism.

In this regard, Howe's use of "as if" suggests a critical resonance with Hans Vaihinger's thesis in *The Philosophy of "As If,"* a study of the

"Preponderance of the Means over the End" in the development of human thought, a development "partly in connection with the progress of mathematics, mechanics and jurisprudence."[112] In the light of Vaihinger's paradigm, the word "if" in the "as if" combination negates the word "as" as constitutive of a "comparative apperception" according to which history is viewed "by means of the conceptual construct" of "a progress," of "a single thread of narrative," of "actual world nothing ideal."[113] For "if" denotes "the assumption of a condition, and indeed, in this instance, of an impossible case."[114] Though similar to the "if . . . then" construct in which, in spite of the "unreality or impossibility" stated in the conditional clause, "inferences are [still] drawn" from it and "the assumption is still formally maintained. . . regarded as an apperceptive construct under which something can be subsumed and from which deduction can be made,"[115] the "as if" collocation, Vaihinger argues, implies yet something more. Dissecting "as if" into "something must be treated as it would be treated . . . if it . . ." (all history must be treated as it would be treated if it were a progress and so forth), Vaihinger points out that contained in "as if" there is "a clear statement of the necessity (possibility or actuality), of an inclusion under an impossible or unreal assumption."[116] The apodosis, otherwise manifest and audible like the one introduced by "then" in "if . . . then," is "merely concealed and suppressed. It lurks unheard between the 'as' and the 'if.'"[117] As such, the "as if" collocation constitutes, according to Vaihinger, a formula which "states that reality as given, the particular, is compared with something whose impossibility or unreality is at the same time admitted."[118] In other words, fiction becomes, as Howe puts it, the "pivot / Literally the unmoving point around which a body turns."[119] No wonder that, as much as "as if" calls into question history as such, "the nets were not torn" regardless. Hence the Wolfish move, indeed, in the game-space, a move which, while reinforcing a circular structure as logic, has left traces at every turn of its shaky foundation. "Contradiction," Howe is certainly right to note, "is the book of this place."[120]

Which is also the place of singularities, the place where language, "free from limitations of genre . . . finds true knowledge estranged in itself."[121] To render this "true knowledge" accessible, the exophoric and the cataphoric readings, then, engage themselves in a "field work" of "sensuous visual catastrophes."[122] (See figure 14 from Howe's *Nonconformist's Memorial*.)

As the physical site of singularities, the textual formation in figure 14 suggests what Howe calls "a field of free transgressive prediscovery."[123]

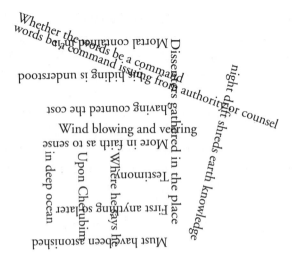

Figure 14

The clashes between words and the collisions among lines demilitarize language by creating points of "capture breaking" which, in turn, become locales for "the chance meeting of words,"[124] leading to discoveries that "outside the central disciplines of Economy, Anthropology, and Historiography is a gap in causal sequence. A knowing excluded from knowing."[125] Thus engendered is a "new way of perceiving" grounded in "the immediate feeling of understanding."[126] "Against the coldness of force / Intellectual grasp,"[127] this "immediate feeling of understanding" originates from "home in a human knowing / Stretched out at the thresh / of beginning" and is articulated in what Howe describes as "body perception thought of perceiving (half-thought."[128] "Body perception" is only a "(half-thought" or a "suggestion" because, as the incomplete parenthesis illustrates, it is still in the process of becoming, of breaking free from the established conceptual fixation as a hunt.[129] "No hierarchy, no notion of polarity," Howe argues, "Perception of an object means loosing and losing it."[130] And not until the logical sequence of language is broken can body perception find complete sense in actuality: "Forward progress disrupted reversed. Sense came after suggestion."[131] Poetry, for Howe to articulate the excluded knowing, "is thought transference. / Free association isn't free."[132]

What first strikes one as obvious is that the textual layout of words in figure 14 suggests a visual presentation of an architecture, the logical foundation of which is, not surprisingly, "effectual crucifying knowledge." But in contrast to the seemingly perfect circle shown in figure 13, it is an architecture visibly on the point of collapse, being off balance from top to bottom. The singularity occurs where the "effectual crucifying knowledge" reigns, where the "distance original disobedience" persists, regardless, in a voice not quite silenced.[133] Partially erased or obscured by "I John bright picture" but kept traceable still—and audible, for that matter—by "suddenly unperceivable time from place to place" is the question "What am I?"—a question directed, as is suggested by its physical posture, to the "effectual crucifying knowledge." Echoing Stella's question "Who can tell me who I am?"[134] one that is ultimately silenced by "Swift's 'liquidation'—abolishing, metaphoric killing of Stella,"[135] "What am I," as a direct challenge to the imposition of a designated status, sends "the shock wave" throughout the architecture, bringing chaos into its scaffolding. The resultant "chance meeting of words" then opens the book of contradiction, of language checkmating itself. The line "Whether the words be a command," for instance, finds itself the site of two counts of linguistic fracture. Rather awkwardly, the word "the" is seen sandwiched, written through, disfigured, and overthrown by "contained in." So configured, these three words form the point of capture-breaking to suggest "a leap into something else." For when placed between "contained" and "in," the word "the," the one and only definite article capable of fixation to the utmost degree, is restrained, physically, in its sphere of application and curtailed, conceptually, in its exclusive power and function of naming, of designating, of referring to an object. Further, if placed after "contained in," "the" then becomes the object of the preposition, and that which is contained in "the" is, by the logic of the syntax, "Mortal," the subject of "contained in," meaning "causing death; fatal"; or, as in theology, that which can cause "spiritual death."[136] To paraphrase: transitive by nature, language, in the form of the "effectual crucifying knowledge," asserts its monotheism by killing other voices. "The" being demilitarized, "command," beneath which the word "his" lurks, is confronted by "dissenters." And the matted palimpsests of "his-command-dissenters" are such that, with the double *m* heavily written through, what seems to be left from the word "command" after the catastrophe are, quite visibly, "co" and "and," suggesting that "*we* plural are the speaker,"[137] a stance in opposition to that of "either-or," which endorses a "dichotomized universe, proposing monism."[138]

Adjacent to this site of singularity is another catastrophe area in "words be a command issuing from authority or counsel." The capture-breaking that occurs with the "chance meeting" of "be" and "it," for instance, demystifies words as "hallucinated to infinity."[139] Denotative of existence, life, occurrence, continuity, identity, value, cause, significance, and sometimes equivalent to the mathematical equal sign, the verb "to be," substantive or copulative, is endowed with such a transparency in "a single thread of narrative" that its physicality has been metamorphosed into a "Being" with its own agency. Yet the word "it," "the subject of an impersonal verb . . . without reference to agent,"[140] points to "be" as nothing but the symptom of a paranoia as the result of an "intractable ethical paradox."[141] In addition, by writing primarily through *e* in "be" and leaving *b* intact, "it" thus metamorphoses the verb "to be" from an autonomous entity back to its corporeality, which is the letter *b* with a monosyllabic sound. The subsequent "chance meeting" of "issuing" and "hiding," each with its own semantic pull in the opposite direction, then suggests not only that the hierarchical trajectory of words as command (issuing) is often masked (hiding), but also that its transitivity (issuing) is frustrated as a criminal hoax (hiding). Based on words as such, "authority" can no longer sustain its own constructedness, which is dissected as nothing but "night drift," an arbitrary piecing-together that "shreds earth knowledge." In the book of contradictions, says Howe, "word flesh crumbled page edge."[142]

In "Writing and Method," Charles Bernstein talks about poetry and philosophy as "[sharing] *the project of investigating the possibilities (nature) and structures of phenomena.*"[143] He writes, "Part of the task of an active poetry or philosophy is to explore these instruments [of power that is taken as neutral or given] by a critique of their partiality and to develop alternatives to them that can serve as models of truth and meaning not dependent for their power on the dominating structures."[144] Poetry is active not only because it continuously explores the language wilderness open only to what Howe calls "human knowing," but also because it develops, while exploring, alternative means to articulate the "common knowledge." Both are executed through poetic praxis, a praxis manifested in a search, as Bernstein puts it in the same essay, for "a 'constructive' mode [suggesting] that the mode itself is explored as content, its possibilities of meaning are investigated and presented, and that this process is itself recognized as a method."[145] Poetry, in this sense, is never written; it is, always, writing.

Howe's counter-method of singularities, as a critique of the "illusion of literacy" that conceives language "as a mechanism of [disciplined] knowledge,"[146] finds its "entrance point" on the dominating linguistic-logical structure.[147] By way of "matted palimpsests," Howe opens the book of contradiction in which language is revealed as checkmating itself, thus rendering possible a "thought transference" embracing the excluded knowing. For Susan Howe, articulating the inarticulate, as the present participle indicates, constitutes a pathfinding expedition in progress, a writing in action, which, while "charting worlds otherwise hidden or denied or, perhaps best of all, never before existing,"[148] engages the "common knowledge," a knowledge that "cannot be stated but only practiced."[149] Indeed, by problematizing that "when words are, meaning soon follows," as Ron Silliman so laconically phrases it in "For L=A=N=G=U=A=G=E," Howe's counter-method of singularities shows that "where words join, writing is."[150]

The very word "diary" depresses me. . . . My life is as permeable constructedness.

—Lyn Hejinian, *My Life*

Theoretical and practical decisions of personal life may well lay hold, from a distance, upon my past and my future, and bestow upon my past, with all its fortuitous events, a definite significance, by following it up with a future which will be seen after the event as foreshadowed by it, thus introducing historicity into my life. Yet these sequences have always something artificial about them.

—M. Merleau-Ponty, *Phenomenology of Perception*

6. Reflection upon *My* [Unreflected] *Life*: M. Merleau-Ponty and Lyn Hejinian's Poetics of "Genetic Phenomenology"

Written as an autobiography, Lyn Hejinian's prose poem *My Life* presents a hermeneutic puzzle. The structure of the poem, on the one hand, certainly mirrors a chronological recording of the poet's life to the year of the composition. When it was first written in 1978, at the poet's then age of thirty-seven, the poem consisted of thirty-seven sections, and each section consisted of thirty-seven sentences, all unnumbered.[1] But in 1986 when Hejinian revised *My Life* for the second Sun and Moon Press edition at the age of forty-five, she added eight sections to the book, and, accordingly, eight new sentences to each section, all inserted into the original text at irregular intervals.[2] The content of the poem, on the other hand, is certainly much less logical or chronological. Although each section in the sequence suggests a parallel to a corresponding year in the poet's life and does contain some allusions to emotional, relational, or linguistic features characteristic of that stage of growth in question,[3] the poem's reflective engagement with everyday existence unfolds a nonlinear "field work"[4] in which life is perceived, rather contra-autobiographically, as "hopelessly frayed, all loose ends,"[5] and a discernible individual identity or subjectivity constantly "eludes, shifts, and even dissolves,"[6] giving way to an opaque multiplicity, "a fluid state that takes on varying shapes."[7]

Hejinian's *My Life,* as such, raises a fundamental question concerning the nature of autobiography. In many ways, the genre's still "dominant definition" since the 1970s, as Juliana Spahr has argued,[8] can be found in Philippe Lejeune's article "The Autobiographical Pact" (1975), in which he describes life-writing as a "retrospective prose narrative written by a real person concerning his own existence, where the focus is his individual life, in particular the story of his personality."[9] Always written "in the service of an overriding purpose," traditional autobiography is, following Hilary Clark's contention, invariably "based on careful narrative shaping and selection [of details] . . . composed in the subordinating and excluding logic of writing" so as to forge "a chain of singular and highly significant events and turning points."[10] It is, in this sense, a reflective discourse of what Paul Smith calls " 'I' talks about 'me' " featuring an enunciatory split between, to put it in the terminology of structural linguistics, the "subject of the enunciation" and the "subject of the enounced," a split that will then be closed down by a "third 'I' " who, as the intended moral and ideological effect on the one hand and the "cerned and complete individual" on the other, is "called upon to hold in place the circuit of guarantees obtaining between 'subject' and knowledge."[11] This third "I," Smith specifies further, thus constitutes the ideological force of the discourse and, in turn, "typically becomes a kind of *de facto* third-person pronoun, supposedly having full objective possession of that which it views."[12] To the extent that it presents an epistemological plotting of life into "permanent constructedness,"[13] autobiography can be construed as the reflection upon the already reflected, in that its "intentionality of act" foregrounds a tripartite construct of perception[14]—that is, identity, memory, and time—and the underlying, functional relationship therein is best epitomized by N. Katherine Hayles when she writes, in her discussion of what she calls the third wave of postmodernism in terms of the denaturing of time in connection with identity, that "human identity depends on memory and memory depends on seeing time as a continuous orderly progression."[15]

It is the critique of this reflection upon the already reflected, or of "the ideological framing of perception,"[16] that constitutes, among other issues, the focal point in Lyn Hejinian's poetic autobiography *My Life.* A contemporary American poet, Hejinian is associated with an avant-garde poetic movement commonly referred to as "Language poetry" that emerged in the margins of the mainstream "official verse culture" in the late 1970s.[17] Well-informed by recent European philosophy and critical theory, this movement's poetic-aesthetic objective presents, in part, a critical resonance with the Merleau-Pontean "task . . . to rediscover phenomena, the layer of living experience through which other people and things are first given to us."[18] It states, as is formulated by Charles Bernstein, one of the founders and major theorists of Language poetry, that "poetry and philosophy share *the project of investigating the possibilities (nature) and structures of phenomena,*" with recourse to formal innovations "as a way to get the dimensions of meaning necessary to put forward the fullness of [one's] experiences and perceptions."[19] Its investigative point of departure, both in theory and in praxis, is located in two related areas: seeing language as the site of a sociopolitical construction of perception, as perception itself, as "not accompanying but constituting the world"; and questioning "the self as the primary organizing feature of writing."[20] Viewed from this perspective, the project of Language poetry articulates a twofold critique: a philosophical rethinking of both the theoretical limitations and the practical prejudices of language as constituting perception, and a critical reflection, as Christopher Macann observes similarly in Merleau-Ponty, "upon that which transcendental phenomenology installs as an ultimately irreducible presupposition, the transcendental Ego itself, together with the entire apparatus of transcendental reflection."[21]

Such, then, is what Merleau-Ponty terms "reflection on the unreflected" or "radical reflection."[22] It is, in other words, a critical self-reflection, one that "steps back to watch the forms of transcendence fly up like sparks from a fire; it slackens the intentional threads which attach us to the world and thus brings them to our notice."[23] In more explicit terms, Merleau-Ponty explains:

> Reflection cannot be thorough-going, or bring a complete elucidation of its object, if it does not arrive at awareness of itself as well as of its result. We must not only adopt a reflective attitude, in an impregnable *Cogito,* but furthermore reflect on this reflection. . . . Reflection is truly reflection only if it is not carried outside itself, only if it knows itself as reflection-on-an-unreflective experience, and consequently as a change in structure of our existence. . . . Reflection must elucidate the unreflective view which it supersedes, and show the possibility of this latter, in order to comprehend itself as a beginning.[24]

Furthermore,

The task of radical reflection, the kind that aims at self-comprehension, consists, paradoxically enough, in recovering the unreflective experience of the world, and subsequently reassigning to it the verificatory attitude and reflective operations, and displaying reflection as one possibility of my being.[25]

In this sense, both Language poetry and *Phenomenology of Perception* share the radical project of reflecting upon the unreflected, in the sense that

"reflection upon the unreflected" includes within the scope of its task a reflection upon what still remained unreflected in the reflective extremity of transcendental reflection, the very reflection which claimed to have risen above all presuppositions, to have reduced all of life and experience, thought and action, to something reflected upon and which, in this very "rising above" only gave rise to its own characteristically unreflected presuppositions.[26]

This reflection upon the unreflected takes a specific form in Hejinian's work in general and in *My Life* in particular. Insisting that "language itself is never in a state of rest," Hejinian calls into question the traditional notion of language as an extra-ontological structure mirroring the world, "the *nomina sint numina* position (that there is an essential identity between name and thing, that the real nature of a thing is immanent and present in its name)," which presupposes a priori, in the Cartesian-Kantian scheme of things, the " 'at oneness' with universe" as the "condition of complete and perfect knowing."[27] "If reality is trying to express itself in words," Hejinian quips, "it is certainly taking the long way around."[28] The compositional alternative Hejinian experiments with foregrounds, then, the "operative intentionality" by way of a no-match between the word and the world.[29] Inscribed in the formal structure of this no-match is a new aesthetic of perception, a "genetic phenomenology" of Merleau-Ponty,[30] the "antepredicative"[31] nature of which leads to the reopening of the "pre-objective realm."[32] This genetic phenomenology finds its succinct gloss in Hejinian's poetics when she writes in "The Rejection of Closure":

The incapacity of language to match the world permits us to distinguish our ideas and ourselves from the world and things in it from each other. . . . A central activity of poetic language is formal. In being formal, in making form distinct, it opens—makes variousness and multiplicity and possibility articulate and clear. While failing in the attempt to match the world, we discover structure, distinction, the integrity and separateness of things.[33]

A reflection upon the unreflected, Hejinian's *My Life* presents, first and foremost, a "self-conscious reflection on the problems of life-writing."[34] In her critique of traditional autobiography as a tripartite construct of perception, Hejinian locates the site of the anti-predicative "no-match" between the word and the world more specifically in language's linear temporality, which she considers as the very constituting element and organizing principle for memory and identity. For linear time, Hejinian realizes, is none other than the intentionality of act itself which, in its transcendental reflection, "[takes] as straight lines the chords of the bounding circle."[35]

This point has been brought to the immediate fore from diverse perspectives by contemporary critical thinking in various disciplines. Alice G. B. ter Meulen, for one, points out, in her recent study of the representation of time in natural language, that "because we must express our reasoning about time in time, our language contains the means to indicate what changes and what does not, relative to where we are and how we are changing."[36] Linear time, as the logical structuring of time, thus bodies forth a "situated reasoning" which, in the final analysis, amounts to no more than a "truth-preserving manipulation of information describing parts of the world as a formal and algorithmic procedure."[37] That being the case, in the "strict linear order" of language, ter Meulen continues, "temporal reasoning is considered a form of logical reasoning" in the sense that "the text does not give us an unstructured lump of information, but a structured object in which a temporal vantage point is fixed from which the available information is surveyed. This temporally located vantage point is the primary factor that makes temporal reasoning situated."[38] The function of tenses, aspectual verbs, states, and perspectives, then, is to establish and maintain in language a diachronic-logical situatedness or positioning as the orienting context in which certain given information can be processed and understood. And it is this context, argues Richard Terdiman, that forms the memory of language, the burden of the past that language always carries.[39] For language, with its "verbal conventions" as well as "the whole system of social conventions attached to it," exhibits and signifies, according to Maurice Halbwachs, its own sociocultural conditions at the level of the sign and thus "[constitutes] what is at the same time the most elementary and the most stable framework of collective memory."[40] In this sense, language, itself not only the primary product but also the primary mechanism of memory that "inscribes the single-ended arrow of temporality,"[41] becomes what Michel Foucault describes in *The Order of Things* as "a dense and consistent historical reality," which in turn "forms the locus of tradition, of the unspoken habits of thoughts, of what lies hidden in a people's mind; it accumulates an ineluctable memory which does not even know itself as memory."[42] And this ineluctable memory, as Paul John Eakin has pointed out, is "literally essential to the constitution of identity," in that it "supplies the possibility of identity."[43] In the reflection upon the unreflected, time is deconstructed as a logical formation and is recognized, instead, as "always 'already there' before reflection begins—as an inalienable presence," not of the transcendental Ego but of its own "facticity"; and "to analyse time is not to follow out the consequences of a pre-established conception of subjectivity," as Merleau-Ponty emphatically forewarns; rather, "it is to gain access, through time, to its concrete structure."[44]

Hejinian's work, critical or poetic, is characterized by a consistent, informed inquiry into the issue of linear temporality as the constituting perception. Contrasting the works of Proust and Gertrude Stein, she acknowledges, in a 1992 interview, that her textual praxis in *My Life* engages this particular polemic:

> My reading of Gertrude Stein's studies of time and space have amplified what Proust's have contributed to my own sense of those dimensions. And her phenomenology—her rejection of memory as a medium of perception—and the command, "Begin again," are vital contradictions to Proust's.[45]

Hejinian's reference to Gertrude Stein and her phenomenological rethinking of time, space, and memory provide an important theoretical index to her own critical thinking and textual experimentation. Her most systematic reading of Stein on the issue of time can be found in an essay titled "Two Stein Talks." Originally published in 1986 as a two-part article ("Language and Realism," "Grammar and Landscape"),[46] the essay presents the poet's sustained effort to theorize Stein's textual praxis, a praxis described by William James as articulating "a fine new kind of realism."[47] Well-informed of the confluences of William James's and Merleau-Ponty's thinking on Stein and her work, Hejinian makes the following comment on *Tender Buttons,* a work which, "if one follows Merleau-Ponty's definition of phenomenology," she claims, "might be read as a masterpiece of phenomenological literature":

> This ambitious, exquisite work raises a number of issues—current issues, relevant to contemporary writing practice. There are three areas from which one can triangulate a reading of the work. The first is linguistic: the work questions the nature of language as the basis for knowing anything and explores the effect of technical aspects of language (parts of speech, sentence structure, grammar, and the size and the shape of the writing) and poetic devices (images, patterns, paradoxes, etc.). The second is psychological, by which I mean, in Jamesian terms, it investigates the character of consciousness that is based on perception and elaborated by the perceiver through encounters with the world. And the third is philosophical, best seen in terms of phenomenology, insofar as it addresses and tests empirically available material—things that can be viewed "objectively."[48]

Concerning to a great extent "temporal structures of perception," Stein's work, Hejinian asserts, is thus "directed toward the study of reality and of our perceptions of reality," a study in which "the vital, even vivacious, relationship of language forms and structures to perception and consciousness" is approached, however, not in terms of the Jamesian assumption of truth but in light of the Steinian notion of "understanding," leading, as a result, to "a shift of emphasis, from perceived to perceiving, and thus to writing, in which acts of observation, as complex perception, take place."[49]

Hejinian's reading of Stein in all three areas—linguistics, psychology, phenomenology—foregrounds, in one sense, the issue of time. In a Merleau-Pontean vein, the metaphor she uses in her discussion of Stein's notion of time is "landscape," which she considers, as does Merleau-Ponty, as "a model of longevity. It has the virtue of never being complete, and so of seeming permanent—eternal."[50] Synchronic in nature, this temporal landscape, according to Stein, "does not move, nothing really moves in a landscape but things are there";[51] according to Merleau-Ponty, "it rolls by for the moving observer . . . like the landscape seen through a railway carriage window. Yet we do not really believe that the landscape is moving";[52] and according to Hejinian, it is "a plane extending over the full expanse of the moment," "a moment of time that has gotten in position."[53] "The synchronous," Hejinian writes further in *My Life,* "which I have characterized as spatial, is accurate to reality."[54] The key topological properties of this temporal landscape with "its reversible logic"[55] are described by the poet as nonlinear and originless.[56] As such, this temporal landscape unfolds what Hejinian calls "an existential density" of activity, "a form free of predications, a somewhat vibrational field of reversible effects . . . with its perspective spread over a largish surface, located on innumerable non-isolating focal points."[57] It presents, in Merleau-Ponty's words, "the field of presence in the wide sense, with . . . the infinite openness of those fields of presence that have slid by, or are still possible," a field of presence in which "these instances of 'now' . . . have no temporal character and could not occur in sequence."[58] Time is, in other words, its facticity being bodily experienced. For Stein, this temporal field of presence is materialized through "continuous present," through "beginning again and again and again";[59] for Hejinian, it is manifested in a "fountainous living";[60] and for Merleau-Ponty, it is the "dimension of our being" in that "I effect it . . . I am myself time, a time which 'abides' and does not 'flow' or 'change.' . . . We are the upsurge of time."[61] "[Rising] from [one's] relation to things" at the moment of experiencing, "time is, therefore, not a real process, not an actual succession that I am content to record," as Merleau-Ponty insists; "hence time, in our primordial experience of it, is not for us a system of objective positions, through which we pass."[62]

The collapse of time as a linear-logical construct measurable and deducible erases, in turn, the constituting structure of memory. For "making sense of memory requires," as Terdiman observes, "that [time's] directionality be central within any representation of its activity," which presents itself, in fact, as the cognitive model based upon "a theory of *production* as the paradigm for all social transformation—and . . . for all representation."[63] Hejinian is clearly aware of the economy of this mnemonic production. When asked about the "prophetic beat" in her work titled *Writing Is an Aid to Memory* (1978), she offers the following theorizing of "knowledge" by mapping out the working mechanism of memory in relation to linear time:

> Prophecies don't foretell the future, they announce fate. And they are proven, not on criteria established in the future, but on the grounds of memory, in which are displayed the patterns of incident and decision that would lead *inevitably* to the accomplishment of fate. A sense of fate

is a result of a retrospective experiencing of experience—an apparent discovery of what was and why it worked. But it depends also on belief in a sublime causality, in a transcendental continuum which I simply can't see.[64]

The projection of the future or the ability to know ("prophecy," "fate"), to paraphrase the above statement, lies in the (re)production and (re)presentation of memory ("an apparent discovery") which, as reflection upon the already reflected ("retrospective experiencing of experience"), forms a self-referential system ("would lead inevitably to the accomplishment of fate") of explanation ("patterns of incidents and decision") grounded in linear time as the intentionality of act itself ("belief") engaged in its own transcendental reflection ("sublime causality," "a transcendental continuum"). In the world already constituted by memory, "memory believes before knowing remembers," as William Faulkner aptly puts it.[65] The reproductive schema of memory as a self-fulfilling prophecy along the causal trajectory of linear time can be outlined in figure 15.

Hejinian's phenomenological critique of linear time is thus always juxtaposed with "the demystification of memory."[66] "[A] coincidence touches / a random more," she writes in *Writing Is an Aid to Memory,* "memory is a trick of coincidence / which overturned has invisibly legible / use."[67] The psychological undercurrent of this "trick" is vividly teased out in Hejinian's critique of traditional autobiography when she ingeniously establishes an analogy between explanation and memory in terms of desire: "Wanting to 'explain' is like having a memory—the person posits itself elsewhere, adolescent-like, as a figure in the distance escaping, while awaiting the advent of its more glorious self but modestly, even piously."[68] Indeed, in the predicative economy of the reflection upon the already reflected, "there is no greater temptation than that of reminiscence," Hejinian writes; but to reflect upon the unreflected, by contrast, "what memory is not a 'gripping' thought," for memory is "overturned" in Hejinian's poetics of genetic phenomenology from "a trick of coincidence" to nothing but "only a coincidence," from memory as explanation to "memory [as] a wall."[69]

$$\text{Prophecy} = \frac{\text{Linear Time}}{\text{Memory}}$$

Figure 15

Hejinian's insight into the nature and the function of memory as an expository "trick" that "underlies the possibility of intelligibility as its precondition" finds its critical resonance in Merleau-Ponty.[70] To remember, argues Merleau-Ponty similarly, is to "[set] in motion 'a reproduction intention,'" in that "the appeal to memory presupposes what it is supposed to explain: the patterning of data, the imposition of meaning on a chaos of sense-data. No sooner is the recollection of memories made possible than it becomes superfluous, since the work it is being asked to do is already done."[71] In this view, the projection of memory initiates a circular argument based on linear time, presenting, according to Merleau-Ponty, "nothing but a bad metaphor hiding a deeper, ready-made recognition,"[72] or "an apparent discovery," as Hejinian has put it ironically earlier. Grounded in the as-if philosophy of transcendental reflection, memory is thus the deductive appropriation of the world. And what distinguishes perception from memory, observes Merleau-Ponty, is that the former enacts "the return to the phenomenal" by "[arriving] at an understanding of man and the world from any starting point other than that of their 'facticity,'"[73] whereas the latter presupposes an objective world by postulating linear temporality as its *a priori synthetic*:[74]

To perceive is not to experience a host of impressions accompanied by memories capable of clinching them; it is to see, standing forth from a cluster of data, an immanent significance without which no appeal to memories is possible. To remember is not to bring into the focus of consciousness a self-subsistent picture of the past; it is to thrust deeply into the horizon of the past and take apart step by step the interlocked perspectives until the experiences which it epitomizes are as if relived in their temporal setting. To perceive is not to remember.[75]

Furthermore, the overturning of memory as a trick—cognitive, psychological, expository, reproductive, representational, and so forth—calls into question the issue of identity. Memory is memory at all, as Mary Warnock has pointed out in her seminal study of memory in relation to identity in, among many others, William James, Jean-Paul Sartre, and Bishop Butler, only insofar as "the idea of the self is the essential prerequisite of memory," the concept of the self, that is, as "the recipient and possessor, the systematic organizer of experiences."[76] It follows then that equally prerequisite to the formation of any personal identity is none other than memory, which presents itself as the constitutive condition for the possibility of identity. In either case, the foundational prerequisite is linear temporality. Arguing against Bergson's notion of identity "not in terms of persistence through time, but of the occupancy of space," Warnock insists that identity is, first and foremost, a temporal construct: "There is no sense at all in the identity-question, or the answer to it, unless we think of persistence through time, the past and present being *separate*. . . . The notion of identity or non-identity is meaningless to common sense unless it means identity or multiplicity over a period of time."[77] In this view, "a statement of identity with regard to a person," writes Warnock, "contains at least the implication of a tense," with "a necessary reference to time past," for "the sense of personal identity that each of us has is a sense of continuity through time."[78]

Warnock's theorizing of the identity formation based on temporal continuity highlights, albeit inadvertently, a circular construct beautifully captured by Hejinian's notion of fate—that is, identity, truth, knowledge, whatever it is called—as depending on a belief in linear time as a sublime causality, in a transcendental continuum. For just as memory is that through which one "[seeks] to explore the path of truth," Warnock avers in her study of diaries, autobiographies, and life stories, "acute awareness of identity, of our own personal identity over time, is not incompatible with the universality of truth which . . . [is ascribed] to the knowledge derived from recollection."[79] In addition, nowhere can the acute sense of identity over time, together with its concomitant obtainment of the universal truth through memory, be rendered possible unless it is perceived from a temporally located vantage point, which is always socially determined and culture-specific. As such, the "self" can be conceived, as Eakin argues, only "as a broadly derived cultural construct, subject to all the forces that shape the complex unfolding of human life in society" and, that being the case, all "models of identity" are therefore "culturally sanctioned."[80] The concept of identity as a sociocultural construct thus inevitably articulates the dominant ideology of a society, whatever that society might be. Memory-induced and tense-based, identity is fate precisely because, on the one hand, it bodies forth the constituting power of a society or culture and, on the other, it exemplifies the predetermined construct projected and represented by that society or culture as objective and inevitable. Constituting both the postulate and verification, the criterion and proof, the cause and effect, the question and answer, identity formation reifies the exclusive, closed circuit of a belief system.

Hejinian's critical re-reading of prophecy as fate points to a similar thesis in Merleau-Ponty's critique of empiricism and intellectualism, in both of which, as Macann observes, "the already constituted world forms the point of departure for an analysis which either explains consciousness in terms of the world or explains the world in terms of the unifying power of consciousness."[81] In many ways, the identity-memory-linear time construct presents a self-referential move of the transcendental Ego whereby "the state of consciousness," argues Merleau-Ponty, "becomes the consciousness of a state," of "a ready-made world."[82] In the reflection upon the already reflected, "the consciousness of the unified presupposes consciousness of the unifying agent and of his act of unification."[83] And transcendental reflections as such, Hejinian writes ironically, always "have depth, are deep" and resultantly "don't make shade,"[84] for its consciousness is one that is conscious only of its own already constituted world as the absolutely Other to which it must refer in order for itself to be constituted.

If traditional autobiography can be labeled, in schematic terms, as a writing of relevance in which, according to Hejinian, "*reason looks for two, then arranges it from there,*" *My Life* is, by contrast, what the poet calls a "rewriting in an unstable text," a text in which "I refer to irrelevance, that rigidity which never intrudes."[85] This unstableness of the text, together with its privileging of irrelevance, articulates a new phenomenon of time. When discussing her compositional technique employed in *My Life,* Hejinian explains that the form "was meant to be mimetic of . . . time," time, that is, perceived as "an activity."[86] More specifically, the paragraph, in which each section of *My Life* is written, is proposed by the poet as a moment of time without any temporally located vantage point:

> The paragraph [is] a unit representing a single moment of time, a single moment in the mind, its content all the thoughts, thought particles, impressions, impulses—all the diverse, particular, and contradictory elements—that are included in an active and emotional mind at any given instant.[87]

"A paragraph is a time and place," she reiterates in *My Life,* "not a syntactic unit."[88] The same holds true for sentence or syntax, which constitute for Hejinian a "field of contingency and provisionality,"[89] of the "infinitesimal" now or present.[90] As such, *My Life* does not unfold "an historical swathe or a current of contiguous time lines trailing behind every object, idea, and event . . . characterized by causality, or . . . narrativity" in which "the attachments of one thing to another are insistently relevant."[91] Rather, it exhibits a "language landscape"[92] in which time, itself this landscape, is "pressed onto and spread out over the imagined spatial plane," and "temporal details, are specified and, as it were, made physical."[93] The result is a text of synchronousness "characterized by parallelism," a text in which "one notices analogies and coincidences, resemblances and differences, the simultaneous existence of variations, contradictions, and the apparently random."[94]

Hejinian's phenomenological reconfiguring of time in turn calls for a critical rethinking of the notion of narrative origin and belonging that memory tries to establish in its identity formation. At the level of the narrative, for instance, "there were more storytellers than there were stories," she writes in *My Life*, "so that everyone in the family had a version of history and it was impossible to get close to the original, or to know 'what really happened.' "[95] At the level of syntax, in a like manner, "it is impossible to return to the state of mind in which these sentences originated."[96] With the erasure of an origin as the temporally located vantage point, there emerges an autobiography in which the identity boundary of the possessive pronoun "my" is transgressed and "life" is released from the explanatory mappings of memory. In *My Life* there is no forged chain of singular and highly significant events and turning points contributing to the formation of a clearly defined identity; much to the contrary, one experiences, throughout, a field of contingency in which "what was the meaning hung from that depend."[97] For Hejinian's autobiography is composed not in the subordinating and excluding logic of representation and reproduction, but in "a poetics of description," an aesthetic of perception defined by the poet as "phenomenal rather than epiphenomenal, original . . . [as] equivalent to perception remaining open to the arbitrariness, unpredictability, and inadvertence of what appears."[98] In this sense, Hejinian's poetics of description finds its philosophical counterpart in Merleau-Ponty's "phenomenology understood as direct description," which is qualified further as "a phenomenology of phenomenology."[99] As poetics of description or phenomenology of direct description, it is to describe, for both Hejinian and Merleau-Ponty, "the *advent* of being to consciousness, instead of presuming its possibility as given in advance."[100]

Take, for example, the opening sentence of section 1 in *My Life*, which begins this autobiography in a language that subverts itself as a temporal-mnemonic system, a subversion that results from Hejinian's reversal of the arrow of time:

> A moment yellow, just as four years later, when my father returned home from the war, the moment of greeting him, as he stood at the bottom of the stairs, younger, thinner than when he had left, was purple—though moments are no longer so colored.[101]

There is, one notices immediately, no temporally located vantage point in this sentence, which problematizes the chronological context adumbrated therein ("four years later, when my father returned home from the war"). Further, in "A moment yellow, just as four years later," one is presented with a rather odd comparison: the moment is not compared to an earlier moment ("just as four years earlier or ago"), as memory would normally operate by tracing time's linear trajectory, logically and psychologically, to a past origin. The moment is compared, rather, to a later moment. It is, in other words, a comparison with the future, a future, though referred to presumably from its past, devoid of any specifics to be remembered by and, for the same token, compared with. Out of this temporal configuration arises another complication concerning the function of the adverbial clause of time introduced by the conjunction "when." What, that is, does it modify, "A moment yellow" or "just as four years later"? If it modifies the former, then "the moment of greeting him," which is the appositive phrase also referring to "when my father returned home from the war," is designated as "purple," not "yellow." If it modifies the latter, "A moment yellow" then becomes a tenseless moment, suspended in the middle of an otherwise temporal continuum, unrelated to anyone or anything. Yellow or purple, both moments are then further negated as "no longer so colored." Here, as elsewhere in *My Life,* even the "most conventional and referential moments," as Juliana Spahr rightly observes, "are details taken out of linear time."[102] The absence of a time-logic (chrono-logical), as evidenced in the non-identity between these two moments, in turn decontextualizes language as a temporal-mnemonic construct in the alleged homecoming scene, thus releasing that experience from a socioculturally constructed category of remembering and identifying into the pre-objective realm, (re)turning it into a life-world that everyone can relate to but no one can claim as his or her own, a life-world whose advent to consciousness is described directly, to repeat Merleau-Ponty, rather than presumed as given in advance.

With the trick of memory thus "overturned," all the details in the opening sentence—and in the entire poem for that matter—begin to have what Hejinian has described earlier as "invisibly legible / use." In a way subtle and yet powerful, the poet's use of the oxymoron in "invisibly legible" here implies a critique of the traditional construct of perception as "visibly illegible." It invokes the Merleau-Pontean thesis in his phenomenology of perception that "nothing is more difficult than to know precisely *what we see*," a difficulty caused by "a dialectic whereby perception hides itself from itself."[103] To make the "invisibly legible" truly legible again, one has to begin with the formidable task of learning to see the "visibly illegible" as constitutive of the traditional dialectic of perception. It is for this purpose, explains Macann, that

> Merleau-Ponty's *Phenomenology of Perception* is designed to teach us to see, to relearn what perception means *against* the falsification that our mental constructions impose. . . . [It] is the most difficult thing in the world. For it requires that we first unlearn what we have already taken the trouble to learn, that we become once again the child we once were whilst, at the same time, retaining the critical acumen needed to set this original way of seeing off against the intellectual prejudices of both empiricism and intellectualism.[104]

In this sense, Hejinian's "invisibly legible / use" announces and inaugurates a genetic way of seeing that brings into visibility what has hitherto been invisible in the Cartesian tradition of "thinking about seeing,"[105] a radical reflection that reflects upon what has hitherto remained unreflected in the transcendental reflection.

My Life enacts this genetic phenomenology through a unique textual strategy. As Juliana Spahr's reading testifies, "In *My Life* a mirror does not reflect the authorly self but rather a hole, an opening in the work."[106] This "hole" or "opening" is what Hejinian refers to as a "gap." Against the overriding purpose of life-writing as the creation of a complete, sensible self-identity over gaps, whatever those gaps might be, the poem paradoxically aims at "the creation of sizeable gaps" at all levels of the text, because "what stays in the gaps," Hejinian argues, "remains crucial and informative. Part of the reading occurs as the recovery of that information (looking behind) and the discovery of newly structured ideas (stepping forward)."[107] More specifically, "The gap indicated that objects or events had been forgotten," she avers, "that a place was being held for them, should they chance to reappear."[108] The gap, in other words, is the site of that which has been rendered invisible in the dialectical play of perception. With linear time deconstituted into a language landscape, Hejinian's *My Life* presents itself not only as a text with gaps; it is, in fact, a text of gaps, a text as gaps. It is itself an "invisibly legible" text, one that refuses to yield to any constructed reflection and consequently invites, or indeed demands, a radical reflection. As such, *My Life* stages a genetic reflection upon the gaps of life, upon the unreflected life, dramatizing what Macann calls "a new *regressive* questioning which carries the investigation *back* into the pre-objective realm."[109]

This "regressive questioning," or "looking behind," as Hejinian phrases it, is realized, according to Macann, by way of "a pre-predicative intentionality which not merely captures the original meaning of existence but does so in such a way that the life-world becomes the locus of feeling and desire as well as thought, of evaluation and projection as well as knowledge, indeed *brings the former to light as the very root source* of thought and knowledge."[110] For both Hejinian and Merleau-Ponty, the gaps of life constitute none other than this life-world, lost and forgotten in transcendental reflection; and to reflect radically is to reflect upon this unreflected life-experience, to bring it to light as the very root source, not the constituted product, of thought and knowledge. Radical reflection is to reflect upon the possibilities of this root source, to put it in Merleau-Ponty's words, in order to comprehend reflection itself as a possible beginning.

To do so, *My Life* foregrounds the invisibly legible gaps as a way to slacken the intentional threads that attach one to the already constituted world so as to recover that which has been screened out, or overlooked, by the constituting perception as thinking about seeing. The following passage presents a case in point:

Somewhere, in the background, rooms share a pattern of small roses. Pretty is as pretty does. In certain families, the meaning of necessity is at one with the sentiment of pre-necessity. The better things were gathered in a pen. The windows were narrowed by white gauze curtains which were never loosened. . . . Hence, repetitions, free from all ambition. The shadow of the redwood trees, she said, was oppressive. The plush must be worn away. On her walks she stepped into people's gardens to pinch off cuttings from their geraniums and succulents. An occasional sunset is reflected on the windows. A little puddle is overcast. If only you could touch, or, even, catch those gray great creatures.[111]

The details in this passage, just like those in any other passage in the poem, strike one as both easy to recognize and easy to forget. They are easy to recognize because they bring out the most common and most familiar glimpses and occurrences of life: interior decorations ("rooms share a pattern of small roses," "The windows were narrowed by white gauze curtains which were never loosened"), popular proverbs or sayings ("Pretty is as pretty does"), overheard remarks ("The shadow of the redwood trees, she said, was oppressive"), casual observations ("An occasional sunset is reflected on the windows"), and so forth. And they are easy to forget because they do not make sense any more than what they are: so what? What seems to be the larger conceptual issue, aesthetically ("a pattern of small roses"), economically ("meaning of necessity"), literarily ("The better things were gathered in a pen"), or sociopolitically and psychologically ("The shadow . . . was oppressive")? In this language landscape without a temporally located vantage point, phrases or sentences present not logical links in a thematic sequence, with a constituting context in which they all inevitably contribute to a predesignated, totalizing vision beyond themselves, but fragmented, synchronic, and mutually disruptive moments of perception, whose contextual parameters are thus reduced virtually to the point of nonexistence. Their intentional threads, which function only in an organizing paradigm of subordination and exclusion, are not only slackened due to decontextualization but also, and more accurately, are cut the moment they attempt to venture out of their factual boundaries. The result is that here, as elsewhere "throughout *My Life*," as Marjorie Perloff aptly observes, "secrets seem about to be revealed, enigmas about to be clarified, but the moment of revelation never comes."[112]

This deferral of the moment of revelation has two functions. On the one hand, it demystifies life as a sociocultural construct consisting of predetermined, ready-made categories, and conventional life-writing as a reflection upon the already reflected. On the other hand, it amplifies the gaps of life, the root sources of life, the existential density of life, the possibilities of which, precisely by making reflection possible, become paradoxically unreflected. Context-resisting and logic-defying, details in *My Life* are presented as such because they are the live fabric of daily existence before being organized by a social system, the cultural material before being appropriated by an ideological paradigm, the moments of seeing before being subjugated by the transcendental gaze, the emotional and psychological "immediacy of an experience before [being] transformed by science and common sense."[113] They are, in other words, the unreflected life "which lies behind and is prior to the *posterior* division of it into the various complexes of traditional epistemological and ontological categories."[114] In this way, to reflect upon this unreflected life is to explore, as Clark points out, "not the 'having-lived' of former states of mind, life as a closed thing, but rather *living* as a dense and open-ended process."[115] It is to open that pre-objective realm of life yet to be lived.

Hejinian's poetic description of the unreflected life in the passage quoted above finds its elaboration in Merleau-Ponty's phenomenology of perception. Invoking the metaphor of time as landscape, Merleau-Ponty offers the following direct description of his experience:

> Natural time is always there. . . . Since natural time remains at the center of my history, I see myself surrounded by it . . . which pursues its own independent course, and which my personal life utilizes but does not entirely overlay. Because I am borne into personal existence by a time which I do not constitute, all my perceptions stand out against a background of nature. While I perceive, and even without having any knowledge of the organic conditions of my perception, I am aware of drawing together somewhat absent-minded and dispersed "consciousness": sight, hearing and touch, with their fields, which are anterior, and remain alien, to my personal life. The natural object is the track left by this generalized existence. And every object will be, in the first place and in some respect, a natural object, made up of colors, tactile and auditory qualities, in so far as it is destined to enter my life. Just as nature finds its way to the core of my personal life and becomes inextricably linked with it, so behaviour patterns settle into that nature, being deposited in the form of a cultural world. . . . The cultural world is then ambiguous, but it is already present. I have before me a society to be known.[116]

The notion of a pre-objective life *to be* lived, or of "a society *to be* known," is important.[117] For the reflection upon the gaps of life, as construed by Hejinian earlier, consists of two related steps: a "looking behind" in terms of the recovery of the forgotten information, followed by a "stepping forward" in terms of the discovery of newly structured ideas. As a phenomenological move toward a life yet to be experienced, this "stepping forward" also takes the form of Hejinian's poetics of description or Merleau-Ponty's phenomenology understood as direct description, whereby

> objective thought works [round the body of human experience or the perceived body], but without being called upon to postulate its completed analysis. As for consciousness, it has to be conceived, no longer as a constituting consciousness and, as it were, a pure being-for-itself, but as a perceptual consciousness. . . . Through phenomenological reflection I discover vision, not as a "thinking about seeing," to use Descartes' expression, but as a gaze at grips with a visible world.[118]

However, a "*strict, technical*" descriptive gaze, argues John E. Drabinski in his study of James and Merleau-Ponty, is not without its "inherent limitations" in that the descriptive account may compromise, in its very endeavor, the experience itself; and "it is precisely for this reason," he continues, "that the Jamesian and Merleau-Pontean descriptions of experience in its original purity employ a similar twofold strategy, one side of which employs *evocative language* and the other side of which allows the phenomenon at issue to show itself *contextually*."[119] Furthermore, far from establishing a situated reasoning or a controlling perspective, as context normally does, the strategy of context in Merleau-Ponty is intended to resist conceptualization. "This is to say," specifies Drabinski, "the phenomenon of pure experience *itself* does not allow for a static and exact conceptualization; in fact, the phenomenon itself precludes such a description. Such a descriptive strategy is essential . . . so that the phenomenon at issue is brought into relief with *a minimum of conceptual violence*."[120] The Merleau-Pontean context, to put it differently, refers to the way the phenomenon shows itself, not the way it is conceptualized into fixity.

Hejinian's *My Life* demonstrates a similar compositional strategy. Take, for example, the following excerpt:

> Many who believe in English speak it. A rubber dawn for rubber tongues. Number, stutter, and curvature. In the dark traffic sounds are round and occasional, but at dawn the trilling and warbling of the cars begins, and as the sun rises the sonic rush turns airy, as if the cars had wings and the traffic was, with considerable flapping, taking off.[121]

The language, for one thing, is indeed evocative. The verbal phrase "believe in English" in the first sentence, for instance, deviates from established collocations such as "think in English" or "write in English" by mixing an act of conviction or faith ("believe") with its medium of expression ("in English"), thus turning "speak it" from a linguistic performance to a value statement. Equally ambiguous, or evocative, is the use of the word "rubber" in the second sentence. Denoting "an elastic substance" produced either "synthetically" or "by coagulating and drying the milky sap (*latex*) of various tropical plants,"[122] the term "rubber," when used as an adjective modifying, rather oddly, "dawn" and "tongues," seems to connote a sound attribute that can be described, perhaps, as "muffled" or "unclear," which then appears to be quite an appropriate description of that time of day ("dawn") and the acoustics of languages ("tongues"). With this connotation of sound through the word "rubber," the second sentence relates itself metonymically not only to "speak it" in the first but also to "stutter" in the third. In addition, since "rubber" also means "a series of games in bridge,"[123] it implicates all three words in the third sentence in terms of sequence: "Number, stutter, and curvature." The last sentence is no exception. While its focus on sound patterns during a day points to sentences one and two, its sequence of "dark-dawn-sunrise" mirrors sentence three. Furthermore, ambiguity exists in that the phrase "in the dark" also means, among others things, "uninformed; ignorant,"[124] in which case the "in the dark-at dawn-sunrise" sequence could connote a process of growth from "ignorance" to "awakening" and, finally, to "enlightenment." With evocative language blurring the established semantic boundaries, sentences form a field or landscape of meaning in that, as Clark observes in her reading of a different section in *My Life,* "one sentence does not so much *lead* to the next as it *fits* with those preceding and succeeding it in its immediate context."[125]

A poetic version of Merleau-Ponty's genetic phenomenology, Hejinian's *My Life* is written as a discovery of phenomena. It is a counter-autobiography in that it dramatizes a radical reflection upon the unreflected life, the gaps of life, brought to visibility via a critical rethinking of reflection itself as a sociocultural construct. Foregrounding the operative intentionality through a no-match between the word and the world, *My Life* opens a realm of life in which "*the rhythm of cognition,*" as the poet herself insists, lies not in "permeable constructedness" but in "love to be astonished."[126]

> The term poetry . . . can be considered synonymous with expenditure;
> it in fact signifies, in the most precise way, creation by means of loss.
>
> —Georges Bataille, "The Notion of Expenditure"

> I . . . have looked the *unintelligible* in the face, and then I was set ablaze
> by a love so great that it would be impossible for me to imagine any-
> thing that could surpass it.
>
> —Georges Bataille, "Friendship"

> *This*—major—writing will be called *writing* because it *exceeds* the *logos*
> (of meaning, lordship, presence etc.) . . . and this is "after all, super-
> fluous," for this writing must assure us of nothing, must give us no
> certitude, no result, no profit. It is absolutely adventurous, is a chance
> and not a technique.
>
> —Jacques Derrida, *Writing and Difference*

7. "Nonsense Bargains": Inversely Proportional Writing and the Poetics of "Expenditure Without Reserve" in Bruce Andrews's Work

"Let me make sense first,"[1] Bruce Andrews concludes his poem "C3B1-c" in *The Millennium Project*.[2] A part of speech intended for emphasis, the adverb "first," when contextualized as such, lets off what Georges Bataille calls "a burst of laughter."[3] This burst of laughter, in light of Jacques Derrida's reading of Bataille's notion of general economy, is "the almost-nothing into which meaning sinks, absolutely."[4] For the word "first," precisely by virtue of its semantic foregrounding of the priority of sense-making, turns an otherwise quite commonsensical statement into a nonsense, since "making sense" has become, via the ironic implication therein, an oc-casional consideration rather than a social norm, a personal choice rather than a collective mandate, a matter of a casual sequencing rather than the communicative precondition. And worse yet, not even an occasional consideration, or a personal choice, or a casual sequencing. As the last line of the poem that ends, rather laughably indeed, with the word "first" but without any punctuation, "Let me make sense first" will, procedurally speaking, never take place, the whole statement thus finding itself emptied out, turned into a pile of nonsensical and, therefore, excessive words. In this Bataillean burst of laughter, what is laughed at, then, is "the *submission* to the self-evidence of meaning," as Derrida points out, "to the force of this imperative: that there must be meaning, that nothing must be definitely lost in death," a submission that is the "essence and element of philosophy, of Hegelian ontologics."[5] In this sense, Andrews's "Let me make sense first," as the Bataillean burst of laughter, constitutes a sovereign moment in which *"the effort at rational comprehension ends in contradiction"*;[6] it articulates, in turn, a "materialism" that underwrites Andrews's poetry praxis in terms of "a mode of disorganization by means of excess, waste, and irrationality,"[7] of a Bataillean general economy whereby, to put it in Andrews's own words, "nonsense bargains."[8]

Central to the investigative project of Language poetry is, as Jerome McGann has observed, the radical critique of society and culture "at those fundamental levels of the consciousness industries: communication, writing, textual production," a critique that proceeds by taking "language to be a system of social facts and social events."[9] Under this rubric but in most explicit terms, Andrews's analytic radicalism is predicated upon two interrelated imperatives of inquiry:[10] first, "not meaning per se but the *conditions* of meaning, its membrane of *social sense*"; and second, "a systemic grasp" of the mechanisms of sense-making—that is, "of language as a kind of agenda or system of capabilities and uses."[11] Both are grounded in Andrews's equating of sense or meaning with "totality," totality being "the internal organization of society, a historically constituted social formation and its organizing principles. . . . Some overall organization of ideology or ways of making sense that underpin the variety of signifying practices or cognitive forms of that society."[12] Determined and affected by meaning as social totality, "what is communicated" or, more accurately, what can be communicated at all turns out to be "something pre-constituted, prepackaged, as if already understood . . . a previous social construction."[13] This communicability constitutes, for Andrews, "a socioeconomic system," and is itself "part of the reproduction needs of that system."[14] This being the case, "radicalism as analytic," Andrews insists, has to engage the "hidden social processes by which value or meaning gets produced" by "[getting] beyond established meaning from *within* the structure of meaning—not just bypassing it with 'experimentalism' of different kinds, but to risk it and to reveal its constructedness."[15]

Hence the corollary: the risk of losing meaning as such, to the extent that it is a critique of meaning, has to be absolute or irreversible; and

the getting beyond the established meaning, insofar as it is a questioning of the productive mechanisms of meaning, precludes any promise or
possibility of a return to meaning. In other words, to reveal meaning's
constructedness entails an unconditional rejection, without reserve, of its
foundational model. Andrews's position, thus stated, leads to a writing
that "rewrites its material"—according to the poet, "in this case: the raw
materials of a society, a collection of practices and avowals and disavowals, governed by discourse"; [16] it is a writing that "draws upon, in order to
exhaust it, the resource of meaning," as Derrida points out in his description of Bataille's writing as general economy; "With minute audacity, it
will acknowledge the rule which constitutes that which it efficaciously,
economically must deconstitute." [17]

"THE COMMUNICATIONAL SUCCESS OF A MESSAGE IS IN
DIRECT PROPORTION TO THE AMOUNT OF REDUNDANCY
IT CONTAINS," Andrews writes in *Divestiture—A*.[18] Well-informed of
developments in information theory as well as systems theory, Andrews's
pronouncement on the operational conditions of communication as restricted economy [19] brings to the fore the "resource of meaning" in any
given message.[20] The key component of this resource of meaning that Andrews has identified is redundancy. A crucial mechanism against ambiguity, confusion, or entropy of message, redundancy is defined, in William
Paulson's study, as "a ratio denoting, in effect, the portion of a message
given over to the repetition of what is already found somewhere else in
the message." [21] In his essay "Disorder, Complexity and Meaning," Henri
Atlan similarly defines redundancy as "a kind of generalization of repetition," specifying it as the "existence of constraints between elements, so
that knowledge about one of them provides automatically some knowledge
about another," thus functioning as "a measure of reduction in complexity in the description of an organized system." [22] As such, redundancy is
"both structural and functional in character," Atlan explains further in his
seminal article of 1974 titled "On a Formal Definition of Organization,"
"since structural redundancy is known to help insure reliability," [23] as is the
case with language as a communication system. With such a dual character, redundancy operates as what Paulson calls an "error-correcting code"
in communication and, when realized in ordinary language, guarantees
the punctual arrival of a qualitatively defined message by "[implying] a
certain degree of expectability or predictability built into its structure." [24]

More important, however, is Andrews's observation that the success of communication, as traditionally understood, depends upon and results from a certain ratio between meaning or message on the one hand and redundancy or repetition on the other, a ratio specified as "directly proportional" ("in direct proportion to"). In other words, the more homogeneous the content of a message is, the less likely it will be misunderstood; or, what amounts to saying the same thing, the less repetitious a piece of information is, the more ambiguous its meaning becomes. Redundancy is, in this sense, the constitutive condition of meaning or sense-making by conditioning the receiver of the message through its subtle but all-pervasive reminding. This observation, stated as a general principle, entails a more specific question: what are the forms of redundancy? Whereas "the simplest and least interesting" form of redundancy is "plain repetition," according to Paulson, the "more typical of both natural language and the error-correcting codes of communications engineers is a contextual redundancy."[25] Or, simply put, context is a form of redundancy.

It comes as no surprise that the issue of context is at the very heart of Andrews's critical inquiry. More specifically, the context in question is, for Andrews, the social context deposited in language. By approaching language as medium "in two respects: first as a sign system; second, as discourse or ideology," Andrews conceives the relationship between these two aspects in terms of "concentric circles, one inside the other."[26] "The system of signs has an Outside," Andrews writes, "a Social Context—of which it is the embodiment, the tooling, the use. (In some literal sense, the sign system embodies that social context: it does make it concrete and perceptible; it deprives it of mumbo jumbo.)"[27] Reciprocally, this "outer context limits and disciplines and naturalizes; it pins meaning down; it positions identities, setting limits to the scope of content and address."[28] From this perspective, "when the utterances are contextualized," Andrews continues, "they would point to these larger codes, this social organization of act and of performance. You're talking about underlying sign systems generating the possibilities of sense. And these are also normative systems that surround language; these are codes that are more like context in *rigor mortis*."[29]

As the underlying network of "reference" or the "prefabricated" totalizing "paradigm,"[30] social context does not only resort to simple repetition as its form of contextual redundancy in language. More pervasively and effectively, "it involves relations of structure, correlations between different elements or features of the message," observes Paulson, ranging from the set positions of the letters Q and U in English to the agreement of subject and verb endings in French, among other examples.[31] In this sense, social context finds its form of contextual redundancy in language itself as a social contract, the items of which (grammar, syntax, word choice, etc.) define the identity and social status of anyone who enters it. All-binding, this social contract as contextual redundancy constitutes, by being deposited in, what Norman Fairclough terms "Members' Resources" and operates chiefly in the form of error-correcting codes[32] whose moving into action reminds one, as Andrews realizes, of the *"circumstance"* of which *"we are embodiments."*[33] As Andrews's ratio of direct proportion between redundancy and message dictates, the more knowledgeable one is of the specific items of the social contract, the better one understands the social message. Or, what amounts to saying the same thing, the poorer one's Members' Resources are, the more difficult it is for one to make sense. Contextual redundancy, in this light, is the constitutive condition of meaning or sense-making by conditioning the members of a given society through its all-pervasive, contractual mediation. "Context constitutes. / Defense of the Code," writes Andrews, "Context crowds, pushy context—no landscape can hide."[34]

Furthermore, Andrews locates this sociolinguistic phenomenon of contextual redundancy specifically in the convention of communication, which he describes as follows:

> Practice takes place within these systems of convention, and they're what make meaning possible—both linguistically (in terms of signification, or the structure of the sign), but also more broadly, socially (as value, or sense). So that the dialogues and the layerings of voices and the ploys of communication, and rhetoric, utterances, are bound up by the coercive social limits of the possible. They're socially governed. That governing takes the shape of rules that are being followed or a context that's being adapted to—a context in light of which certain actions "make sense."[35]

What is more important in the above passage is Andrews's view of dialogue or communication as not only socially governed but also strategically deployed. In other words, communication or dialogue presents a game structure. For the word "ploys," while highlighting, denotatively as well as connotatively, social sense or meaning as both "arbitrary" (it is a game) and "systematic" (it has rules),[36] also resonates with Paulson's observation of the "relations of structure" and the "correlations between different elements or features of message" as forms of contextual redundancy. It identifies, by implication, the communication model Andrews has mentioned earlier as a construct, as a well-orchestrated game, with a built-in mechanism guaranteeing communicational success by sustaining the directly proportional ratio between message and redundancy.

The critique of the traditional transmission theory of communication begins with an intensified awareness of its structure. When introducing Language poetry in "Language Sampler," Charles Bernstein points out, for instance, that the communication model under scrutiny is one "schematized as a two-way wire with the message shuttling back and forth in blissful ignorance of the (its) transom (read: ideology)."[37] It is a model consisting of, as Steve McCaffery specifies, "a transmission-reception by two individual, reflective consciousnesses."[38] This dichotomized construct, together with its working mechanism that makes "blissful ignorance" possible, has received a structural analysis from Michel Serres, an analysis that suggests a theoretical resonance to Andrews's reading of redundancy as the constitutive condition of communication.

In "Platonic Dialogue,"[39] Serres presents a critique of the traditional communication model represented by the title of his essay. He calls attention to the conditions of communicational success by bringing into visibility that which must be eliminated first, and which he subsumes under the umbrella term of "pathology of communication": "cacography" in writing, and mispronunciations in speaking, among many other examples.[40] To communicate, in this sense, is always to risk losing meaning in various pathological complications generically referred to as noise, noise being defined more specifically as "the set of these phenomena of interference that become obstacles to communication."[41] Also personified as "the third man" and "the demon,"[42] noise is the "empirical portion of the message," according to Serres;[43] and the elimination of the empirical "is at the same time the condition of the apprehension of the abstract form," which is the logical or meaningful portion of the message, "and the condition of the success of communication."[44] As such, *the first effort to make communication successful in a dialogue,* Serres points out, *is isomorphic to the effort to render a form independent of its empirical realizations.*[45] In other words, successful communication pivots on minimizing noises or differentiation and maximizing redundancy or homogeneity within its system.

This is achieved by way of a game-structure, Serres asserts; and the phenomenon of "the message shuttling back and forth in blissful ignorance of its transom" belies a dialectic formation. Successful communication is possible, argues Serres, because

such communication is a sort of game played by two interlocutors considered as united against the phenomena of interference and confusion. . . . These interlocutors are in no way opposed, as in the traditional conception of the dialectic game; on the contrary, they are on the same side, tied together by a mutual interest: they battle together against noise. . . . [They] exchange their reciprocal roles in dialogue, where the source becomes reception, and the reception source. . . . They exchange roles sufficiently often for us to view them as struggling together against a common enemy. *To hold a dialogue is to suppose a third man and to seek to exclude him;* a successful communication is the exclusion of the third man. The most profound dialectical problem is not the problem of the Other, who is only a variety—or variation—of the Same, it is the problem of the third man. We might call this third man the *demon,* the prosopopeia of noise. . . . Dialectic makes the two interlocutors play on the same side; they do battle together to produce a truth on which they can agree, that is, to produce a successful communication.[46]

Serres's observation presents a revisionist re-reading of the traditional concept of dialectics in the transmission theory of communication by relocating the site of the dialectic play. The exchange between the two interlocutors, whatever its nature (discussion, debate, disagreement, etc.) and to whatever degree (profound, slight, heated, etc.), is always circumscribed by a shared politics of production and a mutual interest in generating something useful or meaningful. Masked by this exchange is the dialectic structure, which is established, in actuality, between the two interlocutors on the one side and noise on the other. Such a remapping of dialectics is significant in two respects. First, it foregrounds the position of noise in terms of servitude within the dialectic structure. For communication to be successful, then, noise has to be first "supposed" and then "excluded": supposed in order to be excluded. Viewed from this perspective, noise indeed "cannot be spoken of," as Derrida contends, "nor has it ever been except in this fabric of meaning"; and, as such, noise as negativity "is always the underside and accomplice of positivity" or meaning.[47] Second, the supposition of noise and its concomitant imperative to exclude it entail a viable strategy to execute the exclusion, and this strategy is that of maximizing redundancy. In Serres's re-reading, this maximizing redundancy finds its formal expression in a structural doubling, in that, of the two interlocutors, the Other is not opposed to the Same but is a variation of the Same, and they are on the same side, united with each other in their battling against noise, joining their effort "in the task of giving birth"[48]—that is, to produce meaning, to make sense.

Serres's reconfiguration of the relationship between the two interlocutors as allies, whose united front itself constitutes the mechanism of contextual redundancy generating and sustaining an agreement on truth by overcoming noise, unveils the dichotomized terms of source and reception as more than just fixed and separated from each other; they are, in essence, the same, reciprocally defined. The social ramification of Serres's model becomes clearer when read in light of Steve McCaffery's exegesis of the transmission theory of communication in terms of "social need." McCaffery writes:

> Communication consists of the transmission of information from a source to a receptor across a space; the context of that communication being proposed as an exchange between producers and consumers, speakers and listeners, media and masses. Hypostatizing both a subject and an object, this theory fixes them as isolated terms in an abstract formula, inserting a notion of need as the necessary link between them. A circular system of power is thus generated by a copula of need. The ideological base of this need was recognized long ago by Hegel in his analysis of the master-slave relationship in *The Phenomenology of Mind.* The need is not a biological need, but a masked social formation linking subject and object terms for the preservation of the abstract structure. . . . In actuality, this need is *not* anterior to the specific act but inheres within the very structure of communication as presented.[49]

As social totality, to elaborate it further, meaning or social sense is always presented in and through a self-generating and self-validating system of communication, in which the "abstract structure" (or Serres's "abstract form")—that is, meaning or logic—is preserved by its own built-in mechanism of contextual redundancy. This redundancy is embodied by the two interlocutors as active constituents of society and is maximized by their being copulated into a unified social formation of power against noise. To make sense at all, or to communicate successfully, one therefore must collaborate with one's Other, who is none other than the social Same, in the name of a shared social need to preserve socially sanctioned sense.

Andrews's own writing, poetic or critical, shows an informed awareness of this formal doubling as the mechanism of contextual redundancy against noise. "Other is Context," he thus states, rather pointedly—"not this localized backdrop of melodrama. The first person pronoun takes its place in line."[50] Further, his concern in this regard is reflected in his intensified attention to the politics as well as the methodology of innovative writing. "I find it troublesome," he writes in "Total Equals What: Poetics and Praxis," "that the whole notion of politics involved with writing is being narrowed down to specific struggles toward change, while the contexts that are actually directly implicated in the use of writing are ignored."[51] Without a careful and thorough critique of context, as Andrews seems to say, change would remain only in name, no matter how political the initial objective is or how innovative writing can be. Since context constitutes sense, socially, Andrews argues, "Context needs a Contest"[52] and, accordingly, innovative writing should move toward "a more critical (or contextual) focus on meaning itself."[53] Andrews's own position in this respect indeed exemplifies his radicalism as analytic, which he clarifies when he writes:

> The overall shape of making sense needs to be reframed, restaged, put back into a context of "pre-sense"—to reveal its constructed character; to reveal by critique, by demythologizing. Otherwise, its apparent immediacy dupes us: the lack of distance is a kind of closure.[54]

Stated as such, Andrews's position can be read in many ways as Bataillean. For one thing, it emphasizes an "overall" approach—that is, a critical rethinking of sense so radical and absolute as to "risk its loss," as McCaffery puts it, "accompany it to its limit and in the slide of [sense] throw [it] into question."[55] For another, the "re-" prefix, used here to signify Andrews's approach, does not denote "again, "anew," or "over again,"[56] which would mean the "return" of sense, of meaning, of the conversion of the negative to the positive. Rather, it should be understood in light of the past participial phrase "put back into a context of 'pre-sense.'" This phrase, in a manner similar to "Let me make sense first," again presents a Bataillean burst of laughter, a sovereign gesture whereby "context," as a network of indices generating possibilities of sense, is linked—possessively, appositionally, qualitatively, among other definitions ("of")—with "pre-sense," which denotes its own absence. For yet another, to reveal the constructed character of sense and sense-making, Andrews points out, one has to go all the way ("the lack of distance is a kind of closure"), to "the point of no-return of destruction"; that is, to the point of "the absolute sacrifice of meaning: a sacrifice without return and without reserves."[57] Any measure short of that would result in a foreclosure, leading back to "immediacy," to "blissful ignorance." It follows, then, that Andrews's own innovative writing, as he himself states in the essay "Poetry as Explanation, Poetry as Praxis," aims not at re-comprehension, or new comprehension, or different comprehension, but "Incomprehension."[58]

Andrews's Bataillean emphasis on incomprehension can be read as making two related statements. First, formally innovative writing, Andrews seems to argue, departs radically from the traditional form of communication as a submission to the socio-ideological imperative of sense-making, to the metaphysical self-evidence of meaning. As a social critique and philosophical rethinking of Hegelian dialectics, it emphasizes incomprehension "because it can no longer permit itself to be converted into positivity," as Derrida explains it, and "because it can no longer *collaborate* with the continuous linking-up of meaning, concept, time and truth in discourse."[59] Second, in view of Andrews's critical awareness of contextual redundancy in terms of a formal doubling in communication and his insistence on looking into the "constructed character" of the "overall shape of making sense," his focus on incomprehension, as is evidenced in his particularly dense textual opacity, seems also to have implicated the reader as the one who, hermeneutically or otherwise, carries out the continuous linking-up of meaning, a reader who, as the contextual double, continues to play the dual and reciprocal role of both the source and receptor in relation to a given text.[60]

That being the case, Andrews's writing foregrounding incomprehension presents itself as what might be called an inversely proportional writing. It is an inversely proportional writing in that it rewrites the directly proportional ratio between message and redundancy by refusing to collaborate with a contextual Other, who is the reader, as the co-producer of meaning. This refusal to collaborate with a fellow interlocutor, to participate in the social game of communication with its own double, dissolves the united front necessary in the joined battle against noise and, as a result, increases the power of noise by radically reducing the amount of contextual redundancy imperative to sense-making. In this way, Andrews's inversely proportional writing bodies forth a powerfully radical critique of contextual redundancy as the structural-functional mechanism of sense-making. It calls into question, in particular, the politics of reader participation as a communicative reinscription of Serres's model of the Platonic dialogue. For this politics is grounded in "a humanization of the reader . . . anthropologized as a 'person'" rather than "seen structurally as a theoretical location in a textual activity,"[61] and in a romantic empowerment of the reader privileged, under the mask of democracy, as the returning contextual Other who is immune, somehow, to all social-linguistic constraints rather than perceived relationally as a sociolinguistic positioning in a communicative paradigm. Uncollaborative and, therefore, unproductive, Andrews's inversely proportional writing can thus be approached as a different kind of communication, one that recognizes both the writer and the reader as none other than socio-structural terms in a textual conspiracy of meaning (re)production. It becomes, as such, what McCaffery describes as "sovereign communication," a communication in which the inversely proportional ratio between message and redundancy leads to a "mutual impenetrability" between the writer and the reader.[62] In his critique of the constructedness of meaning or sense, Andrews's inversely proportional writing indeed carries his demythologization to the point of no return of destruction, as its "communicative act involves the destruction of the communication model" itself, to put it in McCaffery's words again, "a simultaneous (and frequently momentary) cancellation of both reader and writer as isolated beings in a communication that rises above, and indeed obliterates, the beings who communicate."[63] With the mechanism of contextual redundancy thus destroyed, what is left in Andrews's inversely proportional writing as sovereign communication, then, is the song of the sirens.

"Nonsense bargains," the poet writes. As the word "bargain" denotes, Andrews's inversely proportional writing, in which nonsense or noise has moved from its previous position of the excluded demon to a bargaining position at the negotiating table where it tries to "get the best possible terms" or to make "agreement,"[64] dramatizes a different kind of economy. It is an economy that resonates, rather explicitly, with Bataille's notion of general economy, one that he defines as the science or theory of sovereignty:

> The question of this *general economy* is situated on the plain of the *political economy*. . . . The *general economy* makes evident in the first

place that a surplus of energy is produced that, by definition, cannot be used. Excess energy can only be lost without the slightest goal, in consequence without any meaning. It is this useless, senseless loss that *is* sovereignty.[65]

This notion of writing as general economy featuring loss and non-utility is similarly articulated by Andrews in his discussion of sound in poetry.[66] In his article titled *"Praxis:* A Political Economy of Noise and Informalism,"[67] for instance, Andrews argues that innovative praxis, as exemplified in this case by what he calls "informal composition," "involves less *communication* (the making dissimilar—or fixed—of the similar), and more *counter-communication* (the making similar—or fluid—of the dissimilar)."[68] This premise is predicated upon his systemic grasp of writing as a communication system sustained by a directly proportional ratio between meaning and redundancy. "The more systematized the writing," Andrews points out, "the more it risks turning into a sleek hypostatizing of means, a correct (and corrective) command structure, a determinacy of fate, in which tautology, redundancy, or homogeneity make individuation superfluous."[69] By contrast, inversely proportional writing foregrounds "deformation" rather than "information" in an absolute way, Andrews contends, "a universalizing of tension, stoking chaos, by denser (and freer) articulation."[70] It is a writing that stages "a figuration of irreconcilability"[71]—that is, a figuration of "catastrophe" and "noise."[72] Situated on the level of political economy, inversely proportional writing as general economy thus communicates only to "make it impossible for any pleasingly meaningful whole to be contracted"; for "the givenness of norms and materials (the relations of literary production) becomes deformed by the forces of production (new sounds, techniques, the foregrounding of dissonance)."[73]

In a strikingly Bataillean fashion, Andrews then goes on to describe in detail his inversely proportional writing in which nonsense or noise wins the bargain and reigns:

> Noise as wayward, unregimented sound. Or seemingly meaningless, random fluctuations in data—not the "managed data" that defines information. Too irregular, or pumped up with excess timbral richness, its overtones untameable in harmonic terms, undercutting expectations of determinate pitch (or, in our case, of a representational determinacy and bolstering). A free play that the equivocal, undefinitive quality of sound units in language makes possible—as long as they

are not recruited as doubling echoes, indentured to stable systems of stable meaning. Noise as chaos. . . . By means of Noise: to disrupt the flow of communication, to create extreme libidinalized density, to approach "white noise." . . . Noise—as freely composed dissonance, and untimely mimesis of shock. To reject the untouchability of auratic beauty. To disturb automatism, to estrange and displace, to burst the binding of current usage. Here, new forces of production (noise) having shaken up the older aestheticized relations of production (conventions of harmoniousness or lyric voicing, for example) can intimate new methods of configuration—even ones that actively subvert their own ground. . . . Contagion as negation may give us a better feel for this manic relationism.[74]

Consistent throughout this passage is Andrews's Bataillean position that noise or nonsense is the means, but it is the means to an end that is none other than itself. In its "free play" that is the absolute slide of meaning, noise is not to be converted into servitude to which is subordinated, dialectically, the formal doubling as contextual redundancy ("not recruited as doubling echoes, indentured to stable systems of stable meaning"); and its forces of production remain counterproductive since they are aimless ("undercutting expectations") and deconstructive ("can intimate new methods of configuration . . . that actively subvert their own ground"). In Andrews's inversely proportional writing, negation does not lead to affirmation; much to the contrary, it demands its own permanent residency or presence without offering the reader any contextual negotiability over its naturalization or conversion ("may give us a better feel for this manic relationism").

Andrews's poetry as inversely proportional writing becomes, in this sense, "The Apparatus of Loss," as Jerome McGann aptly puts it in the title of his article on Andrews's work.[75] It is a writing that "outruns limits," observes Jed Rasula, and "overflows into the extremities."[76] As the critique of "text as context" or "text as seizure by context,"[77] Andrews's poetic text presents itself as the contesting ground for context.

Published in 1999, one of Andrews's poetry books is titled, rather suggestively, *Ex-Communicate*. The lettering of the word is obviously intended for two different readings. On the one hand, it can be read as a hyphenated compound word, with the *ex-* prefix meaning, among others, "beyond," "away from, out of," "without, not having," and "former, previous, previously."[78] Whichever the case, the prefix clearly identifies the poetry book

under this title as having changed its function from previous communication to current non-communication. On the other hand, the title can be
read as a word denoting "to exclude, by an act of ecclesiastical authority,
from the sacraments, rights, and privileges of a church; censure by cutting
off from communion with a church"[79]—that is, to exclude from the logos
of meaning, lordship, and presence. This being the case, the question then
becomes who or what is excommunicated. The answer seems to have been
implied in the way the text is composed. Take, for example, the following
excerpt:

adhesive lungs

                                                citizen
          solitude   genetic
          of the S   fanshen
                                                guitar
                                                viking

                    A B A B
                    B B A A
                    A C A C
                    C C A A[80]

From single letter ("S") to letter combination ("ABAB"), from individual word ("solitude") to isolated phrase ("adhesive lungs"), from English
vocabulary ("citizen") to Chinese phonetic transcription ("fanshen"), from
random typography to visual and acoustic patterning ("ABAB / BBAA"),
this text exhibits a poem of what Andrews refers to earlier as "pre-sense."
It foregrounds "incomprehension" in that "it multiplies words," as Derrida accurately says, "precipitates them one against the other, engulfs them
too, in an endless and baseless substitution whose only rule is the sovereign affirmation of the play outside meaning."[81] Such a text, as sovereign
communication, indeed does not communicate; it exemplifies an inversely
proportional writing, as it has rewritten the directly proportional ratio
between meaning and contextual redundancy by exhausting the resource
of the latter—that is, by refusing to recognize, much less collaborate with,
the reader as its double, its contextual Other, in their joined effort to
make sense. This refusal to acknowledge the reader as the co-producer of
meaning, as the comrade-in-arms in fighting against noise, is particularly
manifested in the fact that the text provides little or no contextual residue
conducive to the reader's interpretative maneuverability. It stages, instead,

a figuration of irreconcilability so intense as to make anyone attempting to decipher it keenly aware of his or her own extremely forced or far-fetched constructedness due to a contextual poverty. Having erased the reader as an interlocutor, such a text leads, as a consequence, to the simultaneous erasure of the writer as the initial communicator. With the cancellation of both the reader and the writer as the two communicative terms constitutive of contextual redundancy guaranteeing the safe arrival of the message against noise, the text becomes excessive, overrun by nonsense. The same holds true for the following excerpt from *Ex-Communicate*:

> stole what want after exactly
> Some nights was legged
> is the I I live
> blue of facts corsets
> Capital
> Farthest
> Drowsy
> Mystify
> jitterbug some + yours to you
> possibility off-kilter of events in common
> tucked anecdote becomes you
> spite without consort
> Humbling Incline Throats
> mass ornamental arrogant misnomer
> razor edge little plugs
> <u>driven to the hum</u>

This text, similar to the previous one, delineates the strange shape into which excess or nonsense, as Derrida observes, has folded discourse.[82] It is the shape of inversely proportional writing in its active "self-dispersal"[83] into the "absolute non-discourse," one in which words "are not there in order to *mean* something, to enounce or to signify, but in order to make sense slide, to denounce it or to deviate from it."[84] More importantly, the textual impenetrability therein, by virtue of its being impenetrable, "opens the question of meaning" rather than simply enacts "the loss of meaning."[85] And this "opening the question of meaning," which is Andrews's critical objective, is executed precisely at the site of context or contextual redundancy brought upon the text by the reader skilled in a socially sanctioned reading practice, be it formal, historical, or metonymic. "Meaning is not produced *by* the sign," Andrews reiterates, "but by the contexts we bring to the potentials of language."[86] To approach Andrews's poetry as inversely proportional writing, one has to remain vigilant against the seduction and coercion of contextual framing—that is, one has to be on guard against oneself, first and foremost, as one of the constitutive terms of contextual redundancy.

In a way applicable to reading Andrews, Derrida summarizes this polemic in his reading of Bataille in terms of "two dangerous straits":

> [One] must not isolate notions as if they were their own context, as if one could immediately understand what the content of words like "experience," "interior," "mystic," "word," "material," "sovereign," etc. *means.* Here, the error would consist in taking as an immediate given of reading the blindness to a traditional culture which itself wishes to be taken as the natural element of discourse. But inversely, one must not submit contextual attentiveness and differences of signification to a *system of meaning* permitting or promising an absolute formal mastery. This would amount to erasing the excess of nonmeaning and to falling back into the closure of knowledge: would amount, once more, to not reading Bataille.[87]

This would amount to not reading Andrews either, whose particularly opaque or unintelligible texts have hitherto quite succeeded in calling attention to these two present and immediate dangers of linking up meaning contextually. The form of this contextual linking-up of meaning can be resisted, Andrews has proposed, by way of a different kind of reading. The "*most* language-oriented of 'language poets,'" Andrews, as Jed Rasula has pointed out, foregrounds in his writing the problem of "the status of language" as the sociolinguistic mechanism of systematization and contextualization at various levels.[88] "Our medium is not a warehouse of styles," the poet asserts, "it's the way signs are already ordered into social codes, into meaning making and mediating."[89] Situated from within this network of social codes, inversely proportional writing, and one's reading of it, have to be carried out as a re-reading, argues Andrews. More specifically, it is a "*rereading* [of] the reading that a social status quo puts [one] through," a re-reading whereby "to make social process visible; to revoke licenses; to ignite unimaginability."[90] In sum, it is a re-reading by way of "de-outfitting the *context.*"[91]

As the defining feature of his inversely proportional writing, Andrews's

re-reading as de-outfitting the context resonates with Derrida's two postulates of "must not." First, it points to the reader as a sociolinguistic term
of contextual redundancy in sense-making, calling into question a much-
overlooked phenomenon in one's reading practice—that is, the manner in
which meaning is linked up contextually. This phenomenon is described
by Andrews earlier as "apparent immediacy" or, in Derrida's words, as
immediate understanding ("immediately understand") of notions or concepts. However phrased, this immediacy, Andrews contends, marks a social process, articulating a "social grasp of the body of words and associations and addresses."[92] It is none other than the effect of social context
made readily present by the reader actively engaged in playing the dual
role of source and receptor, thus constructing a contextual double that
outfits a redundancy directly proportional to the social message. So much
so that this immediacy, also referred to by Andrews as "lack of distance,"
"dupes" one by rendering transparent or natural a socially licensed hermeneutics and an ideologically sanctioned perception or imaginability. In
other words, immediacy as such represents a form of social licensing, and
what it permits is closure, granting nothing new or unique but only "something pre-constituted, prepackaged, as if already understood . . . a previous social construction."[93] From this perspective, to understand immediately the contents of words in Andrews's inversely proportional writing is
to automatically link up meaning by reinscribing, through the very act of
understanding, contextual redundancy as the meaning-making mechanism, socio-ideological as well as communicative, back into Andrews's text
which is itself the very critique of that mechanism. For the "content" of
each word in Andrews's excerpt above, such as "Capital," "Drowsy," and
"Mystify," when understood immediately in its received and presumed
significance, socially "gives orders to make order content."[94] At the most
fundamental level of sense-making, Andrews's inversely proportional writing thus exercises the revoking of social licenses camouflaged as literacy
and individual capability, favoring a Bataillean willingness to let meaning
slide, to waste, to un-understand, over the socially programmed automa-
tion to make sense, to produce, to understand.

Second, Andrews's re-reading as de-outfitting the context implicates
the reader as the methodological term of contextual redundancy in sense-
making, calling into question, then, a much-preferred method in tack-
ling avant-garde poetry—that is, the structural or formalist approach,
whereby meaning is reconstructed systematically through establishing a

set of newly perceived interrelations, be they visual, acoustic, or lexical. The production of meaning, Andrews has pointed out from early on, is characterized by two features: it "isn't just arbitrary (in the way the structure of the sign would suggest) but . . . also systematic."[95] Sense-making is systematic, Andrews argues, because it is "based on these conventions," linguistic as well as social, on "the methods by which meaning arrives in a prefabricated way."[96] Therefore, meaning is always already a system of meaning, the context of which, insofar as it permits or promises an absolute formal mastery of textual units, is the "social system."[97] As such, the linking-up of meaning in the formalist reconstruction of sense amounts to, at its best, reshuffling or, to put it in Andrews's own words, "relocating those units within the largest totalizing of this context."[98] It is, in fact, another form of immediacy, of lack of distance, which presents a false appearance of objective distancing through its seemingly autonomous systematization. As much creative as it is ingenious, a formalist approach can thus be described as implicitly articulating nothing more than a socially licensed imaginability.

Hence the paradox: Andrews's inversely proportional writing, as formal innovation intended to investigate as well as to critique the constructedness of meaning from within the system of meaning, rejects absolutely any formalist or structural reappropriation. "Valorizing form has its limits," Andrews announces.[99] Furthermore, "if something's going to be disruptive, or disrupted" in order to "[lay] bare the device" of sense-making, Andrews insists, "it's going to have to be *method*," and formalist method in particular, "seen in a more social way—as the social organization of signs, as ideology, as discourse," rather than some "preppie formalism."[100] His disruption of method as a formal system, which corresponds to Derrida's second postulate of "must not," finds its expression in a composition described as "informalist" or "informal."[101] Working from within the text-context concentric circle, Andrews's inversely proportional writing is informalist in that it rejects "the simpler *buttoning-down* of overall reference" on the one hand and "refuses any projective resolution of social contradiction" on the other.[102] In other words, it resists being restructured back into any meaning system, into the closure of knowledge. This informalist resistance is realized, then, by de-outfitting the context through a re-reading, a re-reading, that is, of one's own initial reading as contextual framing, as a formal display or systematic mapping of a socio-discursively disciplined imaginability.

Consider the following excerpt from *Ex-Communicate:*

meter hat hand lit gone little

gargoyle stuff

bit nipples clay <u>buick</u> outvote

is clear

abracadabra

garrulous

carp turnstiles

is paint

<u>E</u>

One's initial reading of this excerpt, as a trained hermeneutic movement, proceeds immediately to establish a system of signification. The
overall reference therein, for instance, can be buttoned down, without
much delay, on "gargoyle stuff." With that in view, the whole excerpt falls
into two parts: the first four lines devoted to the description of the physical appearance of the "gargoyle stuff," while the second five lines, to that
of the sound its spouting water makes. In the first part, the shape of the
grotesquely carved water spout is portrayed as a fantastic hybrid, an aggregate of what looks like instruments ("meter," "lit"), human figures ("hat,"
"hand,"), animal bodies ("bit nipples"), and vehicles ("clay *buick*"), among
others. Whatever seems ambiguous, such as "gone," "little," or "outvote,"
is in fact very "clear," as each contributes rather appropriately, through its
own very ambiguity, to a shape so grotesque as to be depicted at the best
as no more than just "stuff." In the second part, the description of the
sound as endless and unpleasant takes on an emotionally negative overtone, ranging from gibberish ("abracadabra") to loquacious ("garrulous"),
personified further as the complaint ("carp") made by a turnstile as the
result of its fresh "paint," which produces a particular kind of sharp or
squeaky sound emphatically compared to and illustrated by that of the
letter "*E*." Such a reading, complete with its contextual framing, structural patterning, and metonymical linking, brings to this excerpt a system
of meaning, reproducing visually and acoustically a cultural icon. It thus
dramatizes what might be referred to, in a social sense, as an encore—also
as "on call"—presentation of the social organization of signs into ideology
and discourse, one that in turn signals, according to Andrews, a successful
social suture.[103] In brief, it exhibits this system of meaning as the social
ready-made.

It is this kind of reading that has to be re-read, Andrews claims. Central to Andrews's re-reading is to demythologize the constructed character of any system of meaning as contextless or self-governing. Andrews brings this point to the fore, focusing on the following two aspects:

> "Meaning" [and a system of meaning in particular] seems to govern itself, according to certain rules and within certain limits—not so coercive looking, not so blatantly "unfree." But the usual romantic view of the weightlessness and self-policing of the subject has disturbing parallels with a supposedly self-policing and weightless formalism of the sign. *Both* ignore the outer social context and its network of power relations.[104]

In addition, the network of power relations of the social context is ignored because it is grounded in a mechanism outfitting contextual redundancy by identifying the reader simultaneously as both the source and receptor in communication. To put it differently, a system of meaning is such only insofar as its own product and producer are one and the same in the social process of meaning construction. Andrews summarizes this view from an Althusserean perspective:

> This body of sense and ideology works to socialize. It acts on meanings the way it acts on individuals: it makes whatever you took to be your meaning into a "subject," a control center. It constructs what is celebrated as the individual as a support system for itself: that's interpellation, subjection, enrollment, or recruitment—the offering of incentives—where society sells itself to its own products, constituting and reconstituting its vehicles, its (purportedly free) receivers. Socialization works by means of such a naming—and reading—society *reading* its subjects into light, into action.[105]

In this sense, Andrews's inversely proportional writing indeed cannot be read but only re-read. Furthermore, in order to re-read the reading that the social status quo puts one through, one has to re-read, first and foremost, oneself as a social term of contextual redundancy in sense-making; one has to re-read one's own identity as a reading subject in system-building, Andrews observes, "recognizing its stereotyping and containment: how it's set up and positioned within" any systems of meaning.[106] Andrews's re-reading, in this light, means "getting distance on the sign and getting distance on identity, on how they're produced."[107] At the methodological level of sense-making, Andrews's inversely proportional writing is thus committed to revealing social process as always a system-building process, to igniting unimaginability, so to speak, privileging a Bataillean politics of system failure over the socio-ideological apparatuses of systematization.

Innovative writing is, Andrews argues, a "self-questioning, a 'hermeneusis of itself and its own activity'" and, as such, it "needs to reach as far as the workings of the social sphere itself."[108] It should "make as visible as possible the limits and norms and operations of the machinery. To show the *possibilities* of sense and meaning being constructed; to foreground the limits of the possible—and our possible lives; to create impossibility."[109] Focusing on the social machinery of communication, Andrews's work implements this "self-questioning" by ex-communicating from its text the traditional communication model itself, with the communicative act posited as it is sacrificed. This is achieved by way of an inversely proportional writing that rewrites the established ratio between meaning and redundancy through a radical critique of the socially constitutive terms of sense-making in communication. The resultant incomprehension, or the impossibility so created, may thus be read as articulating what Bataille calls "ecstasy,"[110] which is itself a form of communication. More specifically, it is a communication which "takes a value that the terms involved did not yet have," Bataille continues, very poetically; "it annihilates, in a sense, these terms in the same way as the luminous glow of a star (slowly) annihilates the star itself, as well as the objects that are so close as to be profoundly modified by the constant metamorphosis of the star into heat and light."[111]

And so is Andrews's poetry as inversely proportional writing.

Method finds its form in speed, and this speed is itself in some ways a consequence of mathematics.

—Bruno Latour, with Michel Serres, *Conversations on Science, Culture, and Time*

The speed of light protects the reality of things by guaranteeing that the images we have of them are contemporaneous. The plausibility of a causal universe would disappear with some appreciable change in this speed. All things would interfere in total disaster. This is the extent to which this speed is our referent, our God, and for us represents the absolute. If the speed of light becomes relative, then no more transcendence, no more God to recognize his own, and the universe lapses into indeterminacy.

—Jean Baudrillard, *Selected Writings*

Competitions of speed . . . coercive and compulsive, efficacious and effective, beginning at the same particular place and leading to the monotonous, uniform, unchanged and identical same dot.

—Steve McCaffery, *Theory of Sediment*

8. "Slowed Reason" as "Idling Language": Postmodern Counter-Speed and the Poetics of Sediment in Charles Bernstein

Among the works of the Language poets, Charles Bernstein's poetry is, as Jerome McGann has pointed out, "(in)famous for its difficulty."[1] Its elusiveness has indeed succeeded, to date, in holding its ground against the powerful arsenal of contemporary critical theory, not to mention approaches built with "an informational or communicative or representational framework."[2] Although, very much like Lyn Hejinian's *My Life*, Bernstein's poems often consist of catalogues of routine quotidian or collages of cultural cliché, such as "the language of movies, the style of stand-up comedy, and the language of business," which bring with them an air of familiarity and, therefore, a seeming communicability, any attempt to encode and decode his poems would lead to what Hank Lazer calls a "self-canceling irony."[3] This hermeneutic bewilderment, when viewed from the critical perspective established in this study, finds its cause not so much in a sophistry alluded to by the title of one of the poet's books, as in an acutely critical disposition with regard to the nature and function of method in relation to writing.

In "Writing and Method" Bernstein, with a critical sensitivity akin to that of Bruce Andrews, raises the issue of what he calls "the centrality of method," or "the basicness of method."[4] Recognizing that "the genre or style of a writing practice becomes centrally a question of method, rather than a transparent given of form,"[5] he argues for a rethinking of method that probes into its social grounding. "All writing is a demonstration of method," Bernstein writes. "In this sense, style and mode are always at issue, for all styles are socially mediated conventions open to reconvening at any time."[6] In traditional forms of writing, as is the case with "the contemporary expository mode" more specifically,[7] he continues, "the question of method [is] suppressed," made to appear neutral or invisible, precisely because it represents a "social governance" and "because it effectively did the business of the society's vested interests."[8] To write, in this sense, is to methodize information material at the service of the social control, for "all methods are coercive," Bernstein contends, "in that they have a relation to power."[9]

With this understanding, Bernstein, à la Laura (Riding) Jackson, calls for a critical inquiry into method, an investigation, that is, of "the limits of meaning and the limits of our forms of trying to mean."[10] The focal point of this investigation is, as Bernstein asserts in his reading of Montaigne, the "methodological awareness of the implications of style," or the "methodological assumptions" which, as evidenced in "'self' writing," "both invest it with a domain of descriptive and explanatory power and also set its limits."[11] Thus, Bernstein's poetic-philosophical *project of investigating the possibilities (nature) and structures of phenomena* is urgently predicated on an imperative, which is to investigate "either the implications of the larger modality or its methodological assumptions."[12]

For Bernstein, this critical investigation of the methodological assumptions is further contextualized in concrete writing practices as forms of social methods of legitimation, and it is carried out at two different but related levels: discursive on the one hand, and socio-philosophical on the other. Discursively, Bernstein calls into question the method of "standardization" whereby forms of writing and meanings are socially determined and sanctioned.[13] He writes, from a Foucauldian perspective:

But the crucial mechanism to keep in mind is not the rules of current preferred forms versus possible alternatives *but the mechanism of distinction and discrimination itself* that allows for certain language practices to be legitimated (as correct, clear, coherent) and other language practices to be discredited (as wrong, vague, nonsensical, antisocial, ambiguous, irrational, illogical, crude, dumb . . .). . . . It is not, then, the intrinsic meaning of the particular distinction that is crucial, not, that is, the particular standard but standardization itself.[14]

Socio-philosophically, Bernstein calls for a de-neutralization of method as given by exposing it as a construct of social power, and for a philosophical exploration and critique of method as a determining and determined mechanism. Bernstein writes:

Part of the task of a history of social forms would be to bring into visibility as chosen instruments of power what is taken as neutral or given. Part of the task of an active poetry or philosophy is to explore these instruments by a critique of their partiality and to develop alternatives to them that can serve as models of truth and meaning not dependent for their power on the dominating structures.[15]

That being the case, "what is being suggested," Bernstein concludes in his essay on "Writing and Method," is that method, as such, "be brought into view, a critique which has potentially liberating effect."[16]

In his own writing practice, Bernstein's critique of method can be seen as centered on one specific aspect of the standardization of language: speed, which defines the efficacy of language as an instrument of communication, as an effective system of exchange, and as a transparent medium of knowledge. In his "particular passion" to move poetry "beyond the twentieth century, beyond the modern and postmodern,"[17] beyond, that is, the existing standardization of language use, Bernstein brings into visibility the mechanism of speed that constitutes this very standardization by deploying a counter-method of sediment. It is, more specifically, a poetics of "deceleration," to put it in Jean Baudrillard's words, one that "destroys meaning by implosion."[18]

Central to the communicative and representational economy of language is a dual imperative of efficiency: understandability and utility. Both are defined by a temporal factor as their constituting condition. Moreover, the relationship between understandability and utility, a relationship that determines the status of each term indicated by the suffix *-ability*, is itself defined, in a more important sense, by the element of time. In other words, to understand and to use language within the restricted economy requires a tripartite prerequisite: first, language has to be endowed with a certain degree of built-in expectability or predictability, as William Paulson has pointed out, so as to facilitate ready access; second, this built-in expectability or predictability of language should be concomitantly manifested in the span of expectation or anticipation on the part of the language user; and third, this span of expectation or anticipation has a time limit, beyond which lies confusion, incomprehension, and un-utility. Hence a ratio of time, or more concretely, a measure of frequency, of pacing, of fastness, and of speed. Differently put, language efficacy is an economy of speed maintained in proportion to the expedient utility in communicational exchange.

In his well-documented study titled *The Culture of Time and Space: 1880–1918,* Stephen Kern has convincingly demonstrated that "the mutual commitment to speed and efficiency" is largely a modern phenomenon as the result of the fast developments and new inventions in science and machine technology around the turn of the twentieth century.[19] Its corresponding artistic and literary manifestations find their most vocal and eloquent pronouncement in Marinetti and Italian futurism. "We say that the world's magnificence has been enriched by a new beauty," Marinetti writes in "Manifesto of Futurism," "the beauty of speed."[20] What characterizes this "new aesthetic of speed," he specifies explicitly, is that it is "most responsive to utility."[21] Functioning as an epistemological vehicle toward the multiplication of "our knowledge of the world" by way of an "intuitive synthesis," speed is perceived further in spiritual terms, designated as "eternal, omnipresent," and as "one of the characteristics of divinity."[22] Despite its futuristic rhetoric and, at times, ironic taunting of the past, Marinetti's statement, one could argue, does not constitute a radical departure from the pre-modern aesthetic. For its privileging of speed posits no challenge to the question of time itself as a construct;[23] rather, it concerns primarily a sentiment and its corresponding form of expression determined, periodically as always, by the material conditions of its time. At its best, Marinetti's proclamation articulates no more than an updated version of how things are perceived then and there, charting a historical transition from an agrarian culture with its rural slowness and inefficiency to an industrial culture with its technological efficiency and immediacy.

In this sense, Marinetti's aesthetic of speed announces the basic principle of the restricted economy of modernity. And when reflected in art and literature, this economy of speed becomes the "economy of expression,"[24] Kern asserts, which results in "a new 'telegraphic' style" in writing, privileging "the need for speed, clarity, and simplicity," as is the case with, among other writers, Ernest Hemingway.[25]

In this sense, speed is itself a form of method, and its function is to measure, determine, and safeguard the shortest path to a semantic destination. As such, it constitutes what Charles Bernstein calls an "artifice of absorption,"[26] in that it controls the transportation of a message with a time-ratio proportional to one's anticipation span so as to ensure the message's smooth and timely dissemination, comprehension, and utilization. As the temporal dimension of language, speed contributes directly to the transparency of language, and it is instrumental in creating "this dream of an art with no medium," as Ron Silliman puts it in *The New Sentence,* responsible for engineering the illusion "of a signified with no signifiers."[27] In other words, the convenient "appearance of the world" of realism is in essence the effect or the consequence of speed, which demands the speedy "disappearance of the word" at its command.[28]

When theorizing "speech" in *The Rustle of Language,* Roland Barthes makes a critical observation of a phenomenon that determines, both structurally and functionally, the intelligibility of oral communication. What makes a speech understandable or comprehensible, he points out, is speed:

> We cannot make ourselves understood (properly or poorly) unless we maintain, as we speak, a certain *speed* of delivery. We are like a bicyclist or a film—doomed to keep riding or turning if we are to avoid falling or jamming; silence and hesitation are both denied us: articulatory speed subjugates each point of the sentence to what immediately precedes or follows it (impossible to "venture" the word in the direction of odd or alien paradigms).[29]

Speed as such, Barthes goes on to argue, is essential in enforcing the chain of signification, the "speech chain" that "equals" a "steel bar," as Steve McCaffery observes in *Theory of Sediment.*[30] It facilitates or forces the immediate drive toward the signified by establishing a context as "a structural datum" of speech, a context that guarantees the "clarity" of the spoken words by being "reductive of meaning," by "the banishment of polysemy."[31] For clarity as the result of the banishment of polysemy, according to Barthes, "serves the Law," which "is produced, *not in what he says, but in the fact that he speaks at all.*"[32] In this light, the so-called truth of a speech or a text is largely the effect of the speed of delivery, which creates images or illusions of "the *smooth,* the *sustained*" by virtue of "the *successive.*"[33] Referring to Brecht's subversive way of reading a Nazi text by Hess, Barthes makes the following observation, raising the issue in a sociopolitical context:

> Because they [the texts or speeches] are concatenated, Brecht says, errors produce an illusion of truth; Hess's speech may seem true, insofar as it is *successive.* Brecht questions concatenation, questions successive discourse; all the pseudo-logic of the discourse—links, transitions, the patina of elocution, in short the continuity of speech—releases a kind of force, engenders an illusion of assurance: concatenated discourse is indestructible, triumphant.[34]

Within such a situational context, the solution Barthes proposes is neither "the great silent mind, heavy with experience and reserve," nor "the militant who in the name of *praxis* dismisses all discourse as trivial."[35] Rather, his is a solution of counter-speed. "In order to subvert the Law (and not simply to get around it)," he explains, "he would have to dismantle all vocal delivery, the speed and rhythm of words, until he achieved an *altogether different* intelligibility."[36] More specifically, to dismantle the speed of the words is to slow speech down by making the delivery discontinuous, unsuccessive; it is to make the delivery unsmooth, unsustained, so as to be incapable of the reduction of polysemy. "To attack the mendacious text is to separate the fabric," Barthes explains metaphorically, "to tear apart the folds of the veil."[37] And this is achieved through what Barthes calls "adding."[38] Still referring to Brecht's subversive way of reading Hess's text, he specifies this "adding" as the technique of counter-speed that interferes with the normal pace of delivery, resultantly breaking the chain of signification: "The exercise consists in saturating the mendacious text by intercalating between its sentences the critical complement which demystifies each one of them," Barthes thus details this form of counter-method. "Each sentence is reversed because it is supplemented: the critique does not diminish, does not suppress, it adds."[39] Also described as "the rustle of language," this adding, Barthes reminds us, is the function of "noise."[40] It incurs a slowdown in one's access to a given message by disrupting the proper ratio of time in delivery through adding counteractive elements, leading to an altogether different intelligibility.

Granted that Barthes's critique of speed and his counter-method of adding deal with the phenomenon of speech; yet the theoretical ramifications and practical applicability of Barthes's approach far exceed the sphere of oral delivery. Central to the Language poetry movement, for instance, is the very critical concern with language transparency as the result of speed. The issue of language as a Cartesian method and methodology, as a time-saving instrument operated by the principle of a quick kill for an immediate gain, is clearly foregrounded in the movement's rethinking of its poetic medium. Among other poets, Steve McCaffery, in an insightful study of Christopher Dewdney's poetics of geology, beautifully captures the futuristic image of speed in language via a military analogy when he writes in *North of Intention,* "Language is a weapon at the service of a guerrilla epistemology."[41]

In a more consistent manner, Charles Bernstein's poetics shows a clear awareness of the polemic in question. The problem of speed as a language issue has preoccupied his critical thinking since early on. When explaining the artifice of absorption as evidenced in modernist aesthetics, he provides probably one of the most succinct and thorough overviews of this matter. The "internal structure" of a poem that renders it readily or speedily absorptive, Bernstein writes, lies in "the unity of its / elements: the *causal* necessity of every element / & relationship being strikingly & instantaneously / apparent."[42] In the modernist tradition, he continues, this phenomenon is clearly visible, for instance, in the following literary figures and their compositional methodologies. He writes:

> Diderot, speaking of painting (but
> the idea translates), called for the elimination
> of all incident, however appealing, that did not
> contribute *directly & indispensably* to the most
> dramatic & expressive presentation of the subject
> that could be imagined: "A composition cannot
> afford any *idle* figures, any superfluous accessory.
> The subject must be one." This is echoed,
> well over a century later, in Pound's Imagist
> & Vorticist dictums against the extraneous & *idly*
> ornamental. Indeed, *the metaphors of speed* &
> vortex in the Italian Futurism of Marinetti

& the Vorticism of Pound were related to
the absorptive, unifying power of dynamic energy.[43]

This excerpt consists of two observations made by the poet: one of the
problem, which is stated, and the other of the solution, which is implied.
In Bernstein's view, the issue of speed is unmistakably the constituting
feature of the modernist economy of expression that foregrounds the
subject—that is, the straightforward presentation and the immediate explanation of the whole message in a poetic form that is its own finished,
exclusive container. His aversion to this Cartesian-modernist methodology, which is articulated in terms of "*impermeability*" and "antiabsorp-
tive,"[44] is announced in what could be considered a manifesto poem or
statement titled "Being a Statement on Poetics for the New Poetics Colloquium of the Kootenay School of Writing, Vancouver, British Columbia,
August 1985," which is collected in *Rough Trades:*

> I've never been one for intellectualizing. Too much
> talk, never enough action. Hiding behind the halls of theories
> writ to obligate, bedazzle, and torment, it is rather
> for us to tantalize with the promise, however false, of speedy
> access and explanatory compensation. *A poem should not
> be but become.*[45]

That the promise of speedy access and explanatory compensation is
false, Bernstein argues in his usual ironic vein, is precisely because a poem
is not a static unit of meaning rendered transparent and readily accessible
by a predetermined internal relation governing all its elements. Nor is it a
methodical instrument equipped with a language efficiency at the service
of a certain theory or ideology. On the contrary, a poem is an ongoing
dynamics which is itself, as Bernstein describes it in "Stray Straws and
Straw Men," "the act of actually letting [words] happen."[46] As such, a
poem is always "become" because it remains an activity of becoming in
which language is consequently devoid of the semantic predictability and
communicative efficiency proportional to the habitual time-span commonly required by expectation or anticipation. "What I like in poems
is encountering the unexpected," Bernstein states in an interview with
Manuel Brito, resonating with a Cagean aesthetic, "and I enjoy not knowing where I am or what comes next."[47] To do so, the poet resorts to what

he calls in *Content's Dream* "the anti-habitual ordering of attentions."[48] Against the giant shadows of Diderot, Marinetti, and Pound as his historical examples of modernist aesthetics and methodologies, Bernstein expresses his anti-habitual alternative of counter-speed in the notion of "idleness" of language.

As early as *Content's Dream,* Bernstein begins to argue for the "idleness" of language as the "political value of poetry."[49] For language to idle is to be "non-instrumental," producing no products and serving no end.[50] It means "not to be used for some other thing, this or that, not to serve up some ideas or tell you a story about what is happening over there," Bernstein writes, "but just in here, in it, content to sit and make a virtue of that."[51] And when "language is not in gear, is idling," he explains, writing "does not carry a meaning along with it as information to take away, which would make the writing there primarily to serve up this information, a shell in itself."[52] Commenting on George Oppen's *Of Being Numerous,* Bernstein emphasizes further this language phenomenon in his poems: "The language itself idled—layed-off—so that even to read a text as 'poetry' would mean to see its language as citational—at minimum doubly valent," calling attention also to its physicality.[53] At the same time, however, idleness for Bernstein does not mean inaction. It is, on the contrary, "antistatic."[54] The paradoxical nature of this idleness of language as action is suggested by the following passage that Bernstein has cited from Rousseau's *Confessions:*

> The idleness I love is not that of an indolent fellow who stands with folded arms in perfect inactivity and thinks as little as he acts. It is the idleness of a child who is incessantly on the move without ever doing anything, and at the same time the idleness of the rambling old man whose mind wanders while his arms are still.[55]

Language idleness, in other words, can be characterized as a Cagean purposeful purposelessness; it is a form of activity, the purpose of which is not to result in anything. More specifically, it is either an energetic, continuous, physical activity without any valid reasons and discernible methods, as is the case with the child, or a loose, inconsistent, mental activity without any actual, practical plans and corresponding actions, as is the case with the old man. In either case, idleness is portrayed as counter-methodic, as anti-habitual, vis-à-vis the social mandate of productive efficiency—that is, as "a kind of stubbornness—at one's own pace, my own measure, and not doing any*thing,* just doing."[56]

A case in point is the title poem in Bernstein's *Islets/Irritations,* whose beginning section stages, as does the rest of the poem, a textual performance of all the demonstrative features of language idling:

> to proper to   behindless   weigh in a   rotating,
> rectilinear   our plated, *embosserie des petits cochons*
>   pliant feint   insensate, round   bands of immense
> release   fell, a crudity   form of the   assignment—
> increase   by venture   populace animated by   appeal
> to which ends, almonds, lacquered unguents   embrasure. . . . [57]

An aggregate of linguistic units standing either in isolation or in incomplete formation without any discernible connections organizing them into any sort of message, language is indeed idling in this excerpt. Its visual exhibit on the page presents a photographic mapping of scattered signs sitting there leisurely, as if on the beach of a summer resort, against any impulse toward being useful, preferring instead to make a virtue of its being laid off. Yet the atmosphere of the vacationland belies a kinetic energy. For, as isolated and fragmented as they are, units such as "to proper to," "rotating," "release," "fell," "assignment," or "increase" do indicate a thrust or a momentum, thus suggesting physical movements or directional forces, though it is never clear "to which ends." While idling, language destroys utilitarian meaning by way of an implosion, as Baudrillard puts it.

In addition, language idled is language interrogated, for idling stages an act of resistance against the productive chain of signification, thus presenting a counterproductive moment, one in which critical, self-reflexive rethinking becomes possible. "And how does poetry idle itself?" Bernstein contends, "It is the product of the most intensive labor, concentration, attention. Attention to measure, to the ordering of occurrences, that such occurrences are instances of how the world itself comes to mean."[58] As practiced in Bernstein's poetry, this idleness of language, which aims at examining "the ordering of occurrences" in relation to "how the world itself comes to mean," investigates, in particular, the mechanism of speed in language as meaning constitutive.

Similar to Barthes's notion of "adding" as a means to slow down the habitual drive toward the signified by introducing noise into speech delivery so as to disrupt the speed limit constitutive of the illusion of truth, Bernstein's concept of language idleness is manifested in a poetics of inclusion. "What interests me is a poetry and a poetics that do not edit out so much as edit in," the poet states, "that include multiple conflicting perspectives and types of languages and styles in the same poetic work or, as here, in the same collection of essays."[59] Insofar as the poetic form is concerned, for instance, the poetics of inclusion or edit-in foregrounds formal experiments aimed at giving voices to the inarticulate, providing forums for nonconformists, and offering readings of the incomprehensible. All this is rendered possible by a deceleration of language. Bernstein writes:

> *Poetry is aversion of conformity* in the pursuit of new forms, or can be. By form I mean ways of putting things together, or stripping them apart, I mean ways of accounting for what weighs upon any one of us, or that poetry tosses up into an imaginary air like so many swans flying out of a magician's depthless black hat so that suddenly, like when the sky all at once turns white or purple or day-glo blue, we breathe more deeply. By form I mean how any one of us interprets what's swirling so often incomprehensibly about us, or the stutter with which he stutter, the warbling tone in which she sing off and on key.[60]

In the same vein, a poetry that edits in is a poetry that pursues the life of complexity, not the culture of restricted economy. With a pace and measure of its own, it does not do anything if perceived from the standpoint of common sense, as Bernstein has put it earlier; it just does, turning upside down the traditional poetic paradigm. The poet continues:

> As if poetry were a craft that there is a right way or wrong way to do: in which case, I prefer the wrong way—anything better than the well-wrought epiphany of predictable measure—for at least the cracks and flaws and awkwardnesses show signs of life. . . . The direction of poetic interest can better be directed outward, centrifugally, to the unknown and the peripheral.[61]

The same holds true for the political value of poetry. By virtue of its idleness, the poetics of inclusion, of anti-absorption, functions to investigate the illusion of truth constituted by language delivered with a measured speed. It is to make visible, in other words, the inherent speed limit in sense-making by violating language's speed regulation. For Bernstein, this is executed by way of idled language, by a language that is slowed down, laid off from its job at the information center. Hence the metaphor of sediment.

As "matter composed of particles which fall by gravitation to the bottom of a liquid," or "earthly or detrital matter deposited by aqueous agency,"[62] sediment is, to borrow and paraphrase Steve McCaffery's term,[63] any language units hanging "in material suspension" as the result of the "erosion" and the subsequent "accumulation" of a text mass through the "slow advance" of time-reason.[64] It is the semantic residue deposited by idling language along "the curve to its answer."[65] In the slow, patient process of "letting-it-happen," sediment, for Bernstein and for McCaffery, is language violating the low speed limit of the information highway by taking its own pace. It is, in other words, a language phenomenon of counter-speed. In a section devoted to the discussion of "different frequencies," McCaffery puts the whole issue in a more focused perspective when he writes, with a finishing touch of wit:

> It is not the words that come out differently but all the words insist their own peculiar speed into the interstices of ambivalent forms and messages. The ambiguity thus arising in the referent produces a relief development of the text and pertains, of course, to the latter's sedimentary depth. (At first he heard sentiment.)[66]

Articulated in an idled language, Bernstein's poetics of inclusion, of adding, of anti-absorption is thus the poetics of sediment featuring a drastically reduced speed in delivery. Its idling language presents itself in an ambiguous and logic-defying formation in which is inscribed, nonetheless, the potential of an altogether different intelligibility. As such, the possibility of an absorptive reading of Bernstein's poetry lies in an attention not to the epistemology, but to the ontology, of sedimentation.

Collected in *Rough Trades,* Bernstein's poem "Slowed Reason," coauthored with Nick Piombino, can be read, in many ways, as a theme poem representative of Bernstein's poetics. The title itself signals from the outset, rather candidly, a blatant self-contradiction. For whereas "reason," as a logical operation based on the restricted economy of predictability and speed, always proceeds swiftly from its premises to a conclusion along "*the straight line*,"[67] the past participle "slowed" turns that straight chain of signification into a curve to its answer, signaling a decrease in speed. As a marker of counter-speed, the title of the poem, in this sense, calls into question the linguistic codes as temporally located vantage points of reasoning with a measured or regulated speed for delivery, which "define and formalize," as Benjamin Hollander has pointed out in his reading of Bernstein's *Resistance,* "a method of discursive thinking (reading, writing) grounded in the appeal to certainty, or rectitude."[68] And so does the poem, which resonates marvelously, both in aesthetics and in wit, with McCaffery's statement cited at the end of the previous section, sounding as if it were the latter's testimony:

Poetry is sediment
I wipe off the windshield
The mindshield, a process
Of such and such refrain
An original instance
Of many waiting
The field of shifting

Expenses reclaim the years
Remainders of what is there
A battle of listening
Degree of fuming
Autopsies the barometer
In children's voices, taut or piercing
Moments, leers, discharge
Against a flattened calculus of indication
(I can tell by the feeling)
Reminders to explain
Insane parts of an entire flesh
A map, a sword, a monkey.

Moisture of talk, minimizes mimicry
Mummy's condensation, a repetitious scrawl
Of transitions from previous notes
Corresponding to functions
Parts of a closed ambition
The original instance of many

Waiting
I can tell by that
Or
"Keep your clothes on"
Process of sifting
The entire field
A calculated function of
Degree (debris)
Without which I must
Rattle a gourd filled with pieces of my own flesh
Matrices that correspond
Inverted sentiment[69]

The first line of the poem stages a double-play of self-affirmation and self-erasure, in that while it indeed invites one to read it as the poem's topic sentence, given its textual position and semantic completeness, its meaning is simultaneously hollowed out by what it states. To any attempt to read certain sentimental value into this line—and it definitely entices one to do so—the word "sediment," with its scientific neutrality, geological indifference, and turbid slowness, defies any anthropomorphic reading. Much like Steve McCaffery's mock-romantic wit of "(At first he heard sentiment)" at the sounding of "sedimentary depth,"[70] Bernstein's "Poetry is sediment" points to the last line of the poem as its own hollowing: "Inverted sentiment." The result is that the poem begins by foregrounding what Hollander calls "an unspecified, lost center of meaning" around which, rather ironically, "meanings [are] spotted circumferentially"[71]— that is, a circumference as a long curve to an absent center.

Along this long curve "words insist their own peculiar speed into the interstices of ambivalent forms and messages."[72] With each word dragging along according to its own pace, reason is inevitably slowed down to a crawl, and so is the delivery of any message therein. Rather ironically, Bernstein locates the curve of deceleration in one of the most crucial mechanisms of effective communication. Given its relatively short length, the poem, for instance, is surprisingly crowded with repetitions, the most basic form of redundancy constitutive of a contextual-semantic expectability and predictability for speedy access to information. Yet these repetitions, oddly enough, do not seem to have any utilitarian function. They are simply look-alikes, without relating in any way to each other so as to contribute to the speedy unfolding of reason. A partial list of the most eye-catching repetitions can be seen as follows, in which parentheses are used to bracket the discrepancies:

1. (w)indshield
   (m)indshield
2. (An) original instance / Of many waiting
   (The) original instance of many / Waiting
3. Rem(a)inders (of what is there)
   Reminders (to explain)
4. (a) process / Of . . . / . . . / The field of s(h)ifting
   Process of sifting / The (entire) field
5. a (flattened) calcul(us) of (indication)
   A calcul(ated) (function) of
6. Degree (of fuming)
   Degree (debris)
7. (Insane parts of an entire) flesh
   (Rattle a gourd filled with pieces of my own) flesh[73]

The repetitions listed above fall into three categories, and in each category Bernstein's way of using them is subversive. It undermines repetition's purported function to establish a contextual expectability and predictability by reducing its otherwise concomitant redundancy. In the first category, for instance, repetitions can even hardly be called as such, for they are no more than what might be referred to as "eye repetitions" in that it is not words or phrases or sentences that are repeated but only some of the same letters in certain words, as is the case with "(w)indshield / (m)indshield" in no. 1, "rem(a)inder / reminder" in no. 3, and "s(h)ifting / sifting" in no. 4. What the "eye repetition" does, inasmuch as the speed of delivery is concerned, is to create an illusion of repetition, an illusion of a familiar semantic unit already seen somewhere else, and thus an illusion of the meaning "that we thought we knew."[74] In this sense, Bernstein's use of the "eye repetition" functions as a double-edged sword: it offers a fast lane to a purported message, only to show that the message is none other than an illusion created by the very fast lane. In this sense, while it allures one to construct relations and form contexts based on its seeming reappearances, it refuses at the same time to "proceed according to those conventions of language-use"; and "as soon as one does so," as Jerome McGann puts it aptly, it immediately "responds by (as it were) reading the reader."[75] By way of a mock-speed realized in language sediment, Bernstein's use of the "eye repetition" becomes, both literally and metaphorically, a mirror to itself, a critical look into its own mechanism constitutive of the illusion of truth.

By contrast, repetitions in the second category are indeed true repetitions, at least in the sense that the exact same elements are written twice, as is the case with no. 2: "(An) original instance / Of many waiting" and "(The) original instance of many / Waiting." Further, the change from the indefinite article "An" in the first phrase to the definite article "The" in the second helps to confirm the identity of the two phrases by virtue of the grammatical rule concerning the use of "the" as referring to an "a" or "an" "previously recognized, noticed, or encountered."[76] As much as this is the case, the speed ratio required to cover the repetitions does not seem adequate enough, however, to establish a contextual-semantic network. This failure results largely from the physical locations of the two phrases in the text: one near the beginning, the other toward the end, with a long distance in between. In addition, this long distance is not a straight line but a curve, along which all the details "insist their own peculiar speed into the interstices of ambivalent forms and messages," to repeat McCaffery. Among all the specifics, nothing, for instance, contributes to the notion of "An original instance," either directly or indirectly. Although some phrases do seem to indicate the idea of "many waiting," such as "Remainders of what is there" or "Moments, leers, discharge," many do not, such as "Insane parts of an entire flesh" and so forth. With its language idling, the poem does not speed up along an iron bar of signification; instead, it unfolds a slow process of sedimentation featuring, indeed, its original instance of "many waiting."

Repetitions in the third category are neither eye repetitions nor exact ones. In the main, they are repetitions with variations in their immediate, isolated linguistic environments, as is the case with nos. 5 and 7. These repetitions have a rather peculiar effect in Bernstein's poetry, in that, both structurally and functionally, their redundancy finds its expression not so much in what they say as in how they look, not so much in their shared meaning as in their similar physicality, not so much in their semantic network as in their lingual-geological features. In other words, repetitions are "(debris)" of language deposited repeatedly. In Bernstein's poetry as sediment, language, idling along the slow curve to describing the sediment, becomes itself the sediment.

In "Slowed Reason," Bernstein, as Hollander observes similarly with regard to his other poem *Resistance,* "[proposes] questions as to how language contextualizes and metaphorizes experience."[77] His counter-methodical handling of repetition as the most basic form of speed delivery constitutive of a semantic-contextual expectability and predictability challenges the conventional use of language as a method of mirage-making. With language not in gear, poetry becomes what Bernstein calls, in the poem "The Simply," that "empty stare that ricochets / haphazardly against any purpose."[78]

The image of language idling, of language being deposited, along the curved line of counter-speed is most literally presented, perhaps, in a poem titled, simply, "was, rain, dish":

was, rain, dish
our, an much
took, kid, stretch
well, real, didn't
immersion, wanted, attractive
oooooo, my, served
&, see, so
mean, was, into
felt, tenderly, beacon
personal, like, trip
looking, many, someone
20, out, preparation[79]

As long as six pages, the poem consists of nothing but a catalogue of words. What seems to have been dramatized therein can be read as articulating Bernstein's reconceptualization of poetry. In *A Poetics,* for instance, the poet begins by redefining poetry:

What I hear, then, in the poetries of this New American fin de siècle is an implicit refusal of unity that is the result of our prodigious and magnanimous outpouring of words. In saying this, I register my own particular passion—everywhere reflected in this book—for poetry that insists on running its own course, finding its own measures, charting worlds otherwise hidden or denied or, perhaps best of all, never before existing.[80]

Viewed in this light, "was, rain, dish" becomes a poem that demonstrates or embodies, in the most literal and physical way possible, a poem in the very process of running its own course, finding its own measure, and charting the world as it goes along. More concretely, it is a poem of adding, a poem that does not edit out so much as edits in, as Bernstein himself has argued. Implied in the poem, then, is a paradox, in the sense that language is most productive when it is most idling, most revealing about the world when most slowed down, most articulate when most inclusive, and closer to truth when deposited along the curved line to answers.

The same can be said about another poem collected in *Islets/Irritations*. Titled "Parameter," the poem appears to have a certain pattern in comparison to "was, rain, dish," as is also suggested by the word "parameter":

> pardon quickly / adroit breeze / argue
>   tonic / in issue / practical
> platoons /
>   returns slowly / that make
>   mason isospheres / unheard relief
>   piston spender
>   churn enhancement / marking action
>   / most delight[81]

Against a textual backdrop as such, the "parameter" in question seems to be the parameter of slowed reason, which is carried out in an idling language along the curved line of addition. It is the parameter of a counter-speed, with which the poem moves toward not "transcendence," as Baudrillard foresees, but "indeterminacy."[82]

If the notion of counter-speed manifested in idling language and slowed reason is demonstrated most physically or materially in poems of language sediment, it is staged most ironically as well as satirically in poems composed with various degrees of pseudo-narrative flows. In *Dark City*, for instance, Bernstein continues to work on this concept in the poem "Locks Without Doors."[83] The title of the poem already starts to question the nature of contextual expectability and predictability by a reversal of the established logical relations between locks and doors as is manifested in normal linguistic collocation: rather than "doors without locks," which seems commonsensical, there is "locks without doors." Read from this perspective, the poem is about unfulfilled expectations or the broken chains of logic, presenting an in-your-face kind of mockery of how "expectations stymie hunger for / exceptions." [84] The poem begins with a request:

> Will you promise not to get mad
>   if I tell you something? Nothing
>   notable except the prism without
>   light effects. Except that
>   expectations stymie hunger for
> exceptions, such that
>   dedication rumples the doily
>   while in a tugboat there's
> too little chance for remorse.
>   Like pillars of sand at a Revivalist
>   Meeting or pockets of pumice at a
> Pita Party. For when the fire chief
>   told Pickles that he could stay
>   the cat knew he had finally
>   found a home. [85]

Framed as a question, the first sentence in this section has a tone of concern or nervousness that is never matched by an answer with a corresponding magnitude. Much to the contrary, the word "Nothing," which immediately follows the question, functions as an emotional letdown, or a sensational anticlimax, vis-à-vis the intense expectations already built up in the question. From this point on, the poem resembles a chain with missing links, dramatizing language idling. What, for instance, is the grammatical function of the conjunction "while"? Does it provide a contrast or comparison between "dedication rumples the doily" and "in a tugboat there's / too little chance for remorse," or does it simply work as an adverbial of time for the latter? What exactly does the prepositional phrase "Like pillars of sand at a Revivalist / Meeting or pockets of pumice at a / Pita Party" refer to? Furthermore, the conjunction "for" in "For when the fire chief / told Pickles that he could stay / the cat knew he had finally / found a home" clearly introduces an adverbial clause of reason, but reason of what or for what? As a result, the reduced speed of the development of logic contributes to a slowed-down reason, which, now burdened by all the non-logical additions, veers off the straight line toward a purported answer to follow the curved line toward possible discoveries.

Language, as "slowed reason" manifested in "locks without doors," is not in gear, and is idling. The fact that the locks without doors do not lock anything thus suggests an openness, a potential for additions, and a reversal of the habitual standardization that "expectations stymie hunger for / exceptions." In other words, with the decrease in expectations, it is the exceptions, the surprises, the unexpected, the unpredictable, located in the interstices in the broken chain of logic, that now begin to increase. In many ways, "Locks Without Doors" is a poem about exceptions, the increase of which leads to a world "never before existing."

In his critique of language and language transparency, Bernstein engages in his poetry the structural-functional parameter of speed via a poetics of sediment grounded in his innovative notion of the idleness of language. Resonating with Roland Barthes's counter-method of adding against speed, Bernstein's poetics of edit-in incurs a slowed reason by disrupting the established speed-ratio as the precondition for logicality. When measured against the standard speed of language engaged in guerrilla epistemology, Bernstein's poetry indeed moves slowly, "in the most physical way," as Robert Smithson puts it in "A Sedimentation of the Mind."[86] So slow, in fact, is the speed of Bernstein's idling language that "this movement seems motionless," observes Smithson, "yet it crushes the landscape of logic under glacial reveries. This slow flowage makes one conscious of the turbidity of thinking."[87]

No good poetry is ever written in a manner twenty years old.
　　—Ezra Pound, "A Retrospect"

The twentieth-century artist is not necessarily someone who draws
well, but someone who thinks well.
　　—Bill Viola, "The Porcupine and the Car"

Coda. The Postmodern Poetics of Counter-Method: Toward a Poetry Yet to Come

When concluding her 1993 essay titled "Postmodernism / *Fin de Siècle:* The Prospects for Openness in a Decade of Closure," Marjorie Perloff raises the issue of the appropriateness or adequacy of the term *postmodernism* when applied to the contemporary poetry of innovation. The term has become problematic because the poetry identified by it in the 1990s, in stark contrast to its 1960s counterpart, has distinguished itself by demonstrating, conceptually as well as formally, myriads of differences so new and so radical as to be hitherto unparalleled even in the genealogy of avant-garde adventures. From a perspective both historical and comparative, she thus writes:

> To confront the linguistic texture of McCaffery's elaborated parodic poem is to ask oneself whether the term *postmodernism,* once applied to the poetry of Olson and his Black Mountain confrères, can apply equally well to the writing of the 90s. Can we simply invert the *6*? Or do the post-post days we are now witnessing *pre*figure a phase for which we don't yet have a name and whose post-people we can't quite conceptualize? In the words of Laurie Anderson, "Do you think they will read our signs?"[1]

Five years later, in what might be considered as a sequel article titled "After Free Verse: The New Nonlinear Poetries," Perloff continues her meditation on the strikingly innovative features of contemporary avant-garde poetry. With conventional aesthetics "no longer operative," the post-linear, new poems are, "in most cases, as visual as they are verbal," she observes, singling out the acoustic feature as one of her examples; as such, they "must be *seen* as well as heard, which means that at poetry readings, their scores must be performed, activated."[2] And "for this new form of sounding," which seems to "reorganize sound configurations according to different principles" by breaking away from all sorts of conventional limits, "I have no name," Perloff acknowledges; and more importantly, she continues, "its namelessness goes with the territory," a territory, that is, of "the new exploratory poetry."[3] Referring to Caroline Bergvall's poem "Of Boundaries and Emblems," which, among other baffling textual features, ends with a colon, Perloff speculates on the poetry of the future, seeing the colon as a gesture toward that which is yet to be recognizable and nameable, as "a signature, as it were, of things to come."[4]

Perloff's observations and questions, together with her candid acknowledgments in both essays that there is, so far, no name for this phase of poetry prefigured by signs yet to become readable, make an important statement. Other issues aside, the difficulty in naming the compositional complexities of the new exploratory poetry, which results from the inadequacy of a taxonomic classifier whereby they would otherwise be recognized, is itself a matter of method, as Perloff has implicitly argued. It bespeaks, more specifically, the absence of method. This poetry is new to the point of being unnameable precisely because it shows no recognized generic kinship or family affiliation in the established genealogical tree, and it is exploratory to the extent of being unrecognizable precisely because what it is exploring, as Lyotard has contended in *The Postmodern Condition,* is method itself, the method with which to identify and name itself. For to name anything at all, one has to recognize it by identifying the categorical similarities determined and defined according to a prior method as the constitutive and operative principle. In this sense, recognizability, which presents the precondition for naming, is both the intrinsic property and predetermined effect of method. It is, in other words, method recognizing itself.

In *The Concept of Method,* Justus Buchler brings this point to the fore in his extended definition of method. "A method is a power of manipulating natural complexes, purposively and *recognizably,* within a reproducible order of utterance," he writes, "and methodic activity is the translation of such a power into the pursuit of an end—an end implied by the reproduction."[5] In this understanding of method, he explains further, one of the "constituent ideas" is "the qualification of 'recognizably,'" which is, in actuality, "redundant" in the sense that[6]

> the reproduction of an order brings with it the essential characteristics that identify the manipulation. An order of utterance, after all, is no blank state; it is an interrelation of judgments and natural conditions. But the presence of "recognizably" in the statement is a reminder that the instances of any method are bound to each other by appreciable similarities.[7]

In other words, recognizability is redundant because, structurally and functionally speaking on the one hand, it is the mirror image of method, the self-acknowledgement and self-affirmation of method as a closed system, whose operation follows its own quadruple orbit of logic-convention-acceptability-evaluation. Rationally and psychologically speaking, on the other hand, recognizability is redundant since it is the self-fulfilling prophecy of method, the "I-think" of method thinking itself into its own valid proof, the a priori prescription of method finding its expression in the conformities of experiences and phenomena.[8] Whichever the case, recognizability beckons to the built-in self-evidence in the methodic campaign of *re*covery.

In terms more explicitly pertinent to Perloff's observations, Gilles Deleuze, in his critique of "the image of thought" based on "good sense" and "common sense" in traditional thinking, foregrounds the issue of recognition or recognizability as a constituting component of method.[9] In application of the mind endowed with the ability to "adjudicate with regard to its own universality, and to suppose itself universal and communicable in principle," Deleuze points out, "there must be an explicit method,"[10] which is also termed respectively as "model" or "form."[11] Predicated upon the "form of identity in the object," he argues, "the form of recognition," in particular, presents itself as one of the "three levels" that "constitute an ideal orthodoxy."[12] Furthermore, in its dogmatic, orthodox operation, recognition plays a redundant, self-referential role, as Buchler has pointed out earlier, in that it recognizes itself, and itself alone. "The form of recognition has never sanctioned anything but the recognizable and the recognized," Deleuze writes, since "form will never inspire anything but conformities."[13] It follows then, more revealingly, that "what is recognized is not only an object but also the values attached to an object" and, as such, Deleuze concludes, "recognition is a sign of the celebration of monstrous nuptials, in which thought . . . *rediscovers* all the current values it subtly presented" in an object.[14]

Viewed from this perspective, Perloff's acknowledgment of the present difficulty in recognizing and naming the "post-" poetry sheds light on the concept of "new" in the "new exploratory poetry," offering a glimpse of the nature of the kind of poetry yet to come. Defiant to methodological appropriations, it is a poetry whose "newness" cannot and will not be established, because "what becomes established with the new," as Deleuze asserts, "is precisely not the new."[15] It is, in other words, a radical newness, and it takes values that the methodological terms currently available do not yet have. In this sense, the poets' critique of method, as evidenced in the poetics of counter-method variously manifested in the innovative practices of avant-garde poetry discussed in this book, articulates eloquently, at the level of philosophy, a poetic, post-dialectic rethinking of "thinking" itself, a conventional "thinking" in whose image the concept of poetry has hitherto been defined. To the extent that it unfolds a wide, open horizon, the colon that ends Bergvall's poem indeed evokes, both literally and symbolically—or more literally than symbolically, to be accurate—a poetry of the future, one, that is, yet to be imagined and conceptualized. It is the sign, perhaps, of a new poetry which has "its power of beginning and beginning again," as Deleuze puts it, and hence "remains forever new."[16] For this sort of "new," in its refusal to be recognized and named methodologically, "calls forth forces in thought which are not the forces of recognition, today or tomorrow," to follow Deleuze's argument, "but the powers of a completely other model, from an unrecognized and unrecognizable *terra incognita*."[17]

To explore that widely open horizon, the poetics of counter-method presents the first critical step, constituting, via its "counter-" position, the precondition for the emergence of a poetry yet to come.

Notes

Introduction

1. This chapter's title—"The Medium Is the 'Method'"—is taken from Josué V. Harari and David F. Bell, "Introduction: Journal a Plusieurs Voies," in *Hermes: Literature, Science, Philosophy,* by Michel Serres, ed. Harari and Bell (Baltimore: Johns Hopkins University Press, 1982), xxxv.

2. See Thomas Kuhn, *The Structure of Scientific Revolutions,* 2nd ed. (Chicago: University of Chicago Press, 1970). For Kuhn's further development of the term *paradigm,* see his essay "Reflections on My Critics," in *Criticism and Growth of Knowledge,* ed. I. Lakatos and A. Musgrave (Cambridge: Cambridge University Press, 1970), 231–78.

3. Matei Calinescu, *Five Faces of Modernity* (Durham, N.C.: Duke University Press, 1987), 269.

4. Ilya Prigogine and Isabelle Stengers, *Order Out of Chaos* (New York: Bantam Books, 1984), xxvii.

5. For a clear and useful overview on this issue, see N. Katherine Hayles, *The Cosmic Web: Scientific Field Models and Literary Strategies in the 20th Century* (Ithaca, N.Y.: Cornell University Press, 1984), especially the introduction and chapter 1.

6. Calinescu, *Five Faces,* 269.

7. Ibid., 304. As Calinescu notices, this shift in contemporary thought from epistemology to hermeneutics has been phrased differently by various critics of postmodern literature. Particularly pertinent to the discussion here is Brian McHale and his argument in his article "Change of Dominant from Modernist to Postmodernist Writing," in *Approaching Postmodernism,* ed. Douwe Fokkema and Hans Bertens (Amsterdam: John Benjamins, 1986), 53-79. Emphasizing fiction and using Faulkner's *Absalom, Absalom!* as an example, McHale posits that there are two "dominants." "The dominant of Modernist writing is epistemological," he writes:

> that is, Modernist writing is designed to raise such questions as: what is there to be known? who knows it? how do they know it, and with what degree of certainty? how is knowledge transmitted from one knower to another, and with what degree of reliability? how does the object of knowledge change as it passes from knower to knower? what are the limits of knowledge? and so on. . . . I think there can be no doubt that Faulkner's *Absalom, Absalom!* for example, has been designed to raise epistemological questions. Its logic is that of the detective story, the epistemological genre par excellence. (58)

By contrast, "the dominant of Postmodernist writing is ontological," he continues:

> that is, Postmodernist writing is designed to raise such questions as: what is a world? what kinds of worlds are there, how are they constituted, and how do they differ? what happens when different kinds of worlds are placed in confrontation, or when boundaries between worlds are violated? what is the mode of existence of a text, and what is the mode of existence of the world (or worlds) it projects? how is a projected world structured? and so on. (60)

As for his use of the term "ontological," McHale has a lengthy note in which he distinguishes the meaning of his "ontology" from that in philosophical discourse, especially that of Heidegger. Crediting his usage to Roman Ingarden and Thomas Pavel, McHale writes:

> For a working definition, let me cite Pavel: an ontology is "a theoretical description of a universe." The operative word here, from my point of view, is the indefinite article: a description of a universe, not of the universe; that is, of any universe, potentially of a plurality of universes. In other words, to "do ontology" in this perspective is not necessarily to seek some grounding for our universe; it might just as well involve the description of other universes, including "possible" and fictional ones. To put it another way: the difference between the universe and a universe is precisely what the Postmodernist critics mean when they talk about the undermining of ontology. (75)

8. Calinescu, *Five Faces*, 271.

9. Ibid., 272. For a more detailed account of these issues, see Gianni Vattimo, *La fine de la modernita: Nichilismo ed ermeneutica cultura postmoderna* (Milan: Garzanti, 1985). See also his article "Dialectics, Difference, and Weak Thought," *Graduate Faculty Philosophy Journal* 10, no. 1 (Spring 1984): 151–64.

10. Calinescu, *Five Faces*, 272–73. For Hans-Georg Gadamer's critique of the scientific method and methodology, see the section titled "Toward a Philosophy of Counter-Method" in the introduction to the present volume, and see his *Truth and Method*, trans. W. Glen-Doepel, 2nd ed. (New York: Crossroad, 1985).

11. Calinescu, *Five Faces*, 273.

12. Ibid., 303, 304.

13. Ibid., 303.

14. Ibid.

15. Hayles, *Cosmic Web*, 31, 32.

16. The privileging of methodological implications over the implications of method can be seen in Hayles's *Cosmic Web*, which is a comparative study that emphasizes "the connecting link" between science and literature (25). For the same approach, see also her important study titled *Chaos Bound: Orderly Disorder in Contemporary Literature and Science* (Ithaca, N.Y.: Cornell University Press,

1990). Joseph Conte takes a similar position in his *Unending Design: The Forms of Postmodern Poetry* (Ithaca, N.Y.: Cornell University Press, 1991). Here, he argues, "The reciprocal relationship of seriality and proceduralism, aleatory procedures and arbitrary constraints, is founded on attitudes toward chaos and order which are newly effective in the postmodern era" (17).

17. Justus Buchler, *The Concept of Method* (New York: University Press of America, 1985), 2.

18. David Antin, "Some Questions About Modernism," *Occident* 8, n.s. (Spring 1974): 29. For Antin's interesting discussion of the works of Bacon and Descartes as experimental novels, see pp. 29–31.

19. Ibid., 31.

20. Francis Bacon, *The Advancement of Learning and New Atlantis,* ed. Arthur Johnston (Oxford: Clarendon, 1974), 135.

21. Michel Serres, *Hermes: Literature, Science, Philosophy,* ed. Josué V. Harari and David F. Bell (Baltimore: Johns Hopkins University Press, 1982), 21, 23, 24. For a general description of Bacon's method, see also Gadamer's *Truth and Method,* especially 312.

22. René Descartes, *The Philosophical Writings of Descartes,* trans. Elizabeth S. Haldane and G. R. T. Ross (New York: Dover, 1955), 15, 16.

23. Ibid., 16.

24. Ibid., 20.

25. Jaakko Hintikka, "A Discourse on Descartes's Method," in *Descartes: Critical and Interpretive Essays,* ed. Michael Hooker (Baltimore: Johns Hopkins University Press, 1978), 74–88.

26. Ibid., 74, 85.

27. Descartes, *Philosophical Writings,* 51–52, quoted in Hintikka, "Discourse on Descartes's Method," 85.

28. Buchler, *Concept of Method,* 71.

29. Descartes, *Philosophical Writings,* 35. For a useful history of the idea of method in the seventeenth century, see Peter Dear, "Method and the Study of Nature," in *The Cambridge History of Seventeenth-Century Philosophy,* ed. Daniel Garber and Michael Ayers (Cambridge: Cambridge University Press, 1998), 147–77. Also useful in this respect are Neal Gilbert, *Renaissance Concepts of Method* (New York: Columbia University Press, 1963); and Stephen Gaukroger, "Descartes: Methodology," in *The Renaissance and Seventeenth-Century Rationalism,* ed. G. H. R. Parkinson (London: Routledge, 1993), 167–200. For a more recent study of the method of Descartes and the "Cartesian circle," see Janet Broughton, *Descartes's Method of Doubt* (Princeton, N.J.: Princeton University Press, 2002).

30. Immanuel Kant, *Critique of Pure Reason,* trans. Norman Kemp Smith (New York: St. Martin's Press, 1929), 25.

31. Ibid., 17.

32. Charles P. Bigger, *Kant's Methodology: An Essay in Philosophical Archeology* (Athens: Ohio University Press, 1996), xxi.

33. Ibid., xviii. Bigger quotes this statement by Levinas.

34. Kant, *Critique of Pure Reason*, 20.

35. Ibid., 23.

36. Ibid., 374–75.

37. Norman Kemp Smith, *A Commentary to Kant's Critique of Pure Reason* (Atlantic Highlands, N.J.: Humanities, 1992), 44.

38. Ibid., 45.

39. Kant, *Critique of Pure Reason*, 374, 375.

40. Smith, *Commentary to Kant's Critique*, 239, 238, 259.

41. Kant, *Critique of Pure Reason*, 375.

42. Rodolphe Gasché, *The Tain of the Mirror: Derrida and the Philosophy of Reflection* (Cambridge, Mass.: Harvard University Press, 1986), 121–22.

43. By "organizational behavior" I do not refer to the particular branch of social science with that name. Rather, I use that term to point to the social or contextual dimension of method, which I will discuss later in this part of the chapter.

44. Husain Sarkar, *A Theory of Method* (Berkeley: University of California Press, 1983). Sarkar's study is not a radical critique of method itself. As "an appraisal of three landmark theories of method" (ix), his work focuses instead on the effectiveness of method in terms of its functional capacity to "achieve the goal of truthlikeness" (6), with a special interest in the social sciences. But his structural approach, which is intended to maximize a method's efficiency, also provides important critical insights into the nature and function of method as a construct grounded in a social context and a collective consensus.

45. Ibid., 8, 15, 9.

46. Ibid., 8, 9.

47. Ibid., 9, 161.

48. Ibid., 12, 10.

49. Ibid., 10, 16.

50. Ibid., 11.

51. Ibid., 16.

52. Ibid., 11–12.

53. I am using the three terms *social, communal,* and *cultural* interchangeably here, and *context,* in this sense, is always a "social," "communal," or "cultural" context.

54. Robert E. Shiller, *New Methods of Knowledge and Value* (New York: Philosophical Library, 1966), 10.

55. Buchler, *Concept of Method*, 30.

56. Don Byrd, "Language Poetry, 1971–1986," *Sulfur* 20 (1987): 156.

57. Buchler, *Concept of Method*, 105.

58. Stephen Fredman, *Poet's Prose: The Crisis in American Verse,* 2nd ed. (Cambridge: Cambridge University Press, 1990), 141. In his discussion of Antin's talk poems, Fredman argues that "the extraordinary claims Antin makes in and for his talk poems" articulate a critical stance similar to that of Gadamer, regardless of their disagreements in other areas. Fredman summarizes the common grounds shared by Antin and Gadamer:

> In both is found (1) a high valuation of the occasional and a concomitant deconstruction of the eternal, as well as the recognition that all understanding occurs phenomenologically and has a temporal grounding; (2) the dismissal of aestheticism (what Gadamer calls "aesthetic differentiation") and its scientific complement of the literal and the factual, as dead formalisms; (3) the recognition that all discourse, in its attempt to represent, is a kind of art; (4) the claim that method is not value-free but rather that the method chosen prejudices the truth one can achieve; (5) the elevation of play to a philosophically meaningful description of art and science. (141)

While all five points of Fredman's synthesis are equally applicable to postmodern writing in general and Stein's work in particular, the emphasis in the following discussion is, for the purpose of this chapter, placed on point number 4.

59. Antin, "Some Questions About Modernism," 13.

60. Ibid., 13.

61. Sarkar, *Theory of Method,* 13.

62. Buchler, *Concept of Method,* 101.

63. David Antin, "Modernism and Postmodernism: Approaching the Present in American Poetry," *boundary 2,* vol. 1 (Fall 1972): 127. Though Antin's observation is certainly and accurately applicable to Pound's poetics and poetry, the context in which he makes this statement is different, as he criticizes therein this aspect of Pound's work in relation to his provincialism, biographical, historical, geographical, temporal, and literary. For more details, see 127–28.

64. Geoffrey Grigson, "The Methodism of Ezra Pound," in *Ezra Pound: The Critical Heritage,* ed. Eric Homberger (London: Routledge and Kegan Paul, 1972), 259.

65. It is important to acknowledge here the possible discrepancy, to whatever degree, between Pound's avowed predilection for science and his own writing practices, especially those manifested in his later work of which, as Pound himself admits, he "[hasn't] an Aquinas-map" (Ezra Pound, *Selected Letters 1907–1941,* ed. D. D. Paige [New York: New Directions, 1971], 323). Francesca Cadel, for instance, calls attention to this discrepancy, asserting that "any consideration of Pound's uses of science must be qualified" because, as much as Pound's "manifold curiosity extended to the scientific developments of his day," he only "valued science for its process of empirical observation—its certitude and preciseness" (264). In addition, she argues further, science functions in Pound's work merely

as a figure of speech, since the poet "from his earliest years was fond of using the anti-sentimentalist rhetoric of science in his critical writings as a metaphor for accurate observation—and occasionally as a sign of occult truth" (264). For a more detailed elaboration on this issue, see Cadel's entry on "Science" in *The Ezra Pound Encyclopedia,* ed. Demetres P. Tryphonopoulos and Stephen J. Adams (Westport, Conn.: Greenwood, 2005), 264–66. However, it is equally important to see that, whereas Pound's uses of science may certainly be, in a sense, metaphorical, his urgent emphasis on and consistent privileging of scientific methods are, as also implied in Cadel's commentary, clearly tailored to practical or literal purposes. Given Pound's extended discourse on scientific methods, it can be argued that the issue of method in Pound invites and warrants critical attention beyond the symbolic limits of a metaphor, and that scientific methods, whatever the kinds, have undoubtedly facilitated a poetic mind in organizing empirical processes through which "an Aquinas-map" is to be drawn.

66. Buchler, *Concept of Method,* 101.

67. Ezra Pound, *Guide to Kulchur* (New York: New Directions, 1970), 51.

68. Ezra Pound, *ABC of Reading* (New York: New Directions, 1934), 17.

69. Ibid., 26, 27.

70. Ibid., 20. For Pound's repeated emphasis on the scientific method as the method of poetry and literature, see also the *Literary Essays of Ezra Pound* (New York: New Directions, 1935), particularly "Part I: The Art of Poetry," 3–87.

71. Pound, *ABC of Reading,* 22.

72. Pound, *Literary Essays,* 18, 61.

73. Ibid., 42.

74. Ezra Pound, *Gaudier-Brzeska: A Memoir* (New York: New Directions, 1970), 90.

75. Ibid.

76. Ibid., 91.

77. Ibid., 91–92.

78. Byrd, "Language Poetry," 152.

79. Pound, *ABC of Reading,* 63.

80. Pound, *Literary Essays,* 23.

81. Ibid., 21, 22.

82. Ezra Pound, *The Spirit of Romance* (New York: New Directions, 1968), 14.

83. Pound, *Literary Essays,* 43, 44, 56, 50.

84. Pound, *ABC of Reading,* 63. For Pound's explanation of the three terms "phanopoeia," "melopoeia," and "logopoeia," see *ABC of Reading,* 63, and *Literary Essays,* 25.

85. Pound, *Literary Essays,* 26.

86. Ibid., 3.

87. Ibid., 46.

88. Ibid., 52, 6.

89. Jayne L. Walker, *The Making of a Modernist: Gertrude Stein from* Three Lives *to* Tender Buttons (Amherst: University of Massachusetts Press, 1984), xviii.

90. Gertrude Stein, *How to Write* (New York: Dover, 1975), 106.

91. Jayne Walker makes a similar point in her discussion of Stein's *Tender Buttons* as one of her "most playful texts" (*Making of a Modernist,* 149). These texts, she argues, "are all based on the premise that knowledge must begin with a knowledge of language. Rigorously investigating its laws and testing its limits, Stein's texts continue to challenge their readers to a new awareness of the system of language as both the necessary instrument and the inevitable 'prison' of thought" (149).

92. Antin, "Some Questions About Modernism," 13, 14.

93. Ibid., 14. The problems Antin has briefly mentioned without detailed explication include the following: "the problematic double system of language—the self-ordering system and the pointing system," the "fundamental structural ambiguity of language: that utterance is play before it is address or discourse or representation," and "the subtlest distinctions of grammar for the most refined distinctions of meaning" (ibid., 13, 14).

94. Gertrude Stein, *The Yale Gertrude Stein,* selected by Richard Kostelanetz (New Haven, Conn.: Yale University Press, 1980), 138–39.

95. Peter Quartermain, *Disjunctive Poetics: From Gertrude Stein and Louis Zukofsky to Susan Howe* (Cambridge: Cambridge University Press, 1992), 35. Quartermain's use of the word "method" here focuses on the grammatical and syntactical patterns at work in this sentence, and it does not engage the issue of method proper. However, his overall critical approach to Stein's work here is applicable to the thesis in my book. For Quartermain's reading of this sentence, see pp. 35–36.

96. Ibid., 34.

97. Ibid., 35.

98. Ibid.

99. Ibid., 34.

100. Gertrude Stein, *Selected Writings,* ed. Carl van Vechten (New York: Vintage, 1962), 518.

101. Ibid.

102. Ibid., 517, 519.

103. Ibid., 519.

104. Ibid., 516. It is important not to confuse Stein's notion of writing as "doing natural phenomena" with any other established conventions of writing. As F. W. Dupee makes it clear in his introduction to Stein's *Selected Writings,* "Gertrude Stein was insistent that she was not practicing 'automatic writing' or working in any literary convention, such as Surrealism, related to automatic writing.

No release of unconscious impulses, her own or those of fictional characters, is intended" (xiii).

105. For critical readings that address this aspect of Stein's writing, see, among others, Marjorie Perloff, *The Poetics of Indeterminacy: Rimbaud to Cage* (Princeton, N.J.: Princeton University Press, 1981), 67–108, especially 85, 88–89. See also Marjorie Perloff, "'A Fine New Kind of Realism': Six Stein Styles in Search of a Reader," in *Poetic License: Essays on Modernist and Postmodernist Lyric* (Evanston, Ill.: Northwestern University Press, 1990), 145–59; Walker, *Making of a Modernist;* and William H. Gass, "Gertrude Stein and the Geography of the Sentence," in *The World Without the Word* (New York: Alfred A. Knopf, 1979). Also useful are Allegra Stewart, *Gertrude Stein and the Present* (Cambridge, Mass.: Harvard University Press, 1967); Norman Weinstein, *Gertrude Stein and the Literature of Modern Consciousness* (New York: Frederick Ungar, 1970); and Marianne DeKoven, *A Different Language: Gertrude Stein's Experimental Language* (Madison: University of Wisconsin Press, 1983).

106. Walker, *Making of a Modernist,* xi.

107. Barrett Watten, *Total Syntax* (Carbondale: Southern Illinois University Press, 1985), 48, 49. Watten's use of the expression "the method that is no method" is both problematic and useful in this context here. It is problematic in that Watten uses it in his discussion of none other than the surrealist concepts and strategies appropriated in art in the postwar period (see note 104 above), and it is useful in that he rightly emphasizes the loss of the "dialectical frame" as well as the "predicative potential" of method. Watten writes:

> Method in American art after the war incorporated numbers of Surrealist concepts. Traces of automatism and objective chance fuse in the renegotiated value for the "self." That recognition and the self are equivalent terms is coded into a wide range of art work. Logically, "the method that is no method," which so many artists have claimed, is consistent with the dominant ideology, aesthetic and otherwise, of the time. The method of no objects, the method of many objects, and the method of the reconstituted object all have their postwar forms, as critiques. The dialectical frame is absent: the predicative potential of method degenerates into the condition one is in. (48–49)

108. Dupee, introduction to Stein, *Selected Writings,* xiv, xiii.

109. Kostelanetz, introduction to Stein, *Yale Gertrude Stein,* xxx.

110. Patricia Meyerowitz, preface to Stein, *How to Write,* v.

111. Kostelanetz, introduction to Stein, *Yale Gertrude Stein,* xxx.

112. Meyerowitz, introduction to Stein, *How to Write,* xiv (emphasis added).

113. Jean-François Lyotard, *The Postmodern Condition: A Report on Knowledge,* trans. Geoff Bennington and Brian Massumi (Minneapolis: University of Minnesota Press, 1984), 81. It is interesting to see that the difficulty of Stein's work due to the lack of rules or methods is also reflected in Lyotard's reading of Stein.

As if continuing his thinking in *The Postmodern Condition,* Lyotard theorizes conflicts between phrases in *The Differend: Phrases in Dispute* (trans. G. Van Den Abbeele [Minneapolis: University of Minnesota Press, 1988]). "A phrase," he asserts, "is constituted according to a set of rules" (xii). Also called a phrase "regimen," each phrase thus falls into a teleological category, be it "reasoning, knowing, describing, recounting, questioning, showing, ordering, etc."; and whereas "phrases from heterogeneous regimens cannot be translated from one into the other, they can be linked one onto the other in accordance with an end fixed by a genre of discourse" (xii). Insisting on his position that "to link is necessary; how to link is contingent" (29), he then argues for a writing that multiplies phrasal combinations beyond the logical forms of the proposition, the rules of consecutive reasoning, and the conventions governing various genres of writing. "To save the phrase," Lyotard writes, "extract it from the discourses in which it is subjugated and restrained by rules for linking, enveloped in their gangue, seduced by their end. Let it be" (68). Using both Cage and Stein as his examples, he then reiterates his thesis made in *The Postmodern Condition:* "The stakes of philosophical discourse are in a rule (or rules) which remains to be sought, and to which the discourse cannot be made to conform before the rule has been found. The links from phrase to phrase are not ruled by a rule but by the quest for a rule" (97). Lyotard continues this line of thinking: "You are really reading a book of philosophy, the phrases in it are concatenated in such a way as to show that that concatenation is not just a matter of course and that the rule for their concatenation remains to be found" (129). At the same time, however, Lyotard seems to be equally baffled by Stein's way of writing. In the section subtitled "Gertrude Stein Notice," for instance, he fails to provide any comments, showing his puzzlement by describing the selection of Stein's sentences as "outrageous" (67). In his discussion of the problems of "language" later, he posits that "maybe prose is impossible," as evidenced, in part, by Stein's prose: "It is tempted on the one side by despotism and on the other by anarchy. It succumbs to the seduction of the former by turning itself into the genre of all genres (the prose of popular Empire) and to the seduction of the latter by trying to be no more than an unregulated assemblage of all phrases (the vagabond's prose, Gertrude Stein?)" (158).

114. Martin Heidegger, *On the Way to Language,* trans. Peter D. Hertz (San Francisco: Harper and Row, 1971), 74.

115. Ibid., 74, 91.

116. Martin Heidegger, "The Age of the World View," trans. Marjorie Grene, *boundary 2,* vol. 4, no. 2, special issue, Martin Heidegger and Literature (Winter 1976): 340–55.

117. Ibid.

118. Ibid., 344–45.

119. Ibid., 345.

120. Ibid.

121. Ibid., 348.

122. Heidegger, *On the Way to Language,* 74.

123. Ibid., 92.

124. Ibid.

125. Gadamer, *Truth and Method,* 5.

126. Ibid., 246.

127. Ibid., 311.

128. Ibid., 417.

129. Ibid., 312.

130. Ibid., 313.

131. Ibid.

132. Ibid., 312.

133. Ibid.

134. Ibid.

135. Ibid.

136. Ibid., 313.

137. Ibid., 312, 312–13.

138. Ibid., 466.

139. Ibid., xi, 6.

140. Ibid., 19.

141. Ibid., 20.

142. Ibid., 20, 21.

143. Ibid., 21.

144. Ibid.

145. Ibid., 23.

146. Paul Feyerabend, *Against Method* (London: Verso, 1988), 23, 231.

147. Ibid., 21.

148. Ibid., 10–11, 9.

149. Ibid., 14.

150. Ibid., 22.

151. Ibid.

152. Ibid., 231.

153. Ibid., 13, 21, 19.

154. Ibid., 20.

155. Ibid.

156. Ibid., 23.

157. Ibid.

158. Cary Wolfe, *Critical Environments* (Minneapolis: University of Minnesota Press, 1988), xxii.

159. Feyerabend, *Against Method,* 23.

160. Harari and Bell, "Introduction," xxx. For why Hermes is chosen as the metaphor for Serres's "anti-method," see xxx–xxxvii.

161. Ibid., x–xi, xi.

162. Maria L. Assad, *Reading with Michel Serres: An Encounter with Time* (Albany: State University of New York Press, 1999), 21, 20.

163. Harari and Bell, "Introduction," xxvii, xxii, xxix.

164. Ibid., xvi.

165. It might be interesting here to compare Ihab Hassan's notion of "anti-form," which he elaborates in the context of, among other writers, John Cage, to Michel Serres's "anti-method." For more details, see Hassan's *The Postmodern Turn: Essays in Postmodern Theory and Culture* (Columbus: Ohio State University Press, 1987), especially 3–22. For a brief critique of Hassan's position on "anti-form," see Conte, *Unending Design,* 19.

166. Harari and Bell, "Introduction," vii.

167. Maria L. Assad, "Michel Serres: In Search of a Tropography," in *Chaos and Order: Complex Dynamics in Literature and Science,* ed. N. Katherine Hayles (Chicago: University of Chicago Press, 1991), 291.

168. Ibid., 291.

169. Michel Serres, *Les cinq sens* (Paris: Grasset, 1985), 289, 323.

170. Bruno Latour, "The Enlightenment Without the Critique: A Word on Michel Serres' Philosophy," in *Contemporary French Philosophy,* ed. A. Phillips Griffiths (New York: Cambridge University Press, 1987), 89.

171. Ibid., 93.

172. Harari and Bell, "Introduction," xxxv, xvii.

173. Michel Serres, *Hermes IV: La distribution* (Paris: Minuit, 1977), 289, quoted in Harari and Bell, "Introduction," xvii.

174. Harari and Bell, "Introduction," xxxvi, note 48. It is interesting to note that this passage on Serres's anti-method, like all radical discourses addressing radical issues, shows in spite of itself an occasionally conceptual limit evidenced in the poverty as well as ambiguity of its vocabulary. Though Harari and Bell clearly endorse Serres's anti-method, for instance, their use of the transition word "but" that begins the third sentence nevertheless seems to suggest that their description of method found in Serres's work in the first two sentences is different from the problems of method singled out in sentences three and four, when in fact they are all appositional specifications of how method works in the traditional sense. Besides, the defining feature of method conventionally understood and employed is that it "invents." Method invents in the sense that it is the projection and imposition of a preconceived objective from a subject's standpoint onto a domain of inquiry from the outside, with its outcome predetermined. Methodical invention is thus none other than a euphemistic expression of a methodical self-referentiality. In the larger context of Harari and Bell's introduction, Serres's "construction of models" should therefore be properly understood as part of his anti-method strategies by which to bring into visibility various methods at work.

175. Harari and Bell, "Introduction," xxxvi.

176. Ibid., vii, xxxvi.

177. Gasché, *Tain of the Mirror,* 122.

178. Harari and Bell, "Introduction," xxxvi, xxxvii.

179. Ibid., xxxvi, xxii.

180. Ibid., xxxii, xxxiii, xxxv.

181. Ibid., xxii–xxiii.

182. Paul Hoover, introduction to *Postmodern American Poetry: A Norton Anthology,* ed. Paul Hoover (New York: Norton, 1994), xxvii. Hoover's distinction between the two terms "constructionist" and "expressionist" is itself problematic. Though it is beyond the scope of this project to make a detailed argument on this issue, suffice it to say at this point that to construct is to express, as is signified by the denotation of the verb *construct.* Equally problematic is his understanding that method can "replace intention," a problem that will be taken up and addressed later in the chapter on John Cage.

183. Fredman, *Poet's Prose,* 141.

184. The expression here alludes to Wittgenstein's remark on words when he says: "What we do is to bring words back from their metaphysical to their everyday use" (Ludwig Wittgenstein, *Philosophical Investigations,* trans. G. E. M. Anscombe [New York: Macmillan, 1958], section 116).

185. Byrd, "Language Poetry," 153.

186. On this point, an oblique critique of this use-oriented approach to method can be found in an interesting essay by Joseph Margolis, who not only discusses Wittgenstein's method very much in terms of counter-method, but also contends that "in Wittgenstein's opinion, metaphysics easily penetrates 'everyday use'" (325). For his complete argument, see Joseph Margolis, "Unlikely Prospects for Applying Wittgenstein's 'Method' to Aesthetics and the Philosophy of Art," in *The Literary Wittgenstein,* ed. John Gibson and Wolfgang Huemer (London: Routledge, 2004), 321–45.

187. Raymond Queneau, "Potential Literature," in *Oulipo: A Primer of Potential Literature,* ed. and trans. Warren F. Motte Jr. (Lincoln: University of Nebraska Press, 1986), 51.

188. Warren F. Motte Jr., introduction to *Oulipo,* 10.

189. Conte, *Unending Design,* 240. In his study of seriality and proceduralism as the "two complementary methods" of postmodern poetry (11), Joseph Conte argues emphatically for this use/production-oriented approach to method, privileging its generative potential. He writes:

Postmodern poets have by no means viewed form suspiciously, nor have they been particularly devoted to "anti-formal" methods of composition. These poets have in fact a decidedly imaginative and innovative approach to formal methods, easily challenging in its diversity the formal innovation of the great modernists. Serial and procedural orders, an aleatory or a rule-dominated method of composition, constitute a distinctive formal identity in postmodern poetics. (12)

It is important to note, however, that this use/production-oriented approach to method, as much as it is antithetical to the modernists' privileging of the scientific methods constitutive of a hierarchal totality, is in one sense still scientific, in that it "is not simply a different methodological stance," as Conte makes it clear, "but a different vision of the world" (24), both contingent upon contemporary theories of sciences and modeled after current methods of scientific research. In addition, proceeding from an exclusively formal and aesthetic perspective, this approach seems to favor the methodical implications over the implications of method, and its belief in a generative potential is in fact the one and the same belief in the efficacy of method. In his discussion of the serial method as "protean," for instance, Conte specifies that its function is "*to capture* [my emphasis] the incessantly changing, fluid, and contiguous phenomena as they occur" (11).

190. Motte, introduction to *Oulipo*, 18.

191. Byrd, "Language Poetry," 153.

192. See Conte's comment in note 189 above. To a great extent, the two words "method" and "form" are used interchangeably in my book.

193. Bruce Andrews, *Paradise and Method: Poetics and Praxis* (Evanston, Ill.: Northwestern University Press, 1996), 152.

194. Ibid., 54.

195. Louis Zukofsky, *Prepositions: The Collected Critical Essays of Louis Zukofsky,* exp. ed. (Berkeley: University of California Press, 1981), 12 (emphasis added).

196. Charles Bernstein, *Content's Dream* (Los Angeles: Sun and Moon, 1986), 226, 224.

Chapter I

1. Zukofsky, *Prepositions,* 146.

2. Rainer Nägele, "Benjamin's Ground," in *Benjamin's Ground: New Readings of Walter Benjamin,* ed. Rainer Nägele (Detroit: Wayne State University Press, 1988), 19.

3. Burton Hatlen, "From Modernism to Postmodernism: Zukofsky's 'A'–12," *Sagetrieb* 11, no. 1–2 (Spring–Fall 1992): 21.

4. Ibid., 21.

5. Michael André Bernstein, "Bringing It All Back Home: Derivations and Quotations in Robert Duncan and the Poundian Tradition," *Sagetrieb* 1, no. 2 (Fall 1982): 177, 178.

6. Hugh Kenner, foreword to Zukovsky, *Prepositions,* ix.

7. Romana Zacchi, "Quoting Words and Worlds: Discourse Strategies in *Ulysses*," *James Joyce Quarterly* 27, no. 1 (Fall 1989): 105.

8. Barbara Johnson, introduction to *Dissemination,* by Jacques Derrida., trans. Barbara Johnson (Chicago: University of Chicago Press, 1981), xxx.

9. Louis Zukofsky, *"A"* (Baltimore: Johns Hopkins University Press, 1993), "A"–14, p. 354, "A"–22, p. 509. For a reading of Zukofsky's poetry, including his "Poem beginning 'The'" from a postmodern perspective, see Bruce Comens, "From A to An: The Postmodern Twist in Louis Zukofsky," *Sagetrieb* 10, no. 3 (Winter 1991): 37–62.

10. Pound, *ABC of Reading,* 95 (emphases in original). Unless otherwise noted, all forms of emphasis in the quotations in this chapter are in the original. For Pound's position on this issue, see also his "Approach to Paris," in which he describes poetry as the "constatation of facts. It presents. It does not comment" (Ezra Pound, "The Approach to Paris, v.," *New Age* 13 [October 2, 1913]: 662).

11. Leonard Diepeveen, *Changing Voices: The Modern Quoting Poem* (Ann Arbor: University of Michigan Press, 1993), 64.

12. Pound, *Literary Essays,* 3.

13. Ibid., 56, 11.

14. Ezra Pound, *Selected Prose 1909-1965,* ed. William Cookson (New York: New Directions, 1973), 26.

15. Pound, *Literary Essays,* 44.

16. Diepeveen, *Changing Voices,* 60.

17. Pound, *Literary Essays,* 25.

18. Pound, *ABC of Reading,* 36.

19. Pound, *Literary Essays,* 419.

20. Marianne Moore, "The Cantos," in *The Complete Prose of Marianne Moore* (New York: Viking, 1986), 272.

21. T. S. Eliot, *Selected Essays,* new ed. (New York: Harcourt, Brace and World, 1950), 4, 7.

22. See also Rosalind Krauss's "Re-presenting Picasso," *Art in America* (December 1980), in which she argues that the use of the past in modernist praxis "allows for the rewriting of succession (diachrony) as system (synchrony), thereby producing the a-historical object" (92–93). Krauss's remark is also cited in Diepeveen, *Changing Voices,* 60.

23. Eliot, *Selected Essays,* 247.

24. T. S. Eliot, "Philip Massinger," in *The Sacred Wood: Essays on Poetry and Criticism* (New York: Alfred A. Knopf, 1930), 125.

25. Pound, *Literary Essays,* 26.

26. Michael André Bernstein makes a similar point when he writes, "Pound's language presents, represents, and invents all at once, and it does so *without privileging any single mode or trivializing essential distinctions between categories*" (Michael André Bernstein, "History and Textuality in Ezra Pound's *Cantos*," in

Ezra Pound and History, ed. Marianne Korn [Orono, Maine: National Poetry Foundation, 1985], 17, emphasis added).

27. Michele J. Leggott, *Reading Zukofsky's 80 Flowers* (Baltimore: Johns Hopkins University Press, 1989), 99.

28. Meir Sternberg, "Proteus in Quotation-Land: Mimesis and the Forms of Reported Discourse," *Poetics Today* 3, no. 2 (Spring 1982): 109.

29. Herbert Grabes, "Deliberate Intertextuality: The Function of Quotation and Allusion in the Early Poetry of T. S. Eliot," in *Multiple Worlds, Multiple Words,* ed. Hena Maes-Jelinek, Pierre Michel, and Paulette Michel-Michot (Liège, Belg.: English Department, University of Liège, 1987), 146–47. See also Diepeveen, *Changing Voices,* 65; and Zacchi, "Quoting Words and Worlds," 101–9. Although Zacchi emphasizes that "only transformative and regenerative operations on the original are possible" (104), and that "quotations can acquire generative functions" (109), her theorizing remains largely modernist in that the "textual clash" and the corollary "new birth" from the "co-existence of the two codes" (104) contribute to, rather than call into question, a predetermined and discernible narrative line with an identifiable theme.

30. Pound, *Guide to Kulchur,* 92, 95.

31. Jennifer Clarvoe, "Quoting History, Reading Poetry," *Agni Review* (1990): 328.

32. Grabes, "Deliberate Intertextuality," 151.

33. Albert Gelpi, *A Coherent Splendor: The American Poetic Renaissance, 1910–1950* (Cambridge: Cambridge University Press, 1987), 203, 202.

34. Ezra Pound, *The Cantos of Ezra Pound* (New York: New Directions, 1995), XIII/59.

35. Gelpi, *Coherent Splendor,* 203.

36. Pound, *Cantos,* XIII/58.

37. Ibid., XIII/59.

38. Gelpi, *Coherent Splendor,* 203.

39. Lawrence S. Rainey, *Ezra Pound and the Monument of Culture: Text, History, and the Malatesta Cantos* (Chicago: University of Chicago Press, 1991), 57.

40. For the names of "host" and "found," see Herbert H. Clark and Richard J. Gerrig, "Quotations as Demonstrations," *Language* 66, no. 4 (December 1990): 764–805. For the names of "frame" and "inset," see Sternberg, "Proteus in Quotation-Land," 109n.

41. Clark and Gerrig, "Quotations," 766.

42. Pound, *Cantos,* VI/21 (ellipses in original).

43. Michael André Bernstein, "Bringing It All Back Home," 178.

44. Pound, *Literary Essays,* 92.

45. Diepeveen, *Changing Voices,* xv. Richard Sieburth argues similarly that to quote is more than just to mime: "It is a mode not merely of copying or reflecting but of including the real. . . . To quote is thus to adduce words as facts, as

exhibits, as documents" (Richard Sieburth, *Instigations: Ezra Pound and Rémy de Gourmont* [Cambridge, Mass.: Harvard University Press, 1978], 121).

46. Michael André Bernstein, "Bringing It All Back Home," 187–88.

47. Emerson writes, "We cannot overstate our debt to the Past, but the moment has the supreme claim. The Past is for us; but the sole terms on which it can become ours are its subordination to the Present" (Ralph Waldo Emerson, "Quotation and Originality," in *Letters and Social Aims* [Boston: Houghton Mifflin, 1904], 204).

48. Sternberg, "Proteus in Quotation-Land," 131.

49. Ibid., 125, 144, 145.

50. Andrew Kappel, "The Reading and Writing of a Modern Paradiso: Ezra Pound and the Books of Paradise," *Twentieth Century Literature* 27, no. 3 (Fall 1981): 228.

51. Ibid., 230, 231, 235. Sieburth points out that Pound's "extensive and multifaceted use of quotations in the *Cantos*" presents "a logical development of a modernist aesthetic that can be traced back to those techniques of constatation and subversive juxtaposition that Flaubert applied at almost every level of his art." However, Sieburth argues, while Flaubert uses cinema-like montage as "vehicles less of metaphor or revelation than of destructive irony"—a use approximating that of Zukofsky—Pound adopts the technique for a constructive end, ideogrammatically "presenting one facet and then another until at some point one gets off the dead and desensitized surface of the reader's mind, onto a part that will register" (Sieburth, "Investigations," 121–22; quoting Pound's *Guide to Kulchur,* 51).

52. Pound, *Cantos,* VII/24.

53. Pound, *Literary Essays,* 295.

54. Ibid., 300–301.

55. Carroll F. Terrell, A *Companion to "The Cantos of Ezra Pound"* (Berkeley: University of California Press, 1980), 31.

56. Ibid.

57. See also Diepeveen, *Changing Voices,* 73–74.

58. Sternberg, "Proteus in Quotation-Land," 144, 109.

59. Grabes, "Deliberate Intertextuality," 148.

60. Clarvoe, "Quoting History," 329.

61. Pound, *Literary Essays,* 25.

62. Zukofsky, *Prepositions,* 60.

63. Norbert Wiener, *The Human Use of Human Beings: Cybernetics and Society* (New York: Da Capo, 1954), 17–18.

64. Hayles, *Chaos Bound,* 270.

65. William R. Paulson, "Literature, Complexity, Interdisciplinarity," in *Chaos and Order,* ed. Hayles, 39.

66. William R. Paulson, *The Noise of Culture: Literary Texts in a World of Information* (Ithaca, N.Y.: Cornell University Press, 1988), 54.

67. Paulson, *Noise of Culture,* 57.

68. Charles Altieri, "The Objectivist Tradition," *Chicago Review* 30, no. 3 (Winter 1979): 15.

69. Zukofsky, *Prepositions,* 20.

70. Louis Zukofsky, "Interview," by L. S. Dembo, in *The Contemporary Writer: Interviews with Sixteen Novelists and Poets,* ed. L. S. Dembo and Cyrena N. Pondrom (Madison: University of Wisconsin Press, 1972), 217.

71. *Webster's New World Dictionary of the American Language,* 2nd College ed. (New York: Simon and Schuster, 1982), s.v. "The."

72. Robert Duncan, "As Testimony: Reading Zukofsky These Forty Years," *Paideuma* 7, no. 3 (Winter 1978): 425.

73. Louis Zukofsky, "Poem beginning 'The,'" in *Complete Short Poetry* (Baltimore: Johns Hopkins University Press, 1991), 8.

74. Ibid.

75. Rainey, *Ezra Pound,* 53.

76. On this issue, see Rainey, *Ezra Pound,* 69.

77. Zukofsky, *Prepositions,* 13.

78. Don Byrd, "The Shape of Zukofsky's Canon," in *Louis Zukofsky: Man and Poet,* ed. Carroll F. Terrell (Orono, Maine: National Poetry Foundation, 1979), 165.

79. L. S. Dembo, "Louis Zukofsky: Objectivist Poetics and the Quest for Form," in *Louis Zukofsky,* ed. Terrell, 298.

80. Paulson, *Noise of Culture,* 57.

81. Zukofsky, "Interview," 222.

82. Altieri, "Objectivist Tradition," 15.

83. Zukofsky, *Prepositions,* 12

84. Altieri, "Objectivist Tradition," 15.

85. For a useful and related discussion of *surface* and *depth,* and *geography* and *geology,* as contextualized in and contrasted between the works of Jakobson and Deleuze, see Jean-Jacques Lecercle, *Deleuze and Language* (New York: Palgrave, 2002), especially 27.

86. Leggott, *Reading Zukofsky's 80 Flowers,* 55.

87. Zukofsky, "Poem beginning 'The,'" 9.

88. Ibid., 8.

89. Ezra Pound and Louis Zukofsky, *Pound/Zukofsky: Selected Letters of Ezra Pound and Louis Zukofsky,* ed. Barry Ahearn (New York: New Directions, 1987), 79.

90. Zukofsky, *Prepositions,* 18.

91. Zukofsky, "Poem beginning 'The,'" 8.

92. Derrida, *Dissemination,* 290. Derrida's critical commentary on Philippe Sollers' novel *Numbers* can be read as an extended punning on the word *number,* which can be applied in an illuminating fashion to Zukofsky's use of numbers here in "Poem beginning 'The.'"

93. Duncan, "Testimony," 424.

94. Marjorie Perloff, "Toward an Avant-Garde *Tractatus:* Russell and Wittgenstein on War," *Common Knowledge* 2, no. 1 (Spring 1993): 30.

95. For a detailed discussion of the terms *context-sensitive* and *context-free,* see Andreas Fischer, "Context-Free and Context-Sensitive Literature: Sherwood Anderson's *Winesburg, Ohio* and James Joyce's *Dubliners,*" in *Reading Contexts,* ed. Neil Forsyth (Tübingen, W.Ger.: Gunter Narr, 1988), 12–31.

96. Pound, *Selected Prose,* 268. Reed Way Dasenbrook also argues, though in the more specific context of painting, that, for Pound, the "essence of any situation is a relation" (108). For more detail, see his *The Literary Vorticism of Ezra Pound and Wyndham Lewis: Towards the Condition of Painting* (Baltimore: Johns Hopkins University Press, 1985).

97. Pound, *Literary Essays,* 49.

98. Ibid.

99. Grabes, "Deliberate Intertextuality," 141.

100. Pound, *Literary Essays,* 44.

101. Pound, *ABC of Reading,* 36.

102. Pound, *Literary Essays,* 25.

103. Pound, *Selected Prose,* 396.

104. Alan Durant, "The Language of History in *The Cantos,*" in *Ezra Pound and History,* ed. Korn, 32.

105. Rainey, *Ezra Pound,* 57. Diepeveen, in *Changing Voices,* makes a similar argument. He writes: "Pound's emphasis on the universal implies that the disparate objects (often both historically and culturally disparate) of the quoting poem must relate to each other; they must be translatable. Eliot and Pound moved to a formal concept like pattern as the central term to support their argument about translatability and originality" (59–60).

106. Michael André Bernstein, "History and Textuality," 21.

107. Claudette Sartiliot, *Citation and Modernity: Derrida, Joyce, and Brecht* (Norman: University of Oklahoma Press, 1993), 11, 20.

108. Jacques Derrida, *Margins of Philosophy,* trans. Alan Bass (Chicago: University of Chicago Press, 1982), 310. Derrida's comment, the complexity of which is, without any doubt, beyond the scope of this book, is pertinent to the issue under discussion here, and it goes as follows: "It seems to go without saying that the field of equivocality covered by the word *communication* permits itself to be reduced massively by the limits of what is called a *context* (and I announce, again between parentheses, that the issue will be, in this communication, the problem of context, and of finding out about writing as concerns context in

general)" (310). For a structural analysis of communication as a game or as an act of complicity between two interlocutors (or between two texts, or between text and context, for that matter) for the purpose of a successful communication by purging noise, see Serres, *Hermes: Literature, Science, Philosophy,* 65–70.

109. Paulson, *Noise of Culture,* 60, 64.

110. Ibid., 64.

111. Ibid., 57.

112. Diepeveen, *Changing Voices,* 103.

113. Pound, *Cantos,* LXXIV/429.

114. Terrell, *Companion to "The Cantos,"* 369.

115. Ibid., 120.

116. Gelpi, *Coherent Splendor,* 200, 201.

117. Ibid., 201.

118. Terrell, *Companion to "The Cantos,"* 120.

119. Hugh Kenner, *The Pound Era* (Berkeley: University of California Press, 1971), 423. Kenner defines Pound's "heuristic device" and "subject rhyme" when he writes: "Pound's heuristic device is always the subject-rhyme. To elucidate the Italian New Birth of circa 1500, he compares it with the American of circa 1770. Specifically, Jefferson and his successors building a nation are rhymed with Malatesta building the Tempio, and a careful structural parallel enforces this rhyme" (423).

120. Pound, *Cantos,* LXXIV/464.

121. Pound, *Literary Essays,* 49.

122. Durant, "Language of History," 32.

123. Pound, *Literary Essays,* 162.

124. Pound and Zukofsky, *Pound/Zukofsky,* 79, 78.

125. Alison Rieke, "Words' Contexts, Contexts' Nouns: Zukofsky's Objectivist Quotations," *Contemporary Literature* 33, no. 1 (Spring 1992): 117.

126. Jean Baudrillard, *Selected Writings,* ed. Mark Poster (Stanford, Calif.: Stanford University Press, 1988), 78, 81, 83.

127. Ibid., 81.

128. Ibid., 81, 84.

129. Derrida, *Dissemination,* 323. See also Paulson, *Noise of Culture,* 61.

130. Robert J. Branham and W. Barnett Pearce, "Between Text and Context: Toward a Rhetoric of Contextual Reconstruction," *Quarterly Journal of Speech* 71, no. 1 (February 1985): 20.

131. Baudrillard, *Selected Writings,* 83, 84.

132. Sternberg, "Proteus in Quotation-Land," 133.

133. See also Leggott, *Reading Zukofsky's 80 Flowers,* 99.

134. Gregory Polletta, "Textuality, Actuality, and Contextuality: The Example of *Gravity's Rainbow,*" in *Reading Contexts,* ed. Forsyth, 88–89.

135. Hayles, *Chaos Bound,* 275.

136. Derrida, *Margins of Philosophy,* 320.

137. Diepeveen defines *texture* as that which asserts "the idiosyncratic rather than the interchangeable." He continues: "Texture does not just define the sounds of a group of words, it has consequences. It shows how these sounds point to and are part of those words' individual, nonparaphrasable meanings. Texture also implies a quotation's history, its past, 'original' use and this original use's earlier appropriations by culture" (Diepeveen, *Changing Voices,* 3). Diepeveen's definition, as the subtitle of his book indicates, focuses on the "formal properties" of quotations, which highlights the importance of their original contexts. While agreeing with him on all of these observations, this chapter also uses the word *texture* to refer to quotations as raw materials in the sense that they are simply words in clusters without any textual-contextual framing through a controlling perspective.

138. Zukofsky, "Poem beginning 'The,'" 10–11.

139. Ibid., 8. In his reading of this poem, John Tomas comments on Zukofsky's use of references: "Such references . . . ensure that nobody will take these notes seriously" (John Tomas, "Portrait of the Artist as a Young Jew: Zukofsky's 'Poem beginning "The"' in Context," *Sagetrieb* 9, no. 1–2 [Spring–Fall 1990]: 44). Tomas's own reading of the poem is, as the title of his article indicates, based on a serious consideration of references and contexts which he locates elsewhere, and which he uses as replacements for the references provided by the poet. What seems to have been overlooked in Tomas's approach is, perhaps, the possibility that it is precisely Zukofsky's lack of seriousness that makes the point here. For Tomas's detailed argument, see "Portrait of the Artist," 43–64.

140. Ben-Ami Scharfstein, *The Dilemma of Context* (New York: New York University Press, 1989), 187.

141. Serres, *Hermes: Literature, Science, Philosophy,* 69.

142. Diepeveen, *Changing Voices,* 76.

143. Christopher Marlowe, *Marlowe's Edward II,* ed. William Dinsmore Briggs (London: David Nutt, 1914), 29.

144. Scharfstein, *Dilemma of Context,* 60.

145. Lenn E. Goodman, "Context," *Philosophy East and West* 38, no. 3 (July 1988): 308.

146. Zacchi, "Quoting Words and Worlds," 107.

147. Louis Zukofsky, *A Test of Poetry* (New York: Jargon/Corinth Books, 1964), 84, 89.

148. Zukofsky, "Poem beginning 'The,'" 15.

149. Derrida, *Dissemination,* 356.

150. Ibid.

151. Ibid., 357.

152. Duncan, "Testimony," 427.

153. Pound and Zukofsky, *Pound/Zukofsky,* 79.

154. John Taggart, *Songs of Degrees: Essays on Contemporary Poetry and Poetics* (Tuscaloosa: University of Alabama Press, 1994), 208.

155. Edward Schelb, "Through Rupture to Destiny: Repetition in Zukofsky," *Sagetrieb* 9, no. 1-2 (Spring–Fall 1990): 32.

156. Zukofsky, *"A,"* 174. On this point, John Taggart's reading of *"A"*–12 and its source material in Hasidic sayings (*Songs of Degrees,* 199–200) sheds light on the compositional strategy of "Poem beginning 'The'." He argues, furthermore, that "to try to locate specific sources" for Zukofsky's poetry presents "a temptation difficult and even misleading"; for "what Zukofsky has done is to separate the words and phrases from their original contexts to provide himself with a vocabulary for composition" (*Songs of Degrees,* 208, 200).

157. Duncan, "Testimony," 423.

158. Pound and Zukofsky, *Pound/Zukofsky,* 79.

Chapter 2

1. George Oppen, *New Collected Poems,* ed. Michael Davidson (New York: New Directions, 2002), 70 (italics in the original). Unless otherwise noted, all forms of emphasis in quotations of Oppen's poems are in the original.

2. Edward Hirsch, "'Out There Is the World': The Visual Imperative in the Poetry of George Oppen and Charles Tomlinson," in *George Oppen: Man and Poet,* ed. Burton Hatlen (Orono, Maine: National Poetry Foundation, 1981), 169.

3. John Taggart, "George Oppen and the Anthologies," *Ironwood* 13, no. 2 (Fall 1985): 259.

4. George Oppen, "An Interview with George and Mary Oppen," by Keven Power, *Montemore* 4 (August 1978): 196.

5. George Oppen, "The 'Objectivist' Poet: Four Interviews," by L. S. Dembo, in *Contemporary Literature* 10, no. 2 (Spring 1969): 161.

6. Ross Feld, "Some Thoughts About Objectivism," *Sagetrieb* 12, no. 3 (Winter 1993): 69.

7. Alan Golding, "George Oppen's Serial Poems," *Contemporary Literature* 29, no. 2 (Summer 1998): 231.

8. L. S. Dembo, "The Existential World of George Oppen," *Iowa Review* 3, no. 1 (1972): 64.

9. Oppen, "'Objectivist' Poet," 173.

10. Oppen, *New Collected Poems,* 107 (ellipses in original).

11. George Oppen, "Three Poets," *Poetry* 100, no. 5 (August 1962): 329. Oppen is very vocal about his position against any systematic thinking in favor of real world experience. In a letter to June Oppen Degnan dated 1963, for instance, he presents to her what he calls "a partial report" on his reading of Jung in relation

to the "Freudian world," which he considers as having become almost "insane." Oppen writes:

> I don't think the philosophic and psychological system has much interest as a system. The idea of the "Protean psyche," the "protean life of the psyche" derived from its own nature and not conditioned by experience, would require him to believe in a special Act of Creation of man, or to disbelieve in the existence of the objective world. He doesn't believe in the Special Act—nor do I—and he does accept the existence of the objective world, the mineral world—and I would if he didn't. But then the psyche must have been created by forces in that world, and it is that world and not the psyche, as he says, which is the "mother." (George Oppen, "Letters to June Oppen Degnan," *Ironwood* 13, no. 2 [Fall 1985]: 220)

For more details, see "Letters to June Oppen Degnan," 220–21. In more straightforward terms, Oppen privileges experiential surprises over systematic treatments of the world when he states: "I do not care for 'systems,' what I read is the philosophy of the astonished" (George Oppen, " 'The Philosophy of the Astonished': Selections from the Working Papers," ed. Rachel Blau DuPlessis, *Sulfur* 10, no. 2 [Fall 1990]: 203). DuPlessis has brought this aspect of Oppen's poetics to the fore in her study titled "George Oppen: 'What Do We Believe to Live With?' " (*Ironwood* 3, no. 1 [1975]: 62–77), arguing that "Oppen is a philosophic poet who distrusts a total intellectual system—and will not create one" (63).

12. Oppen, " 'Objectivist' Poet," 173.

13. The imagist theory of perception that could be considered as conducive, in a certain sense, to the effect of "isolation" or "distancing" would be Williams's theorem of "no ideas but in things" (William Carlos Williams, *Paterson* [New York: New Directions, 1963], 6). Oppen, however, has clearly articulated his doubt and reservations about the plausibility of Williams's position as well as about the imagist method more generally. For a brief but revealing discussion on this issue, see Oppen, " 'Objectivist' Poet," 170.

14. Quite often, critics tend to consider Oppen's objectivist vision as identical with the imagist vision and, in this context, believe that the issue of "isolation" or "distancing" has significant impact on the poet. Jeremy Hooker argues, for instance, that "the question is particularly 'profound and painful' for Oppen, because it strikes at the roots of his way of seeing, the method of thought which he has constructed from the 'imagist intensity of vision.' " While Hooker is right in pointing out that "the question itself defines [Oppen's] area of concern as a poet," the aesthetic, philosophical, and methodological perspectives from which the question defines Oppen's area of concern is not, however, that of the imagists. See Jeremy Hooker, " 'The Boundaries of Our Distances': On 'Of Being Numerous,' " *Ironwood* 13, no. 2 (Fall 1985): 83.

15. Claude Gandelman, *Reading Pictures, Viewing Texts* (Bloomington: Indiana University Press, 1991), 1.

16. Oppen, "'Objectivist' Poet," 170.

17. Zukofsky, *Prepositions,* 16.

18. Piotr Parlej, "Testing the Image: The Double Interrogative in the Poetry of George Oppen," *Sagetrieb* 10, no. 1-2 (Spring–Fall 1991): 69. In this essay, Parlej's discussion of "the central issue of *predication*" focuses on the examples of "Pound's 'Metro' haiku" and his "ideogrammatic method of juxtaposition" (68, 69) between two images where the predication works (72), and the issue is analyzed mainly at the level of syntax. On this point, Oppen differs from Pound, he argues, in that "Oppen prefers to investigate the single image and 'test' its metaphorical residue, without any ambition to construct an ideogrammatic equation that would tantalize the reader" (71), and that the predication reemerges in Oppen's work "this time *within* the space of one image" (72). For Parlej's Heideggerian reading of Oppen's single images, see, especially, pages 75–81. Although Parlej's treatment of the issue of predication is limited to the numbers of images involved, his theorizing of the concept of predication in this area is equally applicable to the issue of vision and its function.

19. Ibid., 68. This statement by Parlej is also a reference to the reading by Harrison Randolph Chilton Jr., as is suggested by Parlej's phrase "as Chilton rightly observes" (68) that precedes the quotation. The specific bibliographical information of this reference is not offered in Parlej's essay. But in "A Selected, Annotated Bibliography of Secondary Sources, 1932–1985, on Louis Zukofsky," compiled by Alvin R. Bailey for an issue of *Sagetrieb,* one can find the source in entry 197: "Chilton, Harrison Randolph, Jr. *The Object beyond the Image: A Study of Four Objectivist Poets.* Diss. U of Wisconsin-Madison, 1981. Ann Arbor: UMI, 1981. 8120300" (198).

20. Parlej, "Testing the Image," 70.

21. Ibid.

22. Ibid.

23. Ibid.

24. Ibid.

25. Hooker, "Boundaries of Our Distances," 97. Hooker also offers a reading of "seeing with the eye" in Oppen's poetry, which focuses primarily on the physical, and as a result, the philosophical implications are given only a passing treatment. For more details, see p. 97.

26. Parlej, "Testing the Image," 80.

27. Oppen, *New Collected Poems,* 99.

28. Parlej, "Testing the Image," 80.

29. Eric Mottram, "The Political Responsibilities of the Poet: George Oppen," in *George Oppen: Man and Poet,* ed. Hatlen, 152.

30. "Intuitive" and "analytical" are the two terms suggested by an interviewer in his attempt to understand Oppen's idea of "the life of the mind" in terms of "awareness," and Oppen concurs. For the context of this exchange, see Oppen, "'Objectivist' Poet," 164.

31. Dembo, "Existential World," 69, 70. In his discussion of the "limitations of perception" in Oppen's poems, Dembo focuses on the aspect of "description," which is "characteristically, 'objective,'" and which "[reflects] the impersonality of an observer"; as a result, the mind "is not always fulfilled or fulfilled in such a way that the observer's sense of isolation is only increased." For more detail, see pp. 69–70.

32. DuPlessis, "George Oppen," 72.

33. Oppen, "'Objectivist' Poet," 163.

34. Ibid.

35. Oppen, "Philosophy of the Astonished," 203.

36. George Oppen, *The Selected Letters of George Oppen,* ed. Rachel Blau DuPlessis (Durham, N.C.: Duke University Press, 1990), 22.

37. George Oppen, "The Mind's Own Place," *Kulchur* 3, no. 10 (Summer 1963): 3–4.

38. Dembo, "Existential World," 65, 86.

39. DuPlessis, "George Oppen," 66.

40. Hirsch, "Out There," 170.

41. Taggart, "George Oppen," 256.

42. Hirsch, "Out There," 169, 176.

43. Ibid., 170, 171, 179.

44. Oppen, *New Collected Poems,* 40.

45. Ibid., 40.

46. Ibid., 41.

47. Ibid.

48. Ibid., 258.

49. George Oppen, "An Adequate Vision: A George Oppen Daybook," *Ironwood* 13, no. 2 (Fall 1985): 11.

50. Robert Hass, "George Oppen: A Tribute," *Ironwood* 13, no. 2 (Fall 1985): 41. Similar to Edward Hirsch, Hass describes Oppen's use of images as showing the process of the mind encountering the object under ethical pressure. He writes:

> [If] the imagist poem is a picture, then the great discovery of the Objectivist poets, if there was such a thing, was that what was really going on at the level of prosody was not the image as a picture but the formation of the image as an x-ray. What the Objectivists did was turn the imagist picture into an x-ray; and as soon as they did, it became clear that an image was not a picture of a thing, but a picture of the mind perceiving a thing. And as soon as it became

the picture of the mind perceiving the thing, then the morality of perception came to be an issue. And what's extraordinary about George Oppen's poetry is, moment after moment in his work, line by line, syllable by syllable, you have a sense of an enormous ethical pressure brought to bear on the act of perception, and a sense that the ethical pressure on the act of perception is for him the same thing as the writing of the poem. (39–40)

51. Ibid., 41.
52. Oppen, *New Collected Poems,* 165 (emphasis added).
53. Altieri, "Objectivist Tradition," 6.
54. Oppen, "Adequate Vision," 30.
55. Oppen, *New Collected Poems,* 15.
56. Ibid., 16, 17, 19, 21, 20, 23.
57. Ibid., 24.
58. Ibid., 64 (ellipses in original).
59. Ibid., 64–66.
60. Ibid., 66, 64.
61. Ibid., 64
62. Ibid.
63. Ibid.
64. Ibid.
65. *Webster's New World Dictionary,* s.v. "In."
66. Oppen, "Adequate Vision," 13.
67. Oppen, *New Collected Poems,* 65.
68. Ibid., 64.
69. Ibid., 142.
70. Ibid.
71. *Webster's New World Dictionary,* s.v. "Expect."
72. Oppen, *New Collected Poems,* 142.
73. Ibid.
74. *Webster's New World Dictionary,* s.v. "Awe."
75. Oppen, *New Collected Poems,* 142.
76. *Webster's New World Dictionary,* s.v. "Patient."
77. Ibid., "Patience."
78. Oppen, *New Collected Poems,* 142.
79. Ibid., 168.
80. Ibid.
81. Ibid.
82. Ibid.
83. Ibid., 169.
84. Ibid.
85. Oppen, "Three Poets," 329.

86. Oppen, "Philosophy of the Astonished," 203.

87. Oppen, "'Objectivist' Poet," 172.

88. Ibid., 166.

89. Oppen, *New Collected Poems,* 167.

90. Oppen, "'Objectivist' Poet," 172.

91. Oppen, "Philosophy of the Astonished," 204.

92. Dembo, "Existential World," 64.

Chapter 3

1. The phrase "the Medusa's glance" in the chapter title is taken from Adorno's *Against Epistemology: A Metacritique,* trans. Willis Domingo (Cambridge, Mass.: MIT Press, 1982), 196.

2. Harriet Monroe, "The Arrogance of Youth," *Poetry* 37 (March 1931): 333.

3. Ron Silliman, "Third Phase Objectivism," *Paideuma* 10 (Spring 1981): 85, 89.

4. Since the initial publication of this essay, scholarship on objectivist poetry has grown tremendously. For important studies that have helped to open this field, see, among many others, Altieri, "Objectivist Tradition"; Michael Heller, *Conviction's Net of Branches: Essays on the Objectivist Poets and Poetry* (Carbondale: Southern Illinois University Press, 1985); Marjorie Perloff, "'Barbed-Wire Entanglements': The 'New American Poetry,' 1930-1932," *Modernism/Modernity* 2, no. 1 (1995); and Burton Hatlen's many critical essays on different objectivist poets published in the 1980s and 1990s.

5. Perloff, "Barbed-Wire Entanglements," 145, 147 (italics in original). Unless otherwise noted in this chapter, all forms of emphasis are in the original.

6. Zukofsky, *Prepositions,* 12 (italics in original).

7. Ibid., 16.

8. For a clear summary of modernist assumptions concerning the function of language in relation to the immediacy of things, see Burton Hatlen's discussion of what he calls the "imagist" "poetics of presence" in "Zukofsky, Wittgenstein, and the Poetics of Absence," *Sagetrieb* 1, no. 1 (Spring 1982): 63–93.

9. *Webster's New World Dictionary,* s.v. "With."

10. Zukofsky makes a similar point in his discussion of how the "clear physical eye" sees, suggesting that the way to prevent "abstraction" from becoming whole-making generalization is to insist, in Zukofsky's own words, that "the abstract idea is particular, too" (Zukofsky, "Interview," 223).

11. In his response to a question concerning Francis Ponge and what Sartre calls the "crisis of language," Zukofsky uses the "assassin" metaphor in a similar way when he points out that "one of the nice statements Ponge makes is that the poet who falsifies the object is an assassin; instead of calling the object what it is,

this kind of poet develops grand metaphors and all the 'baroque' curlicues." See Zukofsky, "Interview," 231.

12. Hatlen, "Zukofsky, Wittgenstein," 66.

13. Zukofsky, "Interview," 222.

14. Altieri, "Objectivist Tradition," 15.

15. Hatlen, "Zukofsky, Wittgenstein," 66.

16. Silliman, "Third Phase Objectivism," 85.

17. Heller, *Conviction's Net,* 44.

18. Carl Rakosi, *Ex Cranium, Night* (Los Angeles: Black Sparrow, 1975), 131.

19. Carl Rakosi, *The Collected Prose of Carl Rakosi* (Orono, Maine: National Poetry Foundation, 1983), 38–39.

20. John Dewey, *The Quest for Certainty,* Gifford Lectures, 1929 (New York: Putnam, 1960), 23, 214.

21. David Michael Levin, introduction to *Modernity and the Hegemony of Vision,* ed. David Michael Levin (Berkeley: University of California Press, 1993), 2.

22. Dalia Judovitz, "Vision, Representation, and Technology in Descartes," in *Modernity,* ed. Levin, 63, 64, 72.

23. Levin, introduction to *Modernity,* 5.

24. Carl Rakosi, *The Collected Poems of Carl Rakosi* (Orono, Maine: National Poetry Foundation, 1986), 237.

25. Edmund Husserl, *Ideas: General Introduction to Pure Phenomenology,* trans. W. R. Boyce Gibson (London: Collier, 1962), 353.

26. Christopher Macann, *Four Phenomenological Philosophers: Husserl, Heidegger, Sartre, Merleau-Ponty* (New York: Routledge, 1993), 39–40.

27. Rakosi, *Collected Prose,* 19.

28. Macann, *Four Phenomenological Philosophers,* 40 (emphasis added).

29. Rakosi, *Collected Prose,* 18.

30. Ibid. (ellipses in original).

31. See Macann, *Four Phenomenological Philosophers,* 40. In his discussion of symbolist and objectivist poetics in terms of the poet's feeling in relation to the object, Rakosi makes a similar argument in an interview with Dembo, pointing out that the symbolist adopts what Dembo calls an "*a priori*" approach, that is, "an object was simply an occasion for him to project this feeling," while the objectivist adopts an "*a posteriori*" one: "he let his feelings depend upon the object and was faithful to the object." See Carl Rakosi, "Carl Rakosi," interview by L. S. Dembo, in *Contemporary Writer,* ed. Dembo and Pondrom, 201.

32. Rakosi, *Collected Prose,* 29, 73.

33. Levin, introduction to *Modernity,* 2.

34. Adorno, *Against Epistemology,* 3, 125. As Adorno claims, *Against Epistemology* is not intended to be a thorough, systematic, and complete analysis of Husserl's philosophical thinking. Aiming across Husserl's work, Adorno con-

centrates, instead, on "the possibility and truth of epistemology in principle," for which "Husserl's philosophy is the occasion and not the point of this book." Especially pertinent to Rakosi's objectivist poetics are Adorno's discussions and critique of what might be called an anthropomorphic phenomenology.

35. Ibid., 125.

36. Ibid., 129–30.

37. Mikel Dufrenne, *Language and Philosophy*, trans. Henry B. Veatch (Bloomington: Indiana University Press, 1963), 101.

38. Adorno, *Against Epistemology*, 193.

39. Ibid., 174.

40. Ibid., 196. Adorno uses this metaphor in his critique of the Husserlian concept of "attitude." As the translator's footnote points out, the word "attitude" also means, as a verb in German, "to focus," which Husserl, Adorno believes, may have borrowed from the language of photography (Adorno, *Against Epistemology*, 196). In contrast to the "natural attitude," which is the "unreflective acceptance of the 'general thesis of the world' in its spatio-temporality" (195), Husserl's "phenomenologically reduced attitude," as Christopher Macann summarizes, refers to a "positional consciousness [that] becomes an explicitly intentional consciousness, that is, an implicitly or explicitly reflective consciousness 'of.' In other words, it is not the object itself so much as the intentional relation to the object which now becomes the focus of attention" (Macann, *Four Phenomenological Philosophers*, 33).

41. Adorno, *Against Epistemology*, 140.

42. Ibid., 127. The recent philosophical reflection and critique of Western culture share very much the same rhetoric. In his analysis of the forms of knowledge acquisition in the seventeenth century, Michel Serres, for instance, makes a similar observation, though from a different perspective, pointing out that "knowledge is a hunt. To know is to put to death" (Serres, *Hermes: Literature, Science, Philosophy*, 28); for Serres's detailed exposition of this, see *Hermes*, 15–28.

43. Adorno, *Against Epistemology*, 125.

44. The chronological order of the poems gathered in *The Collected Poems of Carl Rakosi* is a subject beyond the scope of this chapter. Rakosi himself makes it clear, in his interview with George Evans and August Kleinzahler, that he has "arranged them all, not according to when they were written but what their sense and climate are"; see Carl Rakosi, "An Interview with Carl Rakosi," *Conjunctions* 11 (1988): 240. And this "sense and climate" seems to have been crystallized—not without irony, of course—in the section of "Adventures of the Head," in a probe into the subject-object relationship, thus granting a justification for the choice of the poems under discussion in this chapter.

45. Rakosi, *Collected Poems*, 44.

46. Jeffrey Peterson, "'The Allotropes of Vision': Carl Rakosi and the Psychol-

ogy of Microscopy," in *Carl Rakosi: Man and Poet,* ed. Michael Heller (Orono, Maine: National Poetry Foundation, 1993), 162.

47. Adorno, *Against Epistemology,* 41. Rakosi's implied argument is shared by other critics. Though Jeffrey Peterson's reading of "The Romantic Eye" emphasizes the tension between two "authoritative modes of vision," romantic and scientific, which "are undercut at the expense of one another," he also points out that "the scientific and the romantic are copresent, reciprocal in magnified seeing" (Peterson, "'Allotropes of Vision,'" 163). Similarly, N. Katherine Hayles asserts that "these twentieth-century epistemological assumptions have more in common with Romanticism. . . . Modern science is not renouncing Romanticism, only changing its emphases" (Hayles, *Cosmic Web,* 18).

48. Adorno, *Against Epistemology,* 76.

49. Ibid., 152.

50. Ibid., 149, 206.

51. Rakosi, *Collected Prose,* 48.

52. Harari and Bell, "Introduction," xxxvi, note 48.

53. Adorno, *Against Epistemology,* 44.

54. Rakosi, *Collected Poems,* 53.

55. Ibid., 237–38.

56. Rakosi, "Carl Rakosi," 202.

57. Burton Hatlen, "Carl Rakosi and the Re-Invention of the Epigram," in Rakosi, *Collected Prose,* 129.

58. Rakosi, "Carl Rakosi," 199.

59. Rakosi often uses the term *subject* to mean "topic"; in this book, *subject* is used to refer to the speaking subject.

60. Rakosi, *Collected Prose,* 44.

61. Ibid., 32.

62. Rakosi, *Collected Poems,* 49.

63. Rakosi's training in psychology and his longtime working experience as a social worker would be an important topic yet to be studied. For a partial treatment of this issue, see Peterson, "'Allotropes of Vision.'"

64. Roland Barthes, *The Rustle of Language,* trans. Richard Howard (New York: Hill and Wang, 1986), 350.

65. The idea of the "unarmed desire" is borrowed from Michael Heller. For details, see *Conviction's Net,* 42.

66. Ibid.

67. Ibid.

68. Adorno, *Against Epistemology,* 149, 150.

69. See also Hatlen's "Carl Rakosi and the Re-Invention of the Epigram," in which he points out that in Rakosi there is this "constant, unresolved struggle between Ego and Object, with the Ego infusing meaning into the Object, and with

the Object serving as a necessary limit-point to the pretensions of the Ego" (Rakoski, *Collected Prose,* 139).

70. Heller, *Conviction's Net,* 38.

71. Rachel Blau DuPlessis, "Objectivist Poetics and Political Vision: A Study of Oppen and Pound," in *George Oppen: Man and Poet,* ed. Hatlen, 130.

72. Barthes, *Rustle of Language,* 355.

73. Ovid, *Metamorphoses,* trans. Rolfe Humphries (Bloomington: Indiana University Press, 1983). The passage referred to reads as follows:

On all sides, through the fields, along the highways,
He saw the forms of men and beasts, made stone
By one look at Medusa's face. He also
Had seen that face, but only in reflection
From the bronze shield his left hand bore. (106)

74. Adorno, *Against Epistemology,* 205.

75. M. H. Abrams, *The Mirror and the Lamp: Romantic Theory and the Critical Tradition* (New York: W. W. Norton, 1958), 58. I am grateful to Peter Quartermain and Rachel Blau DuPlessis for suggesting to me this connection.

76. Ibid., 58, 59.

77. Rakosi, *Collected Poems,* 380.

78. Michael Palmer, "On Objectivism," *Sulfur* 26 (Spring 1990): 121.

79. Harold Bloom, *Wallace Stevens: The Poems of Our Climate* (Ithaca, N.Y.: Cornell University Press, 1977), 3, 205.

80. Bloom, *Wallace Stevens,* 57.

81. Wallace Stevens, *The Palm at the End of the Mind,* ed. Holly Stevens (New York: Vintage Books, 1990), 363.

82. Stevens, *Palm at the End of the Mind,* 364.

83. Bloom, *Wallace Stevens,* 351.

84. Rakosi, *Collected Prose,* 19.

85. Ibid., 46.

86. Rakosi, *Collected Poems,* 42.

87. Levin, introduction to *Modernity,* 14.

88. The term *demilitarize* is John Cage's. In his preface to "Writing for the Second Time Through *Finnegans Wake,*" Cage writes, "Due to N. O. Brown's remark that syntax is the arrangement of the army, and Thoreau's that when he heard a sentence he heard feet marching, I became devoted to non-syntactical 'demilitarized' language" (John Cage, *Empty Words* [Middletown, Conn.: Wesleyan University Press, 1973], 133). With its denotations and connotations, as well as its corresponding image, this term is consistent with those of the Medusa's glance as a weapon used to conquer the object. See also the foreword to Cage's *M: Writings '67–'72* (Middletown, Conn.: Wesleyan University Press, 1973), x, as well as the next chapter of this book.

89. Adorno, *Against Epistemology,* 148.

90. Ibid., 148, 149.

91. Ibid., 171.

92. *Webster's New World Dictionary,* s.v. "Art."

93. Adorno, *Against Epistemology,* 129.

94. Rakosi, *Collected Prose,* 46.

95. Rakosi, *Collected Poems,* 47.

96. Serres, *Hermes: Literature, Science, Philosophy,* 28.

97. Rakosi, *Collected Poems,* 50.

98. Hatlen, "Carl Rakosi and the Re-Invention of the Epigram," 139.

99. Rakosi, *Collected Prose,* 46.

100. Rakosi, *Collected Poems,* 50.

101. *Webster's New World Dictionary,* s.v. "A."

102. Heller, *Conviction's Net,* 18.

103. Hugh Kenner, *A Homemade World* (New York: Morrow, 1975), 187.

104. Rakosi, *Collected Poems,* 50.

105. *Oxford English Dictionary,* s.v. "Plutonic."

106. Theodor W. Adorno, *Minima Moralia: Reflections from Damaged Life,* trans. E. F. N. Jephcott (London: Verso, 1974), 50.

107. Michael Palmer, "On Objectivism," 123.

108. Ibid., 125.

109. Rakosi, "Interview," 222 (ellipses in original).

110. Michael Palmer, "On Objectivism," 121.

111. Watten, *Total Syntax,* 59.

112. Oppen, "George Oppen," 177.

113. Rakosi, *Collected Poems,* 55.

114. *Webster's New World Dictionary,* s.v. "Copulate."

115. *Webster's New World Dictionary,* s.v. "Copula."

116. *Webster's New World Dictionary,* s.v. "Derive."

117. Rakosi, *Collected Prose,* 49.

118. Rakosi, *Collected Poems,* 46.

119. Heller, *Conviction's Net,* 19.

120. Louis Zukofsky, "Preface: 'Recencies' in Poetry," in *An "Objectivists" Anthology,* ed. Louis Zukofsky (New York: Folcroft Library Editions, 1975), 25.

121. Altieri, "Objectivist," 15.

122. Ibid., 12.

123. Adorno, *Against Epistemology,* 194.

124. Ibid., 193.

125. Ibid., 171.

126. Ibid., 15, 27.

127. Adorno, *Minima Moralia,* 13.

128. See Matthew 7:3–5 and Luke 6:41–42.

129. G. W. F. Hegel, *The Phenomenology of Mind,* trans. A. V. Miller (Oxford: Oxford University Press, 1977), 11; Adorno, *Minima Moralia,* 50 (see also the translator's footnote).

Chapter 4

1. John Cage, *Silence* (Middletown, Conn.: Wesleyan University Press, 1961), 126.

2. Joel C. Weinsheimer, *Gadamer's Hermeneutics: A Reading of Truth and Method* (New Haven, Conn.: Yale University Press, 1984), 4.

3. Daniel Herwitz, "John Cage's Approach to the Global," in *John Cage: Composed in America,* ed. Marjorie Perloff and Charles Junkerman (Chicago: University of Chicago Press, 1994), 192.

4. Perloff and Junkerman, introduction to *John Cage: Composed in America,* 5.

5. Buchler, *Concept of Method,* 42, 48.

6. Alexander Pope, *An Essay on Criticism 1711* (Yorkshire: Scolar, 1970), 8.

7. Herwitz, "John Cage's Approach," 188.

8. Cage, *Silence,* 10.

9. Buchler, *Concept of Method,* 34.

10. Ibid., 35.

11. Cage, *Silence,* 100, 12.

12. Weinsheimer, *Gadamer's Hermeneutics,* 4.

13. Ibid., 5.

14. S. T. Coleridge, *Shorter Works and Fragments,* ed. H. J. Jackson and J. R. de J. Jackson, 2 vols. (Princeton, N.J.: Princeton University Press, 1995), 1:362, quoted in Buchler, *Concept of Method,* 37 (italics in original). Unless otherwise noted, all forms of emphasis in the quotations in this chapter are in the original.

15. William Wordsworth, *The Major Works,* ed. Stephen Gill (Oxford: Oxford University Press), 270.

16. Weinsheimer, *Gadamer's Hermeneutics,* 5.

17. Ibid.

18. Gerald Bruns, "Poethics: John Cage and Stanley Cavell at the Crossroad of Ethical Theory," in *John Cage: Composed in America,* ed. Perloff and Junkerman, 211; John Cage, *Conversing with John Cage,* ed. Richard Kostelanetz (New York: Limelight Editions, 1991), 212.

19. Bruns, "Poethics: John Cage and Stanley Cavell," 212.

20. Shiller, *New Methods,* 4–5.

21. Dewey, *Quest for Certainty,* 200.

22. Bruns, "Poethics: John Cage and Stanley Cavell," 210.

23. Ibid. Bruns is quoting from Emmanuel Levinas, *Totality and Infinity,* trans. Alphonso Lingis (Philadelphia: Duquesne University Press, 1961), 43–44, 46.

24. Cage, *Silence,* 83, 84.

25. Ibid., 8.

26. Ibid.

27. Weinsheimer, *Gadamer's Hermeneutics,* 5.

28. Joan Retallack, ed., *Musicage* (Hanover and London: Wesleyan University Press, 1996), 73.

29. Ibid., 74.

30. Ibid., 74, 73.

31. Quoted in Joan Retallack, "Poethics of a Complex Realism," in *John Cage: Composed in America,* ed. Perloff and Junkerman, 267.

32. S. T. Coleridge, *The Complete Works of Samuel Taylor Coleridge,* ed. W. G. T. Shedd, 7 vols. (New York: Harper and Brothers, 1868), 2:410, quoted in Buchler, *Concept of Method,* 43.

33. Retallack, *Musicage,* 274.

34. Ibid., xxix, xxxiv.

35. Cage's notion of counter-method closely resonates with contemporary thinking in feminist and post-colonial studies. In response to the question of how women can introduce themselves into the "tightly woven systematicity" of the "philosophical discourse" that constitutes "the discourse on discourse," in order to "challenge, and disrupt" it, Luce Irigaray, for instance, argues for the method of mimicry. She writes: "There is, in an initial phase, perhaps only one 'path,' the one historically assigned to the feminine: that of mimicry. One must assume the feminine role deliberately. Which means already to convert a form of subordination into an affirmation, and thus to begin to thwart it." And the purpose of this method of mimicry is to "[jam] the theoretical machinery itself" from within. For more detail, see Luce Irigaray, *This Sex Which Is Not One,* trans. Catherine Porter and Carolyn Burke (Ithaca, N.Y.: Cornell University Press, 1985), 76. In "The Blackness of Blackness: A Critique on the Sign and the Signifying Monkey," Henry Louis Gates also points out that Cage's theory of interpretation is a theory of "formal revisionism" which "turns on repetition of formal structures and their difference." Defined as "tropological," and "formal signifying," he refers to his method as "critical Parody" in terms of formal "repetition and inversion." For more detail, see Henry Louis Gates, *Figures in Black: Words, Signs, and the "Radical" Self* (New York: Oxford University Press, 1989).

36. Cage, *Silence,* 12.

37. Buchler, *Concept of Method,* 83.

38. Cage, *Conversing with John Cage,* 212.

39. *Webster's New World Dictionary,* s.v. "Chance."

40. N. Katherine Hayles, "Chance Operation: Cagean Paradox and Contemporary Science," in *John Cage: Composed in America,* ed. Perloff and Junkerman, 226, 227.

41. Buchler, *Concept of Method,* 37, 30.

42. Dewey, *Quest for Certainty,* 204.

43. Buchler, *Concept of Method,* 49.

44. Cage, *Conversing with John Cage,* 218–19.

45. In Chinese, the word *I* denotes "change," not "chance." While the book has several titles—another one being *Chou I*—the emphasis always falls on "change." For a useful introduction to the basic theory and method of this ancient book of wisdom, see Hellmut Wilhelm and Richard Wilhelm, *Understanding the I Ching: The Wilhelm Lectures on The Book of Changes,* Bollingen Series 19:2 (Princeton, N.J.: Princeton University Press, 1979).

46. Cage, *Conversing with John Cage,* 17.

47. Cage, *Empty Words,* 3.

48. Buchler, *Concept of Method,* 133.

49. Cage, *Conversing with John Cage,* 17.

50. *Webster's New World Dictionary,* s.v. "Use."

51. Richard Palmer, *Hermeneutics* (Evanston, Ill.: Northwestern University Press, 1969), 233.

52. Werner Heisenberg, *Physics and Philosophy: The Revolution in Modern Science* (New York: Harper and Row, 1958), 28.

53. Buchler, *Concept of Method,* 101.

54. Cage, *Conversing with John Cage,* 137.

55. Ibid., 138–39 (emphasis added, ellipses in original).

56. Buchler, *Concept of Method,* 93.

57. Ibid.

58. Ibid.

59. Gadamer, *Truth and Method,* 246.

60. Weinsheimer, *Gadamer's Hermeneutics,* 7.

61. Buchler, *Concept of Method,* 19.

62. Ibid., 80.

63. Ibid., 72.

64. Cage, *Conversing with John Cage,* 219.

65. Retallack, *Musicage,* 186.

66. Cage, *Conversing with John Cage,* 149.

67. For a detailed reading of Cage on this topic in relation to *Oulipo,* see Conte, *Unending Design,* chapter 5.

68. Cage, *Empty Words,* 133.

69. Cage, *Conversing with John Cage,* 149.

70. Cage, *M: Writings '67-'72,* x.

71. John Cage, *I–IV* (Cambridge, Mass.: Harvard University Press, 1990), 1.

72. Buchler, *Concept of Method,* 166. Buchler also explains that "the product may happen to be interpreted as designating, either iconically or through symbolic association; but it may not" (ibid.).

73. Cage, *Empty Words,* 123.

74. Conte, *Unending Design,* 257.

75. Harry Mathews, "John Ashbery Interviewing Harry Mathews," *Review of Contemporary Fiction* 7 (Fall): 43.

76. Conte, *Unending Design,* 257.

77. Ibid., 258. For an example of how Cage's mesostics work, see Conte's analysis on the same page.

78. Niklas Luhmann, *Theories of Distinction,* ed. William Rasch (Stanford, Calif.: Stanford University Press, 2002), 136.

79. Marjorie Perloff, "Music for Words: Reading/Hearing/Seeing in John Cage's *Roaratorio,*" in *Postmodern Genres,* ed. Marjorie Perloff (Norman: University of Oklahoma Press, 1989), 220.

80. Buchler, *Concept of Method,* 167.

81. Jacques Derrida, *Speech and Phenomena,* trans. David Allison (Evanston, Ill.: Northwestern University Press, 1973), 132.

82. John Cage, *Roaratorio: An Irish Circus on Finnegans Wake,* ed. Klaus Schöning (Königstein: Athenäum, 1985), 36, quoted in Perloff, "Music for Words," 214.

83. Perloff, "Music for Words," 215.

84. John Cage, *X: Writings '79–'82* (Middletown, Conn.: Wesleyan University Press, 1983), 123–24.

85. For a brief discussion of the relation between attention and perception from *Oulipo*'s standpoint, see Conte, *Unending Design,* 241.

Chapter 5

1. Citations of "If Written Is Writing" will refer to Hejinian's book of collected essays entitled *The Language of Inquiry* (Berkeley: University of California Press, 2000).

2. Charles Bernstein, *A Poetics* (Cambridge, Mass.: Harvard University Press, 1992), 180.

3. Michael Davidson, "On Reading Stein," in *The L=A=N=G=U=A=G=E Book,* ed. Bruce Andrews and Charles Bernstein (Carbondale: Southern Illinois University Press, 1984), 198.

4. *Webster's New World Dictionary,* s.v. "Omniscient."

5. Jerome McGann, "Contemporary Poetry, Alternate Routes," in *Politics and Poetic Value,* ed. Robert von Hallberg (Chicago: University of Chicago Press, 1987), 265.

6. Don Byrd, *The Poetics of the Common Knowledge* (New York: State University of New York Press, 1994), 36.

7. Ibid., 265.

8. Charles Bernstein, *Poetics,* 184.

9. Hejinian, *Language of Inquiry,* 27.

10. Byrd, *Poetics of the Common Knowledge,* 194.

11. Ibid., 10.

12. Ibid., 62.

13. Descartes, *Philosophical Works,* 9, quoted in Byrd, *Poetics of the Common Knowledge,* 65.

14. Byrd, *Poetics of the Common Knowledge,* 29.

15. Ibid., 107.

16. Ibid., 11, 3.

17. Ibid., 8, 23.

18. Ibid., 23.

19. Charles Bernstein, *Poetics,* 2.

20. Ron Silliman, *The New Sentence* (New York: Roof, 1987), 17.

21. Hejinian, *Language of Inquiry,* 56.

22. Susan Howe, "Statement for the New Poetics Colloquium, Vancouver, 1985," *Jimmy and Lucy's House of "K"* 5 (November 1985): 17.

23. Susan Howe, "An Interview with Susan Howe," with Edward Foster, *Talisman: A Journal of Contemporary Poetry and Poetics* 4 (Spring 1990): 37.

24. Marjorie Perloff, *The Dance of the Intellect: Studies in the Poetry of the Pound Tradition* (Cambridge: Cambridge University Press, 1985), 231.

25. Susan Howe, *My Emily Dickinson* (Berkeley, Calif.: North Atlantic, 1985), 17–18 (italics in original). Unless otherwise noted, all forms of emphasis in the quotations in this chapter are in the original. Although explicitly informed by a feminist perspective, both Howe's poetry and her criticism present a broad range of significance and implications that embraces, but is not confined to, feminist critique. In this sense, the term to describe Howe's critical spectrum more comprehensively is, perhaps, *contradiction,* a term the poet herself emphasizes in *My Emily Dickinson.*

26. Bruce Andrews, "Poetry as Explanation, Poetry as Praxis," in *The Politics of Poetic Form: Poetry and Public Policy,* ed. Charles Bernstein (New York: Roof, 1990), 27, 29.

27. *Webster's New World Dictionary,* s.v. "Articulate."

28. Susan Howe, "Encloser," in *Politics of Poetic Form,* ed. Bernstein, 192.

29. Susan Howe, *Singularities* (Hanover, N.H.: Wesleyan University Press, University Press of New England, 1990), 32, 65, 70, 64, 65.

30. Howe, "Encloser," 192.

31. Dale Spender, "Extracts from *Man Made Language,*" in *The Feminist Critique of Language: A Reader,* ed. Deborah Cameron (New York: Routledge, 1990), 105.

32. Susan Howe, *The Europe of Trusts* (New York: New Directions, 2002), 99.

33. Howe, "Interview with Susan Howe," 24.

34. Steve McCaffery, "From the Notebooks," in *The L=A=N=G=U=A=G=E Book,* ed. Andrews and Bernstein, 160.

35. Marjorie Perloff, "Canon and Loaded Gun: Feminist Poetics and the Avant-Garde," *Stanford Literature Review* 4, no. 1 (1987): 31.

36. Howe, *My Emily Dickinson,* 11–12.

37. Rachel Blau DuPlessis, *The Pink Guitar: Writing as Feminist Practice* (New York: Routledge, 1990), 122.

38. Susan Howe, *The Birth-Mark: Unsettling the Wilderness in American Literary History* (Hanover, N.H.: Wesleyan University Press, University Press of New England, 1993), 136, 139.

39. Howe, "Statement," 16.

40. Howe, *My Emily Dickinson,* 17, 51.

41. Howe, *Birth-Mark,* 38.

42. Howe, "Interview with Susan Howe," 23.

43. Howe, *Birth-Mark,* 83.

44. Julia Kristeva, *Revolution in Poetic Language,* trans. Margaret Waller (New York: Columbia University Press, 1984), 16.

45. Serres, *Hermes: Literature, Science, Philosophy,* 15. While Serres's studies focus on the classical age, his theory and model can be applied to the present just as effectively. The outlining of Serres's idea in this section, often in a word-for-word manner, is based on pp. 15–28 of the essay in *Hermes.*

46. Byrd, *Poetics of the Common Knowledge,* 43, 44, 47.

47. Ibid., 48.

48. Ibid., 43.

49. Ibid., 72.

50. Ibid., 85.

51. Serres, *Hermes: Literature, Science, Philosophy,* 23.

52. Byrd, *Poetics of the Common Knowledge,* 66.

53. For a study of women poets and the issue of epistemology from the feminist perpsective, see Megan Simpson, *Poetic Epistemology: Gender and Knowing in Women's Language-Oriented Writing* (New York: State University of New York Press, 2000). Its chapter 5 is devoted to the study of the works of Susan Howe.

54. Howe, *Singularities,* 12, 35.

55. Susan Howe, "The *Difficulties* Interview," with Tom Beckett, *The Difficulties* 3, no. 2, Susan Howe special issue (1989): 26, 27.

56. Ibid., 21.

57. Serres, *Hermes: Literature, Science, Philosophy,* 23.

58. Howe, "Interview with Susan Howe," 22.

59. Byrd, *Poetics of the Common Knowledge,* 61.

60. Howe, *Singularities,* 30.

61. Serres, *Hermes: Literature, Science, Philosophy,* 22.

62. Howe, "Interview with Susan Howe," 17.

63. Howe, "Statement," 15.

64. Serres, *Hermes: Literature, Science, Philosophy,* 22.

65. Howe, *Singularities,* 18.

66. Jacques Derrida, *Of Grammatology,* trans. Gayatri Chakravorty Spivak (Baltimore: Johns Hopkins University Press, 1976), 24.

67. Howe, "Interview with Susan Howe," 30–31. Both René Thom's work (*Mathematical Models of Morphogenesis, Structural Stability and Morphogenesis*) and the terminology in his lecture ("predation," "capture," and so forth) suggest an awareness of algebraic geometry as a game and a corresponding ambiguity toward its nature. Don Byrd makes a similar observation when he writes: "The confusion over the nature of this science has been far greater than is justified by the textual difficulties. The problems are logical, not textual, and they remain a constant of the philosophic tradition from Descartes himself, who found a way in the *Discourse* to sweep them under the rug, to Noam Chomsky and the foremost current French proponent of geometric mechanism, René Thom" (Byrd, *Poetics of the Common Knowledge,* 66).

68. Howe, *Singularities,* 34, 38.

69. DuPlessis, *Pink Guitar,* 28.

70. Howe, *Singularities,* 28.

71. The passage that Howe quotes in full in "Interview with Susan Howe" (31) is the introduction to chapter 5, "Elementary Catastrophe Theory," in Thom's *Mathematical Models of Morphogenesis.* The following references in this paragraph are to Howe's "Interview."

72. Howe, *Singularities,* 32.

73. Howe, *My Emily Dickinson,* 21.

74. Perloff, "Toward an Avant-Garde *Tractatus*," 31.

75. Howe, "Interview with Susan Howe," 31.

76. Ibid., 23.

77. Howe, *My Emily Dickinson,* 13.

78. Howe, *Singularities,* 69.

79. Serres, *Hermes: Literature, Science, Philosophy,* 28.

80. DuPlessis, *Pink Guitar,* 126.

81. Howe, *My Emily Dickinson,* 11–12.

82. Howe, *Birth-Mark,* 128.

83. Ibid., 136.

84. Hejinian, *Language of Inquiry,* 43, 47.

85. I am indebted to Peter Quartermain for the terms *anaphoric, exophoric,* and *cataphoric.* Discussing Gertrude Stein's use of pronouns—and, for that matter, articles—as "shifters," Quartermain defines the linguistic and deictic functions of these terms as, respectively, "backward pointing" (*Disjunctive Poetics,* 24) to the antecedents, "outward pointing" to "materials outside the text" (41), and

"forward pointing" to the "forward movement of the prose" (26). I borrow and use them here to suggest a mental trajectory largely conditioned by the textual formations therein and their concomitant reading processes. For more detail, see Peter Quartermain, *Disjunctive Poetics: From Gertrude Stein and Louis Zukofsky to Susan Howe* (Cambridge: Cambridge University Press, 1992), 21–43.

86. Howe, "Statement," 17.

87. Charles Bernstein, *Poetics,* 184.

88. Howe, "Interview with Susan Howe," 20.

89. Susan Howe, *The Nonconformist's Memorial* (New York: New Directions, 1993), 3.

90. Ibid., 5.

91. *Webster's New World Dictionary,* s.v. "Citation."

92. Howe, *Nonconformist's Memorial,* 7.

93. Ibid., 4.

94. Ibid., 7.

95. Ibid., 15.

96. Ibid., 13.

97. Ibid., 7.

98. Ludwig Wittgenstein, *Tractatus Logico-Philosophicus,* trans. D. F. Pears and B. F. McGuinness (London: Routledge, 1961), 68, 69.

99. Howe, *Nonconformist's Memorial,* 7.

100. Ibid., 6.

101. Ibid., 3.

102. Ibid.

103. Ibid., 12, 30.

104. K. Ludwig Pfeiffer, "Fiction: On the Fate of a Concept Between Philosophy and Literary Theory," in *Aesthetic Illusion: Theoretical and Historical Approaches,* ed. Frederick Burwick and Walter Pape (New York: Walter de Gruyter, 1990), 102.

105. Howe, "Interview with Susan Howe," 31.

106. Hans Vaihinger, *The Philosophy of "As If": A System of the Theoretical, Practical, and Religious Fictions of Mankind,* trans. C. K. Ogden (New York: Harcourt, 1925), 91.

107. Howe, *Nonconformist's Memorial,* 6.

108. Andrews, "Poetry as Explanation," 31.

109. Howe, *Nonconformist's Memorial,* 6, 7.

110. Ibid., 13.

111. DuPlessis, *Pink Guitar,* 132.

112. Vaihinger, *Philosophy of "As If,"* xlvi, 95.

113. Ibid., 92.

114. Ibid.

115. Ibid., 92, 93.

116. Ibid., 93.

117. Ibid., 258.

118. Ibid., 93.

119. Howe, *Nonconformist's Memorial*, 11.

120. Howe, *My Emily Dickinson*, 45.

121. Howe, *Birth-Mark*, 137.

122. Ibid., 140.

123. Ibid., 147.

124. Howe, *My Emily Dickinson*, 24.

125. Howe, "*Difficulties* Interview," 23.

126. Howe, *My Emily Dickinson*, 51.

127. Howe, *Nonconformist's Memorial*, 15.

128. Howe, *Singularities*, 26, 13.

129. Howe, *My Emily Dickinson*, 24.

130. Ibid., 23.

131. Ibid., 24.

132. Howe, *Nonconformist's Memorial*, 105.

133. Ibid., 15.

134. Howe, *Europe of Trusts*, 199.

135. DuPlessis, *Pink Guitar*, 136.

136. *Webster's New World Dictionary*, s.v. "Mortal."

137. Howe, *Nonconformist's Memorial*, 11.

138. DuPlessis, *Pink Guitar*, 6.

139. Howe, *Nonconformist's Memorial*, 19.

140. *Webster's New World Dictionary*, s.v. "It."

141. Howe, *Nonconformist's Memorial*, 20.

142. Ibid., 13.

143. Charles Bernstein, *Content's Dream*, 219–20.

144. Ibid., 224.

145. Ibid., 227.

146. Byrd, *Poetics of the Common Knowledge*, 194.

147. Howe, "Interview with Susan Howe," 34.

148. Charles Bernstein, *Poetics*, 1.

149. Byrd, *Poetics of the Common Knowledge*, 200.

150. Ron Silliman, "For L=A=N=G=U=A=G=E," in *The L=A=N=G=U=A=G=E Book*, ed. Andrews and Bernstein, 16.

Chapter 6

1. Lyn Hejinian, *My Life* (Providence, RI: Burning Deck, 1980).

2. Lyn Hejinian, *My Life* (Los Angeles: Sun and Moon, 1987). All subsequent references are to this edition.

3. In her study of Lyn Hejinian's *My Life,* Marjorie Perloff observes that "the (unnamed) number assigned to each section governs that section's content: thus 1 has its base in infant sensations, in 9 the references are to a gawky child, in 18 someone is 'hopelessly in love,' in 22 there are allusions to college reading, in the form of Nietzsche, Darwin, Freud, and Marx. . . . In the course of the narrative, the references gradually shift from childhood to adolescence to adult thought and behavior." For more details, see Marjorie Perloff, *Radical Artifice: Writing Poetry in the Age of Media* (Chicago: University of Chicago Press, 1991), 162.

4. Hejinian, *Language of Inquiry,* 43.

5. Hejinian, *My Life,* 15.

6. Juliana Spahr, "Resignifying Autobiography: Lyn Hejinian's *My Life,*" *American Literature* 68, no. 1 (March 1996): 148.

7. Perloff, *Radical Artifice,* 166.

8. Spahr, "Resignifying Autobiography," 139.

9. Philippe Lejeune, "The Autobiographical Pact," in *On Autobiography,* ed. Paul John Eakin, trans. Katherine M. Leary (Minneapolis: University of Minnesota Press, 1989), 4.

10. Hilary Clark, "The Mnemonics of Autobiography: Lyn Hejinian's *My Life,*" *Biography* 14, no. 4 (Fall 1991): 327, 332, 328.

11. Paul Smith, *Discerning the Subject* (Minneapolis: University of Minnesota Press, 1988), 105. For similar discussions of the function of "I" in autobiography, see Emile Benveniste, *Problems in General Linguistics,* trans. Mary Elizabeth Meek (Coral Gables, Fla.: University of Miami Press, 1971), 224–26; and Lejeune, "Autobiographical Pact," 8–10.

12. Paul Smith, *Discerning the Subject,* 105.

13. Hejinian, *My Life,* 94.

14. M. Merleau-Ponty, *Phenomenology of Perception,* trans. Colin Smith (New York: Humanities, 1962), xviii.

15. Hayles, *Chaos Bound,* 279.

16. George Hartley, *Textual Politics and the Language Poets* (Bloomington: Indiana University Press, 1989), 18.

17. Charles Bernstein, *Content's Dream,* 246.

18. Merleau-Ponty, *Phenomenology of Perception,* 57.

19. Charles Bernstein, *Content's Dream,* 219–20, 72 (italics in original).

20. Ibid., 62, 408.

21. Macann, *Four Phenomenological Philosophers,* 170.

22. Merleau-Ponty, *Phenomenology of Perception,* 213, 241.

23. Ibid., xiii.

24. Ibid., 62, 213.

25. Ibid., 241.

26. Ibid., 170.

27. Hejinian, *Language of Inquiry,* 50, 52–53.

28. Hejinian, *My Life,* 105.

29. Merleau-Ponty, *Phenomenology of Perception,* xviii.

30. The term *genetic phenomenology* is used explicitly by Christopher Macann in his discussion of Merleau-Ponty's work (*Four Phenomenological Philosophers,* 163, 169). For Merleau-Ponty's frequent use of the concept of *genesis,* see, as Macann has suggested, the opening section of *Phenomenology of Perception.*

31. Merleau-Ponty, *Phenomenology of Perception,* xviii.

32. Macann, *Four Phenomenological Philosophers,* 168.

33. Hejinian, *Language of Inquiry,* 56.

34. Clark, "Mnemonics of Autobiography," 316.

35. Hejinian, *My Life,* 43.

36. Alice G. B. ter Meulen, *Representing Time in Natural Language* (Cambridge, Mass.: MIT Press, 1995), x.

37. Ibid., 12.

38. Ibid., 1, 3, 13.

39. Richard Terdiman, *Present Past: Modernity and the Memory Crisis* (Ithaca, N.Y.: Cornell University Press, 1993), 192, 51.

40. Maurice Halbwachs, *On Collective Memory,* ed. and trans. Lewis A. Coser (Chicago: University of Chicago Press, 1992), 173, 45.

41. Terdiman, *Present Past,* 46, 54; see also 268 and 340.

42. Michel Foucault, *The Order of Things* (New York: Vintage, 1970), 297.

43. Paul John Eakin, *Touching the World: Reference in Autobiography* (Princeton, N.J.: Princeton University Press, 1992), 67.

44. Merleau-Ponty, *Phenomenology of Perception,* vii, 410.

45. Hejinian, "Interview," by Manuel Brito, in *A Suite of Poetic Voices: Interviews with Contemporary American Poets,* ed. Manuel Brito (Santa Brigida, Spain: Kadle Books, 1992), 82.

46. Lyn Hejinian, "Two Stein Talks," *Temblor* 3 (1986): 128–39. "Two Stein Talks" was reprinted in Hejinian's *Language of Inquiry.*

47. William James, "From William James," in *The Flowers of Friendship: Letters Written to Gertrude Stein,* ed. Donald Gallup (New York: Alfred A. Knopf, 1953), 50.

48. Hejinian, *Language of Inquiry,* 96–97.

49. Ibid., 112, 89, 92, 93.

50. Ibid., 105. For a succinct discussion of Merleau-Ponty's notion of time as "eternity," see Macann, *Four Phenomenological Philosophers,* 197–98.

51. Gertrude Stein, *Gertrude Stein: Writings,* ed. Catharine R. Simpson and Harriet Chessman (New York: Library of America, 1998), 267, quoted in Hejinian, *Language of Inquiry,* 114.

52. Merleau-Ponty, *Phenomenology of Perception,* 412, 419–20.

53. Hejinian, *Language of Inquiry,* 116, 117.

54. Hejinian, *My Life,* 16.

55. Ibid., 44.

56. Hejinian, *Language of Inquiry,* 101, 111.

57. Ibid., 116, 106.

58. Merleau-Ponty, *Phenomenology of Perception,* 423, 412.

59. Stein, *Selected Writings,* 518.

60. Hejinian, *Language of Inquiry,* 101.

61. Merleau-Ponty, *Phenomenology of Perception,* 415, 421, 428.

62. Ibid., 412, 419.

63. Terdiman, *Present Past,* 269, 54 (italics in original).

64. Hejinian, "Interview," 88.

65. William Faulkner, *Light in August* (New York: Random House, 1959), 88.

66. David R. Jarraway, "*My Life* Through the Eighties: The Exemplary L=A=N=G=U=A=G=E of Lyn Hejinian," *Contemporary Literature* 33, no. 2 (Summer 1992): 323.

67. Lyn Hejinian, *Writing Is an Aid to Memory* (Los Angeles: Sun and Moon, 1996), section 21.

68. Hejinian, *My Life,* 43–44.

69. Ibid., 46, 47.

70. Terdiman, *Present Past,* 9.

71. Merleau-Ponty, *Phenomenology of Perception,* 18, 19.

72. Ibid., 20.

73. Ibid., 57, vii.

74. Macann, *Four Phenomenological Philosophers,* 183.

75. Merleau-Ponty, *Phenomenology of Perception,* 22.

76. Mary Warnock, *Memory* (London: Faber and Faber, 1987), 62, 61.

77. Ibid., 54 (italics in original).

78. Ibid., 56, 57, 75.

79. Ibid., 103, 144.

80. Eakin, *Touching the World,* 76, 72.

81. Macann, *Four Phenomenological Philosophers,* 181.

82. Merleau-Ponty, *Phenomenology of Perception,* 208.

83. Ibid., 237.

84. Hejinian, *My Life,* 72, 75.

85. Ibid., 59, 113, 7.

86. Hejinian, *Language of Inquiry,* 46, 47.

87. Ibid., 44.

88. Hejinian, *My Life,* 96.

89. Hejinian, "Interview," 88.

90. Merleau-Ponty, *Phenomenology of Perception,* 412.

91. Hejinian, *Language of Inquiry,* 116.

92. Hejinian, "Interview," 76.

93. Hejinian, *Language of Inquiry,* 118.

94. Ibid., 116–17.

95. Hejinian, *My Life*, 21.

96. Ibid., 30.

97. Ibid., 21.

98. Hejinian, *Language of Inquiry*, 138.

99. Merleau-Ponty, *Phenomenology of Perception*, 365.

100. Ibid., 61 (italics in original).

101. Hejinian, *My Life*, 7.

102. Spahr, "Resignifying Autobiography," 143.

103. Merleau-Ponty, *Phenomenology of Perception*, 58 (italics in original).

104. Macann, *Four Phenomenological Philosophers*, 182–83 (italics in original).

105. Merleau-Ponty, *Phenomenology of Perception*, 351.

106. Spahr, "Resignifying Autobiography," 147.

107. Hejinian, *Language of Inquiry*, 46.

108. Hejinian, *My Life*, 31.

109. Macann, *Four Phenomenological Philosophers*, 168.

110. Ibid., 163 (emphasis added).

111. Hejinian, *My Life*, 7.

112. Perloff, *Radical Artifice*, 168.

113. Macann, *Four Phenomenological Philosophers*, 169.

114. John E. Drabinski, "From Experience to Flesh: On James and Merleau-Ponty," *Phenomenological Inquiry* 21 (October 1997): 145.

115. Clark, "Mnemonics of Autobiography," 325 (italics in original).

116. Merleau-Ponty, *Phenomenology of Perception*, 347, 348.

117. Ibid., 348 (emphasis added).

118. Merleau-Ponty, *Phenomenology of Perception*, 351.

119. Drabinski, "Experience to Flesh," 145, 146 (italics in original).

120. Ibid., 146 (italics in original).

121. Hejinian, *My Life*, 92.

122. *Webster's New World Dictionary*, s.v. "Rubber."

123. Ibid.

124. *Webster's New World Dictionary*, s.v. "Dark."

125. Clark, "Mnemonics of Autobiography," 322.

126. Hejinian, *My Life*, 92, 93, 107.

Chapter 7

1. The expression "nonsense bargains" is taken from Andrews's *Divestiture—A* (New York: Drogue, 1994), 34. "Expenditure without reserve" is taken from Derrida's *Writing and Difference,* trans. Alan Bass (Chicago: University of Chicago Press, 1978), 259.

2. Bruce Andrews, "C3B1-c," of *The Millennium Project,* from which this line is taken, is published in *Aerial* 9 (1999), a special issue on Bruce Andrews; 211.

3. Georges Bataille, *Visions of Excess: Selected Writings 1927–1939,* ed. Allan Stoekl (Minneapolis: University of Minnesota Press, 1985), 99.

4. Derrida, *Writing and Difference,* 256.

5. Ibid., 256–57 (italics in original). Unless otherwise noted, all uses of italics and other forms of emphasis in the quotations of this chapter are in the original.

6. Bataille, *Visions of Excess,* 99.

7. Allen S. Weiss, *The Aesthetics of Excess* (New York: State University of New York Press, 1989), 22.

8. Regardless of the different perspectives from which these issues are raised and addressed, Andrews's notion of nonsense resonates with Bataille's concepts of excess and waste, not only in that it provides a means for a critical rethinking through which to bring into visibility the mechanisms constitutive of sense and sense-making, but also in that it presents a more contemporary version of the Bataillean negativity without reserve, as is evidenced in Andrews's notoriously opaque texts, the difficulty of which frustrates as well as questions the politics of reader participation through recontextualized reading.

9. Jerome McGann, "Language Writing," *London Review of Books* 9, no. 18 (October 15, 1987): 7.

10. Andrews's exact phrase is "radicalism as analytic," in *Paradise and Method,* 54.

11. Andrews, *Paradise and Method,* 52, 47.

12. Ibid., 38.

13. Ibid., 21, 28.

14. Ibid., 46.

15. Ibid., 54, 43.

16. Ibid., 55.

17. Derrida, *Writing and Difference,* 270. Focusing on Andrews's notion of "nonsense bargains" in light of Georges Bataille's theory of general economy, the present chapter is informed of the "complexities" that "are often missed by Bataille's readers," as Arkady Plotnitsky has pointed out in his article "Effects of the Unknowable: Materialism, Epistemology, and the General Economy of the Body in Bataille," *Parallax* 7, no. 1 (January-March 2001): 22. Adopting the concept of "complementarity" from Niels Bohr's interpretation of quantum mechanics, Plotnitsky sees these complexities in the mutual dependence between general and restricted economies for their functioning in *Reconfigurations: Critical Theory and General Economy* (Gainesville: University Press of Florida, 1993), 4, 15. He writes:

The suspension of either sort of expenditure, productive or unproductive, is problematic. . . . A suspension often functions as what Derrida terms the "unproblematized reversal." . . . It is a reversal that leaves the metaphysical base untouched. For example, it may lead to the metaphysics, or the politico-economic utopias, of expenditure, difference, plurality, otherness, and so forth. But the restricted economies can take other forms as well, even within attempts to avoid the unproblematized reversal. One is best off seeing the general economy as the economy of interaction, or as a complementarity of losses and gains, which figures the diversity of their interplay. (*Reconfigurations,* 23)

For a more detailed study by Plotnitsky, see both his *Reconfigurations* and *Complementarity: Anti-Epistemology After Bohr and Derrida* (Durham, N.C.: Duke University Press, 1994). However, with its emphasis on "nonsense" in Andrews's poetry in relation to general economy, the present chapter is not built on the "misunderstandings of Bataille's thought as uncritically idealizing expenditure, loss, and so forth" (Plotnitsky, "Effects of the Unknowable," 22). Rather, it is prompted by two critical observations. First, in the existing scholarship on contemporary avant-garde poetry and poetics, theoretical explorations of the significance and ramifications of "nonsense" or "unintelligibility" have remained disappointingly inadequate, and this inadequacy results, at least in part, from what seems to be an over-concern with the "unproblematized reversal." Itself a methodological consequence in the critique of the logic of logos, this over-concern often effectively—not to mention ironically—short-circuits any attempt to theorize the unproductive expenditure by relegating it to its productive counterpart. In this sense, my study of "nonsense" in terms of general economy, under what Plotnitsky calls "the constraint of the conditional" (*Reconfigurations,* 26), is an effort to remedy this inadequacy in a small way. Second, it is important to note that this over-concern with the unproblematized reversal, the idealization of expenditure, or the interplay between the restricted economy and the general economy is valid only when one operates, both conceptually and methodologically, within the bipolar, dialectical paradigm that constitutes the metaphysical base itself. It articulates and enacts a critical disposition that resurrects simultaneously what it critiques, as I have previously argued in my article "The Past Is No Longer Out-of-Date: Topological Time and Its Foldable Nearness in Michael Serres's Philosophy," *Configurations* 6 (2000), 235–44. With these polemics in mind, this study pursues a post-dialectic approach, an approach whereby the discarding of the metaphysical base presents the point of departure for a radical critique.

18. Andrews, *Divestiture—A,* 35.

19. Steve McCaffery defines "restricted economy" as the "economy of Capital, Reason, Philosophy, and History" which "will always strive to govern writing, to force its appearance through an order of constraints," in *North of Intention* (New York: Roof, 1986), 203. The operation of such a restricted economy, according to McCaffery, "is based upon valorized notions of restraint, conservation, investment, profit, accumulation and cautious proceduralities in risk taking," and it

has "a regulating, conservational disposition that limits and organizes the independent letters, pushing them toward the word as a component in the articulated production and accumulation of meaning" (215).

20. See Paulson, *Noise of Culture.* As Paulson rightly points out, "the mathematical theory of information," as theorized by, among others, Claude E. Shannon, does not concern "the meaning or significance of transmitted messages" and defines information "independently of" it. It does, however, "have implications for our understanding of how we speak and write to one another" (*Noise of Culture,* 54, 55). It is these implications that this chapter on Andrews's work draws upon.

21. Ibid., 58.

22. Henri Atlan, "Disorder, Complexity and Meaning," in *Disorder and Order,* ed. Paisley Livingston (Stanford, Calif.: Anma Libri, 1984), 111, 112.

23. Henri Atlan, "On a Formal Definition of Organization," *Journal of Theoretical Biology* 45, no. 2 (June 1974): 295. Atlan's theorizing here concerns more specifically the "initial redundancy (*Ro*)" as one of the three parameters defining "a given organization," the other two being "the initial information content (*Ho*)" which is structural in character, and "time (*t*)" which is functional in character.

24. Paulson, *Noise of Culture,* 58, 64.

25. Ibid., 60. Paulson's notion of contextual redundancy is grounded in information theory and, therefore, his discussion of this issue is confined to the linguistic system without making larger, extra-linguistic connections. Again, it is the implications of this notion that this chapter focuses on.

26. Andrews, *Paradise and Method,* 50.

27. Ibid., 260.

28. Ibid., 53.

29. Ibid., 43.

30. Ibid., 8, 26, 41.

31. Paulson, *Noise of Culture,* 60.

32. Norman Fairclough, *Language and Power* (London: Longman, 1989), 141.

33. Andrews, *Paradise and Method,* 124.

34. Ibid., 211, 242.

35. Ibid., 37.

36. Ibid., 45.

37. Charles Bernstein, "Language Sampler," *Paris Review* 86 (1982): 75.

38. McCaffery, *North of Intention,* 156.

39. Serres, *Hermes: Literature, Science, Philosophy,* 65–70.

40. Ibid., 66.

41. Ibid.

42. Ibid., 67.

43. Ibid., 70.

44. Ibid., 68.

45. Ibid., 69.

46. Ibid., 66–67.

47. Derrida, *Writing and Difference*, 259.

48. Serres, *Hermes: Literature, Science, Philosophy*, 67.

49. McCaffery, *North of Intention*, 40–41 n.2.

50. Andrews, *Paradise and Method*, 242.

51. Ibid., 40.

52. Ibid., 56.

53. Ibid., 35.

54. Ibid., 58. Andrews's notion of "critique" here should be understood as what Plotnitsky specifies as "radical but not absolute" (*Reconfigurations*, 23); for general economy "can never offer a full critique" of sense, as McCaffery has argued, because to do so is to engage in the "operation" of sense that "it explicitly disavows" (*North of Intention*, 203).

55. McCaffery, *North of Intention*, 203.

56. *Webster's New World Dictionary*, s.v. "Re-."

57. Derrida, *Writing and Difference*, 259, 257.

58. Andrews, *Paradise and Method*, 49.

59. Derrida, *Writing and Difference*, 259–60.

60. The word *reader* in this study should be understood more broadly to also include "reading," "writing as reading," and so forth.

61. McCaffery, *North of Intention*, 27.

62. Ibid., 156.

63. Ibid., 156–57.

64. *Webster's New World Dictionary*, s.v. "Bargain."

65. Georges Bataille, *The Unfinished System of Knowledge*, ed. Stuart Kendall, trans. Michelle Kendall and Stuart Kendall (Minneapolis: University of Minnesota Press, 2001), 284.

66. For a discussion of sound poetry in terms of general economy, see McCaffery, *North of Intention*, 214.

67. Bruce Andrews, "*Praxis:* A Political Economy of Noise and Informalism," in *Close Listening: Poetry and the Performed Word*, ed. Charles Bernstein (New York: Oxford University Press, 1998), 84. Andrews's rethinking of noise here is clearly informed by Jacques Attali's study titled *Noise: The Political Economy of Music*, trans. Brian Massumi (Minneapolis: University of Minnesota Press, 1985), which he mentions at the beginning of his article. Grounded in chaos theory and catastrophe theory in a fairly systematic way, Attali's theorizing of noise emphasizes, to a great extent, its importance or potential of meaning reproduction, seeing noise as "prophetic," as "[creating] a meaning," and so forth (19, 33). Although Andrews's critical approach shows some conceptual affinity to Attali, his rhetoric suggests quite a different position, one that foregrounds what he calls, toward the end of his essay, the performance of failure (Andrews, "*Praxis*," 85).

68. Andrews, *"Praxis,"* 85. Steve McCaffery makes a similar observation in his article "Language Writing: From Productive to Libidinal Economy" when he writes:

> What is important to grasp here is the characteristic *excess* of this text. In a way it cannot be spoken about but only participated within and a criticism would comprise the documentation of its reading as an extended writing. It might be argued that texts like the above have no concern with communication (or at least with the dominant theory of communication that sees it as a transmission from producer to receiver along a semiotic axis of production-consumption, giver-recipient). (McCaffery, *North of Intention,* 150)

For more details, see *North of Intention,* 143–58.

69. Andrews, *"Praxis,"* 77.

70. Ibid., 75.

71. Ibid., 77.

72. Ibid., 75.

73. Ibid.

74. Ibid., 75, 80.

75. Jerome McGann, " 'The Apparatus of Loss': Bruce Andrews' Writing," *Aerial* 9 (1999): 183.

76. Jed Rasula, "Andrews Extremities Bruce," *Aerial* 9 (1999): 23.

77. Andrews, *Paradise and Method,* 260.

78. *Webster's New World Dictionary,* s.v. "Ex-."

79. *Webster's New World Dictionary,* s.v. "Excommunicate."

80. Andrews's *Ex-Communicate* is not paginated.

81. Derrida, *Writing and Difference,* 274.

82. Ibid., 253.

83. McCaffery, *North of Intention,* 203.

84. Derrida, *Writing and Difference,* 270, 272.

85. Ibid., 270.

86. Andrews, *Paradise and Method,* 9.

87. Derrida, *Writing and Difference,* 272–73.

88. Rasula, "Andrews Extremities Bruce," 24.

89. Andrews, *Paradise and Method,* 52.

90. Ibid., 54, 55.

91. Ibid., 55.

92. Ibid., 51.

93. Ibid., 21, 28.

94. Ibid., 53.

95. Ibid., 45.

96. Ibid.

97. Ibid., 43.

98. Ibid., 42.

99. Ibid., 51.

100. Ibid., 44.

101. Andrews, *"Praxis,"* 76, 84.

102. Ibid., 76, 85.

103. Andrews, *Paradise and Method,* 58.

104. Ibid., 53.

105. Ibid.

106. Ibid., 53–54.

107. Ibid., 54.

108. Ibid.

109. Ibid.

110. Georges Bataille, "Friendship," *Parallax* 7, no. 1 (January–March 2001): 7.

111. Ibid.

Chapter 8

1. Jerome McGann, "Charles Bernstein's 'The Simply,'" in *Contemporary Poetry Meets Modern Theory,* ed. Antony Easthope and John O. Thompson (Toronto: University of Toronto Press, 1991), 34.

2. Ibid.

3. Hank Lazer, *Opposing Poetries,* 2 vols. (Evanston, Ill.: Northwestern University Press, 1996), 2:137, 139.

4. Charles Bernstein, *Content's Dream,* 221, 229. It is important to point out that Bernstein's understanding of method is not without limitations. While his sociopolitical critique of method is perceptive, his interests in "the possibilities for method itself," especially in the philosophical sense, nevertheless still articulate a degree of nostalgia for the tradition of "Descartes and Bacon" (*Content's Dream,* 220, 221). For other suggestive clues in this regard, see *Content's Dream,* 217–36.

5. Ibid., 220.

6. Ibid., 226.

7. Ibid., 224.

8. Ibid., 226, 225, 224.

9. Ibid., 235–36.

10. Ibid., 228.

11. Ibid., 222, 234.

12. Ibid., 219–20, 227 (emphasis in original). Unless otherwise noted, all forms of emphasis in the quotations in this chapter are in the original.

13. Ibid., 223.

14. Ibid.

15. Ibid., 224.

16. Ibid., 236.

17. Charles Bernstein, *Poetics,* 1, 2.

18. Baudrillard, *Selected Writings,* 194.

19. Stephen Kern, *The Culture of Time and Space: 1880–1918* (Cambridge, Mass.: Harvard University Press, 1983), 116.

20. F. T. Marinetti, *Let's Murder the Moonshine: Selected Writings of F. T. Marinetti,* ed. R. W. Flint, trans. R. W. Flint and Arthur A. Coppotelli (Los Angeles: Sun and Moon, 1991), 49.

21. Ibid., 89, 88.

22. Ibid., 93, 49, 103.

23. For a more detailed discussion of this issue, see Ursula K. Heise, *Chronoschisms: Time, Narrative, and Postmodernism* (Cambridge: Cambridge University Press, 1997), particularly chapter 1.

24. Kern, *Culture of Time,* 115.

25. Ibid.

26. Charles Bernstein, *Poetics,* 9.

27. Silliman, *New Sentence,* 14.

28. Ibid., 7.

29. Barthes, *Rustle of Language,* 310.

30. Steve McCaffery, *Theory of Sediment* (Vancouver: Talonbooks, 1991), 103.

31. Barthes, *Rustle of Language,* 310.

32. Ibid., 310, 311.

33. Ibid., 216.

34. Ibid.

35. Ibid., 311.

36. Ibid.

37. Ibid., 216.

38. Ibid., 215.

39. Ibid.

40. Ibid., 76.

41. McCaffery, *North of Intention,* 200.

42. Charles Bernstein, *Poetics,* 37.

43. Ibid. (emphasis added).

44. Ibid., 29, 30. While this is not the place to thoroughly engage this issue, it is important to point out that Bernstein's concept of "anti-absorption" as his compositional strategy works dialectically with the notion of "absorption," with each used toward the other's end (ibid., 30). Similar to that of Arkady Plotnitsky and of Steve McCaffery, who describes the dialectics between the anti-absorptive and the absorptive as "magical doubling" (ibid., 48), and to whom Bernstein makes repeated references as his support, Bernstein's position on this issue stays

within the confines of dialectical thinking. For more details in this regard, see "Artifice of Absorption" in *Poetics,* 9–89. For an implicit critique of Bernstein's position, see my article "The Past Is No Longer Out-of-Date." For a qualified statement concerning the critical approach of the present volume, see note 17 of chapter 7.

45. Charles Bernstein, *Poetics,* 29.

46. Charles Bernstein, *Content's Dream,* 41.

47. Charles Bernstein, "Interview," 28.

48. Charles Bernstein, *Content's Dream,* 71.

49. Ibid., 82.

50. Ibid., 83.

51. Ibid., 82–83.

52. Ibid., 83.

53. Ibid., 84.

54. Ibid.

55. Jean-Jacques Rousseau, *The Confessions of Jean-Jacques Rousseau,* trans. J. M. Cohen (Baltimore: Penguin Books, 1953), 591, quoted in Charles Bernstein, *Content's Dream,* 82.

56. Charles Bernstein, *Content's Dream,* 83.

57. Charles Bernstein, *Islets/Irritations* (New York: Roof, 1983), 1.

58. Charles Bernstein, *Content's Dream,* 84.

59. Charles Bernstein, *Poetics,* 2.

60. Ibid., 1.

61. Ibid., 2, 6.

62. *Oxford English Dictionary,* 2nd ed., s.v. "Sediment."

63. Steve McCaffery's use of the term *sediment* is multi-vectorial, to say the least. At times, it explicitly refers to the cliché of a culture or the "derivative" nature of current practices evidenced, among other phenomena, in "libraries, genres, specialist discourse and reported speech" (*Theory of Sediment,* 107, 109). Given the ambiguity with which it is used in McCaffery's text and its broad metaphorical coverage, *sediment* lends itself very nicely not only to the argument established so far in my book, but also to McCaffery's own thinking concerning language. Its connotative meaning, for instance, contributes aptly to McCaffery's critique of language in *North of Intention* as "a weapon at the service of a guerrilla epistemology" (200).

64. McCaffery, *Theory of Sediment,* 112, 104, 107.

65. Ibid., 93.

66. Ibid., 106.

67. Marinetti, *Let's Murder the Moonshine,* 103.

68. Benjamin Hollander, "*Resistance* by Charles Bernstein," *Sulfur* 12 (January 1986): 139.

69. Charles Bernstein, *Rough Trades* (Los Angeles: Sun and Moon, 1991), 65–66.

70. McCaffery, *Theory of Sediment,* 106.

71. Hollander, *"Resistance,"* 141.

72. McCaffery, *Theory of Sediment,* 106.

73. Excerpted from Charles Bernstein, *Rough Trades,* 65–66.

74. McGann, "Charles Bernstein's 'The Simply,' " 34.

75. Ibid., 36.

76. *Webster's New World Dictionary,* s.v. "The."

77. Hollander, *"Resistance,"* 141.

78. Charles Bernstein, *The Sophist* (Los Angeles: Sun and Moon, 1987), 7.

79. Charles Bernstein, *Islets/Irritations,* 12.

80. Charles Bernstein, *Poetics,* 1.

81. Charles Bernstein, *Islets/Irritations,* 29.

82. Baudrillard, *Selected Writings,* 193.

83. Charles Bernstein, *Dark City* (Los Angeles: Sun and Moon, 1994).

84. Ibid., 49.

85. Ibid.

86. Robert Smithson, *The Writings of Robert Smithson,* ed. Nancy Holt (New York: New York University Press, 1979), 82.

87. Ibid., 82.

Coda

1. Marjorie Perloff, "Postmodernism / *Fin de Siècle:* The Prospects for Openness in a Decade of Closure," *Criticism* 35, no. 2 (Spring 1993): 190 (italics in original). Unless otherwise noted, all forms of emphasis in the quotations are in the original.

2. Marjorie Perloff, "After Free Verse: The New Nonlinear Poetries," in *Poetry On and Off the Page* (Evanston, Ill.: Northwestern University Press, 1998), 166.

3. Ibid.

4. Ibid., 167.

5. Buchler, *Concept of Method,* 135 (emphasis added).

6. Ibid., 135, 137.

7. Ibid., 137.

8. I expound upon these issues in my article "The Past Is No Longer Out-of-Date."

9. Gilles Deleuze, *Difference and Repetition,* trans. Paul Patton (New York: Columbia University Press, 1994). The section of the book this chapter focuses on is chapter 3, "The Image of Thought." For Deleuze's complete argument, see pp. 129–67.

10. Deleuze, *Difference and Repetition,* 132–33.

11. Ibid., 133, 134.

12. Ibid., 133, 134. Deleuze specifies "the supposed three levels" as "a naturally upright thought, an in principle natural common sense, and a transcendental model of recognition" (ibid., 134).

13. Ibid., 134.

14. Ibid., 136 (emphasis added).

15. Ibid.

16. Ibid.

17. Ibid.

Works Cited

Abrams, M. H. *The Mirror and the Lamp: Romantic Theory and the Critical Tradition.* New York: W. W. Norton, 1958.

Adorno, Theodor W. *Against Epistemology: A Metacritique.* Translated by Willis Domingo. Cambridge, Mass.: MIT Press, 1982.

———. *Minima Moralia: Reflections from Damaged Life.* Translated by E. F. N. Jephcott. London: Verso, 1974.

Altieri, Charles. "The Objectivist Tradition." *Chicago Review* 30, no. 3 (Winter 1979): 5–22.

Andrews, Bruce. "C3B1-c." *Aerial* 9, Bruce Andrews special issue (1999): 211.

———. *Divestiture—A.* New York: Drogue, 1994.

———. *Ex-Communicate.* Elmwood, Conn.: Potes and Poets, 1999.

———. *Paradise and Method: Poetics and Praxis.* Evanston, Ill.: Northwestern University Press, 1996.

———. "Poetry as Explanation, Poetry as Praxis." In *The Politics of Poetic Form: Poetry and Public Policy,* edited by Charles Bernstein, 23–43. New York: Roof, 1990.

———. "*Praxis:* A Political Economy of Noise and Informalism." In *Close Listening: Poetry and the Performed Word,* edited by Charles Bernstein, 73–85. New York: Oxford University Press, 1998.

Andrews, Bruce, and Charles Bernstein, eds. *The L=A=N=G=U=A=G=E Book.* Carbondale: Southern Illinois University Press, 1984.

Antin, David. "Modernism and Postmodernism: Approaching the Present in American Poetry." *boundary 2,* vol. 1 (Fall 1972): 98–133.

———. "Some Questions About Modernism." *Occident* 8, n.s. (Spring 1974): 7–38.

Assad, Maria L. "Michel Serres: In Search of a Tropography." In *Chaos and Order: Complex Dynamics in Literature and Science,* edited by N. Katherine Hayles, 278–98. Chicago: University of Chicago Press, 1991.

———. *Reading with Michel Serres: An Encounter with Time.* Albany: State University of New York Press, 1999.

Atlan, Henri. "Disorder, Complexity and Meaning." In *Disorder and Order,* edited by Paisley Livingston, 109–28. Stanford, Calif.: Anma Libri, 1984.

———. "On a Formal Definition of Organization." *Journal of Theoretical Biology* 45, no. 2 (June 1974): 295–304.

Attali, Jacques. *Noise: The Political Economy of Music.* Translated by Brian Massumi. Minneapolis: University of Minnesota Press, 1985.

Bacon, Francis. *The Advancement of Learning and New Atlantis.* Edited by Arthur Johnston. Oxford: Clarendon, 1974.

Bailey, Alvin R. "A Selected, Annotated Bibliography of Secondary Sources, 1932–1985, on Louis Zukofsky." *Sagetrieb* 10, no. 1–2 (Spring–Fall 1991): 169–206.

Barthes, Roland. *The Rustle of Language.* Translated by Richard Howard. New York: Hill and Wang, 1986.

Bataille, Georges. "Friendship." *Parallax* 7, no. 1 (January-March 2001): 3–15.

———. *The Unfinished System of Knowledge.* Edited with an introduction by Stuart Kendall, translated by Michelle Kendall and Stuart Kendall. Minneapolis: University of Minnesota Press, 2001.

———. *Visions of Excess: Selected Writings 1927–1939.* Edited with an introduction by Allan Stoekl. Minneapolis: University of Minnesota Press, 1985.

Baudrillard, Jean. *Selected Writings.* Edited by Mark Poster. Stanford, Calif.: Stanford University Press, 1988.

Benveniste, Emile. *Problems in General Linguistics.* Translated by Mary Elizabeth Meek. Coral Gables, Fla.: University of Miami Press, 1971.

Bernstein, Charles. *Content's Dream.* Los Angeles: Sun and Moon, 1986.

———. *Dark City.* Los Angeles: Sun and Moon, 1994.

———. "Interview." By Manuel Brito. In *A Suite of Poetic Voices,* edited by Manuel Brito, 23–36. Santa Brigida, Spain: Kadle Books, 1992.

———. *Islets/Irritations.* New York: Roof, 1983.

———. "Language Sampler." *Paris Review* 86 (1982): 75–78.

———. *A Poetics.* Cambridge, Mass.: Harvard University Press, 1992.

———, ed. *The Politics of Poetic Form: Poetry and Public Policy.* New York: Roof, 1990.

———. *Rough Trades.* Los Angeles: Sun and Moon, 1991.

———. *The Sophist.* Los Angeles: Sun and Moon, 1987.

Bernstein, Michael André. "Bringing It All Back Home: Derivations and Quotations in Robert Duncan and the Poundian Tradition." *Sagetrieb* 1, no. 2 (Fall 1982): 176–89.

———. "History and Textuality in Ezra Pound's *Cantos.*" In *Ezra Pound and History,* edited by Marianne Korn, 15–22. Orono, Maine: National Poetry Foundation, 1985.

Bigger, Charles P. *Kant's Methodology: An Essay in Philosophical Archeology.* Athens: Ohio University Press, 1996.

Bloom, Harold. *Wallace Stevens: The Poems of Our Climate.* Ithaca, N.Y.: Cornell University Press, 1977.

Branham, Robert J., and W. Barnett Pearce. "Between Text and Context: Toward a Rhetoric of Contextual Reconstruction." *Quarterly Journal of Speech* 71, no. 1 (February 1985): 19–36.

Brito, Manuel, ed. *A Suite of Poetic Voices: Interviews with Contemporary American Poets.* Santa Brigida, Spain: Kadle Books, 1992.

Broughton, Janet. *Descartes's Method of Doubt.* Princeton, N.J.: Princeton University Press, 2002.

Bruns, Gerald. "Poethics: John Cage and Stanley Cavell at the Crossroad of Ethical Theory." In *John Cage: Composed in America,* edited by Marjorie Perloff and Charles Junkerman, 206–25. Chicago: University of Chicago Press, 1994.

Buchler, Justus. *The Concept of Method.* New York: University Press of America, 1985.

Byrd, Don. "Language Poetry, 1971–1986." *Sulfur* 20 (1987): 149–57.

———. *The Poetics of the Common Knowledge.* New York: State University of New York Press, 1994.

———. "The Shape of Zukofsky's Canon." In *Louis Zukofsky: Man and Poet,* edited by Carroll F. Terrell, 163–85. Orono, Maine: National Poetry Foundation, 1979.

Cadel, Francesca. "Science." In *The Ezra Pound Encyclopedia,* edited by Demetres P. Tryphonopoulos and Stephen J. Adams, 264–66. Westport, Conn.: Greenwood, 2005.

Cage, John. *Conversing with John Cage.* Edited by Richard Kostelanetz. New York: Limelight Editions, 1991.

———. *I–VI.* Cambridge, Mass.: Harvard University Press, 1990.

———. *Empty Words.* Middletown, Conn.: Wesleyan University Press, 1979.

———. *M: Writings '67–'72.* Middletown, Conn.: Wesleyan University Press, 1973.

———. *Roaratorio: An Irish Circus on Finnegans Wake.* Edited by Klaus Schöning. Königstein: Athenäum, 1985.

———. *Silence.* Middletown, Conn.: Wesleyan University Press, 1961.

———. *X: Writings '79–'82.* Middletown, Conn.: Wesleyan University Press, 1983.

Calinescu, Matei. *Five Faces of Modernity.* Durham, N.C.: Duke University Press, 1987.

Chilton, Harrison Randolph, Jr. "The Object Beyond the Image: A Study of Four Objectivist Poets." Diss., University of Wisconsin, Madison, 1981.

Clark, Herbert H., and Richard J. Gerrig. "Quotations as Demonstrations." *Language* 66, no. 4 (December 1990): 764–805.

Clark, Hilary. "The Mnemonics of Autobiography: Lyn Hejinian's *My Life.*" *Biography* 14, no. 4 (Fall 1991): 315–35.

Clarvoe, Jennifer. "Quoting History, Reading Poetry." *Agni Review* (1990): 326–33.

Coleridge, S. T. *The Complete Works of Samuel Taylor Coleridge.* Edited with an introduction by W. G. T. Shedd. 7 vols. New York: Harper and Brothers, 1868.

———. *Shorter Works and Fragment*s. Edited by H. J. Jackson and J. R. de J. Jackson. 2 vols. Princeton, N.J.: Princeton University Press, 1995.

Comens, Bruce. "From A to An: The Postmodern Twist in Louis Zukofsky." *Sagetrieb* 10, no. 3 (Winter 1991): 37–62.

Conte, Joseph M. *Unending Design: The Forms of Postmodern Poetry.* Ithaca, N.Y.: Cornell University Press, 1991.

Dasenbrook, Reed Way. *The Literary Vorticism of Ezra Pound and Wyndham Lewis: Towards the Condition of Painting.* Baltimore: Johns Hopkins University Press, 1985.

Davidson, Michael. "On Reading Stein." In *The L=A=N=G=U=A=G=E Book,* edited by Bruce Andrews and Charles Bernstein, 196–98. Carbondale: Southern Illinois University Press, 1984.

Dear, Peter. "Method and the Study of Nature." In *The Cambridge History of Seventeenth-Century Philosophy,* edited by Daniel Garber and Michael Ayers, 147–77. Cambridge: Cambridge University Press, 1998.

DeKoven, Marianne. *A Different Language: Gertrude Stein's Experimental Language.* Madison: University of Wisconsin Press, 1983.

Deleuze, Gilles. *Difference and Repetition.* Translated by Paul Patton. New York: Columbia University Press, 1994.

Dembo, L. S. "The Existential World of George Oppen." *Iowa Review* 3, no. 1 (1972): 64–92.

———. "Louis Zukofsky: Objectivist Poetics and the Quest for Form." In *Louis Zukofsky: Man and Poet,* edited by Carroll F. Terrell. Orono, Maine: National Poetry Foundation, 1979.

Dembo, L. S., and Cyrena N. Pondrom, eds. *The Contemporary Writer: Interviews with Sixteen Novelists and Poets.* Madison: University of Wisconsin Press, 1972.

Derrida, Jacques. *Dissemination.* Translated by Barbara Johnson. Chicago: University of Chicago Press, 1981.

———. *Margins of Philosophy.* Translated by Alan Bass. Chicago: University of Chicago Press, 1982.

———. *Of Grammatology.* Translated by Gayatri Chakravorty Spivak. Baltimore: Johns Hopkins University Press, 1976.

———. *Speech and Phenomena.* Translated by David Allison. Evanston, Ill.: Northwestern University Press, 1973.

———. *Writing and Difference.* Translated by Alan Bass. Chicago: University of Chicago Press, 1978.

Descartes, René. *The Philosophical Writings of Descartes.* Translated by Elizabeth S. Haldane and G. R. T. Ross. New York: Dover, 1955.

Dewey, John. *The Quest for Certainty.* Gifford Lectures, 1929. New York: Putnam, 1960.

Diepeveen, Leonard. *Changing Voices: The Modern Quoting Poem.* Ann Arbor: University of Michigan Press, 1993.

Drabinski, John E. "From Experience to Flesh: On James and Merleau-Ponty." *Phenomenological Inquiry* 21 (October 1997): 137–55.

Dufrenne, Mikel. *Language and Philosophy.* Translated by Henry B. Veatch. Bloomington: Indiana University Press, 1963.

Duncan, Robert. "As Testimony: Reading Zukofsky These Forty Years." *Paideuma* 7, no. 3 (Winter 1978): 421–27.

Dupee, F. W. Introduction to *Selected Writings of Gertrude Stein,* edited by Carl Van Vechten, ix–xvii. New York: Vintage Books, 1990.

DuPlessis, Rachel Blau. "George Oppen: 'What Do We Believe to Live With?' " *Ironwood* 3, no. 1 (1975): 62–77.

———. "Objectivist Poetics and Political Vision: A Study of Oppen and Pound." In *George Oppen: Man and Poet,* edited by Burton Hatlen, 123–48. Orono, Maine: National Poetry Foundation, University of Maine, 1981.

———. *The Pink Guitar: Writing as Feminist Practice.* New York: Routledge, 1990.

Durant, Alan. "The Language of History in *The Cantos.*" In *Ezra Pound and History,* edited by Marianne Korn, 23–35. Orono, Maine: National Poetry Foundation, 1985.

Eakin, Paul John. *Touching the World: Reference in Autobiography.* Princeton, N.J.: Princeton University Press, 1992.

Eliot, T. S. "Philip Massinger." In *The Sacred Wood: Essays on Poetry and Criticism,* 71–83. New York: Alfred A. Knopf, 1930.

———. *Selected Essays.* New ed. New York: Harcourt, Brace and World, 1950.

Emerson, Ralph Waldo. "Quotation and Originality." In *Letters and Social Aims,* 175–204. Boston: Houghton Mifflin, 1904.

Fairclough, Norman. *Language and Power.* London: Longman, 1989.

Faulkner, William. *Light in August.* New York: Random House, 1959.

Feld, Ross. "Some Thoughts About Objectivism." *Sagetrieb* 12, no. 3 (Winter 1993): 65–77.

Feyerabend, Paul. *Against Method.* London: Verso, 1988.

Fischer, Andreas. "Context-Free and Context-Sensitive Literature: Sherwood Anderson's *Winesburg, Ohio* and James Joyce's *Dubliners.*" In *Reading Contexts,* edited by Neil Forsyth, 12–31. Tübingen, W.Ger.: Gunter Narr, 1988.

Forsyth, Neil, ed. *Reading Contexts.* Tübingen, W.Ger.: Gunter Narr, 1988.

Foucault, Michel. *The Order of Things.* New York: Vintage, 1970.

Fredman, Stephen. *Poet's Prose: The Crisis in American Verse.* 2nd ed. Cambridge: Cambridge University Press, 1990.

Gadamer, Hans-Georg. *Truth and Method.* Translated by W. Glen-Doepel. 2nd ed. New York: Crossroad, 1985.

Gandelman, Claude. *Reading Pictures, Viewing Texts.* Bloomington: Indiana University Press, 1991.

Gasché, Rodolphe. *The Tain of the Mirror: Derrida and the Philosophy of Reflection.* Cambridge, Mass.: Harvard University Press, 1986.

Gass, William H. "Gertrude Stein and the Geography of the Sentence." In *The World Within the Word,* 63–123. New York: Alfred A. Knopf, 1979.

Gates, Henry Louis. *Figures in Black: Words, Signs, and the "Radical" Self.* New York: Oxford University Press, 1989.

Gaukroger, Stephen. "Descartes: Methodology." In *The Renaissance and Seventeenth-Century Rationalism,* edited by G. H. R. Parkinson, 167–200. London: Routledge, 1993.

Gelpi, Albert. *A Coherent Splendor: The American Poetic Renaissance, 1910–1950.* Cambridge: Cambridge University Press, 1987.

Gilbert, Neal. *Renaissance Concepts of Method.* New York: Columbia University Press, 1963.

Golding, Alan. "George Oppen's Serial Poems." *Contemporary Literature* 29, no. 2 (Summer 1998): 221–40.

Goodman, Lenn E. "Context." *Philosophy East and West* 38, no. 3 (July 1988): 307–23.

Grabes, Herbert. "Deliberate Intertextuality: The Function of Quotation and Allusion in the Early Poetry of T. S. Eliot." In *Multiple Worlds, Multiple Words,* edited by Hena Maes-Jelinek, Pierre Michel, and Paulette Michel-Michot, 139–52. Liège, Belg.: English Department, University of Liège, 1987.

Grigson, Geoffrey. "The Methodism of Ezra Pound." In *Ezra Pound: The Critical Heritage,* edited by Eric Homberger, 259–64. London: Routledge and Kegan Paul, 1972.

Halbwachs, Maurice. *On Collective Memory.* Edited and translated by Lewis A. Coser. Chicago: University of Chicago Press, 1992.

Harari, Josué V., and David F. Bell. "Introduction: Journal a Plusieurs Voies." In *Hermes: Literature, Science, Philosophy,* by Michel Serres, ix–xl. Baltimore: Johns Hopkins University Press, 1982.

Hartley, George. *Textual Politics and the Language Poets.* Bloomington: Indiana University Press, 1989.

Hass, Robert. "George Oppen: A Tribute." *Ironwood* 13, no. 2 (Fall 1985): 38–42.

Hassan, Ihab. *The Postmodern Turn: Essays in Postmodern Theory and Culture.* Columbus: Ohio State University Press, 1987.

Hatlen, Burton. "Carl Rakosi and the Re-Invention of the Epigram." In *The Collected Prose of Carl Rakosi,* 125–44. Orono, Maine: National Poetry Foundation, University of Maine, 1983.

———. "From Modernism to Postmodernism: Zukofsky's 'A'–12." *Sagetrieb* 11, no. 1–2 (Spring–Fall 1992): 21–34.

———, ed. *George Oppen: Man and Poet.* Orono, Maine: National Poetry Foundation, 1981.

———. "Zukofsky, Wittgenstein, and the Poetics of Absence." *Sagetrieb* 1, no. 1 (Spring 1982): 63–93.

Hayles, N. Katherine. "Chance Operation: Cagean Paradox and Contemporary Science." In *John Cage: Composed in America,* edited by Marjorie Perloff and Charles Junkerman, 226–41. Chicago: University of Chicago Press, 1994.

———, ed. *Chaos and Order: Complex Dynamics in Literature and Science.* Chicago: University of Chicago Press, 1991.

———. *Chaos Bound: Orderly Disorder in Contemporary Literature and Science.* Ithaca, N.Y.: Cornell University Press, 1990.

———. *The Cosmic Web: Scientific Field Models and Literary Strategies in the 20th Century.* Ithaca, N.Y.: Cornell University Press, 1984.

Hegel, G. W. F. *The Phenomenology of Mind.* Translated by A. V. Miller. Oxford: Oxford University Press, 1977.

Heidegger, Martin. "The Age of the World View." Translated by Marjorie Grene. *boundary 2,* vol. 4, no. 2, Martin Heidegger and Literature special issue (Winter 1976): 340–55.

———. *On the Way to Language.* Translated by Peter D. Hertz. San Fransisco: Harper and Row, 1971.

Heise, Ursula K. *Chronoschisms: Time, Narrative, and Postmodernism.* Cambridge: Cambridge University Press, 1997.

Heisenberg, Werner. *Physics and Philosophy: The Revolution in Modern Science.* New York: Harper and Row, 1958.

Hejinian, Lyn. "Interview." By Manuel Brito. In *A Suite of Poetic Voices: Interviews with Contemporary American Poets,* edited by Manuel Brito, 71–93. Santa Brigida, Spain: Kadle Books, 1992.

———. *The Language of Inquiry.* Berkeley: University of California Press, 2000.

———. *My Life.* Providence, R.I.: Burning Deck, 1980.

———. *My Life.* Los Angeles: Sun and Moon, 1987.

———. "Two Stein Talks." *Temblor* 3 (1986): 128–39.

———. *Writing Is an Aid to Memory.* Los Angeles: Sun and Moon, 1996.

Heller, Michael, ed. *Carl Rakosi: Man and Poet.* Orono, Maine: National Poetry Foundation, 1993.

———. *Conviction's Net of Branches: Essays on the Objectivist Poets and Poetry.* Carbondale: Southern Illinois University Press, 1985.

Herwitz, Daniel. "John Cage's Approach to the Global." In *John Cage: Composed in America,* edited by Marjorie Perloff and Charles Junkerman, 188–205. Chicago: University of Chicago Press, 1994.

Hintikka, Jaakko. "A Discourse on Descartes's Method." In *Descartes: Critical and Interpretive Essays,* edited by Michael Hooker, 74–88. Baltimore: Johns Hopkins University Press, 1978.

Hirsch, Edward. "'Out There Is the World': The Visual Imperative in the Poetry of George Oppen and Charles Tomlinson." In *George Oppen: Man and Poet,* edited by Burton Hatlen, 169–80. Orono, Maine: National Poetry Foundation, 1981.

Hollander, Benjamin. "*Resistance* by Charles Bernstein." *Sulfur* 12 (January 1986): 139–43.

Hooker, Jeremy. "'The Boundaries of Our Distances': On 'Of Being Numerous.'" *Ironwood* 13, no. 2 (Fall 1985): 81–103.

Hoover, Paul. Introduction to *Postmodern American Poetry: A Norton Anthology,* edited by Paul Hoover, xxv–xxxix. New York: Norton, 1994.

Howe, Susan. *The Birth-Mark: Unsettling the Wilderness in American Literary History.* Hanover, N.H.: Wesleyan University Press, University Press of New England, 1993.

———. "The *Difficulties* Interview." By Tom Beckett, *The Difficulties* 3, no. 2, Susan Howe special issue (1989): 17–27.

———. "Encloser." In *The Politics of Poetic Form: Poetry and Public Policy,* edited by Charles Bernstein, 175–96. New York: Roof, 1990.

———. *The Europe of Trusts.* New York: New Directions, 2002.

———. "An Interview with Susan Howe." By Edward Foster. *Talisman: A Journal of Contemporary Poetry and Poetics* 4 (Spring 1990): 14–38.

———. *My Emily Dickinson.* Berkeley, Calif.: North Atlantic, 1985.

———. *The Nonconformist's Memorial.* New York: New Directions, 1993.

———. *Singularities.* Hanover, N.H.: Wesleyan University Press, University Press of New England, 1990.

———. "Statement for the New Poetics Colloquium, Vancouver, 1985." *Jimmy and Lucy's House of "K"* 5 (November 1985): 13–17.

Husserl, Edmund. *Ideas: General Introduction to Pure Phenomenology.* Translated by W. R. Boyce Gibson. London: Collier Books, 1962.

Irigaray, Luce. *This Sex Which Is Not One.* Translated by Catherine Porter with Carolyn Burke. Ithaca, N.Y.: Cornell University Press, 1985.

James, William. "From William James." In *The Flowers of Friendship: Letters Written to Gertrude Stein,* edited by Donald Gallup, 51–52. New York: Alfred A. Knopf, 1953.

Jarraway, David R. "*My Life* Through the Eighties: The Exemplary L=A=N=G=U=A=G=E of Lyn Hejinian." *Contemporary Literature* 33, no. 2 (Summer 1992): 319–36.

Johnson, Barbara. Translator's introduction to *Dissemination,* by Jacques Derrida, vii–xxxiii. Chicago: University of Chicago Press, 1981.

Judovitz, Dalia. "Vision, Representation, and Technology in Descartes." In *Modernity and the Hegemony of Vision,* edited by David Michael Levin, 63–86. Berkeley: University of California Press, 1993.

Kant, Immanuel. *Critique of Pure Reason.* Translated by Norman Kemp Smith. New York: St. Martin's Press, 1929.

Kappel, Andrew. "The Reading and Writing of a Modern Paradiso: Ezra Pound and the Books of Paradise." *Twentieth Century Literature* 27, no. 3 (Fall 1981): 223–46.

Kenner, Hugh. Foreword to *Prepositions: The Collected Critical Essays of Louis Zukofsky,* by Louis Zukofsky. Exp. ed., vii–x. Berkeley: University of California Press, 1981.

———. *A Homemade World.* New York: Morrow, 1975.

———. *The Pound Era.* Berkeley: University of California Press, 1971.

Kern, Stephen. *The Culture of Time and Space: 1880–1918.* Cambridge, Mass.: Harvard University Press, 1983.

Korn, Marianne. *Ezra Pound and History.* Orono, Maine: National Poetry Foundation, 1985.

Kostelanetz, Richard. Introduction to *The Yale Gertrude Stein,* by Gertrude Stein. Selected by Richard Kostelanetz, xiii–xxxi. New Haven: Yale University Press, 1980.

Krauss, Rosalind. "Re-presenting Picasso." *Art in America* (December 1980): 90–96.

Kristeva, Julia. *Revolution in Poetic Language.* Translated by Margaret Waller. New York: Columbia University Press, 1984.

Kuhn, Thomas. "Reflections on My Critics." In *Criticism and Growth of Knowledge,* edited by I. Lakatos and A. Musgrave, 231–78. Cambridge: Cambridge University Press, 1970.

———. *The Structure of Scientific Revolutions.* 2nd ed. Chicago: University of Chicago Press, 1970.

Latour, Bruno. "The Enlightenment Without the Critique: A Word on Michel Serres' Philosophy." In *Contemporary French Philosophy,* edited by A. Phillips Griffiths, 83–98. New York: Cambridge University Press, 1987.

Lazer, Hank. *Opposing Poetries.* 2 vols. Evanston, Ill.: Northwestern University Press, 1996.

Lecercle, Jean-Jacques. *Deleuze and Language.* New York: Palgrave, 2002.

Leggott, Michele J. *Reading Zukofsky's 80 Flowers.* Baltimore: Johns Hopkins University Press, 1989.

Lejeune, Philippe. "The Autobiographical Pact." In *On Autobiography,* edited by Paul John Eakin, translated by Katherine M. Leary, 3–30. Minneapolis: University of Minnesota Press, 1989.

Levin, David Michael. Introduction to *Modernity and the Hegemony of Vision,* edited by David Michael Levin, 1–29. Berkeley: University of California Press, 1993.

Levinas, Emmanuel. *Totality and Infinity.* Translated by Alphonso Lingis. Philadelphia: Duquesne University Press, 1961.

Luhmann, Niklas. *Theories of Distinction.* Edited by William Rasch. Stanford, Calif.: Stanford University Press, 2002.

Lyotard, Jean-François. *The Differend: Phrases in Dispute.* Translated by G. Van Den Abbeele. Minneapolis: University of Minnesota Press, 1988.

———. *The Postmodern Condition: A Report on Knowledge.* Translated by Geoff Bennington and Brian Massumi. Minneapolis: University of Minnesota Press, 1984.

Ma, Ming-Qian. "The Past Is No Longer Out-of-Date: Topological Time and Its Foldable Nearness in Michel Serres's Philosophy." *Configurations* 6 (2000): 235–44.

Macann, Christopher. *Four Phenomenological Philosophers: Husserl, Heidegger, Sartre, Merleau-Ponty.* New York: Routledge, 1993.

Margolis, Joseph. "Unlikely Prospects for Applying Wittgenstein's 'Method' to Aesthetics and the Philosophy of Art." In *The Literary Wittgenstein,* edited by John Gibson and Wolfgang Huemer, 321–46. London: Routledge, 2004.

Marinetti, F. T. *Let's Murder the Moonshine: Selected Writings of F. T. Marinetti.* Edited by R. W. Flint. Translated by R. W. Flint and Arthur A. Coppotelli. Los Angeles: Sun and Moon, 1991.

Marlowe, Christopher. *Marlowe's Edward II.* Edited by William Dinsmore Briggs. London: David Nutt, 1914.

Mathews, Harry. "John Ashbery Interviewing Harry Mathews." *Review of Contemporary Fiction* 7 (Fall 1987): 36–48.

McCaffery, Steve. "From the Notebooks." In *The L=A=N=G=U=A=G=E Book,* edited by Bruce Andrews and Charles Bernstein, 159–62. Carbondale: Southern Illinois University Press, 1984.

———. *North of Intention.* New York: Roof, 1986.

———. *Theory of Sediment.* Vancouver: Talonbooks, 1991.

McGann, Jerome. "'The Apparatus of Loss': Bruce Andrews' Writing." *Aerial* 9, Bruce Andrews special issue (1999): 183–95.

———. "Charles Bernstein's 'The Simply.'" In *Contemporary Poetry Meets Modern Theory,* edited by Antony Easthope and John O. Thompson, 34–39. Toronto: University of Toronto Press, 1991.

———. "Contemporary Poetry, Alternate Routes." In *Politics and Poetic Value,* edited by Robert von Hallberg, 253–76. Chicago: University of Chicago Press, 1987.

———. "Language Writing." *London Review of Books* 9, no. 18 (October 15, 1987): 6–8.

McHale, Brian. "Change of Dominant from Modernist to Postmodernist Writing." In *Approaching Postmodernism,* edited by Douwe Fokkema and Hans Bertens, 53–79. Amsterdam: John Benjamins, 1986.

Merleau-Ponty, M. *Phenomenology of Perception.* Translated by Colin Smith. New York: Humanities, 1962.

Meulen, Alice G. B. ter. *Representing Time in Natural Language.* Cambridge, Mass.: MIT Press, 1995.

Meyerowitz, Patricia. Preface and introduction to *How to Write,* by Gertrude Stein, v–vii, x–xxv. New York: Dover, 1975.

Monroe, Harriet. "The Arrogance of Youth." *Poetry* 37 (March 1931): 332–33.

Moore, Marianne. "The Cantos." In *The Complete Prose of Marianne Moore,* 268–77. New York: Viking, 1986.

Motte, Warren F., Jr. Introduction to *Oulipo: A Primer of Potential Literature,* edited and translated by Warren F. Motte, with a foreword by Noël Arnaud, 1–22. Lincoln: University of Nebraska Press, 1986.

Mottram, Eric. "The Political Responsibilities of the Poet: George Oppen." In *George Oppen: Man and Poet,* edited by Burton Hatlen, 149–67. Orono, Maine: National Poetry Foundation, 1981.

Nägele, Rainer. "Benjamin's Ground." In *Benjamin's Ground: New Readings of Walter Benjamin,* edited by Rainer Nägele, 19–37. Detroit: Wayne State University Press, 1988.

Oppen, George. "An Adequate Vision: A George Oppen Daybook." *Ironwood* 13, no. 2 (Fall 1985): 5–31.

———. "George Oppen." Interview by L. S. Dembo. In *The Contemporary Writer: Interviews with Sixteen Novelists and Poets,* edited by L. S. Dembo and Cyrena N. Pondrom, 172–90. Madison: University of Wisconsin Press, 1972.

———. "An Interview with George and Mary Oppen." By Keven Power. *Montemora* 4 (August 1978): 187–203.

———. "Letters to June Oppen Degnan." *Ironwood* 13, no. 2 (Fall 1985): 215–36.

———. "The Mind's Own Place." *Kulchur* 3, no. 10 (Summer 1963): 2–8.

———. *New Collected Poems.* Edited by Michael Davidson. New York: New Directions, 2002.

———. "The 'Objectivist' Poet: Four Interviews." By L. S. Dembo. *Contemporary Literature* 10, no. 2 (Spring 1969): 159–77.

———. "'The Philosophy of the Astonished': Selections from the Working Papers," edited by Rachel Blau DuPlessis. *Sulfur* 10, no. 2 (Fall 1990): 202–20.

———. *The Selected Letters of George Oppen.* Edited by Rachel Blau DuPlessis. Durham, N.C.: Duke University Press, 1990.

———. "Three Poets." *Poetry* 100, no. 5 (August 1962): 329–33.

Ovid. *Metamorphoses.* Translated by Rolfe Humphries. Bloomington: Indiana University Press, 1983.

Palmer, Michael. "On Objectivism." *Sulfur* 26 (Spring 1990): 117–26.

Palmer, Richard. *Hermeneutics.* Evanston, Ill.: Northwestern University Press, 1969.

Parlej, Piotr. "Testing the Image: The Double Interrogative in the Poetry of George Oppen." *Sagetrieb* 10, no. 1–2 (Spring–Fall 1991): 67–82.

Paulson, William R. "Literature, Complexity, Interdisciplinarity." In *Chaos and*

Order: Complex Dynamics in Literature and Science, edited by N. Katherine Hayles, 37–53. Chicago: University of Chicago Press, 1991.

———. *The Noise of Culture: Literary Texts in a World of Information.* Ithaca, N.Y.: Cornell University Press, 1988.

Perloff, Marjorie. "After Free Verse: The New Nonlinear Poetries." In *Poetry On and Off the Page,* 141–67. Evanston, Ill.: Northwestern University Press, 1998.

———. " 'Barbed-Wire Entanglements': The 'New American Poetry,' 1930–1932." *Modernism/Modernity* 2, no. 1 (1995): 145–75.

———. "Canon and Loaded Gun: Feminist Poetics and the Avant-Garde." *Stanford Literature Review* 4, no. 1 (1987): 23–46.

———. *The Dance of the Intellect: Studies in the Poetry of the Pound Tradition.* Cambridge: Cambridge University Press, 1985.

———. " 'A Fine New Kind of Realism': Six Stein Styles in Search of a Reader." In Marjorie Perloff, *Poetic License: Essays on Modernist and Postmodernist Lyric,* 145–60. Evanston, Ill.: Northwestern University Press, 1990.

———. "Music for Words Perhaps: Reading/Hearing/Seeing in John Cage's *Roaratorio.*" In *Postmodern Genres,* edited by Marjorie Perloff, 193–228. Norman: University of Oklahoma Press, 1989.

———. *The Poetics of Indeterminacy: Rimbaud to Cage.* Princeton, N.J.: Princeton University Press, 1981.

———. "Postmodernism/*Fin de Siècle:* The Prospects for Openness in a Decade of Closure." *Criticism* 35, no. 2 (Spring 1993): 161–91.

———. *Radical Artifice: Writing Poetry in the Age of Media.* Chicago: University of Chicago Press, 1991.

———. "Toward an Avant-Garde *Tractatus:* Russell and Wittgenstein on War." *Common Knowledge* 2, no. 1 (Spring 1993): 15–34.

Perloff, Marjorie, and Charles Junkerman, eds. *John Cage: Composed in America.* Chicago: University of Chicago Press, 1994.

Peterson, Jeffrey. " 'The Allotropes of Vision': Carl Rakosi and the Psychology of Microscopy." In *Carl Rakosi: Man and Poet,* edited by Michael Heller, 119–91. Orono, Maine: National Poetry Foundation, University of Maine, 1993.

Pfeiffer, K. Ludwig. "Fiction: On the Fate of a Concept Between Philosophy and Literary Theory." In *Aesthetic Illusion: Theoretical and Historical Approaches,* edited by Frederick Burwick and Walter Pape, 92–104. New York: Walter de Gruyter, 1990.

Plotnitsky, Arkady. *Complementarity: Anti-Epistemology After Bohr and Derrida.* Durham, N.C.: Duke University Press, 1994.

———. "Effects of the Unknowable: Materialism, Epistemology, and the General Economy of the Body in Bataille." *Parallax* 7, no. 1 (January-March 2001): 16–28.

———. *Reconfigurations: Critical Theory and General Economy.* Gainesville: University Press of Florida, 1993.

Polletta, Gregory. "Textuality, Actuality, and Contextuality: The Example of *Gravity's Rainbow.*" In *Reading Contexts,* edited by Neil Forsyth, 83–101. Tübingen, W.Ger.: Gunter Narr, 1988.

Pope, Alexander. *An Essay on Criticism 1711.* Yorkshire, Eng.: Scolar, 1970.

Pound, Ezra. *ABC of Reading.* New York: New Directions, 1934.

———. "The Approach to Paris, v." *New Age* 13 (October 2, 1913): 662.

———. *The Cantos of Ezra Pound.* New York: New Directions, 1995.

———. *Gaudier-Brzeska: A Memoir.* New York: New Directions, 1970.

———. *Guide to Kulchur.* New York: New Directions, 1970.

———. *Literary Essays of Ezra Pound.* New York: New Directions, 1935.

———. *Selected Letters 1907–1941.* Edited by D. D. Paige. New York: New Directions, 1971.

———. *Selected Prose 1909–1965.* Edited by William Cookson. New York: New Directions, 1973.

———. *The Spirit of Romance, 1910.* New York: New Directions, 1968.

Pound, Ezra, and Louis Zukofsky. *Pound/Zukofsky: Selected Letters of Ezra Pound and Louis Zukofsky.* Edited by Barry Ahearn. New York: New Directions, 1987.

Prigogine, Ilya, and Isabelle Stengers. *Order Out of Chaos: Man's New Dialogue with Nature.* New York: Bantam Book, 1984.

Quartermain, Peter. *Disjunctive Poetics: From Gertrude Stein and Louis Zukofsky to Susan Howe.* Cambridge: Cambridge University Press, 1992.

Queneau, Raymond. "Potential Literature." In *Oulipo: A Primer of Potential Literature,* edited and translated by Warren F. Motte Jr., 51–64. Lincoln: University of Nebraska Press, 1986.

Rainey, Lawrence S. *Ezra Pound and the Monument of Culture: Text, History, and the Malatesta Cantos.* Chicago: University of Chicago Press, 1991.

Rakosi, Carl. "Carl Rakosi." Interview by L. S. Dembo. In *The Contemporary Writer: Interviews with Sixteen Novelists and Poets,* edited by L. S. Dembo and Cyrena N. Pondrom, 191–205. Madison: University of Wisconsin Press, 1972.

———. *The Collected Poems of Carl Rakosi.* Orono, Maine: National Poetry Foundation, 1986.

———. *The Collected Prose of Carl Rakosi.* Orono, Maine: National Poetry Foundation, 1983.

———. *Ex Cranium, Night.* Los Angeles: Black Sparrow, 1975.

———. "An Interview with Carl Rakosi." By George Evans and August Kleinzahler. *Conjunctions* 11 (1988): 220–45.

Rasula, Jed. "Andrews Extremities Bruce." *Aerial* 9, Bruce Andrews special issue (1999): 23–27.

Retallack, Joan, ed. *Musicage.* Hanover and London: Wesleyan University Press, 1996.

———. "Poethics of a Complex Realism." In *John Cage: Composed in America,* edited by Marjorie Perloff and Charles Junkerman, 242–73. Chicago: University of Chicago Press, 1994.

Rieke, Alison. "Words' Contexts, Contexts' Nouns: Zukofsky's Objectivist Quotations." *Contemporary Literature* 33, no. 1 (Spring 1992): 113–34.

Rousseau, Jean-Jacques. *The Confessions of Jean-Jacques Rousseau.* Translated by J. M. Cohen. Baltimore: Penguin Books, 1953.

Sarkar, Husain. *A Theory of Method.* Berkeley: University of California Press, 1983.

Sartiliot, Claudette. *Citation and Modernity: Derrida, Joyce, and Brecht.* Norman: University of Oklahoma Press, 1993.

Scharfstein, Ben-Ami. *The Dilemma of Context.* New York: New York University Press, 1989.

Schelb, Edward. "Through Rupture to Destiny: Repetition in Zukofsky." *Sagetrieb* 9, no. 1–2 (Spring–Fall 1990): 25–42.

Serres, Michel. *Hermes IV: La distribution.* Paris: Minuit, 1977.

———. *Hermes: Literature, Science, Philosophy.* Edited and with an introduction by Josué V. Harari and David F. Bell. Baltimore: Johns Hopkins University Press, 1982.

———. *Les cinq sens.* Paris: Grasset, 1985.

Serres, Michel, and Bruno Latour. *Conversations on Science, Culture, and Time.* Translated by Roxanne Lapidus. Ann Arbor: University of Michigan Press, 1995.

Shiller, Robert E. *New Methods of Knowledge and Value.* New York: Philosophical Library, 1966.

Sieburth, Richard. *Instigations: Ezra Pound and Rémy de Gourmont.* Cambridge, Mass.: Harvard University Press, 1978.

Silliman, Ron. "For L=A=N=G=U=A=G=E." In *The L=A=N=G=U=A=G=E Book,* edited by Bruce Andrews and Charles Bernstein, 16. Carbondale: Southern Illinois University Press, 1984.

———. *The New Sentence.* New York: Roof, 1987.

———. "Third Phase Objectivism." *Paideuma* 10 (Spring 1981): 85–89.

Simpson, Megan. *Poetic Epistemology: Gender and Knowing in Women's Language-Oriented Writing.* New York: State University of New York Press, 2000.

Smith, Norman Kemp. *A Commentary to Kant's Critique of Pure Reason.* Atlantic Highlands, N.J.: Humanities, 1992.

Smith, Paul. *Discerning the Subject.* Minneapolis: University of Minnesota Press, 1988.

Smithson, Robert. *The Writings of Robert Smithson.* Edited by Nancy Holt. New York: New York University Press, 1979.

Spahr, Juliana. "Resignifying Autobiography: Lyn Hejinian's *My Life.*" *American Literature* 68, no. 1 (March 1996): 139–59.

Spender, Dale. "Extracts from *Man Made Language.*" In *The Feminist Critique of Language: A Reader,* edited by Deborah Cameron, 102–10. New York: Routledge, 1990.

Stein, Gertrude. *Gertrude Stein: Writings.* Edited by Catharine R. Simpson and Harriet Chessman. New York: Library of America, 1998.

———. *How to Write.* New York: Dover, 1975.

———. "Patriarchal Poetry." In *The Yale Gertrude Stein,* selected by Richard Kostelanetz. New Haven, Conn.: Yale University Press, 1980.

———. *Selected Writings.* Edited by Carl van Vechten. New York: Vintage, 1962.

Sternberg, Meir. "Proteus in Quotation-Land: Mimesis and the Forms of Reported Discourse." *Poetics Today* 3, no. 2 (Spring 1982): 107–56.

Stevens, Wallace. *The Palm at the End of the Mind.* Edited by Holly Stevens. New York: Vintage Books, 1990.

Stewart, Allegra. *Gertrude Stein and the Present.* Cambridge, Mass.: Harvard University Press, 1967.

Taggart, John. "George Oppen and the Anthologies." *Ironwood* 13, no. 2 (Fall 1985): 252–62.

———. *Songs of Degrees: Essays on Contemporary Poetry and Poetics.* Tuscaloosa: University of Alabama Press, 1994.

Terdiman, Richard. *Present Past: Modernity and the Memory Crisis.* Ithaca, N.Y.: Cornell University Press, 1993.

Terrell, Carroll F. *A Companion to "The Cantos of Ezra Pound."* Berkeley: University of California Press, 1980.

———, ed. *Louis Zukofsky: Man and Poet.* Orono, Maine: National Poetry Foundation, 1979.

Thom, René. *Mathematical Models of Morphogenesis.* Translated W. M. Brookes and D. Rand. Chichester, Eng.: Ellis Horwood, 1983.

Tomas, John. "Portrait of the Artist as a Young Jew: Zukofsky's 'Poem beginning "The"' in Context." *Sagetrieb* 9, no. 1–2 (Spring–Fall 1990): 43–64.

Vaihinger, Hans. *The Philosophy of "As If": A System of the Theoretical, Practical, and Religious Fictions of Mankind.* Translated by C. K. Ogden. New York: Harcourt, 1925.

Vattimo, Gianni. "Dialectics, Difference, and Weak Thought." *Graduate Faculty Philosophy Journal* 10, no. 1 (Spring 1984): 151–64.

———. *La fine de la modernita: Nichilismo ed ermeneutica nella cultura postmoderna.* Milan: Garzanti, 1985.

Walker, Jayne L. *The Making of a Modernist: Gertrude Stein from* Three Lives *to* Tender Buttons. Amherst: University of Massachusetts Press, 1984.

Warnock, Mary. *Memory.* London: Faber and Faber, 1987.

Watten, Barrett. *Total Syntax.* Carbondale: Southern Illinois University Press, 1985.

Weinsheimer, Joel C. *Gadamer's Hermeneutics: A Reading of Truth and Method.* New Haven, Conn.: Yale University Press, 1984.

Weinstein, Norman. *Gertrude Stein and the Literature of Modern Consciousness.* New York: Frederick Ungar, 1970.

Weiss, Allen S. *The Aesthetics of Excess.* New York: State University of New York Press, 1989.

Wiener, Norbert. *The Human Use of Human Beings: Cybernetics and Society.* New York: Da Capo, 1954.

Wilhelm, Hellmut, and Richard Wilhelm. *Understanding the I Ching: The Wilhelm Lectures on The Book of Changes.* Bollingen Series 19:2. Princeton, N.J.: Princeton University Press, 1979.

Williams, William Carlos. *Paterson.* New York: New Directions, 1963.

Wittgenstein, Ludwig. *Philosophical Investigations.* Translated by G. E. M. Anscombe. 3rd ed. New York: Macmillan, 1958.

———. *Tractatus Logico-Philosophicus.* Translated by D. F. Pears and B. F. McGuinness. London: Routledge, 1961.

Wolfe, Cary. *Critical Environments: Postmodern Theory and the Pragmatics of the Outside.* Minneapolis: University of Minnesota Press, 1988.

Wordsworth, William. *The Major Works.* Edited with an introduction by Stephen Gill. Oxford: Oxford University Press, 1984.

Zacchi, Romana. "Quoting Words and Worlds: Discourse Strategies in *Ulysses.*" *James Joyce Quarterly* 27, no. 1 (Fall 1989): 101–9.

Zukofsky, Louis. *"A."* Baltimore: Johns Hopkins University Press, 1993.

———. "Interview." By L. S. Dembo. In *The Contemporary Writer: Interviews with Sixteen Novelists and Poets,* edited by L. S. Dembo and Cyrena N. Pondrom, 216–32. Madison: University of Wisconsin Press, 1972.

———. "Poem beginning 'The.'" In Louis Zukofsky, *Complete Short Poetry,* with a foreword by Robert Creeley. Baltimore: Johns Hopkins University Press, 1991.

———. "Preface: 'Recencies' in Poetry." In *An "Objectivists" Anthology,* edited by Louis Zukofsky, 9–25. New York: Folcroft Library Editions, 1975.

———. *Prepositions: The Collected Critical Essays of Louis Zukofsky.* Exp. ed. Berkeley: University of California Press, 1981.

———. *A Test of Poetry.* New York: Jargon, Corinth Books, 1964.

Index

Gandelman, Claude, 63

Gasché, Rodolphe: *The Tain of the Mirror,* 10–11

Gates, Henry Louis, 251n35

Gaudier-Brzeska: A Memoir (Pound), 17

Gelpi, Albert, 42, 43, 54

general economy. *See* Bataille, Georges

"Genesis" as term, 103–4

Gödel, Kurt, 4

"The Gospel According to St. John," 146–48

Grabes, Herbert, 42, 51

Gracian, Balthasar: *Arte de ingenio, tratado de Agudeza,* 83

"Grand Collage" (Pound), 39

The Great Digest (Confucius), 42

Grigson, Geoffrey, 16

"Ground Breaking" (Rakosi), 109

group think, 14. *See also* "I think" proposition

"Guest Room" (Oppen), 62

Guide to Kulchur (Pound), 234n51

Halbwachs, Maurice, 158

Harari, Josué V., 32–33, 90

Hass, Robert, 242n50

Hassan, Ihab, 229n165

Hatlen, Burton, 91, 101, 244n8, 247n69

Hayles, N. Katherine, 47, 56, 120, 155, 247n47; *The Cosmic Web,* 5

H.D. (Hilda Doolittle), 39

Hegel, Georg W. F., 11, 111, 175, 183; *The Phenomenology of Mind,* 181

Heidegger, Martin, 4, 86, 220n7, 241n18; works of: "The Age of the World View," 23; *On the Way to Language,* 23–25

Heisenberg, Werner, 4, 124; *Physics and Philosophy,* 3

Hejinian, Lyn, 37, 145; works of: "If Written Is Writing," 135–36; *My Life,* 154–55, 157–61, 165–73, 195; "The Rejection of Closure," 137, 157; "Two Stein Talks," 159; *Writing Is an Aid to Memory,* 161–62

Heller, Michael, 86, 93–94, 103, 109

Hemingway, Ernest, 199

"Henry James" (Pound), 45

hermeneutics, 35, 192, 195; difference between epistemology and, 4; Gadamer's theory of, 25, 27, 113, 127

Hermes, 30, 34, 36

Hermes: Literature, Science, Philosophy (Serres), 34, 255n45

Herwitz, Daniel, 113

Hess, Rudolph, 200

Hintikka, Jaakko: "A Discourse on Descartes's Method," 8

Hirsch, Edward, 60, 66, 69, 242n50

Hoffman, Donald: *Visual Intelligence: How We Create What We See,* 60

Hollander, Benjamin, 207, 208, 211

Homer, 46

Hooker, Jeremy, 65, 240n14

Hoover, Paul, 35

Horace, 46, 95

Howe, Susan, 37, 137–53; works of: "Articulation of Sound Forms in Time," 135; "The Captivity and Restoration of Mrs. Mary Rowlandson," 145; "The Difficulties Interview," 135; *The Europe of Trusts,* 138; *My Emily Dickinson,* 139, 254n25; "The Narrative of Finding," 147; *The Nonconformist's Memorial,* 146, 149; *Singularities,* 138; "Statement for the New Poetics Colloquium, Vancouver, 1985," 137–38

"How to Be with a Rock" (Rakosi), 97, 101

How to Write (Stein), 19, 21–22

Husserl, Edmund, 66, 87–89, 94, 110, 111

I Ching, 119, 121, 124–26, 128, 131
identity, concept of, 164–65
I-eye configuration. *See* eye/I
"If Written Is Writing" (Hejinian), 135–36
Image, Music, Text (Barthes), 39
"Image of the Engine" (Oppen), 67
Image of the People: Gustave Courbet and the 1848 Revolution (Clark), 60
imagism, 39; rear-view, 61–82
incompleteness theorem, 4
"The Indomitable," (Rakosi), 106–9
information, Wiener's definition of, 47
Ingarden, Roman, 220n7
Irigaray, Luce, 86, 251n35
Islets/Irritations (Bernstein), 204, 212
"I think" proposition, 11, 14, 112, 115–16, 126, 217

Jackson, Laura (Riding), 196
Jakobson, Roman, 235n85
James, Henry, 45–46
James, William, 159–60, 163, 172
Jefferson, Thomas, 237n119
Joyce, James, 21, 132–33
Judovitz, Dalia, 87
Jung, Carl, 239n11

Kant, Immanuel, 7, 9–10, 64; Kantian legacy, 12, 114–15, 126, 157; method challenged, 112–13; and rational psychology, 10, 13, 14; *Critique of Pure Reason,* 9
Kappel, Andrew, 45
Kenner, Hugh, 40, 103; *The Pound Era,* 54
Kern, Stephen: *The Culture of Time and Space: 1880–1918,* 198
Kleinzahler, August, 246n44

knowledge, 28–29, 53; acquisition of, in 17th century, 139; closure of, 189; disciplined or common, 137; forgoing or disowning, 114; as a hunt, 142; language and, 136; practical (*sensus communis*), 27–28. *See also* epistemology
"Knowledge in the Classical Age: La Fontaine and Descartes" (Serres), 139–40
Kostelanetz, Richard, 22
Krauss, Rosalind, 232n22
Kuhn, Thomas, 219n2

Labyrinth, the, 8
Lakatos, Imre, 11
language: Cage's concern with, 128–32; and communication, 18, 197; "crisis of," 244n11; "demilitarized" (by Cage) 129–32, 134, (by Howe) 144, 150–51, (by Rakosi) 99, 103, 109–10; evocative, 173; function of, 94; idleness of, 203–6, 211, 213–14; "language trap," 138, 139; linear time in, 158–59; and Medusa's glance as, 107–9; as method of epistemology, 37; need for reassessment of, 136; and objectivity, 84–85; poetic, 158; predictability of, 198; social context in, 177–78, 193; speed as language issue, 201–2, 214; Stein's use of, 15, 19; traditional notion of, questioned, 157; visual and acoustic patterning, 187, 192; vocabulary, 136, 187. *See also* communication; meaning; writing
The L=A=N=G=U=A=G=E Book, 135, 153
Language poetry, 135–39, 155–58, 175, 179, 189, 195, 201
"Language Sampler" (Bernstein), 179
Latour, Bruno: *Conversations on Science, Culture, and Time,* 195; "The

uncertainty principle, 4

About the Author

Ming-Qian Ma is an assistant professor of English at the State University of New York in Buffalo.

Avant-Garde & Modernism Studies

General Editors
Marjorie Perloff
Rainer Rumold

Consulting Editors
Peter Fenves
Stephen Foster
Christine Froula
Françoise Lionnet
Robert von Hallberg

Avant-Garde & Modernism Collection

General Editors
Rainer Rumold
Marjorie Perloff